HOUSEHOLD HORROR

THE YEAR'S WORK:
STUDIES IN FAN CULTURE AND CULTURAL THEORY

Edward P. Comentale and Aaron Jaffe, *Editors*

HOUSEHOLD HORROR

Cinematic Fear and the Secret Life of Everyday Objects

Marc Olivier

INDIANA UNIVERSITY PRESS

This book is a publication of

Indiana University Press
Office of Scholarly Publishing
Herman B Wells Library 350
1320 East 10th Street
Bloomington, Indiana 47405 USA

iupress.indiana.edu

© 2020 by Marc Olivier

All rights reserved
No part of this book may be reproduced or utilized in any form or by any means, electronic or mechanical, including photocopying and recording, or by any information storage and retrieval system, without permission in writing from the publisher. The paper used in this publication meets the minimum requirements of the American National Standard for Information Sciences—Permanence of Paper for Printed Library Materials, ANSI Z39.48-1992.

Manufactured in the United States of America

Cataloging information is available from the Library of Congress.

ISBN 978-0-253-04655-0 (hdbk.)
ISBN 978-0-253-04656-7 (pbk.)
ISBN 978-0-253-04659-8 (web PDF)

1 2 3 4 5 25 24 23 22 21 20

CONTENTS

Acknowledgments vii

Introduction 1

Part I Kitchen/Dining Room

  1 Refrigerator 11

  2 Microwave 29

  3 Telephone 44

  4 Dining Table 75

Part II Living Room

  5 (Sleeper) Sofa 95

  6 Remote 110

  7 Sewing Machine 126

  8 Houseplant 154

Part III Bedroom

  9 Bed 183

  10 Typewriter 211

  11 Armoire 237

Part IV Bathroom

12 Radiator *253*

13 Pills *268*

14 Shower Curtain *296*

Conclusion . . . *311*

Filmography *313*

Bibliography *317*

Index *331*

ACKNOWLEDGMENTS

To Michelle, Max, Lucas, and Eva, for keeping me from turning into Jack Torrance. To my parents, Miriam and Bob Winegar, for actual thoughts and prayers. To dog Jack, for clearing my mind during ponderous midnight walks in his final year. To movie group friends Craig Mangum, Nicholus Chugg, Rob McFarland, Ed Cutler, and Corry Cropper, who brainstormed films and objects with me as this offbeat project teetered at the precipice. To my colleague-consultants, especially Sara Phenix, Bob Hudson, Daryl Lee, Scott Miller, Van Gessel, Jack Stoneman, and again, Corry Cropper. Thanks to the Society for Cinema and Media Studies for providing a fruitful venue to present research in progress. Thanks to the generous Ludwig-Weber-Siebach Professorship and the Humanities Fellowship awarded by the College of Humanities at Brigham Young University. To Richard Daniels and the Stanley Kubrick Archive for letting me read "All work and no play . . ." thousands of times over. Special thanks to Indiana University Press; to the peer reviewers of the manuscript, who provided helpful comments; to the series editors, Edward P. Comentale and Aaron Jaffee; to Leigh McLennon for copyediting; and to Janice E. Frisch, who convinced me immediately that this was the perfect series for my book. And to Brooke Gladstone, whose voice I imagine as a litmus test for readability.

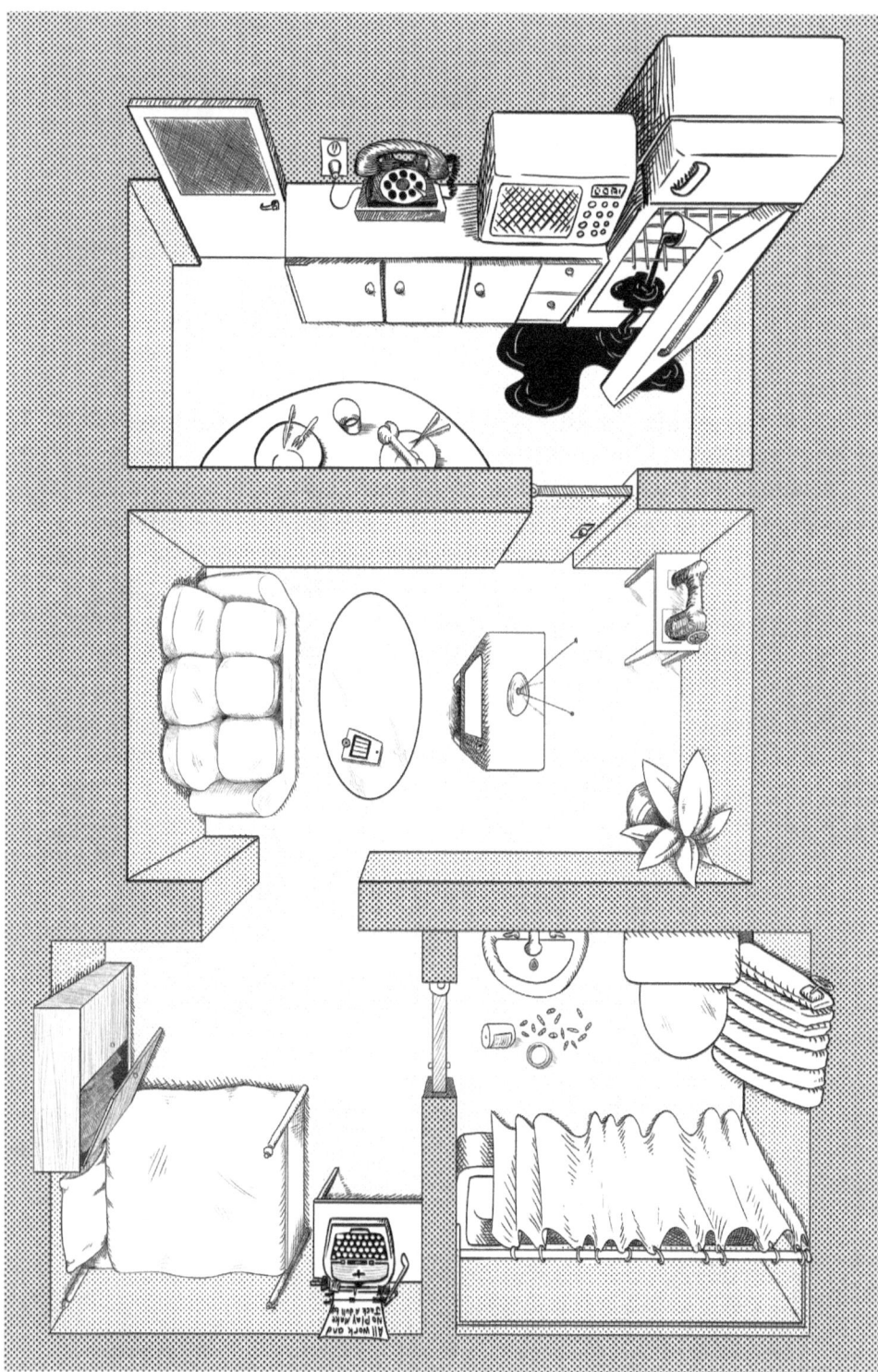

HOUSEHOLD HORROR

INTRODUCTION

Complete the sentence: "In the great green room / There was a telephone / And a red balloon / And a picture of—" Chances are, if you were a child, parent, or babysitter any time after 1947, you recognize that inventory of domestic objects. Margaret Wise Brown's *Goodnight Moon* is the quintessential object-oriented book. Like many books for young children, *Goodnight Moon* is unburdened by the constraints of character development and plot. It's more of a chant, really—a ritualized bedtime peace treaty with objects that will soon go dark and haunt the room with their unrecognizable shapes. *Goodnight Moon* names a series of objects in a room and then says good night to each of them. *Household Horror* is the insomniac's answer to *Goodnight Moon*; it is a story about straining to see objects in the dark. In *Household Horror*, there is a telephone call coming from inside the house, a sewing machine working on Carrie's prom dress, a typewriter that makes Jack a dull boy, a possessed bed, a refrigerator best left unopened, and other household objects that refuse to sleep no matter how many times you tell them good night.

This is an object-centered book, but it is not strictly speaking a book about object-oriented ontology (OOO) or other strains of philosophy that acknowledge the being of things. I am nevertheless deeply influenced by the "nonhuman turn" of the twenty-first century. I consider Ian Bogost the patron saint of this book, given that my idea to look at objects in horror films emerged from a discussion of Bogost's *Alien Phenomenology* with students in my theory class. Most of the students simply could not conceive of a world in which objects are endowed with their own being as much as any human—a "flat ontology" in OOO speak. My guess is that it had been a while since any of them had read *Goodnight Moon*. Let me echo Bogost in *The Nonhuman Turn* to explain my feelings about what OOO accomplishes: "So much of object-oriented ontology is, to me, a reclamation of a sense of wonder often lost in childhood."[1] To wonder, I will add a reclamation of awe, or wonder mixed with fear. Horror recovers the wonder and fear of objects in a way that approaches the sincerity of a child frightened by the shapes of objects in the dark. My object-focused view of horror decenters the human in a similar manner to OOO and speculative realism. Nevertheless, I have no desire to write about how Kant got it wrong (a critique of correlationism being the first station of the OOO cross at which one must genuflect, followed by methodic attention to philosophers whose last names begin with the letter *H*). Instead, I start from a position of belief in the dehierarchizing principles of object-centered thought, and then I see how the objects in scary movies take on new dimensions when seen through 3-O lenses. I agree with the object-oriented crowd that "cautious anthropomorphism" is a useful weapon in the fight against anthropocentrism.[2] Therefore, I try to place objects on equal par with humans by arguing in all sincerity that a sleeper sofa is as much the star of Brian De Palma's *Sisters* (1973) as Margot Kidder (chap. 5, "[Sleeper] Sofa"), that *The Exorcist* (1973) is about a possessed bed (chap. 9, "Bed"), and that *Rosemary's Baby* (1968) is a conflict between herbal shakes and prenatal vitamins (chap. 13, "Pills").

Household Horror includes canonical works, cult classics, mainstream franchises, and films not generally associated with the genre. Many of the films are Western productions (especially, US or UK), but chapter 4 ("Dining Table") focuses on an object in Japanese cultures, and chapter 11 ("Armoire") looks at a Western object in a South Korean film. Horror fans stand to be alternately thrilled and aggravated by my inclusions and omissions. *What! Two films by De Palma and nothing by Cronenberg?* Auteur worshippers will find some of the standards such as Hitchcock (chap. 14, "Shower Curtain," naturally), Lynch (chap. 12, "Radiator"), and Kubrick (chap. 10, "Typewriter") and deeper cuts such as Zulawski (chap. 1, "Refrigerator"). Chronologically, the approach varies. Chapter 8 ("Houseplant") is a double bill of features from two different genres that opened only a week apart—the sci-fi horror remake *Invasion of the Body Snatchers* (1978) and the feel-good documentary *The Secret Life of Plants* (1978). Chapters 3 ("Telephone"), 7 ("Sewing Machine"), and 13 ("Pills") take on works from at least three decades each to explore changes in specific object-human and object-object interactions over time. In brief, traditional strategies of coherence such as chronology, country, director, and subgenre are present to some degree in this book, but these categories are secondary to the manner in which the works permit access to an otherwise overlooked household object.

Household Horror is organized by room (sections) and by object (chapters). As a reader, you are free to roam about the house (or more accurately, the one-bedroom apartment) in any order you choose. Each chapter can stand alone. I do not aim to present a point-by-point argument that progresses from one chapter to the next in order to arrive at one grand theory of "The Object." Accordingly, there are many conclusions but no traditional "Conclusion." My purpose is to explore the presence of objects in cinema regardless of the status of those objects as symbols or as "characters"—a critic's favorite anthropomorphic compliment to bestow on objects that demand attention (e.g., "The house is *almost a character* in that film"). I treat objects as beings that surpass the roles given to them as props or decor. Objects do more than prop up humans. If I succeed, then what OOO philosopher Graham Harman says of essayist Clement Greenberg's prose should also be true of this book, that it "retrieves relevant objects from the shadows of indifference, and makes them the target of our awareness in a plausible way."[3] In short, I wish to spark curiosity more than to author an exhaustive treatise. As OOO philosopher Timothy Morton writes, "No solo ever exhausts the trumpet—there is that feeling that there is always more of the object than we think."[4] An object, according to Morton, is like Doctor Who's TARDIS: "bigger on the inside than it is on the outside."[5] My project has more in common with cubism's multiplication of viewpoints or with the Renaissance rhetoric of abundance (*copia*) than with classicist ideals.

I encourage readers to use this book as a point of departure for object-centered readings of other media texts. Consider gaps as invitations. The "Houseplant" chapter, for example, does not include *The Little Shop of Horrors* (1960), counter to the expectations of every person to whom I spoke while writing it. Nor do cult films such as *Garden of Death* (a.k.a. *The Gardener*, 1974) and *The Freakmaker* (a.k.a. *The Mutations*, 1974) fit within the limitations of a single chapter. Nevertheless, my "Houseplant" double feature foregrounds plant sentience in a manner applicable to those and many other media texts. I apply a variety of approaches to suggest how objects resonate beyond their roles in a given film. Chapter 6 ("Remote") adopts a fragmentary format that mirrors the use of the device. Chapter 14 ("Shower Curtain") uses YouTube comments, Reddit threads, and Amazon customer reviews as film commentary. One recurring strategy in this book begins with the simplest of devices—the list. Chapter 4 ("Dining Table") adapts the anthropological term *food event* as *table event* and then lists the twenty table events in *Noriko's Dinner Table* (2006) as an interpretive framework that puts the object first. An inventory of the beds in *The Exorcist* (chap. 9, "Bed") and a list of all the phone calls in *Black Christmas* (chap. 3, "Telephone") likewise employ simple tools to reclaim the grammar of objects so pervasive in childhood picture books and yet so quickly forgotten once human narratives take center stage. The simple recognition of an object's presence in a list (*There is a child's bed. There is a hospital bed. There is a bed made of wood. There is a bed made of metal*, etc.) is enough to decenter the human.

I note in chapter 9 ("Bed") how "there is," as described by Emmanuel Levinas, has become a beloved philosophical concept among OOO philosophers, even if the purposes of Levinas do not always align with their own. As first described by Levinas, "there is" (*il y a*) evokes the "menace of pure and simple presence" felt by the insomniac who notices how objects (humans included) almost melt into the blanket of being that seems to take over as night falls. Dylan Trigg classifies "there is" as a "nocturnal ontology" that "threatens the singularity of the subject."[6] As things go dark, a rustling presence strips the subject down to a partly formed status that Trigg describes as "present to itself while also being simultaneously conscious of its own effacement: in a word, *unhuman*."[7] "I do not stay awake: 'it' stays awake," says the Levinasian insomniac.[8]

Philosophers have adapted the Levinasian *il y a* in different ways, but here, I use it as part of my concept of this book as *Goodnight Moon* for insomniacs. Margaret Wise Brown's book begins by acknowledging the presence of the objects in a room, which, it so happens, are grouped in rhyming pairs, often with one animate or anthropomorphic object coupled with one inanimate object (e.g., kittens/mittens, bears/chairs), as if Brown were in the business of flattening hierarchies of being. Next, *Goodnight Moon* tells each object good night, whereupon, presumably, the bunny and all surrounding objects are now free to retire for the night as equals. Now imagine, in place of the bunny, the insomniac described by Levinas. Rather than say *good night*, the unfocused gaze of the insomniac senses that under the moonlight, the objects take on an otherworldly aura, a buzzing, a strangely diffuse density. The awareness that there is more to these objects than meets the eye becomes more certain even as the objects become less clear. Soon, the insomniac's own sense of self is objectified as an "it" that does not sleep.

In horror, "it" proliferates, especially as a shape-shifting form such as those in the *It* adaptations (1990, 2017, 2019) and in *It Follows* (2014). "It" conjures a sense of "there is" without a knowable, stable object. "It" is nevertheless something. "It" is a surplus of being, a "plus one" object that disturbs the universe, according to Morton.[9] "It" is arguably as much

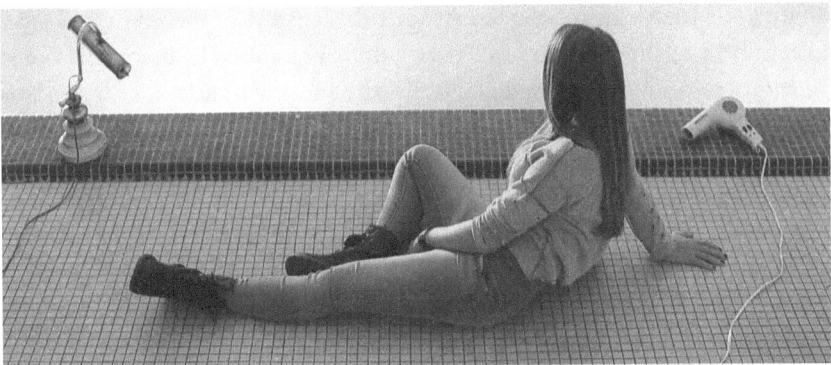

Fig. 0.2. Poolside with objects in *It Follows* (2014).

a function as a thing. Consider *It Follows*, where a shape-shifting "it" stalks and kills adolescents unless they pass the curse on to a sexual partner. "It" creates object awareness. *It Follows* has a surprisingly *Scooby-Doo* style goofiness to its climactic showdown between a group of teens and whatever "it" is. Presumably, the myriad plug-in household objects stuffed in duffel bags and carted to an old Detroit indoor swimming pool are part of the teens' electrocution-based booby trap. But however ill-conceived the plan, the moments leading up to the object-centered battle with "it" take on an unexpected poignancy when considered in light of the film's final lines, quoted from Dostoyevsky's *The Idiot*: "But the most terrible agony may not be in the wounds themselves but in knowing for certain that within an hour, then within ten minutes, then within half a minute, now at this very instant—your soul will leave your body and you will no longer be a person, and that this is certain; the worst thing is that it is *certain*."[10] Looking back to the silent poolside vigil during which the slow pan of the camera places the teens as equals with office lamps, typewriters, hair dryers, and radios, the Dostoyevsky quote suggests that one of the most terrifying aspects of objects is that human superiority over them is at best temporary. The it-function is twofold: first, it introduces a paranoia about objects that points to the larger truth that all objects are unknowable, and second, it flattens ontology—that is, it returns people to the community of objects. In that regard, *It Follows* is less about death than it is about the fact that all things are objects—lamps, hair dryers, typewriters, and even horny teenagers.

Horror accomplishes the it-function with or without shape-shifters, but not all horror is truly object focused. Films featuring possessed objects are among the least object oriented in spirit because they merely use objects to reinforce anthropocentrism. Creepy dolls are a case in point. In *Annabelle* (2014), a demon possesses a doll—the most aspirationally human of objects—as a stepping-stone to its true object of desire, the human soul. "Demons can sometimes use objects as conduits to achieve their desire," explains a priest. Consequently, in *Annabelle* and similar films, anything not human is no more than the means to a human-centered end. The demon in *The Exorcist* (chap. 9, "Bed") and the alien invaders in *Invasion of the Body Snatchers* (chap. 8, "Houseplant") are similarly human obsessed. My analysis of those two films recuperates the stepping-stone objects as things worthy of deeper consideration. Rather than forget that Regan MacNeil's bed is possessed before Regan or that plants are the first victims of an alien invasion, I propose a look at how those objects interact with humans in ways that make them good choices for demonic or alien instrumentalization in the first place.

The tension between object-centric and anthropocentric horror is present in every chapter, but as an overview of that struggle, the immensely successful but critically underappreciated *Final Destination* franchise merits mention here in the introduction. Although the *Final Destination* movies use "Death" to personify causality, the real stars of the show are objects interacting with other objects. Each feature stages a series of elaborate set-piece freak accidents that claim the lives of people who have cheated death. In the first *Final Destination* (2000), the death of high school teacher Valerie Lewton (Kristen Cloke) stems from the following series of object interactions: Ms. Lewton puts on a John Denver album, fills a teakettle at the kitchen sink, wipes off water drops from the kettle with a dish towel, throws the towel on a knife block, and lights the gas stovetop burner, which blows out. She strikes a match to relight the burner, at which point an extreme close-up and its sonic equivalent draw our attention to the blue flames as a menacing presence that saps Ms. Lewton of her privileged position as the dominant force behind all action. The teakettle heats up and performs its teakettle version of a horror scream queen. Lewton then pours the hot water into a mug, gets spooked, and throws the water onto the floor. Opting for cold vodka instead of hot tea, Lewton places ice cubes in the mug and pours. An extreme close-up shows a crack appear on the mug due to the sudden temperature shift. Vodka drips along the floor as Lewton moves from the kitchen to the living room. Lewton holds the mug over her computer, and vodka drips through the ventilation slots on top of the monitor.

Fig. 0.3. Vodka leaks into a computer monitor in *Final Destination* (2000).

A shot inside the computer follows the combustible liquid as it flows over the circuitry. Smoke exits the vents, and an electrical spark turns explosive, sending a shard of glass into Lewton's jugular. Grasping her neck, Lewton stumbles past the turntable, which restarts "Rocky Mountain High." As Lewton moves to the kitchen, the electrical fire ignites the vodka in a trail that leads to the gas stove, where the nearby vodka bottle becomes a Molotov cocktail in a burst that throws Lewton to the floor. While bleeding out, Lewton reaches up and pulls the dish towel, which in turn pulls the knife block, which releases its charge of knives into her supine body.

What *Final Destination* shows is a chain of events commonly called a "freak accident." But what are accidents if not object interactions stripped of human intentionality? Death, with its aura of personification, is arguably the most reassuring figure in the *Final Destination* films. The more frightening reality is that objects act without us, that they exist not only for us, and that sometimes their actions can result in our death. The horror of objects is subdued by demons, aliens, ghosts, or other anthropocentric entities, who, if anything, borrow the power of an object's being to augment their own menacing presence. The truth is that it is easier to ascribe being to a gremlin than to the microwave that destroys it, easier to look for a ghost in a hotel than to ponder the authority of a typewriter on a desk, easier to recognize objects as tools for supernatural beings than to recognize the depth of being that is already there. To rephrase Dostoyevsky, the most terrible agony may not be in wounds inflicted by supernatural figures but in the recognition of a fact known to all children: that the objects in our homes are more than tools and that our coexistence with them is perpetually under negotiation.

Until 2005, Margaret Wise Brown's author photo on *Goodnight Moon* included a cigarette. The cancer stick has since been deemed inappropriate for children and consequently has been photoshopped into oblivion. Around the time I first began working on this book, I learned that sitting is the new smoking, that the chair I was sitting in to write these words, like the one you may be sitting in while reading, is draining precious hours from my life. These thoughts are enough to keep a person up at night. Hello, moon.

Notes

1. Bogost, "The Aesthetics of Philosophical Carpentry," 85.
2. Shaviro, 61.
3. Harman, *Weird Realism*, 43.
4. Morton, *Realist Magic*, 23.
5. Ibid., 49.
6. Trigg, *The Thing*, 50.
7. Ibid., 53.
8. Levinas, quoted in Trigg, *The Thing*, 48.
9. Morton, *Realist Magic*, 126.
10. Dostoyevsky, 22–23.

PART I

KITCHEN/DINING ROOM

1

REFRIGERATOR

THE KITCHEN IS A HUB OF DOMESTICATED MICROCLIMATES: the arctic cold of the freezer, the chill of the refrigerator subdivided into zones according to food type, the variable heat of the conventional oven, the misunderstood microwave radiation that bounces around a smaller oven, the circular hot zones of the stovetop, the storms of the dishwasher, and other no less dramatic shifts in temperature brought about by other appliances such as the coffee maker, the Crock-Pot, the pressure cooker, the ice cream maker, and the toaster. Heat and cold—or, more correctly, heat and various degrees of its absence—regulate essential functions of the domestic ecosphere. Each room of a house may be subject to heating and cooling systems not unlike those of ovens and refrigerators, but the kitchen harbors some of the most potent examples of matter impacted by energy transfer. The kitchen's microclimates participate in sustaining, preserving, destroying, or otherwise altering organic life.

The Cold Womb

More often than not, the kitchen has been designated as a feminine space. Kitchen appliances, in turn, are often seen as extensions of the female body to which a range of temperatures and climatic conditions (ice cold, frigid, smoking hot, wet, dry, etc.) are disproportionately attributed. The colloquial expression for pregnancy "to have a bun in the oven," though not complimentary insofar as it equates a pregnant woman with a household appliance, provides a telling example of a long-standing link between procreation, gestation, and kitchen technology. The phrase imagines the womb as an oven and, by the same logic, the oven as a womb, similar to "The Gingerbread Man" and other folktales of high-carb homunculi cooked up by women in the kitchen. Andrzej Zulawski's *Possession* (1981), "a fairytale for grown-ups" according to the director, falls within that tradition, although instead of a bun in the oven, the story features a body in the refrigerator, and instead of piping-hot runaway baked goods, the woman of the house prepares a tentacular, glutinous golem through a miscarriage of groceries and bodily secretions expelled in the tunnels of the Berlin U-Bahn during an ecstatic trance.[1] The aberrant offspring of a body in crisis disrupts a marriage, an affair, and two kitchens. When considered in relation to perishable food distribution, refrigerator-related household duties, and the desire of a woman to say "I" for herself, the miscarriage-birth emerges as an abject expression of identities both human and nonhuman, of a woman who runs hot and cold, and of refrigerators and their unspeakable contents.

"*Possession* is a fable whose moral I do not understand," says Zulawski.[2] And the director is not alone in his confusion. *Possession* was reportedly the most controversial film at the 1981 Cannes Film Festival.[3] The French newspaper *Le Monde* wrote that it "traumatized" festival audiences.[4] Invariably (and usually unfavorably), French critics linked the film to the Grand Guignol tradition of sensationalist theatrical horror, whereas Zulawski had imagined his work too serious to be mistaken for the disfavored genre.[5] The French newspaper *Libération* called *Possession* "a cocktail of Polish obscurantism and Hitchcockian effects."[6] The *New York Times* characterized it as "an intellectual horror film," adding, "That means it's a movie that contains a certain amount of unseemly gore and makes no sense whatsoever."[7] Isabelle Adjani, rewarded at Cannes for her leading roles as both Anna (the woman who gives birth to, cares for, and copulates with the monster) and Helen (her kindhearted schoolteacher double), called the film "emotional pornography," which, truth be told, is as good an explanation as any.[8] Thoroughly rational attempts to unravel the plot are doomed because incomprehension is as essential to Zulawski's project as it is to symbolist poetry or surrealism. During production, Zulawski often told people that *Possession* was a film about God—a concept that also escapes him. "I don't know what God is," says Zulawski. "I believe that if I did know, I wouldn't make art."[9] *Possession* is not an atheistic attack on the notion of a divine being but rather a "quarrel against God" that Zulawski compares to a child crying to a father or an injured party facing a lawmaker.[10]

"Anyone can make a film, but making a film that has a soul is very difficult," says Zulawski. "It is as if I were trying to make a golem."[11] And rumor had it, during preproduction, that Zulawski was in fact going to Berlin with Isabelle Adjani to make a film about a golem.[12] Once the film was released, however, plot synopses forgot about the golem and attempted to couch the story along the lines of a bizarre bourgeois melodrama. Outlined as such, the plot follows Mark (Sam Neill) as he returns home from some sort of espionage mission in East Berlin to his wife, Anna (Isabelle Adjani), and son, Bob (Michael Hogben), in their West Berlin apartment, which faces the Berlin Wall. He soon learns that Anna has been having an affair with a man named Heinrich (Heinz Bennent). Fights ensue (so many that the *Times* called the film "a veritable carnival of nosebleeds"), the couple's young son is neglected, Mark sleeps with Helen, and Anna cheats on both her husband and her lover with a cephalopodan six-foot phallic monster that she keeps in a love hideaway with a view of the Wall.[13] The creature continues to transform as the body count rises. A head, hands, and feet soon stock the refrigerator shelves. The film spirals to its climax as the main characters ascend a staircase (meant to evoke Jacob's ladder), and the drama ends in nothing less than the sounds of an impending apocalypse. The story is not your average tale of conjugal strife, but dialogue borrowed from Zulawski's own failed marriage pierces through the narrative absurdity with the genuine agony of a relationship in crisis. *Possession* is indeed a domestic psychodrama, but it is also Zulawski's film about the golem—not the clay golem of the director's native Poland but something more intimate, something that must be understood in connection to banal domestic objects such as groceries and refrigerators.

Outlined to better represent nonhuman actors, *Possession* becomes a story of perishable groceries that participate in the creation of a golem. The creature not only materializes Anna's emotions but also connects the cold chain network of food distribution to the home refrigerator as abject horror's answer to the oven-womb. As absurd as it seems to consider how a kitchen appliance might react to a film (a thought experiment no less irrational than the film's plot), one can imagine that if appliances could dream, then Zulawski's golem, born from an oozing discharge of spilled milk, yogurt, eggs, and human bodily secretions—a half-baked, imminently perishable yet ever-thriving and metamorphosing entity—would surely haunt a refrigerator's nightmares. Anthropomorphism aside, the refrigerator is an active prop in the film. Just as Anna and Helen are nearly identical human doubles with different souls, Anna's two apartments have nearly identical refrigerators with radically different contents. The first holds eggs, milk, meat, and even clothing at one point. The second contains body parts and flowers from a lover. The first is often gripped by Mark, who admires and caresses its bright exterior when Helen sleeps over and cleans up. The second stuns and terrifies both Mark and Heinrich. Like all refrigerators, the appliances defy nature through climate control—an act of suspended animation or suspended decomposition depending on one's point of view. Both of *Possession*'s refrigerators reside in apartments that face the Berlin Wall, which draws attention to how "cold" borderline conflicts can take on material forms.

In *Possession*, the refrigerator is a woman's domain and serves as the primary signifier of domesticity, its failures, and its perversions. All of the characters seem to agree that a good woman keeps her refrigerator well stocked and clean. Helen, always clothed in white, is the picture of sanitary housekeeping. When Helen stops by to discuss concerns about Bob's behavior at school, Mark puts her to work without a second thought. She gets Bob out of the bath, tucks him in bed, and then heads to the kitchen to clean up Anna's mess. Mark enters the kitchen and runs his hand across the top of the refrigerator with a look of wonder. Twice he caresses the pristine cleanliness of the appliance while Helen washes the meat and blood from the electric knife that Anna had used earlier (in a domestic act that quickly spiraled into self-harm). Helen's house, seen only at the end of the film, is modern, spacious, and impeccably clean. She feeds Bob a king's breakfast on a gleaming white table. "Look at the kitchen," says Zulawski to Daniel Bird in the DVD audio commentary. "It's white. It's clinical. We do try to make our surroundings clinically beautiful, clinically clear, or artistically clear, because we are lost. And this thread of being lost, lost, lost, lost between the Berlins, the politics, the morals, it's at the core of the film."[14] In an interview at the time of the film's release, Zulawski explains that he associates the color white with Helen as a marker of "lucidity, goodness, heart" and the only real chance that Mark could have had to get out of his destructive relationship with Anna: "The more [Helen] was white, the more she colored the other story with intensity."[15] And yet when perfect Helen cleans up Anna's mess in the kitchen and Bob asks Mark which woman he prefers, Mark replies, "Our mummy," and Bob smiles. Like Zulawski, the father and son find clinical and artistic clarity less satisfying than colorful chaos.

Anna is almost never without bags of groceries. She is always stocking refrigerators but failing to do so properly. All of Anna's domestic acts go awry even as her insistence on performing them intensifies. At one point, she gathers piles of clothes and shoves them into the refrigerator yelling, "I'm sorting out his things to take to the laundry!" Mark watches as she moves from stocking the fridge with clothes to emptying food from the cupboards. He tries to calm her. "But it's my job!" she screams. "I'm better at it!" Anna's many attempts at idealized domesticity are interrupted, malfunctioning, and short-lived. When Mark returns home from a confrontation with Anna's lover, he finds Anna with Bob in the kitchen—a sentimental tableau of mother and child at a small table eating and singing "Baa-Baa Black Sheep." But Mark's arrival disrupts the scene, Bob exits the kitchen, and the fighting begins. While Mark yells, Anna continues to perform housework by madly putting things in the fridge. The argument ends violently, nosebleed oblige. Later, Anna returns and heads straight to the kitchen with bags of groceries. As Mark again yells at her, she unpacks meat, gets the electric knife and the meat grinder, and furiously cuts and grinds as if making hamburger were the most important thing in the world. Mark grips the refrigerator tightly while firing off accusatory questions. Anna turns the electric knife against herself—and Mark, after bandaging her neck, performs the same stunt on his arm. "It doesn't hurt," says Anna as she prepares to leave. A high-angle shot dwarfs Mark, who broods like a neglected child at Bob's kitchen table. Outside, a private investigator trails Anna straight to the supermarket, where she buys two more bags of groceries for her other apartment. At Anna's hideaway, foodstuffs become weapons. A broken wine bottle cuts the detective's throat; yogurt in a bag becomes a makeshift mace to pummel a foe. Her refrigerator looks more like a morgue than a food-storage device.

Anna's most intense perversion of refrigerator-linked duties occurs on a trip home from the supermarket. She carries a string bag filled mostly with milk, eggs, and yogurt—groceries that need refrigeration and that all clearly allude to fertility and procreation. She stops in a church and kneels before a statue of Christ on the cross, her string bag hanging at the level of her uterus. She lifts her eyes and moans almost like a woman in labor. This is the beginning of what she terms a miscarriage of "Sister Faith." She exits the church and walks into the subway. Alone in the underground passage, she begins to convulse and scream in a fit as raw as anything in *The Exorcist* (1973). Her string bag, that external womb of eggs, yogurt, and milk, bursts against the wall as she convulses. She thrashes about in an ecstatic frenzy and then kneels as she did in the church minutes earlier.[16] Viscous fluids spill from her body and coalesce into streams alongside the spilled groceries. Anna's convulsive possession does not come from an external entity as in most possession films. The thing that her body now rejects has

Fig. 1.1. Anna's miscarriage of groceries and faith in *Possession* (1981).

grown inside her. Among the dozen-or-so quotes in the film's press booklet from Cannes, a verse from the Gospel of Thomas stands out almost like a warning to Anna: "If you bring forth [*matérialisez*] that which is within you, that which is within you shall save you. If you do not bring forth that which is within you, this which you do not bring forth will destroy you."[17] Anna's hysterical fit brings forth her very weak faith, which, as she explains to Mark, is what she is trying to protect in her secret apartment.

Zulawski had intended to present Anna's subway miscarriage of faith and birth of the golem in a clearer chronology, first as "something gluey in the subway," then as an entity that would gradually take shape at home.[18] The director had also planned on having Anna tell the subway story in three different versions to three separate people, but he decided to use only one version. In an interview, Zulawski explains that in one of the two alternatives, Anna was to mix the eggs and other groceries with sand and make a paste "like the paste of the Golem, like the paste of Adam"—a biblical golem, according to the director.[19] Zulawski does not take the interviewers' bait to philosophize, but had he responded, he might have mentioned that last-minute alterations to the monster were made with glue and film stock—a poetically ideal medium for a director's golem.[20] Zulawski's creature thus emerges literally from the stuff of his trade, just as Anna's golem takes form from the forces that govern her life: her own body and the refrigerated dairy aisle of the supermarket.

The Abject Refrigerator

To better appreciate how the refrigerator figures into this fable, we need to consider another tentacular creature known to the food industry as the cold chain. Science writer Tom Jackson explains the often-overlooked cold chain network with a plant metaphor: "We do not consider that our kitchen fridge is the very tip of a chilled tendril, one of millions more that make up a network known in food-industry circles as the cold chain. The cold chain, with its myriad nodes and branches, entangles the globe, creating a temperature-controlled transport corridor that connects the farmer's field and the trawler's hold to every grocery store chiller."[21] The term *cold chain* was coined in 1908 to describe the refrigerated storage facilities and mobile units that transport perishable foods from sites of production to places of consumption.[22] Around that time, ice manufacture, brewing, and the meat trade made up three-quarters of all of the refrigerating capacity in the world. Dairy and vegetables eventually overtook meat, but before 1914, a typical "cold chain" might begin at an abattoir, then move through sea or land to port or city, and finally arrive at a retail location.[23] The cold chain dilates the temporospatial conditions of food distribution. By slowing spoilage, refrigeration changes food's geographical boundaries and extends the seasons. Without refrigeration, sashimi in Japan would have remained a seaside specialty rather than a national dish.[24] Without refrigeration, we would not be eating apples in May or June, we would not expect eggs all year round, and supermarkets as we know them would not exist.[25] Without the cold chain, the consumption of "seasonal" or "locally sourced" food would be a given rather than a conscious effort infused with ideological principles. The cold chain allows us to consume products from around the globe, form new eating habits that alter our bodies, change the ecosphere, and endanger or propagate entire species of plants and animals. And those changes do not begin to account for the impact of refrigeration on non-food-related areas such as particle physics, weapons manufacturing, engineering, pharmaceuticals, fertility, organ transplants, and other areas that this chapter does not explore.

The cold chain is the triumph of the artificial. The heat pumps of refrigeration are like a fist raised in defiance to the heavens—a quarrel with God.

Jackson calls heat pumps "tiny acts of rebellion against the conformity of the universe" because they seem to disrupt the laws of thermodynamics by pushing heat against the universal flow.[26] Like the promethean theft of fire, refrigeration technology steals "cold" from the weather. And it all begins with manufactured ice. Once harvested like a crop from the frozen water of lakes and rivers, ice in the age of refrigeration becomes "artificial" or "mechanical."[27] In the 1880s, enormous steam-powered machines weighing as much as 220 tons were the heart of ice and cold storage facilities. Those machines controlled the vaporization and condensation of a refrigerant (e.g., in early machines, ammonia, carbon dioxide, sulfur dioxide, methyl chloride, or ethyl chloride) to absorb heat in one place and move it to another, typically with the help of a compressor. The technology is common to both ice machines and refrigerators. The cycle of compression and expansion occurs within a closed system so that costly, toxic, and flammable refrigerants can do their work without leaking into the environment and risking explosions or death by poisoning.

The introduction of artificial cold into the home begins with the adoption of artificial ice. Of course, the cold of manufactured ice is no more artificial than the cold of ice from a frozen lake, but the means of production extricates artificial ice from any climatic context. Furthermore, the discourse that made artificial ice preferable to natural ice paved the way for the artificial cold of refrigeration technology. Americans, who to this day are ice obsessed compared to Europeans, took to ice and the icebox quickly by the turn of the twentieth century, even though iceboxes required constant cleaning and restocking. Before there were "bow chicka wow wow" pizza delivery boy jokes or stories of affairs with the milkman, there were muscular icemen (whence "the iceman cometh" double entendre behind the title of the Eugene O'Neill play) who hoisted giant blocks of ice on their broad shoulders to stock iceboxes that ranged from no-frills containers to ornate cabinetry. Fear of cuckoldry, however, was less a factor in the emerging preference for the artificial than was the fear of germs. First came the scares of "villainously impure" natural ice linked to typhoid.[28] Then came the marketing opportunists. Among the many creative advertisements devoted to showing off the crystalline clarity of artificial ice, one unintentionally creepy photo manipulation features the smiling head of a woman frozen in a block of ice alongside other blocks of suspended frozen food.[29] Finally, as manufactured ice overtook natural ice, artificial cold became the next logical step in mechanizing the cold chain.

The ability to make one's own ice was the feature that turned artificial cold into the hot new trend. Ice cubes were the "killer app" of the refrigerator, as Jackson put it.[30] How magical the power to make one's own ice! No more ice deliveries, cubes on command—for early adopters, the appeal outweighed the risk of death from leaking toxic refrigerant. The annual sales of refrigerators in the United States in 1914 was a mediocre 600, but only fourteen years later, annual sales had reached 468,000.[31] Those "chilled tendrils" grew in the kitchen only after a worldwide industry had set root. Once the refrigerator began to replace the icebox in the home, the adoption took hold faster than other household technologies such as the television or the washing machine.[32] By 1957, more than 90 percent of US homes had a refrigerator, compared to 14 percent in West Germany, the setting of *Possession*.[33] Just three years later, nearly 54 percent of German households boasted ownership of a refrigerator.[34] By the 1970s, the number of homes with refrigerators in Germany reached 95 percent.[35] Even a sparsely furnished apartment such as Anna's love nest would be expected to include a refrigerator to be considered livable. Today, at least three-quarters of all homes on the planet have a refrigerator.[36] Defying nature through artificial cold has become the norm.

Anna's U-Bahn miscarriage/golem birth scene reveals the no-man's-land (in both senses in *Possession*, where only women carry groceries) between the final steps of the cold chain—that is, between the supermarket and the home refrigerator. What occurs in that scene is a textbook case of the crisis in boundaries and identity known as the abject in the philosophy of Julia Kristeva. The spilled dairy of the scene and the bodily fluids are in fact central ingredients in Kristeva's explanation of the "deep psycho-symbolic economy" that evolves from the process of expelling and rejecting as a primal form of expressing subjectivity.[37] If ever there were a key to Anna's psychological journey, the abject would be it. Even though this is a chapter more about refrigerators than about Anna's identity crisis, her abjection serves as a model of a structural system that need not be restricted to human psychology. Anna's abject miscarriage is entwined with the abjection of refrigeration. And although Kristeva's intent was not to explain the identity of kitchen appliances, her model possibly explains as much about refrigerators as it does about the human psyche.

Kristeva turns to milk to illustrate how spasms, retching, and vomiting emblematize the construction of the symbolic self through expulsion. Her description is nearly as visceral and drawn out as Adjani's trance, but it bears quoting at length for its imagery of violent expulsion as a form of self-birth:

> Food loathing is perhaps the most elementary and most archaic form of abjection. When the eyes or the lips touch that skin on the surface of milk—harmless, thin as a sheet of cigarette paper, pitiful as a nail paring—I experience a gagging sensation, and still farther down, spasms in the stomach, the belly; and all the organs shrivel up the body, provoke tears and bile, increase heartbeat, cause forehead and hands to perspire. Along with sight-clouding dizziness, *nausea* makes me balk at that milk cream, separates me from the mother and father who proffer it. "I" want none of that element, sign of their desire; "I" do not want to listen, "I" do not assimilate it, "I" expel it. But since the food is not an "other" for "me," who am only in their desire, I expel *myself*, I spit *myself* out, I abject *myself* within the same motion through which "I" claim to establish *myself*. . . . I give birth to myself amid the violence of sobs, of vomit.[38]

Kristeva's example of retching at milk skin is a figure of how the self emerges through a primal scene of expulsion. "I" emerge in opposition to what I reject, which in Kristeva's psychoanalytic economy is a fundamental paradox that relies on a dual movement of expulsion and repression. In the move away from the semiotic system of the mother into the symbolic system of the father, the child objectifies, or *abject*ifies, things to which she had previously been connected, things that stand in opposition to the symbolic, representational "I" that cannot exist without that split. In a sense, "I" gives birth to itself by deciding what is not itself, but herein lies the paradox: there was no detached "I" making that decision. The "I" emerges only through the expulsion or exclusion that creates a border between those two modalities of being. "I" cannot exist without that exclusion, that othering, and that exclusion cannot take place without a repression of its primal connectedness. A repression forms a border that maintains my identity. When I encounter the abject, as in loathing an item of food or seeing a corpse, that border is put in a state of crisis and the body responds with a visceral rejection that maintains my difference from it. "My body extricates itself, as being alive, from that border," writes Kristeva.[39] The abject is about disturbing but also preserving "identity, system, order."[40]

Anna's development after the subway miscarriage can be read as a narrative enactment of Kristevan philosophy. The lover, Heinrich, is the nurturing mother figure from which Anna will eventually separate herself. He is an incubator. Anna tells Heinrich, "That's why I'm with you. Because you say 'I' for me. Because you say 'I' for me." After the abject miscarriage, Anna

Fig. 1.2. An abject refrigerator in *Possession* (1981).

forms her own identity even as she begins to nurture the "other" that she has expelled from herself. Her secret apartment facing the Wall is the place of her border construction. That space where Anna begins to say "I" for herself might be compared to Kristeva's reimagining of the *chora*—a term borrowed from Plato's *Timaeus*.⁴¹ The chora is a sealed receptacle, a chaotic space of becoming, and the primal semiotic site where the "I" emerges. When a detective trails Anna to her chaotic flat and encounters the partially formed creature of white and bloody ooze, he exclaims "My God!" as if to signify both abjection and awe. "He's very tired," says Anna. "He made love to me all night." Anna's incestuous communion with her own abject expulsion is beautiful to her because it is the precondition of her own coming into being. That is why Heinrich, who says "I" for Anna, is so repulsed, incapacitated, and blinded by the creature. That is why Anna's first impulse is to lead her shocked soon-to-be-ex-lover to the kitchen to show him the head and hands inside her abject refrigerator. "Meat!" she calls him as she thrusts a knife into him, twists it, and pulls it out. The codevelopment of Anna and the expelled other that she nurtures into being must lead to a rejection of Heinrich, who now opposes Anna's "I."

The final visitor to Anna's chora by the Wall is Mark, who comes to understand Anna and reconciles with her after this experience. Mark arrives and finds the door to the abject refrigerator ajar. He looks inside with shock and begins to convulse with the same movements of Anna's subway trance. He goes to the balcony and looks out at the border as if to underscore the apartment's border-generating function; then he returns to the kitchen, turns on the gas stove, and opens the refrigerator door to consider its contents. Mark has understood. He rushes to meet wounded Heinrich in the restroom of a bar. "It wasn't even human," says Heinrich. "It was—" Mark interrupts, "Divine?" Mark recognizes the sacred process and can now murder Heinrich and blow up the apartment not merely as a cover-up for Anna's crimes but also as a sign that they have served their purpose. Anna is almost there. Back at the couple's apartment, Mark and Anna have a postcoital chat on the kitchen floor. Anna leans her bare back against the clean and proper fridge and says, "Oh, I've cleaned all the mess, I washed the floor, I made the bed." Kristeva's "identity, system, order" are emerging along with Anna. The process of identity formation helps explain what Mark witnesses later that night: Anna makes love to the now half-human, half-cephalopodan creature and cries out orgasmically, "Almost . . . almost . . ." Mark watches from the corner of the room with amazement rather than jealousy and utters, "Yes." The other that has given Anna so much joy now half-resembles Mark.

Zulawski's own artistic struggle with the divine involves a similar process of creation as expulsion and doubling. Literature, music, painting, and film all serve to question the nature of God, according to Zulawski. But as for the artist, the director asks, "To whom does he address the question?" His answer resides in the same liminal space as the border Kristeva imagines between two modes of being: "*I* ask myself the question. Which means that I am not alone. Who is therefore this other? It is God, no doubt. That is why I have taken to writing nothing but moral fables. Everything I do is a function of this other thing inside of me, that listens, and sometimes answers."[42] Zulawski's formulation of the divine exists within a rupture that manifests nonverbal meaning within reflexive interrogation. "I" ask "myself." Like Kristeva, who sees the chora not as an empty vessel but rather as something swirling with the divine chaos of the maternal, Zulawski also opens a space of meaning at the border of the fractured self. The ability to ask oneself a question requires a wall within the self but also necessitates a divine and dangerous game of border crossing that makes the split vulnerable. That "thread of being lost, lost, lost, lost, lost between the Berlins, the politics, the morals" that Zulawski says is at the core of the film is inseparable from the primal border of being lost between modes of being. That is the sense of the nonsense of *Possession*.

Surprisingly, Kristeva's "psycho-symbolic economy" withstands a nearly complete evacuation of human consciousness. *Possession*'s refrigerators—all refrigerators—are the embodiment of coming into being through expulsion. Refrigerators say "I" through lack. Cold, their raison d'être, we too quickly forget, exists purely as lack. Cold is the absence of heat. The ingenious heat pumps that quarrel with the laws of thermodynamics do so by expelling heat. *A refrigerator extricates itself into being*, Kristeva might say if she were locked in a Home Depot with nothing but her thoughts. Without refrigerant flowing through its veins, sopping up heat in one part and releasing it in another, the appliance is nothing but an expensive cupboard, an icebox without ice. Heat must be perpetually thrust aside in order for the refrigerator to live. A power outage is all it takes to realize how quickly a refrigerator can flatline. Refrigerators too become abject cadavers. Witness the post-Katrina refrigerator graveyards. Historian Jonathan Rees recalls the spectacle of refrigerators "too filthy to restore to regular use" after Hurricane Katrina.[43] Victims of the hurricane duct-taped up their maggot-infested refrigerators and put them outside on the curb, often with messages like "Do Not Open: Cheney Inside." And the rot inside the fridge-cadavers may as well have been human. To a refrigerator, the point is moot. Leave the disgust to the humans. As Kristeva says, "It is thus not lack of cleanliness or health that causes abjection but what disturbs identity, system, order."[44] The "I" of the refrigerator is expelled when it can no longer expel heat. Mark's encounter with the refrigerator at the hideaway is abject both for its contents and for the fact that the door has stood ajar for too long like a gaping wound.

Conveniently, for those dumping the abject appliance, a refrigerator is its own coffin. And the association between refrigerators or freezers and coffins has gripped the imagination in real and fictitious crime for as long as bodies have been "iced." Jeffrey Dahmer's refrigerator was set to go up for auction in 1996, but a group of businesspeople paid $407,225 to the families of his victims to destroy the abject appliance instead.[45] The Ultraline Professional freezer/fridge of Patrick Bateman (Christian Bale) in *American Psycho* (2000) chills both the eye mask of his beauty regime and the head of one of his victims. Everything you need to know about Bateman is contained in his freezer. A fan of superhero comics created a "Women in Refrigerators" website after noticing how often superheroines end up stuck

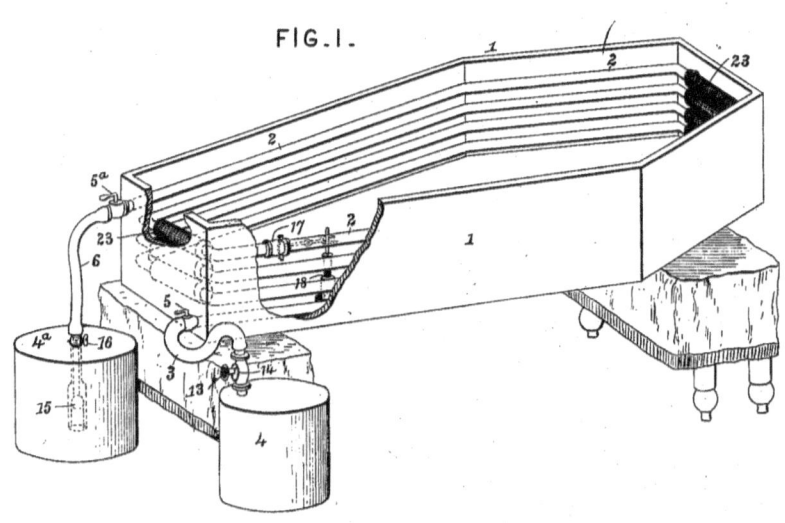
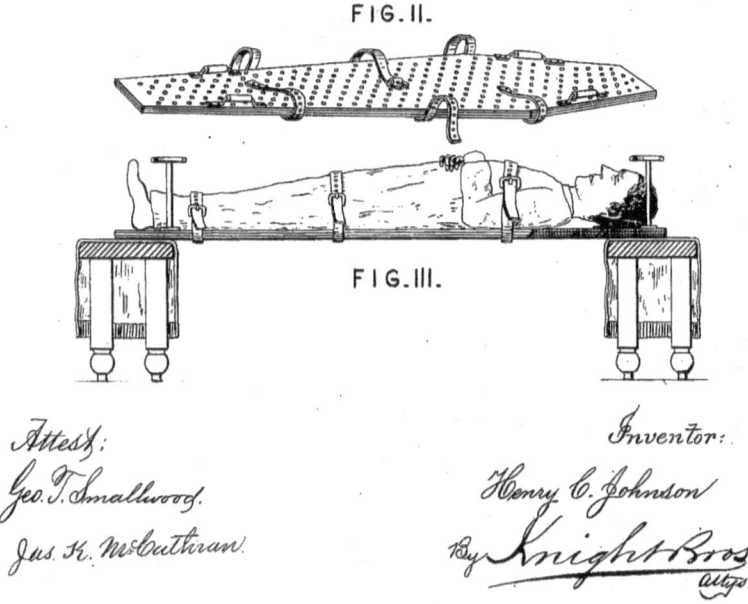

Fig. 1.3. 1885 patent for a "corpse cooler."

in a refrigerator.⁴⁶ Those abject uses of the refrigerator are not merely perversions of an appliance; they are part of its heritage. In the 1880s, forty years before home refrigerator sales started to take off, the "corpse cooler" entered a branch of the cold chain that people tend to avoid thinking about. Embalming the dead was uncommon, so putting a body on ice (the origin of the euphemism for murder "to ice someone") was a popular scheme for preserving bodies before burial. Numerous patent models show casket-shaped refrigerators for the dearly departed.⁴⁷ Refrigeration technology helped freeze corpses in morgues as early as 1878.⁴⁸ Essentially, the refrigerator-coffin is a progenitor of the home refrigerator.

To the human observer, the corpse cooler is an abject refrigerator; to the refrigerator, as long as heat is being expelled, the device is simply doing its job. The abject manifests differently depending on whether we consider it from the human psychological point of view or as a structural model. Anna's abject refrigerator disturbs the human border between medical refrigeration and domestic refrigeration. Human body parts in a refrigerator are abject to humans as "death infecting life," as Kristeva says, and also abject as encounters with the repressed fact that all refrigerated goods occupy a shadowy limbo of extended decomposition.⁴⁹ One disconcerting effect of the cold chain from a human point of view is the radical separation between points of production and points of consumption. As much as the family-run farms of a food service such as Blue Apron appease the consumer, the source still functions as an abstract idea. The concept of "sourcing" ingredients is a reaction to an industrialized, refrigeration-based food economy. The loss of a rich sensorial connection to food manifests in institutional interventions such as "best by" dates. Just as the human child moves from a semiotic to a symbolic realm according to Kristeva's Lacanian-based structure, so also does food enter the symbolic in the era of refrigeration. Text, in the form of packaging and labeling, mediates what we consume. For many, the stamped date on food is enough to justify its expulsion. One extreme example of text-mediated food abjection was reported by CNN during relief efforts in Haiti after the 2010 earthquake. Earthquake survivors, confusing "sell by" dates with expiration dates, reportedly began to throw away nutritional biscuits despite their dire need for food.⁵⁰ With the shorter life span of chilled perishables, textually determined food expulsion occurs regularly in home refrigerators.

The refrigerators of *Possession* register as abject through the human psyche. As receptacles, they contain both life and death. The eggs, each in its own plastic nest in the refrigerator door, suggest uterine presubjectivity while the body parts cause us to confront what it means to no longer be human. The before and the after of the "I" sit in the chill of artificial cold. To the refrigerator, however, the abjection of border disturbance occurs each time the door opens. Heat rushes into the body of the appliance like water into a drowning human. The body of the refrigerator responds to the forces of heat sink, always expelling what seeps in at its opening. "Refrigerators do seem to breathe," says semiotician Deborah Smith-Shank. "Of all the appliances we have, that's the one that's most alive."[51] Refrigerators hum, whine, click, and exhale. We hear them working to say "I." They are extensions of the cold chain, and they rely on the power grid for their survival. Electric utilities, realizing this, sold refrigerators at a loss.[52] The companies crushed the quieter gas-absorption refrigerator, leaving most homes with machines that breathe out heat with the help of electric pumps, compressor lungs that need around-the-clock life support from an electrical outlet.[53] When the power goes out, when the refrigerator door is left open, when a compressor fails, a refrigerator begins to drift into the horror of abject otherness.

Zulawski did not set out to make a film about a refrigerator; he set out to make a film about a golem—a moral fable, a quarrel with God. A Cold War climate and a divided city give a larger material and ideological backdrop to an intimate crisis of a marriage and identity. The less evident but more expansive material backdrop of the cold chain connects intimate domestic life to a great, tentacular other—a Leviathan on the seas, a Behemoth on land, a beast that defies nature and snakes into nearly every kitchen, where it consumes energy and exhales hot breath to stave off the inevitable rot that makes us retch and reminds us of death. A refrigerator is an ally in a continual fight against the abject, but one not far removed from the corpse cooler—a device to temporarily house an object no longer considered a living thing. *Possession* troubles the identity of the refrigerator and puts the appliance to perverse uses. As the golem approaches its final form, the two refrigerators of the film meet opposite fates: the one in Anna and Mark's apartment is returned to its clean and proper state, and the other, having served its purpose, bleeds out all of its "cold" and dies in an explosion. Zulawski did not intend to make a refrigerator film, but from eggs and milk nestled in the door to rotting flesh on a shelf, the refrigerator is both womb and coffin, both life-giving and abject. If ever an appliance were a golem, it would be the refrigerator.

Notes

1. For Zulawski's comments on the film as fairy tale, see Stéphane du Mesnildot, "Andrzej Zulawski: À la recherche de la matière noire," *Cahiers du cinéma*, September 2013, 62–63.
2. Pierre Montaigne, "Zulawski: Fantasmagorie au pied du mur de Berlin," *Le Figaro*, August 27, 1980 (translation mine).
3. See Annie Coppermann, "*Possession*," *Les Echos*, June 2, 1981.
4. Jean de Baroncelli, "'*Possession*,' d'Andrzej Zulawski," *Le Monde*, May 27, 1981.
5. Marie-Elisabeth Rouchy, "Andrzej Zulawski: '*Possession*' doit se mériter," *Matin*, May 25, 1981.
6. G. R., "'*Possession*' de Zulawski," *Libération*, May 27, 1981 (translation mine).
7. Vincent Canby, "Film: '*Possession*,' Blood and Horror, with Isabelle Adjani," *New York Times*, October 28, 1983.
8. Quoted in Monique Pantel, "A Berlin-Ouest, pour '*Possession*' Zulawski met Adjani en transe," *France Soir*, August 8, 1980 (translation mine).
9. Jean-Luc Doulin, "Entretien avec Adrzej Zulawski," *Télérama*, no. 1637, May 27, 1981 (translation mine).
10. Ibid.
11. Chion, *Le Cinéma et ses métiers*, 48 (translation mine).
12. See Jacqueline, Bruller, "Impressions de Pologne," *Cahiers du cinéma*, March 1980, 39.
13. Canby.
14. Andrzej Zulawski and Daniel Bird, DVD audio commentary, *Possession*, Mondo Vision Blu-ray Limited Edition, 2014.
15. Pascal Bonitzer and Serge Toubiana, "Entretien avec Andrzej," *Cahiers du cinéma*, July–August 1981, 47 (translation mine).
16. Finding Zulawski's single piece of direction ("fuck the air") unhelpful, Adjani reports having practiced macumba sexual trances with a Brazilian makeup artist named Renaldo in her trailer. See Michel Braudeau, "'Adjani' la folie lui va si bien," *L'Express*, May 22–28, 1981, 38.
17. Cannes Press Booklet for *Possession*, May 25, 1981, n.p. (translation mine).
18. Zulawski, DVD audio commentary.
19. Bonitzer and Toubiana, 43 (translation mine).
20. See DVD audio commentary.
21. Jackson, 10.
22. See Thévenot, 105.
23. Ibid., 88.
24. Ashkenazi and Jacob, 11.
25. Rees, *Refrigeration Nation*, 101.
26. Jackson, 11.
27. See Rees, *Refrigeration Nation*, 30.
28. Quoted from a 1903 issue of the *Detroit Tribune* in Rees, *Refrigeration Nation*, 61.
29. See Donaldson and Nagengast, 143.
30. Jackson, *Refrigeration Nation*, 182.
31. Rees, *Refrigeration Nation*, 147.
32. Ibid., 163.
33. Ibid., 179.

34. Ibid., 178.
35. See Thévenot, 347–48.
36. Rees, *Refrigeration Nation*, 60–61.
37. Kristeva, 68.
38. Ibid., 2–3.
39. Ibid., 3.
40. Ibid., 4.
41. Ibid., 14.
42. Doulin (translation mine).
43. Rees, *Refrigeration Nation*, 182.
44. Kristeva, 4.
45. Reuters, "Serial Killer's Possessions to Be Destroyed," *New York Times*, June 15, 1996, http://www.nytimes.com/1996/06/15/us/serial-killer-s-possessions-to-be-destroyed.html?mcubz=3.
46. Gail Simone, "Women in Refrigerators," http://lby3.com/wir/index.html.
47. Donaldson and Nagengast, 148.
48. Thévenot, 127.
49. Kristeva, 4.
50. Chris Lawrence, Eric Marrapodi, and Rick Hall, "Haiti Aid Efforts Hindered in Critical Hours," CNN, January 16, 2010, http://www.cnn.com/2010/WORLD/americas/01/15/haiti.international.aid/index.html.
51. Quoted in Rees, *Refrigerator*, 22.
52. Rees, *Refrigeration Nation*, 146.
53. Cowan, 142.

2

MICROWAVE

Roger Ebert's review of *Gremlins* (1984) divides the film into a good half and a nasty half. In the good half, we meet an "unbearably cute" creature that looks like "a cross between a Pekingese, Yoda from *The Empire Strikes Back*, the Ewoks from *Return of the Jedi*, and kittens."[1] The cuddly, wide-eyed pet "mogwai" comes from a shop in Chinatown, where down-on-his-luck inventor Randall Peltzer (Hoyt Axton) has been peddling his malfunctioning gadgets and Christmas shopping for his son, Billy (Zach Galligan). Gizmo, as Mr. Peltzer calls the new pet, comes with a few care instructions: avoid bright light (sunlight will kill it), keep the creature away from water, and never feed it after midnight. Until those rules get broken, the Spielberg-produced movie looks like a successor to *E.T.* (1982). We know things are about to change, however, when a splash of water on Gizmo spawns five mischievous new mogwai. After tricking Billy into giving them an after-midnight snack, Gizmo's progeny enter a pupal stage that resembles a cross between the pods from *Invasion of the Body Snatchers* (1956) and the eggs from *Alien* (1979). From the pupae emerge mayhem-seeking, reptilian-skinned, gargoylesque mutations called gremlins. And this, writes Ebert, is where "the movie itself turns nasty."[2]

Especially nasty, according to Ebert, is the scene in which Billy's mother, Lynn Peltzer (Frances Lee McCain), slams a gremlin into a microwave and cooks the creature until it explodes in a death so gruesome that the kitchen massacre took its place alongside the heart-ripping human sacrifice in *Indiana Jones and the Temple of Doom* (1984) as an argument for the creation of a PG-13 rating.[3] Although Mrs. Peltzer exterminates one gremlin in a guts-splattering food processor assault and another in a frenzied knife attack ripped straight from *Psycho* (1960), Ebert singles out the explosive microwave death as a plausible threat to impressionable young minds: "I had the queasy feeling that before long we'd be reading newspaper

Fig. 2.1. A gremlin gets "nuked" in a microwave in *Gremlins* (1984).

articles about kids who went home and tried the same thing with the family cat."[4] Ebert had little reason to fear, as not a single *Gremlins*-inspired microwave attack on a family pet followed. Nevertheless, he was right to single out the oddball appliance as a greater source of anxiety or fascination than the mundane chef's knife or the weaponized food processor. The microwave moves violence beyond the blade and cooking beyond fire. Microwave radiation transcends the connection between primitive tools and the modern kitchen. The microwave is a gremlin-sized chamber of atmospheric terror rooted in wartime research, embroiled in spy scandals and health scares—it is an inspirer of tabloid stories and urban legends and possibly the least understood device in the kitchen.

Weaponizing an Appliance

Gremlins did not invent death by microwave. Stories about exploding microwaved dogs and cats had been circulating since the 1970s, when sales of the appliance began to take off. Folklorists added "The Microwaved Pet" to the canon of urban legends in 1979.[5] The most popular version of the tale features an old woman whose son gives her a new microwave for Christmas. Accustomed to drying her pet poodle in her conventional oven set to "warm," the woman decides to upgrade her grooming technique with the new gadget. She pops the poodle in the machine and turns it on, and the pet explodes.[6] By the time *Gremlins* was in theaters, many viewers would have recognized the exploding gremlin as a reference to the legend rather than as a novel idea. Not coincidentally, Mrs. Peltzer makes the gremlin recoil and stumble into the microwave by blinding it with a spray can labeled "Flea and Tick Killer for Your Cats and Dogs." In homage to the legend, the pet-grooming product remains in frame by the microwave window for the final blow.

The explosive gremlin scene takes a twisted cautionary joke about misunderstood technology and repurposes the punchline as a demonstration of how to weaponize a kitchen appliance. Intent replaces naivete in *Gremlins*, and although no one comes out of the theater with a better understanding of technology, the movie represents a significant turn in the microwaved-pet narrative. Given the film's commercial success—a domestic gross of more than $153 million by 1985—we can safely assume that viewers such as Ebert, who may have been unaware of the microwaved pet legend, now not only were in on the joke but had seen it emerge, gremlin-like, in a new, malicious form. Indeed, when Mrs. Peltzer sets the timer and selects from the "special functions" control panel, as if already familiar with the proper setting to cook a gremlin, her ruthlessness moves us, however momentarily, to pity the creature that whimpers and presses its hands against the glass door of its death chamber. The executioner's unflinching stare into the flickering oven, the neon-like buzz of electricity mixed with the plaintive mewling of the sizzling, bloating little devil, and the final explosion of its soupy innards modulates the comedy for a fleeting moment into visceral horror.

Of the many films that task the microwave with horrific deeds—*Superstition* (1982), *Microwave Massacre* (1983), *Evil Laugh* (1986), *The Willies* (1990), *Ghost in the Machine* (1993), *Urban Legend* (1998), and *Final Destination 2* (2003), among others—the closest parallel to the kitchen scene in *Gremlins* is the 2009 remake of Wes Craven's controversial vigilante justice film *The Last House on the Left* (1972). The gravity of the crimes in *The Last House on the Left* has nothing in common with the playful mayhem of *Gremlins*, but the use of kitchen appliances to dispose of unwelcome guests puts both films in a similar narrative framework. In *Gremlins*, the offending parties have made a mess of Lynn's freshly baked gingerbread man cookies, whereas in *The Last House on the Left*, the criminal visitors have murdered the daughter of their hosts. As punishment befitting the murderers' crimes, the 2009 remake adds a microwave to the already kitchen-centric bevy of improvised torture devices (a chef's knife, a toaster, a garbage disposal, etc.).

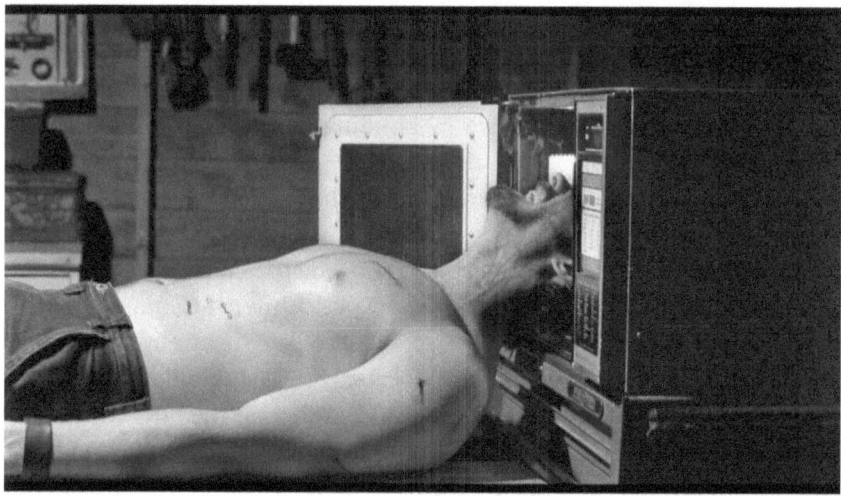

Fig. 2.2. Vigilante justice by microwave in *The Last House on the Left* (2009).

The microwave is not new but an old countertop model of the same vintage as the one in *Gremlins*, the kind with the wood veneer to match the family station wagon.[7] As luck would have it, a malfunctioning safety latch allows the vigilante father to operate the device with the door open. Bad news for Krug (Garret Dillahunt), paralyzed, duct-taped to a table, the top of his head positioned in the oven. The father hits "Start." There's a sizzling sound, and then Krug's head begins to smoke. He tries to cry out "Help!" but can only produce a truncated groan that sounds like "hell, hell." A minute later, his head explodes.

Twenty-five years after *Gremlins*, the climactic microwave execution in *The Last House on the Left* demonstrates the staying power of the appliance as a means of delivering a particularly cruel and unusual death. The enduring myth that a microwave cooks from the inside out conjures an imperceptible yet thoroughly invasive form of penetration far more brutal and punishing (at least by the standards of vigilante movie parents) than anything the human hand can do with a gun or knife. The consequent explosion from within has more in common with the "chestburster" scene in *Alien* than with an external attack. While the chef's knife is easily the most ubiquitous self-defense weapon in horror films, the microwave's spectacular appeal makes it something of a nuclear option in the heart of the home—a rare and impactful death blow delivered at the push of a button.

Another common misunderstanding, the association between microwave energy and the properties of nuclear radiation, further heightens the perceived stakes of misuse. The vernacular expression "to nuke"—defined by *Urban Dictionary* as, first, "to attack with a nuclear weapon" and, second, "to cook a foodstuff in a microwave oven"—promotes an affinity between the most feared modern weapon of mass destruction and the unassuming machine that reheats leftovers.[8] Beneath the playful use of the verb dwells uncertainty about what, exactly, happens in those two or three minutes before the timer beeps.

Consider the experience of reheating a bowl of soup. Put the soup in a pot on a burner, and the heating process more or less resembles cooking practices that are thousands of years old. With a microwave, the analogous relation to fire disappears. Rather than stir the soup while cooking, the user can peer through a glass door and watch the bowl rotate on a turntable like a car at an auto show. Forced separation from the food during operation suggests danger, as does the mysterious mesh on the glass. With a conventional oven, the threat of burns is evident through both sight and touch. A microwave oven, in contrast, offers no warning to the senses, no burst of hot air when opening the door, no glowing element or flame. And yet some unseen hazard requires complete shutdown the second the door is unlatched—a safety measure not taken for conventional ovens, blenders, mixers, or other kitchen appliances. Most children learn firsthand through accidents or curiosity that touching the burner of a hot stove is a bad idea, but the microwave has no equivalent cautionary rite of passage. The danger of a microwave must be imagined vicariously through nonhuman material rather than registered by the skin. The angry fireworks caused by the unadvised introduction of a piece of aluminum foil, a fork, or the handle of a Chinese takeout box manifest the wrath incurred by disobedience to the machine's material preferences. Likewise, a bowl of leftover soup, cold one minute, a splattering mess the next, indicates that the forces at work inside the box are highly temperamental.

No one buys a microwave because it heats evenly. The true appeal of the machine is not culinary but temporal, as advertisers have invariably understood. The microwave is to cooking what time-lapse photography is to film—a celebration of technological power over temporal regimes. "Bakes a cake in 3 minutes, cooks a 5-pound roast in 30 minutes. . . . Heats a TV dinner in 4 minutes," exclaims the 1967 *House Beautiful* ad for the Tappan "Time Machine."[9] Time-lapse cooking obliterates the exclusive claim, forged over millennia, between cooking and thermal radiation. Tappan skirts any technical explanation of that monumental shift by removing heat from the picture and comparing the appliance to the TV—another electronic object that had already subsumed the social functions of fire. "We call it the 'cool oven' because it cooks with *microwaves* instead of heat. (The same thing that makes your TV work)," explains Tappan simplistically.[10] Granted, we would be surprised if the same ad executives who decided to advertise their modern product with a woman in a white apron and pink gingham dress had considered explaining, in place of the TV metaphor, that a magnetron hidden in the side of the machine generates sinusoidal electromagnetic fields that change direction about 2.45 billion times per second (or 2.45 GHz) and that those waves, once directed into the oven chamber, interact with water molecules in the food, which attempt to reorient themselves to match the oscillation, thereby causing the molecular agitation we would define as heat.[11] Instead, a photo of an apron-clad woman entranced by the fourteen-pound turkey that will be roasted in a mere seventy-five minutes helps the reader imagine the kinship between the microwave, nostalgia, and television.

While Tappan was promoting their "Time Machines," the Raytheon Company was making their "Radarange" more affordable. Introduced by Raytheon in 1947, the first microwave oven was a 750-pound refrigerator-sized contraption that cost more than the average person made in a year and was better suited for commercial settings such as ocean liners, trains, and hospitals than for the home. Thanks to a 1955 licensing agreement with Raytheon, the Tappan Stove Company brought the microwave to home consumers, but with a hefty $1,300 price tag. In 1967, Raytheon became Tappan's biggest rival by selling a countertop Radarange for only $495. As for branding, the Radarange name also happened to reflect the oven's technological heritage even better than the Tappan Time Machine television metaphor. As the origin story goes, magnetron tube specialist Percy Spencer was working to improve radar systems when microwave radiation emitted by the magnetron melted a chocolate bar in his pocket.[12] The following day, Spencer made the first-ever batch of microwave popcorn. Raytheon then patented Spencer's invention, laying the groundwork for a company as successful with home cooking as with radar and missiles. During the war, the company was making more than 2,600 magnetrons a day for radar; during the 1970s, they were putting out 2,000 magnetrons a day for Radarange ovens.[13]

Although advertisers failed to explain in one sentence how radar technology could prepare a meal, the market began to warm up to the idea of waging war against long cooking times. Less than 1 percent of US households owned a microwave at the start of 1971. By the mid-1980s, some estimates put microwave ownership in the United States at over 50 percent.[14] During a period of exponential growth, when a technology reaches a large consumer base but is not yet taken for granted, rumors circulate about the hidden dangers of the gizmo and the possible consequences of misuse—a phenomenon French sociologist Jean-Bruno Renard calls the "Gremlins effect."[15] Like a cuddly pet mogwai, the new object might be a sought-after purchase and may even enter the home as a gift, but manufacturing defects or half-understood owner's manuals can lead to disaster. Consumers rush to buy the product during this phase even as they pore over alarmist stories in the press. Thus, in the 1970s through the mid-1980s, while middle-class *House Beautiful* subscribers were eyeing the magazine's regular "Microwave Corner" cooking columns and pondering the miracle of the four-minute baked potato, stories of poodle mishaps and health threats were multiplying like wet gremlins.

When it comes to fears about new technologies, urban legends and the press enjoy a symbiotic relationship. Rumors lay the groundwork for a confirmation bias that makes anecdotes newsworthy, and news stories offer facts that give rise to new legends or reinforce the ones we already know. The 1987 *Daily Mail* headline "Horror of Babies 'Roasted Alive in Microwave Ovens,'" for example, is a variant of the urban legend known as "The Baby-Roast" (a.k.a. "The Cooked Baby" or "The Hippy Babysitter") in which a negligent, drugged-up babysitter or an abusive or mentally ill mother either accidentally or intentionally puts a baby in a conventional or a microwave oven.[16] Although the legend predates the microwave, the novelty of the appliance provides a twist that boosts the circulation of rumored accidents and abuse. In the United Kingdom, where microwave sales lagged behind those in the United States, the "horrific new form of child abuse" made for a good invasion narrative in which US influence and technological influence were conspiring to fashion a destructive new trend. "With so many microwaves in Britain there are fears that the torture will spread here," warns the report.[17] Sadly, an article published that same year by the American Academy of Pediatrics documents two cases of microwave oven burns (neither fatal) as child abuse, one involving a babysitter and the other an abusive mother—confirmation of the urban legend that had been circulating for a decade.[18]

A recurring theme in microwave fearmongering is the insidious nature of the damaging rays. A *Daily Mail* story from 1964, "Strange Case of the Oven 'Death Ray,'" warns the public to fear microwave ovens years before they became affordable. According to the story, a worker in a microwave oven factory had been slowly cooking from the inside and did not realize the cause of his illness until it was too late. "People caught in such radiation have no idea that they are being burned," writes the news correspondent.[19] To his credit, the reporter adds in the final paragraph that microwave radiation "has nothing to do with nuclear radiation," but that reassurance is cold comfort tacked onto the end of a story about a man whose own kidneys are cooked without his knowledge.[20] A 1981 *New York Times* report on the first legally validated case of "microwave sickness" in the United States similarly feeds apprehension about damage from microwave exposure. The article centers on a worker's compensation case that blamed the death of a telecommunications technician on prolonged exposure to microwaves. Although an unusual case, the journalist jumps to relate the story to microwave home cooking. "Unshielded, even relatively low-power microwaves can be sufficiently intense at short range to readily penetrate and cook meat, as in microwave ovens."[21] The assertion that microwaves could have a cumulative negative impact on health "at powers well below those that would 'cook' an exposed person" raised concerns that microwaves might be the new asbestos.[22]

International differences in standards for microwave exposure stirred up public concern in the United States, largely due to confusion about oven radiation leakage measurements. That confusion channeled ideological debates through the kitchen, setting up the microwave as a material critique of the inadequate consumer protections of capitalism. Soviet regulations were reportedly one thousand times stricter than those in America.[23] The frequently cited comparison is misleading, however, as it is built on the erroneous assumption of a common measurement standard. US regulations are based on total leakage from the oven, whereas the Russian measurements count only how much radiation reaches the human body, making the net effect in real-world use roughly the same.[24] But standards mean little without good monitoring, and independent testing by the Consumers Union (the publisher of *Consumer Reports*) in 1974 concluded that the federal Food and Drug Administration's Bureau of Radiological Health was not doing its job. The FDA became defensive when *Consumer Reports* officially recommended against buying microwave ovens that year, but warning labels about oven door safety were added the following year to microwaves sold in the United States.[25] Even so, health concerns about microwave sickness continued to make the news for years—more often than not, in articles referencing superior Soviet radiation leakage standards.

Just as sales began to skyrocket in 1976, a diplomatic scandal embroiled microwaves in a story of Cold War espionage with potentially far-reaching health implications. According to a State Department report, the Soviet Union had been beaming microwaves at the American Embassy building in Moscow for fifteen years, either to eavesdrop or to prevent eavesdropping.[26] When the State Department realized what the Russians had been doing, the United States installed aluminum screens on all of the embassy windows to block the waves in the same way that the mesh Faraday cage shielding in the glass door of a microwave oven prevents waves from passing through the glass. In essence, the Kremlin had turned the embassy building into a nine-story microwave, and although the new screens were meant to keep the waves out, not in, the boxy edifice now resembled an oversized kitchen appliance. Stranger than any urban legend, the scandal of the microwaved embassy made the front page of major newspapers more than once. The thought that Russia, whose scientists acknowledged microwave sickness as a threat, had been slowly nuking Americans for fifteen years made the act all the more repellent.

The nefarious Kremlin microwave scandal fueled speculation about the health hazards of low-level radiation. According to the *Times*, the ambassador was suffering from bleeding in his eyes and nausea.[27] According to *Boston Globe*, the condition was "a mysterious blood ailment" resembling leukemia.[28] Officials downplayed health concerns, but a medical investigation found elevated lymphocyte counts in one-third of the embassy employees tested. Four months later, two young girls living in the embassy were sent back to the United States to be treated for "unusual blood conditions," followed a year later by a preschool-age boy with similar anomalies.[29] Science writer Paul Brodeur reported on the Moscow microwave crisis for the *New Yorker* and in 1977 expanded his work into the book *The Zapping of America*. Brodeur lists cataracts, male infertility, genetic damage, cancer, and a host of other infirmities among the many risks of exposure. Backed by journalistic credibility, Brodeur's claim to have uncovered "a conspiracy of silence about the potential hazards of microwave radiation" carried weight.[30] Even allegations about classified experiments with microwave-based mind control research had appeal that reverberated beyond the tinfoil hat crowd.[31]

Brodeur understood better than most the connections between geopolitical, corporate, natural, and home environments. Brodeur had worked counterintelligence for the US Army at an underground storage depot for nuclear weapons in Germany before landing a job as a staff writer for the *New Yorker*. In 1968, his reporting brought unprecedented attention to asbestos-related diseases and the conspiracy to cover up the known dangers. A spate of lawsuits followed. In 1971, Brodeur turned his attention to the hazards of enzyme detergents, prompting the FDA to investigate. Major manufacturers promptly removed the enzyme from their products. On the heels of the asbestos scandal and the detergent story, Brodeur's *Zapping of America* completed a trifecta of household hazards: lethal dust, flesh-eating cleaning products, and now, killer microwaves. The bubble of the domestic sphere, it seemed, was insulated with carcinogens, kept clean with the help of injurious enzymes, and irradiated by a Pandora's box that also happened to make popcorn in record time.

Microwave "Atmoterror"

Brodeur's reporting participates in what German philosopher Peter Sloterdijk calls the "demonic nature of the explicit"—an "explication" process or summoning to the foreground of background circumstances such as "the air we thoughtlessly breathe" or the atmospheres in which we are immersed.[32] The acceleration of the explication process is what terrorism, design, and environmentalism have in common, according to Sloterdijk, as first manifest in the twentieth-century by the German poison chlorine gas attack near Ypres on April 22, 1915.[33] By aiming at the enemy's environment, gas warfare brought the "climatic and atmospheric premises of human existence" to the foreground.[34] The need to design against the atmosphere had never been so urgent. As atmoterrorism (to use Sloterdijk's term) entered the theater of war, opposing nations rushed to construct immunity spheres for their troops. Millions of gas masks traveled from the production lines to the front lines. Soldiers took on an insectoid appearance, their human features hidden behind the proboscis-like housing for the air filters that had become as important to defense as trenches.[35]

Between wars, Germany turned the products of atmoterror against insects. Berlin chemists waged assaults on bed bugs, lice, moths, and gnats. The cyanide-based fumigation product Zyklon B, which emerged from post-WWI German research, nearly monopolized the world market for pest control. The Germans piled carpets, upholstery, and other textiles into mobile or stationary "disinfestations chambers" to be gassed and then aired out once the vermin had been eradicated.[36] When Hitler proposed his "Final Solution," the rhetoric for pest control dehumanized Jews, and Zyklon B took part in the project of genocidal extermination. In one night, using the same concentration recommended for delousing, SS officers at Auschwitz forced 1,492 Jews deemed "unfit for work" into Morgue I of Crematorium II and gassed them to death with six kilograms of Zyklon B.[37] Some of the gas chambers at Majdanek continued to serve the clothing fumigation needs of German citizens even as neighboring gas chambers used the same products to kill the men, women, and children labeled vermin by their government.

In the United States during the same period, political cartoons and pesticide advertisements under the banner of patriotism conflated humans and insects as infestations. A magazine for the US Marines calls for the complete annihilation of the "Louseous Japanicas," while ads by insecticide manufactures graft enemy heads onto bug bodies to elevate the heroism of their product. However humorous the intent of the cartoons, historian Edmund P. Russel notes, the "calls for annihilation of human enemies had, by the end of the war, become realistic."[38] The carpet-bombing techniques of pest control, the incendiary carpet-bombing of cities, and the indiscriminate devastation of the atomic bombing of Hiroshima and Nagasaki are signs that the atmoterror of World War I had reached its apotheosis in World War II.

When Mrs. Peltzer sprays flea and tick killer into the eyes of a gremlin, slams the door of the microwave chamber closed, and then "nukes" the creature, her instinctive combat technique connects wartime atmoterror to household products and appliances. Billy Peltzer likewise shows an instinct for war-tested extinction techniques when all of the creatures gather at the local movie theater to watch Disney's *Snow White and the Seven Dwarfs* (1937). As the gremlins sing "Heigh-ho, heigh-ho," Billy and his friend Kate sneak down to the boiler room and open the gas valves. As gas fills the theater, Billy lights a wad of newspaper. The gremlins notice and give chase. Gizmo in tow, the couple exits through the alleyway door. Gremlins claw for escape, their arms reaching wildly through the closing door as Kate and Billy force it closed. Billy and Kate take cover behind a car at a safe distance and watch what they believe to be the complete extinction of the gremlin race.

Does this make Billy Hitler? The fact that he drives a VW Beetle (the Third Reich's answer to the affordable American car) does him no favors, should one wish to pursue that reading. On the other hand, the Peltzer surname ties Billy to Ashkenazi Jews in Germany. Thus, in one reading the gremlins are Jews, and in the other the gremlins are Nazis and the theater scene a precursor to Tarantino's cinema massacre in *Inglourious Basterds* (2009). Ultimately, deciding on a single label for the gremlins is a fool's errand. As critic Jonathan Rosenbaum noted in his 1985 review, the possibilities are infinite: "The evil beasties can be plausibly read at various times as (a) adolescents, (b) blacks, (c) Native Americans, (d) good ole boys, (e) people who like Walt Disney (or Steven Spielberg) movies, (f) mischievous kids, (g) hoboes, (h) monsters—anyone can add to the list."[39] Director Joe Dante's copious quotation of popular cinema (no fewer than sixty cinematic references according to his own statements to the press) complicates a static reading of the creatures.[40] More important here than resolving their identity is understanding how thoroughly the monsters are steeped in the conditions of atmoterror brought to the foreground by twentieth-century warfare and subsequently domesticated in products such as flea spray and microwaves.

Gremlin symbolism may be slippery, but gremlin provenance is clear. One need only lend an ear to the resident unemployed drunken xenophobe of Kingston Falls, Mr. Futterman, to see that gremlins, like microwaves, are creatures of World War II: "That's the same gremlins that brought down our planes in the big one. That's right. World War Two . . . good old WWII. You know, they're still shipping 'em over here. They put them in the cars, they put them in the TV, they put them in the stereos, and in the radios you stick in your ears, they put 'em in there. They put 'em in your watches; they got little teeny gremlins." Although no one is inclined to pay attention to a man who rants excessively and drives a combine around town, he is right about the connection between gremlins and World War II. Gremlin mythology comes from pilots of the Royal Air Force, and if Walt Disney had been able to copyright the critters, the gremlins in the Kingston Falls movie theater might have been watching an animated feature about themselves rather than *Snow White and the Seven Dwarfs*.

Roald Dahl, author of *James and the Giant Peach*, *Charlie and the Chocolate Factory*, and other beloved children's books, claimed to have invented gremlins during his time as a fighter pilot for the RAF, although a more accurate statement would be that Dahl was the first to fully flesh out the gremlin lore that had been circulating among RAF pilots for some time. Dahl was injured in 1940 when his plane crashed in the Sahara desert.

While recovering, he wrote *The Gremlins*, a story about a pilot downed by gremlin sabotage. The pilot meets one of the gremlins, learns of their history, and eventually founds a Gremlin Training School where the creatures learn to repair planes rather than destroy them. Dahl's gremlins are not evil critters sent by foreigners but rather spritely forest folk displaced by the construction of a factory that builds airplanes for the war. Without the war's negative ecological impact, the gremlins would have steered clear of humans and their machines. Dahl's gremlins, like Dante's, are victims of war technology.

In 1942, Disney put out a seven-page spread in *Cosmopolitan* magazine called "Meet the Gremlins."[41] *Punch* and *Life* magazines ran their own gremlin stories the same year. *Punch* describes the gremlin as a large-eared, twenty-inch-high, seventeen-pound creature that looks like a cross between a North American jackrabbit and a bull terrier—a portrait nearly identical to Dante's gremlins. "Gremlins are found literally everywhere," says *Punch*, and getting rid of them is nearly impossible.[42] *Life* maintains that no one but aviators has ever seen a gremlin, but "gremlins are just as real for aviators as, for instance, Santa Claus is for children."[43] Gremlins have never caused fatal accidents, and pilots have "warm feelings for them," as they make convenient scapegoats for every mishap.[44] Not one report of gremlins has emerged from Germany, states the *Life* article, as if having gremlins were a badge of honor for the Allies, which it was, quite literally. For although the Disney movie never saw the silver screen, the gremlin characters proliferated on military insignia, and the Women Airforce Service Pilots (WASP) adopted Fifinella, the female gremlin, as their mascot.[45] Gremlins are both an annoyance and a source of pride, like a system of checks and balances that permits the coexistence of civilization and its discontents.

Dante's gremlins, too, present a necessary counterweight to the unbearable cuteness of gizmos. Nasty as they are, gremlins provide an inescapable and vital demonic explication of the latent effects of technological objects purchased and adopted without a clear understanding of the stakes. No one needs a gremlin to understand the futility of Mr. Peltzer's inventions, which are, like Kingston Falls, already broken before the little devils spawn. The power of gremlins is in their interaction with those objects that seem to function smoothly and harmlessly in the background. The gremlin that meets its explosive demise in Mrs. Peltzer's kitchen does not destroy the microwave but rather brings to the foreground the machine's efficiency as an atmoterror device. Just as Russian spying scandals and health scares were fading from public consciousness, an exploding gremlin gave the horrified families who perhaps thought they had come to see the next *E.T.* a taste of what a microwave can do. Malfunction in the case of the microwaved gremlin is not about a machine functioning badly but rather about the bad functions that reside in the machine. The microwave, like *Gremlins*, divides into a good half and a nasty half. The good half makes popcorn or reheats leftovers, and the nasty half nukes pets, inflicts abuse, spies on you, cooks you from the inside out, alters your blood, and metes out vigilante justice should the need arise.

Notes

1. Roger Ebert, review of *Gremlins*, Warner Bros./Amblin, *Chicago Sun-Times*, June 8, 1984, http://www.rogerebert.com/reviews/gremlins-1984.

2. Ibid.

3. Richard Zoglin, Meg Grant, and Timothy Loughran, "Gremlins in the Rating System," *Time*, June 25, 1984, 94.

4. Ebert.

5. See Brunvand, 412–13.

6. That version of tale was brought to the screen six years after *Gremlins* as "Poodle Soufflé" in the prologue sequence to the horror comedy *The Willies* (1990).

7. The *Gremlins* microwave is a prop that was built to accommodate the puppet, but the control panel and wood veneer typifies the style of countertop models from the late 1970s and early 1980s.

8. Carl Willis, "Nuke," *Urban Dictionary*, March 12, 2005, http://www.urbandictionary.com/define.php?term=nuke.

9. Tappen advertisement, *House Beautiful*, October 1967, 139.

10. Ibid.

11. To be more precise, the frequencies called microwaves include a range from 300 MHz to 300 GHz, and although the standard is now 2.45 GHz, there were also microwaves at 915 MHz. For an overview of how a microwave works, see Buffler, 14–31.

12. While the melting chocolate bar narrative is the canonical version of the story, Spencer must not have been very surprised, given that many radar technicians were well aware of the heating properties of the microwave.

13. Earls and Edwards, 24, 79.

14. See Buffler, ix. Liegey, for the Bureau of Labor Statistics, puts the number at 25 percent, but the article references a study about how many households had both a microwave *and* a VCR.

15. Renard, 101.

16. Brunvand, 44. Another variant of the legend can be found as recently as 2000, in the *Daily Mail* story about an epileptic mother who microwaves her baby instead of milk while in the throes of a seizure and then comes to when the timer beeps to indicate the heating is done. See Mail Foreign Service, "Microwave Tragedy," *Daily Mail* (London, England), September 12, 2000, 17 (via *Daily Mail Historical Archive*).

17. "Horror of Babies 'Roasted Alive in Microwave Ovens,'" *Daily Mail* (London, England), December 9, 1987, 8 (via *Daily Mail Historical Archive*).
18. See Randell, Surrell, and Cohle.
19. Hugh McLeave, "Strange Case of the Oven 'Death Ray,'" *Daily Mail* (London, England), February 17, 1964, 10 (via *Daily Mail Historical Archive*).
20. Ibid.
21. Barnaby J. Feder, "Microwaves: Are They a Peril?," *New York Times*, April 21, 1981, D1.
22. Ibid.
23. A similar appeal to the rigors of Soviet science was used during the seventies by advocates of houseplant sentience and psychic abilities (see chap. 8, "Houseplant").
24. Buffler, 111.
25. Ernest Dickinson, "Microwave Sales Sizzle as the Scare Fades," *New York Times*, May 2, 1976, F1.
26. Bernard Gwertzman, "Moscow Rays Linked to U.S. Bugging: Moscow Radiation Is Now Linked to Jamming of U.S. Buskin," *New York Times*, February 26, 1976, 1.
27. Ibid.
28. William Beecher, "Did Soviet Microwaves Cause Envoy's Illness?," *Boston Globe*, February 16, 1976.
29. Associated Press, "Third Child at Moscow Embassy Is to Be Sent to U.S. for Tests," *New York Times*, January 21, 1977, 23.
30. Brodeur, 318.
31. One cannot help but wonder if Trump senior counselor Kellyanne Conway had some vague memory of the Russian microwave scandal or Brodeur's book in mind when she made the meme-worthy statement in 2017 that the Obama administration had been using "microwaves that turn into cameras" to spy on Trump.
32. Sloterdijk, 62–66.
33. Ibid., 85.
34. Ibid., 97.
35. World War II gas masks featured asbestos filters, making them the catch-22 of respiratory defense. See McDonald, Harris, and Berry.
36. See Sloterdijk, 108.
37. Ibid., 118.
38. E. Russell, 119.
39. Jonathan Rosenbaum, "Gremlins (1985 review)," December 19, 1985, https://www.jonathanrosenbaum.net/2018/12/gremlins-1985-review/.
40. See Lafond, 36.
41. Sturrock, 180.
42. "Gremlins, Aircrews, for the Use Of," *Punch* (London, England), November 11, 1942, 396 (via *Punch Historical Archive*).
43. "Gremlins," *Life Magazine*, November 16, 1943, 93.
44. Ibid.
45. See Maltin's introduction to the 2006 reissue of Dahl, viii.

3

TELEPHONE

The Telephonic Eye

"I saw what you did, and I know who you are," teenage Libby Mannering (Andi Garrett) purrs into the receiver in her best version of a seductive grown-up voice. She has been making prank phone calls with her friend while her parents are away. Little does she know that she has just reached a murderer who will stop at nothing to silence her. The harmless phone prank gone horribly wrong is the premise for William Castle's *I Saw What You Did* (1965). Critical reaction to the film was one of bewilderment at the uneven tone created by the presence of Joan Crawford, whose character seems to have stumbled onto the set of a *Gidget* popcorn flick and hijacked the movie for top billing.[1] Indeed, as Ned Schantz has observed, the film seems unable to decide "if it is a light teen-comedy or a vicious horror flick."[2] Nevertheless, when read as a "telephonic film" (to use Schantz's term), *I Saw What You Did* marks a pivotal moment in the cultural portrayal of communications technology. Castle's telephonic tug-of-war between an erstwhile noir persona and a chatty teenage girl makes *I Saw What You Did* a precursor to an entire home-alone-with-a-phone slasher subgenre that popped up in the 1970s with *Black Christmas* (1974), *Halloween* (1978), and *When a Stranger Calls* (1979). Castle updates what I have called the "phone fatale" of film noir and repurposes it as an important transitional object in the lives of American teenage girls.[3] In so doing, Castle suggests a sinister counterpoint to Ma Bell's rhetoric of enchanted technology and a reimagining of Little Red Riding Hood for an electronically mediated oral culture in which to speak is to tiptoe along wire paths amid a forest of telephone poles.

The idea of the telephonic forest is one crafted by Ma Bell herself in countless advertisements, company-generated histories, and educational films shown in millions of classrooms across America. One such epic

Fig. 3.1. Libby and Kit up to no good on the phone in *I Saw What You Did* (1965).

narrative, authored by the Information Department of AT&T in 1942, invites readers to imagine telephone poles as both a fence and a forest: "*Poles.* More than 15,000,000 of them, enough to build a solid transcontinental fence 30 feet high from New York to San Francisco. Fifteen million poles represent a forest over 800 square miles in extent."[4] Like the railroad and the highways whose paths they often line, the physical signs of telephony represent an integral part of the American landscape and the country's conquest of time and space. Stretching across the country like Paul Bunyan–sized fence posts, the poles stake out and domesticate the land. In the words of a popular AT&T ad from the 1920s and 1930s, "the continent that became a neighborhood" did so by planting poles and stringing lines.[5]

Phone company films and literature from the first half of the twentieth century invariably adopt a rhetoric of the technological sublime. Bell System's *Long Distance* (1941), for example, admires "the graceful drapery of the cables" along the "highways of wire" that form "vital transcontinental arteries" stretching "where the covered wagon made its plodding and heroic way." Films such as *Our Shrinking World* (1946), *The World at Your Call* (1950), and *The Nation at Your Fingertips* (1951) promise dreams of conquest and exploration all made possible while tethered safely to home. Even "a few spoken words from the depths of an Oregon forest" can reach across the nation to find friends and family waiting. And yet the conquest of one

Fig. 3.2. The forest primeval moves to Main Street (*American Magazine*, 1923).

forest is made possible by the creation of another—a hybrid that grafts the modern onto the ancient and embeds technology in nature.

In a headline as eerily uncanny as it is optimistic, a 1923 ad proclaims, "The forest primeval moves to Main Street."[6] The accompanying image of a toppling tree over which floats a graphic of telephone poles lining the street seeks to exemplify technological mastery over nature but unintentionally conveys a disquieting confrontation of the natural and civilized worlds. The declaration that a primeval forest is moving to town quite literally evokes the return of the repressed. For what is Main Street if not the antithesis of the "forest primeval?" The dangers of the forest are precisely what a town pushes away as civilization defines itself in opposition to the untamed wild. In that light, the eight-hundred-square-mile forest—which today (underground lines notwithstanding) has grown to ten times that size—substitutes itself for the enchanting and threatening forest of folklore and fairy tale.

Outside the control of phone propaganda, modern tales of dangerous phones abound. Most famously, the film noir genre employs the telephone as a metaphor for isolation, violence, and alienation—a phone fatale that creates bonds at once alluring and deadly. The prologue to one of the best-known examples, *Sorry, Wrong Number* (1948), tells how "in the tangled networks of a great city, the telephone is the unseen link between a million lives. . . . It is the servant of our common needs—the confidante of our inmost secrets. . . . Life and happiness wait upon its ring . . . and horror . . . and loneliness . . . and *death*." J. P. Telotte's study of the "tangled networks" of film noir concludes that in *Sorry, Wrong Number*, the phone embodies the core anxiety of modernity, binding individuals within a common "nexus of potential communication" such that all hope is qualified by a "possibly fatal vulnerability in every effort to speak of this condition."[7] In Hitchcock's *Dial M for Murder* (1954), the title alone implicates the technology as an accessory to homicide, and in *Detour* (1945), a man accidentally strangles a woman in an adjoining hotel room by pulling on the cord.

I Saw What You Did echoes the noir tradition of telephonic peril, but with a teenage twist. The film merges the idyllic existence of a country adolescent with the dark and murderous world of the city. Thanks to the phone, fifteen-year-old Libby Mannering need only choose at random a number from the directory and adopt the breathy voice of a starlet, and she becomes the femme fatale in a drama of her own creation. Life on the farm becomes less dull.[8] When Libby's new friend, Kit (Sara Lane), comes over for the evening, Libby and kid sister Tess (Sharyl Locke) proudly introduce their phone game. "Pick a name, Kit," says Tess, offering the phone book like a magician holding out a deck of cards. Kit chooses William Harrison, and the show begins:

"Hello," says Libby in a breathy voice. "Is Bill there?"

"Who is this?" asks the woman at the other end of the line.

"This is Alice. I've been waiting for him. Almost an hour."

"*Waiting* for him?"

"Yes. At the Green Garter Club. He promised to be on time."

"Well, this is *Mrs.* Harrison. I'll be sure to tell him!"

The girls burst into laughter. "Oh. This is his wife? I'm sorry; I must have the wrong number." A film noir theme becomes a teenage prank.

The success of the girls' pranks can be measured by their ability to access and control the adult sphere. Young Tess best achieves that control by playing a stranded child who has just spent her last dime on a call meant to reach her mother. She then persuades the woman to come to her rescue by making the call for her. Although Libby repeatedly tells Tess to "grow up" throughout the film, the prank calls provide the sole arena for Tess to assume a role of complete dependence with Libby's approval. Libby, in turn, must play the mother to complete the drama. A maternal role is never Libby's preferred disguise, but her convincing performance highlights the protean possibilities of disembodied communication. Libby prefers to play the promiscuous woman, and the phone grants her that fantasy in a way that real-world dress-up cannot deliver. Wearing the telephone as a disguise, the two sisters are able to flee the disenfranchised limbo of adolescence in opposite chronological directions.

Libby's real-life frustrated attempts at independence take center stage at the beginning of the film when the sitter cancels at the last minute. Although reluctant to leave a fifteen-year-old in charge, Libby's mother (Patricia Breslin) capitulates, her worries assuaged only by the belief that she will be able to monitor her children long-distance via telephone. Tying up the line with pranks therefore gives Libby complete freedom from parental interference. Her use of the phone is a conduit to adulthood just as the corresponding denial of phone contact from her mother is a way to "cut the cord." When Mrs. Mannering contacts the switchboard operator to ask why she has been getting a busy signal for two hours, the operator does no more than confirm that the number is busy. Libby's empowerment by phone coincides with the phone service's failure to allow remote mothering. Mrs. Mannering is left

Fig. 3.3. William Castle's eye mask in *I Saw What You Did* (1965).

with the ambiguity of the busy signal, which for her indicates distress but for her husband provides reassurance. "So they're talking. So everything's perfectly normal."

Libby's path to teenage emancipation strays into noir drama when the girls pick the name Steve Marak (John Ireland) from the phone book. Libby once again dons her sexy persona, unaware that her call has reached a marriage in crisis. At Libby's insistence, Mrs. Marak goes to find Steve in the bathroom, where a confrontation ends in her death. Meanwhile, oblivious to the violence sparked by their phone call, the girls hang up and decide to call back later. The call to Steve Marak signals a shift in tone characterized by one critic as "a redundant middle chapter involving the aroused, snarling killer, played by John Ireland, and his predatory, love-hungry neighbor, Miss Crawford."[9] Seconds after Steve has washed the blood off his hands, Amy (Joan Crawford) knocks on the door and complains, "I tried to call you three times, but your line was busy." The phone has not served Amy any better than it has Libby's mother. The phone lines clearly belong to a younger generation in this film.

The tension established between Libby and Amy is based on two modes of access to the same man. On one side is the teen with the phone, and on the other, the neighbor who can knock on the door or peer out her window. The film's title, *I Saw What You Did*, puts vision center stage, or more properly, it puts the *illusion* of vision center stage—a claim to sight via a telephonic eye. The pretitle sequence establishes the conflation of phone and eye by framing Libby and Kit in a pair of giant eyes as they talk on the phone. Rather than opt for the typical split-screen phone call, Castle masks each girl in her own "eye" so that when Libby places a call, her eye (on the left) opens, and when Kit answers, the right eye opens to reveal her in her room. Whenever a girl hangs up, the corresponding eye closes. This clever gimmick literally overlays the visual onto the aural, as if to say that hearing is seeing or, more specifically, that telephoning is seeing. The effect is alternately playful and menacing. As the first eye opens to show Libby making the call, Castle seems to be winking at the viewer. The second eye opens, and the effect is that of filming through a ski mask. The mask view lends an immediate sense of voyeurism to telephonic communication and replaces the objective lens with a subjective point of view—not that of a murderous stalker, as we might first expect, but that of the telephone or, more specifically, that of acoustic sight.

"We simply are not equipped with earlids," writes Marshall McLuhan.[10] And yet the humorous neologism seems to best describe Castle's opening phone sequence. For McLuhan, sight and sound represent two distinct cultural and technological modes of relating to time and space. He associates sight with print culture and sound with oral culture. As the dominant mode of cultural production since Gutenberg, print organizes the world through a rational, linear, and visually oriented means of communication. In contrast, oral culture exists in a mode of simultaneity that McLuhan associates with the primitive: "Until writing was invented, man lived in acoustic space: boundless, directionless, horizonless, in the dark of the mind, in the world of emotion, by primordial intuition, by terror."[11] Writing favors the eye; writing visualizes sound and orders the world. Conversely, "the ear favors no particular 'point of view.'"[12] In McLuhan's mind, the telephone is by nature related more to primitive emotion than to centuries of literary rationality because it takes us back to acoustic space.[13] From his vantage point (to use a visual metaphor), print culture conditions society to impose rational, linear, sight-driven thinking on any new media. In spite of that conditioned response, the inherent message of acoustic technologies subverts the singular viewpoint. In the context of those two competing cultural modes, Castle's conflations of eye and ear—his "earlids"—are symptomatic of the profound conflict between old media models and new extensions of the self.

I Saw What You Did personifies the visual/acoustic dissonance most powerfully in the rivalry between the two "women" of the film—Libby's persona, "Suzette," and Amy—or, more properly, between the woman Steve hears and the woman Steve sees. The section of the film that comes across as generically confused is, in fact, a battle that pits the physical gaze (Amy) against the telephonic eye (Libby). The shift toward female power occurs when Amy becomes an eyewitness. In a shot reminiscent of Hitchcock's *Rear Window* (1954), Amy peeks out her window and spies Steve dragging something into the trunk of his car. The film cuts back to the country house where Libby is playing her phone games. The juxtaposition immediately establishes the competing acoustic "sight" mode. Even the film's rewording of the prank from the novel's "I know who you really are, and I know what you did" to "I saw what you did" foregrounds the visual.[14] When the girls pick up the phone, they are attempting to open an acoustic window.

After Steve returns, we find Amy emboldened rather than scared by the suspicious activity she has witnessed. And yet just as she begins to plan her future life with Steve, a ringing telephone competes for attention. "Let it ring!" yells Amy with the kind of melodramatic desperation normally reserved for a standoff between competing love interests. By commanding attention, the telephone has already won the power struggle between sight and sound. Even before Libby's alter ego "Suzette" speaks, she has already pulled Steve into the terror of the acoustic. She is the invisible woman-telephone, whereas Amy is detached from the network. In spite of her status as an eyewitness, Amy's physical presence limits her claim to power. Thus, Steve's sole preoccupation is to separate "Suzette" from her phone. "Where are you calling from? Where can I reach you?" he says, while Amy jealously waits. "Wouldn't you like to know," taunts Libby before hanging up.

After Amy fails to win Steve's attention with promises of love and money, she quietly heads to the bedroom, where a second telephone allows her to eavesdrop on the next call. One might expect Amy's use of the phone to put her on equal footing with "Suzette," perhaps giving her information to leverage against Steve or to destroy her rival. Instead, Amy's interaction with the phone is brief and her eavesdropping redundant. She can already hear Steve's side of the conversation through the door, and she learns nothing new about Suzette by listening in. Her momentary eavesdropping appears so pointless that the act of placing the receiver back on the hook takes on more significance than the use of the phone. The shot of Amy holding the receiver recalls the iconic still of Barbara Stanwyck in the quintessential telephonic film noir *Sorry, Wrong Number*.[15] Less an homage than an acknowledgment of impotence, the abandonment of the phone midconversation reminds the viewer that the technology in this film belongs to another woman and another generation. Amy has already lost, even before Steve puts her out of the picture.

For Libby, the uncertainty of acoustic space allows access to eroticism and danger. "What a sex maniac! He does wanna date!" she tells Kit while covering the receiver. Steve pushes for a time and a place, but Libby hangs up, leaving them to imagine how "exciting" and "sexy" Steve must be. "His voice was so deep. So exciting! It's like he was running his hand down my back. Real slowly," says Libby. Libby's gross misinterpretation of Steve's motives generates the suspense of the film in the same way that the noir tradition underscores the insufficiency of telephonic communication, but with the crucial difference that Libby's actions are fueled by adolescent sexual desire. She is not a femme fatale but rather a Little Red Riding Hood in a telephonic forest.

The folkloric Little Red Riding Hood, as Jack Zipes observes, "was not just a warning tale, but also a celebration of a young girl's coming of age."[16] Later versions changed to reflect different value systems and various civilizing discourses. Perrault's literary version transforms the brave peasant girl of the folk tradition into a spoiled brat to warn little girls that they "could be 'spoiled' in another way by a wolf/man."[17] The Grimms' version adds the happy ending and emphasizes the Christian moral of avoiding carnal temptation. Film adaptations have also varied over time. Zipes divides the adaptations into two phases: the first beginning with Méliès in 1901 and continuing through 1979, and the second beginning with the publication of "The Company of Wolves" (adapted for film in 1984) and continuing to the present day. The first phase focuses on the need for "policing by an armed huntsman," whereas films in the second phase depict "a more forceful young woman intent on following her desires and breaking with the male gaze of domination."[18]

I Saw What You Did clearly follows the morality of Riding Hood's literary traditions, as Libby concludes their adventure by telling her sister, "We're not going to be using the phone for a long, long time."[19] Even the "wolf" delivers the didactic message of telephone safety in Castle's tale.

Once Steve arrives at Libby's house and sees her in person, he declares, "You're not Suzette. You're just a kid." Libby explains that it was just a game. Steve then scolds her and threatens to tell her parents. Before he turns to leave, he gives one last piece of advice: "Don't use the phone for fun and games anymore!" Steve's function is that of the wolf, who, as Zipes observes, "is *sent* to teach her and the audience a lesson."[20] In the best-known literary versions of the tale, that lesson "was both Christian and male."[21] Here, that message is the same, but the dangerous forest has been replaced by telephony. Once the phone is taken out of the equation, Steve reasserts his dominance and assures their mutual security. Without a phone, Libby is "just a kid," and Steve is just another adult with her best interest at heart.

The phone triggers the final scenes of violence just as it had set in motion the initial murder earlier that night. Kit calls Libby to warn her about Steve, but in so doing, she alerts the killer. Now the would-be prey of a knife-wielding maniac, Libby escapes thanks to the male authority figure of a policeman. Less the rite of passage of the early Riding Hood folktales and more the didactic cautionary tale of the literary tradition, Libby's wanderings through the telephonic forest have led her back to a life on the farm without telephone privileges. After Libby's vow of telephonic chastity, the mood abruptly changes—the two sisters laugh, and the teen beach party genre music used at the beginning of the film lightens the mood. The camera pulls back to a crane shot above the trees, the picture dissolves to a shot of a telephone pole laden with phone lines, and the happy soundtrack is replaced by the chipmunk-like chatter of all the people still connected to the telephonic forest. Then, at normal speed, a female voice says, "Sorry. You have reached a disconnected number." Finally, the words "The End of the Line" appear before the final credits.

Castle's walk into the telephonic forest is as much a warning to adults about disruptions to the civilizing process as it is a cautionary tale to adolescents about the abuse of telephone privileges. *I Saw What You Did* revolves around teenage access to communications technology and the resulting conflict between generations, genders, and genres when adult control of that sphere diminishes. For more than half of the movie, the teenage girls are the predators. Without their prank calls, Steve's wife could have taken her already-packed suitcase and left, Amy would not have been driven by rivalry with "Suzette," and Steve would have had no reason to escalate his violent behavior. Despite Libby's disavowal of technological mischief, the final shot of telephone poles, the accompanying sound of high-speed chatter, and the cyclical return to happy-go-lucky beach party music suggest an eternal return of telephonic disruption not unlike the inevitable reappearance of Michael Myers, Jason Voorhees, or Freddy Krueger in slasher franchises.

Castle's promotional trailers and stunts are warnings not about making calls but rather about receiving them. "Don't Answer It!" the trailer warns three times as various (adult) arms reach for a ringing phone. "Your Name Is in This Book! It Could Happen to You!" it continues—a warning more logically relevant to adults in light of most telephone listings at the time.[22] Contrary to the moralizing conclusion of the movie, Castle's promotions actively encouraged teenagers to use the phone for entertainment. As a tie-in with phone companies, Castle placed huge plastic phones in front of theaters advertising his movie and put ads in newspapers with numbers for people to call. "Upon dialing, a girl's voice answered and whispered sexily, 'I saw what you did, and I know who you are,' and then made a date to meet the potential customer at whatever local theater was showing the picture."[23] In retaliation for the rash of crank calls set off by the campaign, the telephone company took away the giant phones and threatened to disconnect Castle's home line, thus mirroring the denial of phone privileges shown in the film. If the big bad wolf's message—"Don't use the phone for fun and games anymore"—is the moral of Castle's story, then *I Saw What You Did* is a spectacular failure. A more accurate characterization is given by Castle himself: "The telephone was the star . . . and the telephone companies around the country were my main target."[24] In spite of Joan Crawford's top billing, hers was not the career Castle rescued from petrification. By wresting the phone from the hands of its noir predecessors, *I Saw What You Did* marks an important if awkward transition toward a teenage-oriented libidinization of telephony in horror films and a recasting of folk narrative tropes for a new generation. The connecting link between generations of modern film heroines in peril may well be a phone line.

"The Calls Are Coming from the House!"

The first cinematic use of the "call coming from the house" is the sorority slasher *Black Christmas* (1974), which features no fewer than eighteen phone calls, six of which come from a psychopath living secretly in the sorority house attic.[25] *Black Christmas* does not present naive teenagers or indulge in exploitation. Instead, it features sexually liberated but fully clothed,

Fig. 3.4. Jess waits for her tormentor to call in *Black Christmas* (1974).

career-driven students. Released less than a year after *Roe v. Wade*, *Black Christmas* focuses on a timely issue through a protagonist, Jess (Olivia Hussey), who has decided to terminate an unwanted pregnancy in order to focus on her studies. This is a far cry from the teenagers of *I Saw What You Did*, who are at once naive and audaciously predatory. Socially speaking, Jess and Libby are worlds apart. Telephonically, Libby is the more active of the two. Libby makes fourteen calls, whereas Jess does little more than answer the phone. Of the eighteen calls in *Black Christmas*, only one is outgoing from a sorority girl: call seven from Jess to the police. Mapped out by caller, we get the following additional calls: two calls from parents checking on children, two from an angry boyfriend to Jess, five from Billy (a.k.a. "the moaner"), and eight related to the phone tap and trace. Jess is central to twelve of the calls—calls related to policing and monitoring, calls meant to influence her reproductive choice, and calls that make sexually explicit threats. What served as a transitional object of exciting and dangerous connections to adulthood for the teens of *I Saw What You Did* is reduced in *Black Christmas* to a point of vulnerability. Jess is not so much skipping through a telephonic forest as she is trapped by it, waiting for the huntsmen at the telephone company and police station to locate the wolf.

Black Christmas positions the four murders inside the sorority in juxtaposition to a tragedy that has occurred outside in a wooded park.

Parents (to sorority house)
call 1: Barb's mother to Barb
call 4: Clare's father looking for Clare

Threats
call 2: "the moaner"* to Jess/Barb
call 5: "the moaner" to Jess
call 6: "the moaner" to Jess
call 11: "the moaner" to Jess
call 17: "the moaner" to Jess

*"the moaner"= Billy and/or Agnes

Phone Company (to Police)
call 9: Graham to Fuller
call 14: Graham to Fuller
call 15: Graham to Fuller

Phone Company (to self)
call 8: Graham to phone exchange
(setting up tap)

Boyfriend
call 3: Peter to Jess
call 13: Peter to Jess

Jess
call 7: Jess to Police

Police
call 10: Fuller [to unidentified]
call 12: Fuller to Jess
call 16: Fuller to Jess
call 18: Officer Nash to Jess
"The calls are coming from the house!"

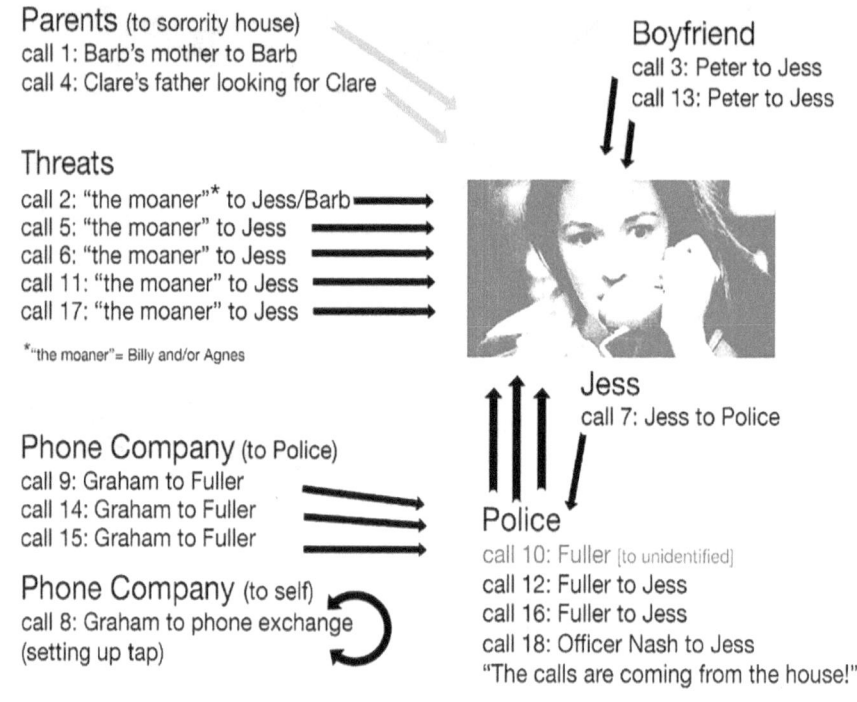

Fig. 3.5. The phone calls of *Black Christmas* (1974).

A fifteen-year-old "townie" named Janice has gone missing. As locals search the park, a student named Clare, back at the sorority, struggles to breathe through a plastic bag held tightly around her head by the psychopathic prank caller, Billy. When a girl from the search party discovers Janice's body, her scream cuts to Clare's gaping mouth, shrink-wrapped by her own dying gasps for air, then back to the park, where Janice's mother has just approached the crime scene. The mother opens her mouth to scream, and once again the film cuts to the sorority, substituting the human voice with the mechanical demand for attention coming from Billy inside the house. The cuts from outside to inside use the townspeople as a foil for the telephone.

A sense of benign urgency surrounds a ringing telephone in the eyes of the townsfolk and perhaps in the attitude of all landline subscribers in the era before caller ID. An interrupted porch conversation between a local woman and Jess concerning the tragic murder at the park typifies the deference paid to the device. "Your phone is ringing," says the woman mid-conversation, fully expecting its demands to receive priority. In the social hierarchy of conversations, the ringing phone stands in for every person not immediately present and thereby trumps face-to-face interaction. Indeed, even later innovations such as caller ID and haptic feedback do not eliminate the demand to check the phone. Far from annoyed at the interruption, the woman on the porch looks at Jess with a judgmental eye, as if Jess had been irresponsible not to notice the telephone and tend to its needs. The comparison that philosopher Vilém Flusser makes between a ringing telephone and "a hysterically whining child that must get its way on the spot before it will quiet down" is especially pertinent here, where motherhood is very much on the line.[26]

A second doorway conversation between Jess and members of the local search party demonstrates by omission the perceived limits of the telephone's invasive power. "You just keep your doors and windows locked and you'll be safe," say the two goofy men. Safe, because the telephone's power to open domestic space to the outside world presupposes a distance that precludes risk of bodily harm. Therefore, the police initially dismiss Jess's report of threatening calls as a problem best handled by the phone company. Lieutenant Fuller intervenes on a hunch that the murder in the park, a missing-persons report, and the prank calls share a connection. The hunch warrants a tap, which means that Fuller, too, must turn to the phone company for help. Enter phone technician Graham as the unlikely equivalent of the huntsman. Graham sets up a tap at the sorority—the first allusion to the hidden recesses of hardware—and outfits the police station with a matching phone whose mouthpiece has been disabled to prevent ambient station noise from reaching the caller. Consequently, Lieutenant Fuller can do little more than listen to Jess's attempts to keep the caller on the line while Graham follows the trail of the machine-to-machine conversation back at the telephone exchange.

The electromechanical exchange in *Black Christmas*, a "step-by-step" Strowger exchange, was already outdated in the 1970s, but the process of replacing mechanical systems with electronic switching systems (ESS) was expensive and slow.[27] The paths that huntsman Graham must trace in the telephonic forest are determined by the mechanical steps in the switching mechanism that connect one caller to another. In a step-by-step exchange, a call is connected one "step" at a time with each digit dialed. When the caller lifts the receiver, a "line finder" at the station connects the caller's

Fig. 3.6. Graham does the trace race at the telephone exchange in *Black Christmas* (1974).

line in circuit with a first selector, which returns a dial tone. Each release of the rotary dial sends a corresponding number of pulses that tell a selector to hunt for an idle circuit and connect to the next selector. The "trunk hunting" process works as follows: if a caller's finger dials a "3," the selector arm moves up to the third semicircular row of circuits and then across horizontally until it finds an idle circuit on that row. The next digit moves to the next selector, where the process repeats—up to the level demanded by the digit, and then across horizontally to find an idle circuit in the connector bank of that row. Each "step" (or dialed digit) determines a path through a combination of user input (i.e., the finger in the dial speaking telephone) and the "decisions" of the machine based on what other selectors serving other callers are doing at that very moment. Underlined type in a 1954 training manual emphasizes the volition of the machine in the search for an idle circuit: "The selector will move up to the specified level under the influence of the customer's dial and will proceed to find an idle trunk *of its own accord*."[28] Otherwise stated, the pathway of a phone call is vertically predictable but horizontally poetic. Humans have built the grammar, but the machine makes the rhetorical choices that move the switching pathway from line finder to final selector.

The "trace race" of an electromechanical switching station requires the machine to be caught in the act once it has passed through the connector bank and into the caller's terminal. Absent a call history record (at that time, rarely available for local calls), the tracks of a call evaporate the moment one of the parties hangs up. The familiar one-minute "keep him on the line" formula is an estimate of how long it takes a human to run the course of the connection path backward, like following a string through a maze. In that regard, the formula is plausible. Had *Black Christmas* been made a decade later, when ESS could do Graham's work in an instant, the "keep him on the line" trope would have been a complete anachronism. Even in the electromechanical system depicted in *Black Christmas*, a diode inserted into the proper test point could eliminate the need to keep the malicious caller on the line by essentially freezing the path of the call (the switch train) in place even after the caller hangs up. Thus, from a technical standpoint, *Black Christmas* takes a theoretically accurate but inefficient approach for dramatic purposes, one that highlights the ephemeral nature of telephone switching.[29] The persistence of the trope in films decades beyond real-world practice demonstrates to what extent telephony resides in the "black box" of the technological unknown.

Telephone sets inside homes and telephone lines strung across poles outside yield a misleading tin-can-and-string analogy for phone service. In contrast, the telephone exchange in *Black Christmas* bombards us with a cacophony of machines that we have not been metaphorically equipped to grasp. Rarely do we see the insides of an exchange. In its most familiar cinematic (and scholarly) depictions, a telephone exchange tends to revolve around the bygone figure of the female operator who manages tangles of lines and sockets with arachnid-like dexterity. The iconic "telephone girl" offers rich analytic possibilities for discussing the gendering of communication networks or the role of women as mediators, but the appeal of that imagery, like the trace race, has far outlasted real-world practice. The persistence of human-centered representations of telephone switching acts as a psychological buffer against intimidating encounters with machines in themselves.

If "a heightening of contact with the universe of things is traumatic," as Stephen Shaviro asserts, *Black Christmas* succeeds at inducing that trauma by placing the heart of the chase in what looks to be a foreboding, empty technopolis.[30] At times, only a portion of telephone technician Graham's head is visible through the rows of selector switches held in their 11'5" frames. Relay racks, selector frames, connector frames, and line finder frames dwarf the human presence, and the sounds of electromechanical speech burst like jarringly percussive machine-gun fire. Ladders that reach vertically out of frame allude to the canopy of iron bars high overhead that help anchor the towering rows in place. Graham must squeeze past the iron ladders to navigate the narrow aisles that separate row upon row of gray machinery. His lone pursuit of current through the exchange gives the impression of a city chase scene in Fritz Lang's *M* (1931) emptied of all the people. And arguably, *Black Christmas* is a descendent of the telephone-centric *M*, whose initial child abduction sequence concludes with a shot of a balloon caught in the telephone and electrical wires overhead. In both films, crime insinuates itself into the mechanisms of modernity, and the forces of law soon follow. In *M*, the physical pursuit of the criminal takes place on foot but is also followed remotely by telephone. In *Black Christmas*, the physical pursuit led by the townsfolk outside is made tangential to the hot pursuit conducted by Graham at the switching station. As the townsfolk of *Black Christmas* bumble about the periphery of the film like keystone cops, popping up every now and then at the sorority house door, the space of the town loses relevance.

The move toward telephonic space does not, for all of its incomprehensibility, negate its physicality. Telephony is not ghostly in *Black Christmas*; it is overwhelmingly material. *Black Christmas* relies neither on the techno-gothic haunted media trope nor on the crossed lines and missed connections of the noir tradition to generate horror. Instead, the film alludes to a technological space occulted by design but not haunted. The switching station multiplies the objects of telephony while keeping the protagonist and the lieutenant in their own separate locations, unable to seize the full picture. More unnerving than the notion that a ghost might speak through a machine in the manner of a living human is the fact that telephony exceeds anthropocentric volition at its connective core. The realization that the call is taking place at "group 140, terminal 55" as much as it is happening at "6 Belmont Street" is as uncanny as any peripheral glimpse of a presence only half-there. The switching station pulsates with constant expansion and collapse as connections and disconnections run their course along rows of machinery, changing paths with each call. Graham's race to the terminal adds its own dizzying effect by refusing the elision encouraged by the reductive tin-can-and-string metaphor. The call is taking place not only at two ends of a phone line but also at a police station and in a switching station. The sense of disequilibrium created by the spatial strain gives way to horror when the completed trace snaps all focus back to one physical location. Suddenly, only the house matters.

Borrowing a term from medicine, we might regard telephonic horror as a form of peripheral vertigo—an imbalance or dizzying excess of perceived movement caused by problems of the inner ear. In its most common form, benign paroxysmal positional vertigo (BPPV), a sense of imbalance is caused by dislodged calcium carbonate crystals floating in the inner ear canal, which confuse the brain with an excess sense of movement such that a person might be standing still physically yet moving perceptually. Telephony is vertiginous by definition, but its movements have been normalized. Telephonic horror recovers the disorientation of telephony; it jostles the system and puts telephonic space simultaneously out of reach and too close for comfort.

We could chart analogies between the telephone system and the vestibular system by comparing the vestibular labyrinth of the inner ear to the mechanisms of a telephone switching station (the semicircular structures that convey movements through electrical impulses) or the ear drum to the diaphragm of the transmitter with its grains of carbon excited by current. Phone company education departments have done as much in their instructional films. The technological history of the telephone-ear correspondence, however, exceeds pedagogical comparisons. Historian Jonathan Sterne has shown that the origins of psychoacoustic research are tied directly to Bell's efforts to expand the telephone system. The phone company has defined "what it means to hear and the notion of the hearing subject that subtends most audio technologies today."[31] Thanks to its research funding, by 1924, Bell quadrupled phone line capacity by identifying and selectively eliminating "surplus" frequencies, or frequencies judged unnecessary to the intelligibility of human speech.[32] Corporate-funded research sliced up the audio spectrum for profit, making Ma Bell the first acoustic slasher.

Sterne provides a disturbingly literal example of the conflation of the ear and mechanical telephony in the 1929 research experiment of Ernest Wever and Charles Bray, who attached electrodes to a cat's body and its auditory nerve, hooked them to a vacuum tube amplifier via sixty feet of shielded cable in a soundproof room, and then spoke into the cat's ear in one lab while a researcher listened through a telephone receiver in another. Sterne writes, "What we claim to know scientifically of hearing-in-itself—and how we know it—passes through the modern technological formation of sound."[33] Otherwise stated, it is not so much that the telephone is like an ear as it is that the ear has been treated as a telephone. Stern has the scholarly equivalent of a "calls are coming from inside the house" moment when he concludes, "There is no 'outside the system,' at least not for these cats, because media are already inside them."[34] By the same logic, we may also say that hearing is already *outside* of us, in the hardware of mouthpieces, switching stations, and wires and in software that determines which frequencies are relevant to conversation and music and which frequencies count only as noise. The ear and the "boundless, directionless, horizonless" acoustic space of McLuhan's pretypographic man encounter discipline, therefore, in frequency modulations and other channels of control built into the telephone system. Like the telegraph before it, the telephone system demands legibility of its medium, even if the literate elite is the line technician and the act of reading amounts to the conversion of a few numbers into a street address.

Once phone technician Graham races to group 140, terminal 55, and translates the numbers of the open circuit into the corresponding street address for the police, the presupposition of telephonic safety-through-distance collapses. Sergeant Nash radios Fuller with the news: "The phone company is on the other line, sir. They say they got a trace on this one. . . . He says the calls are coming from Number Six, Belmont Street." Fuller assumes Nash has misunderstood. "That's where the calls are going into," he says. Nash insists, "That's where they're coming from too, sir." A dissonant musical cue and a tense ticking sound fill the silence as Fuller realizes that the seemingly paradoxical proposition is true. The sorority housemother has a separate line in her room upstairs. The house has been divided against itself all along through two separate subscriber lines. Stuck in his car with only a police radio, Fuller must rely on Nash to call Jess and get her to exit the house.

Sergeant Nash delivers the panicked warning: "The caller is in the house! The calls are coming from the house!" Nash's two exclamatory statements correspond to two coexisting horrors. The first, and most obvious, is the menace of physical presence—the murderer is inside the house. The second is the shock of the house calling itself. Nash's omission of "inside" in the second statement, however negligible it may seem, provides an anthropomorphic boost to the climactic revelation and a commentary on the power of telephonic horror. The two sentences begin with two separate subjects: "The caller" and "The calls"—the embodied and the disembodied sources of fear, or the human and the telephone. Telephonic horror, thus understood, is not merely an extension of the killer but also a manifestation of the primordial terror hidden in the device itself, or in telephony as an object. Thus, even when we might expect a final chase and physical battle with the killer, Billy keeps to the shadows, peering through a crack in the door, a disembodied, telephonic eye. From the darkened room, he speaks as if making a call to the wrong party: "Agnes, it's me, Billy." Even as the final credits roll over a crane shot of the sorority house where Jess sleeps in vulnerable exhaustion, and where Billy still lurks in the attic, the dread looms not from approaching footsteps or the gleam of a knife but from the ring of an unanswered phone. No haunting score accompanies the final shot, only the background noises of the street and thirteen rings of a telephone.

"I haven't the right to think of anything but this telephone. It is a monster, a tower and a character," writes French filmmaker and theorist Jean Epstein in his seminal work on the close-up.[35] Epstein speaks of a "new rhetoric" concealed in the close-up and calls cinema "a cyclopean art, a unisensual art, an iconoscopic retina."[36] Sight wins out over sound every time for Epstein, but his choice of the telephone—the "acoustical pigeon house . . . from which everything good or bad may issue"—is a brilliant sleight of hand to demonstrate the magic of visual cinematic language.[37] For whether Epstein wants to say so or not, he well knows that every telephone comes preloaded with its own jarring soundtrack. Thanks to its ring, every telephone is a jump scare waiting to happen. Epstein's argument for the power of the close-up thus borrows sound (or its time-bomb-like potentiality) to assert the primacy of the visual. This argument is a cruel disservice to sound, but what better way to vaunt the photogenic prowess of the lens than to fix its gaze on the device associated with the monstrosity of acoustic sight?

As numerous close-ups of the device in telephonic slashers attest, the telephone itself is the source of fear as much as it is a metonymic link to a killer. *Halloween* (1978) makes this clear with Laurie's reactions to phone calls of her friends Annie and Lynda. Early in the film, before Halloween night, Laurie answers her phone and hears nothing. "Hello? Hello? Who is this?" she asks, distraught, and then hangs up violently. The phone rings again. Apprehensive, Laurie picks up. It's Annie. "You scared me to death!" cries Laurie. "I thought it was an obscene phone call!" Annie explains that she was chewing a sandwich. Later that night, Laurie mistakes a wordless call from Lynda as a prank from Annie. Michael Myers strangles Lynda with her telephone handset cord and then drops her lifeless body to the floor as Laurie's voice through the receiver says, "Annie? Annie?" Then, in one of the most haunting shots of the film, the figure considers the receiver

Fig. 3.7. Michael Myers says nothing on the phone in *Halloween* (1978).

almost quizzically and then lifts it to his masked face.[38] The silent presence of the connection reaches out to Laurie like the shadow of a menacing hand. She pulls the receiver away from her ear and stares at it as if compelled to consider the object before placing it back on the hook.

Even when Laurie is wrong about the obscene call, she is right, in that all phone calls are obscene—obscene in the Latin sense of *obscenus*, or that which is offstage. The absent-presence—the obscenity—of a phone call adds a dimension of violence to every call, no matter how friendly. Tellingly, three of the four "theological categories" Flusser uses to describe the position of the recipient in relation to a ringing phone involve fear. In the first, the absence of an awaited ring "evokes a tension that in extreme cases can lead to real existential crisis if the caller is not the one who was expected or if there is a bad connection."[39] The second category is the ring that interrupts attention to a person or object. Flusser equates this invasion of public space into private space to a break-in. The third category is the ring that aggressively interrupts a relaxed or sleeping person "like a knife in the stomach or heart."[40] Only in the fourth category, that of the phone in a station or an office, does Flusser speak of the ring as "an organic part of the life world it pierces"; only in this public space does he describe a natural openness to calls.[41]

Once the receiver is lifted, the telephone demands its own scripted, telephonic speech. Users must pass through mechanized, rote phrases ("hello," "who's there," "it's me," etc.) or obligatory "ritual words" before moving on to what Flusser calls "extratelephonic language."[42] The tension between those two modes and our haste to pass from the one to the other help explain one of the most powerful weapons of the obscene call: silence. Obscene silence keeps the recipient asking for an intolerable length of time, "Hello? Hello? Who is this? Who's there? Is that you? Who is calling?" In that dead air thrives an uncomfortable excess of the medium itself—a presence that extratelephonic language seeks to drown out. Most of us have experienced the slightest hint of that obscene horror in the lag time between our "hello" and the recorded voice of a telemarketing message. In that extra beat, we feel the unwelcome touch of nonhuman presence as it brushes by. Like the glimpse of a dark figure in the corner of one's eye, telephonic horror is peripheral and fleeting: begin a conversation, switch to extratelephonic speech, and it seems to vanish. Move from a threatening call to an on-scene chase with an embodied killer, and acoustic terror is eclipsed by the visual. But in *Black Christmas*, Billy, the cyclopean acoustic eye behind the door, keeps telephonic language on equal ground with the visual, and with each of the final thirteen rings during the credits, the telephone reasserts its obscene terror.

"Have You Checked the Children?"

Although *Black Christmas* is the first film to use the "call coming from the house" trope, *When a Stranger Calls* (1979) most faithfully replicates "The Babysitter and the Man Upstairs" urban legend that emerged in the 1970s.[43] The widely circulated tale features a babysitter subjected to a series of harassing phone calls from a man who asks, "Have you checked the children?" For whatever reason, the babysitter does not go upstairs to check, and so the calls continue. The frightened sitter dials the police, who tell her to keep the caller on the line so they can trace the calls, which, it turns out, are *coming from inside the house!* The police arrive in time to save the babysitter (or not, depending on the version), but the children have already been dead for several hours.

The first act (roughly the first twenty-two minutes) of *When a Stranger Calls* replicates the legend, filling in a couple of logical holes along the way such as why the babysitter does not go upstairs to check the children (the mother has instructed her not to disturb them because they are getting over bad colds) and how the calls from inside the house are technically possible (the father has an office line, and the police discover a third line left active by the previous owners).[44] The remainder of the film follows the detective

(Charles Durning) seven years later, now retired to the private sector and still traumatized by that gruesome night. When the killer (Tony Beckley) escapes from the asylum where he has been subjected to a regime of electroshock therapy and medication, the detective sees an opportunity to satisfy his need for vigilante justice. Confused but still able to elude capture, the psychopath unravels amid a skid row backdrop. Former babysitter Jill (Carol Kane), meanwhile, lives a peaceful life with her husband and their two children in a charming suburban home complete with white picket fence and gabled dormer windows. Unaware of the killer's escape, Jill leaves her children with a babysitter for a night out with her husband. At the restaurant, the maître d' tells Jill that she has a call. She answers, hears the familiar voice, screams, and collapses to the floor. Police officers find no sign of an intruder. Later that night, the lurking killer attacks Jill, but the detective bursts in and shoots the maniac in the nick of time.

The meandering second act of the film appeals to increasing social consciousness in the 1970s surrounding mental health care, addiction, and homelessness. The film humanizes the killer as we follow his confused wanderings. As his medication wears off, the killer's mental disintegration elicits our fear but also our sympathy. We share his point of view through violent flashbacks to the night of the crime. The killer cowers in anguish at the onslaught of memories, and we see, for the first time, a shot of him covered in blood sitting on the bed in the children's room, telephone in hand. By the time the film returns to suburbia, however, what little humanity had been established in the killer evaporates, quite literally, in a zoom out and dissolve during which he repeatedly denies his own existence. Once again, the psychopath is the stock figure from the "man upstairs" legend. He has no motive, only a drive to enact violence with the telephone as an accomplice. He is reduced once again to the maniacal telephone voice that asks the nagging question, "Have you checked the children?"

The seven-year leap that sees Jill move from the position of babysitter to that of mother projects the theme of babysitting as an attenuated form of motherhood into its actualization as a supposed inevitability. The babysitters of today are the mothers of tomorrow, the film seems to say, and even those who sit downstairs talking about boys on the phone while the children upstairs are slaughtered will one day become mothers and hire babysitters of their own. The haunting line "Have you checked the children?" therefore belongs not only to the voice of the maniac but also to that of the babysitter herself as a future mother. Grown-up Jill addresses the babysitter she has hired in words not so different from those of the maniac seven years earlier: "Sharon, please do me a favor; just tell me truthfully, when was the last time you checked my children?" In contrast to whatever sexually liberating qualities the telephone holds for adolescent girls, the disciplinary voices of absent parents and future children interfere with that freedom almost as incessantly as the harassing calls of a stranger.[45] Similarly, in the nonbabysitter movie *Black Christmas*, the voice of the unborn child is allied with the voice of the maniac, whose initial sexual calls later give way to taunts that echo Peter's angry objections about Jess's decision to abort. "Just like having a wart removed," the voice says as the police lieutenant listens in.

In telephonic horror, control of the telephone is tied to control over the reproductive potential of the female body. Pregnant women, too, are babysitters, and their phones participate in the struggle of access to their bodies. *Rosemary's Baby* (1968), also a telephone-centric horror film, features close-ups of Rosemary's bedroom telephone handset cord alongside her pregnant belly—a clear umbilical visual reference. As Jill holds her young girl while on the phone with her husband, we see the same umbilical reference of a phone cord tethering mother and child. In Rosemary's case, the threat from inside the house comes from her conspiratorial husband and from the demonic seed growing inside her. Access to the telephone corresponds to control of Rosemary's uterus, and her alienation from her home phone corresponds to her complete loss of control. Significantly, the cutting of Rosemary's phone line and the removal of the phone from her hands is the final action before the delivery of Rosemary's demon son and her subsequent separation from the baby. Phone cord and then umbilical cord, two connections between child and mother, are severed. Whether manifest in calls to or from an expectant mother, a babysitter, a coed dealing with an unwanted pregnancy, or a worried parent, the telephone is never indifferent to motherhood.

Once a babysitter and now a mother of two, Jill finds herself counting on the phone as a surveillance device and a safety net, a connection to her babysitter and to the police. In full embrace of traditional patriarchy, she relies on the phone as a connection between her kitchen and her husband's office. We first see the seven-years-later Jill in the kitchen at the stove, an apron tied around her waist. The kitchen phone rings. "Maybe it's Daddy," she says, and her son runs to answer. Indeed, it is Daddy, and he has called to tell Mommy some good news: "You know that dress I got you for your birthday? Well, now's your chance to wear it, 'cause I'm taking you out to

68 | *Household Horror*

Fig. 3.8. The umbilical phone cord in *Rosemary's Baby* (*top*, 1968) and *When a Stranger Calls* (*bottom*, 1979).

dinner tonight." We can safely assume that a recent newspaper article about Jill's community service did not receive the same dress-worthy celebratory treatment. Sharon, the babysitter, however, mentions the article the minute Jill comes downstairs for the date: "I saw your picture in the paper the other day. Congratulations!" Jill responds with self-deprecating modesty that the photo is awful (a tactical redirection from her accomplishment to her appearance). After Jill writes down the number for the restaurant and gives Sharon instructions about calling 911 for emergencies, the couple leaves, and the babysitter heads straight to the phone. As the sitter lifts the telephone from its place on the side table, the camera zooms in on the aforementioned clipped article ("Jill Lockhart Chairs Community Fundraiser"), which had been covered by the device now associated with the demands of motherhood.

Jill's days of frivolous phone use are long gone. "She is Mrs. John Lockhart now," declares the script.[46] As such, she is more Donna Reed than Gloria Steinem. Her big night out in celebration of her husband's promotion has her giggling with giddy delight at his success. Her newspaper article pales in comparison to a job promotion, but the recognition outside of the home has not gone unnoticed by the killer. A shot of the maniac's hand bending to pick up a crumpled newspaper from the gutter tells us that no lapse in domestic responsibility will go unpunished. Were it not for her picture in the paper, Mrs. Lockhart might never have been found. That voice asking if she has checked the children might never have come back.

The seven-year leap during which Jill has married and had children of her own also marks a transition for telephony. New push-button phones were replacing old rotary dials.[47] Touch-tone dialing was well on its way to becoming the norm. By 1976, 70 percent of Bell System lines offered touch-tone service to subscribers.[48] Behind the scenes, upgrades to switching stations ushered in what Bell Laboratories dubbed the "Service and Feature Era."[49] Jill mentions one of the most important of those new services in her instructions to the babysitter: "And you know the number for police and emergencies is 911, right? You know that?" To the modern viewer, the reminder about 911 reads as a case of paranoid parental overprotection, but in 1979 (the year of the film's release), only 26 percent of US households had access to that service. Bell System had rolled out the new service code in 1968, but the adoption of emergency service switchboards was much slower than expected, complicated by the "lack of coincidence between the telephone exchange and political (town, city, etc.) boundaries."[50] In practical terms, the telephone system needed to find ways to align with preexisting political systems of control in order to serve as a three-digit superguardian. Before 911 services, the telephone was an unreliable babysitter.

With the move to ESS, calls could be identified and routed to a proper bureau in ways not possible in electromechanical exchanges such as the one in *Black Christmas*.[51] While ESS meant little or nothing to the average telephone subscriber, the changeover allowed for unprecedented memory access and program controls, making the "Service and Feature Era" a victory for McLuhan's Gutenberg man over the terrifying illegibility of acoustic space. And more than any other service or feature, 911 inscribes law and memory into telephony. In roughly the same time frame in which Jill the babysitter becomes Jill the attentive wife and mother, the telephone system partnered with the forces of law and order for the sake of security and protection. This is not to say that a phone company can *69 or 911 its way out of the perils of acoustic space, but every move toward legibility saps just a little more of the forest primeval from those telephone poles on Main Street. Fast-forward a few decades to ubiquitous texting and live video, and visual culture increasingly gains the upper hand in matters of remote communication.

Once we move beyond the nearly extinct domestic object now qualified as the "landline" telephone, the relations between the visual and the acoustic in telephony undergo shifts beyond the scope of this chapter. The nomadic domain of the mobile phone puts the very notion of domesticity into question and offers new confines within cellular freedom. In horror, the best example of a transitional film that cuts the cord and moves into cell-hell is without a doubt *Scream* (1996). Like *I Saw What You Did*, which toys with the conventions of the phone fatale of an earlier era, *Scream* dips back into the landline horror archive before repositioning the telephone within contemporary adolescent culture. *Scream* opens with a scream, a couple of rings, and a landline phone shown in close-up. The opening sequence featuring Drew Barrymore as a home-alone-with-a-phone girl, Casey, includes a transitional trinity of a landline, a cordless, and a mobile phone in a telephonic death match in six rounds. Calls one and two pit Casey and her corded landline phone against a playfully maniacal scary movie superfan (or two) with a mobile phone. Once things get serious, Casey steps it up a notch and moves to the cordless phone in the kitchen—still a landline, but one that allows her to roam freely about the house and yard. Call three introduces the passage from telephonic sight to actual vision when the caller tells Casey, "I want to know who I'm looking at."[52] By call five, Casey knows she is being watched, and during call six, Casey meets her demise, clutching her clunky cordless landline phone until the bitter end. Adding insult to mortal injury, Casey's grasp on the cordless extension ties up the line and prevents her parents from calling the police.

The mobile phone wins the battle, but not without moving telephonic horror into another awkward pubescence, unsure how to cope with its strange new powers. From a materialist and technological standpoint, most cell phone horror has been exceedingly chaste, completely unwilling to look at what's going on down there. In reaction to the untethered phone, horror films have "ghosted" the technology in two ways. The first way is through repetition of the time-honored "haunted media" narrative that reduces media to a conduit for immaterial, supernatural forces.[53] Dozens of ghost-in-a-mobile stories such as *Pulse* (*Kairo*, 2001, and its 2006 remake), *Phone* (*Pon*, 2002), and *Txt* (2006) "ghost" away the materiality of wireless service.[54] Second, and by far the most common way to "ghost" the mobile, is denial of service—the scripted negation of the technology through signal loss, dying batteries, or any means necessary to recover the helplessness once achieved by snipping a telephone line. Alexandre Aja's 2006 remake of Wes Craven's *The Hills Have Eyes* (1977) pokes fun at the denial strategy by making one of the cannibal-besieged suburbanites a cell phone salesman who complains, "Ninety-seven percent nationwide coverage and we find ourselves in that three percent!" A popular 2009 YouTube supercut featuring more than sixty examples of "the most overused horror-cinema plot device, post 2000" indicates viewer fatigue with the denial strategy.[55] Even cellular service providers have been in on the joke, airing television ads that parody both ghostly phone usage and dropped service clichés.[56] Once, the telephone was a domestic object; now, every horror movie set in the present must contend with the phone. Like it or not, all modern horror is telephonic horror. The trick is to figure out what that means. Once we charge the batteries, get a better coverage plan, and chase away the ghosts, what still lurks in the shadows?

Notes

1. An interview with Castle from the 1970s exemplifies the critical indifference to the film. As the interviewer pursues questions about *Homicidal* and *Strait-Jacket*, Castle attempts to use Joan Crawford, the star of *Strait-Jacket* (1964), as a segue to *I Saw What You Did*: "But getting back to Crawford, I did another film with her as soon as I could, a picture that I like and one of my best: *I Saw What You Did*." See Derry, 355. The interviewer refuses to take the bait, and not a word more is said about the film.

2. Schantz, 62.

3. I use *fatale* in the feminine (in spite of the male gender of the noun) because the telephone has been socially gendered in the feminine in the films discussed. My discussion of *I Saw What You Did* in this chapter is adapted from my earlier article. See Olivier, "Gidget Goes Noir."

4. American Telegraph and Telephone Company, "The Telephone in America," 17.

5. Advertisement in *World's Work*, November 1930, 16.

6. Advertisement in the *American Magazine*, 1923, 122.
7. Telotte, 47.
8. This echoes years of advertising claiming that the telephone could save the sanity of farmer's wives by reducing their solitude. See C. Fischer, 211–33.
9. Howard Thompson, "The Dark Intruder: Thriller Double Bill," *New York Times*, July 22, 1965, https://www.nytimes.com/1965/07/22/archives/thriller-doublebill.html.
10. McLuhan and Fiore, 111.
11. Ibid., 48.
12. Ibid., 111.
13. Ibid., 63.
14. Curtiss, 5.
15. Castle has another connection to noir through Stanwyck, who had just starred in his film *The Night Walker* (1964) the year before *I Saw What You Did*.
16. Zipes, *Trials*, 9.
17. Ibid.
18. Zipes, *The Enchanted Screen*, 135.
19. Ibid., 181.
20. Zipes, *Trials*, 16.
21. Ibid.
22. "I Saw What You Did (1965) Trailer," YouTube video, 2:10, original promotional trailer for *I Saw What You Did*, posted by alifeatthemovies, July 2, 2015, https://www.youtube.com/watch?v=vvbXDqIQfwg.
23. Castle, 181.
24. Ibid., 179.
25. The silent film *Whispering Wires* (1926), in which a killer lurks in the basement and uses an electronically activated device inside a telephone receiver to fire a bullet, merits consideration as a predecessor to the "call coming from inside the house" tradition. See Soister et al., 642–44.
26. Flusser, 135.
27. The first large-scale implementation of ESS was in Succasunna, New Jersey, in May 1965, but many cities would have to wait until as late as the 1980s to see upgrades. See Keister, 197. A useful case study can be seen on Will Cardwell's site, "Atlanta Telephone History" (http://www.atlantatelephonehistory.info/part5.html). For a corporate overview of the switching technology, see Joel. For an overview of telephone switching history from its origins to the period discussed in this chapter, see Chapuis.
28. Western Electric Company, 48.
29. A special thanks to Mike Sanders, whose more than four decades of telephone switching experience provided me with knowledge of real-world practice that is not included in available trade manuals or academic sources. Mike was kind enough to reach out to me via AT&T Tech Channel archives on YouTube. To briefly summarize pertinent points of the longer explanation (which can be found in the comments section of "AT&T Archives: The Step-by-Step Switch," https://www.youtube.com/watch?v=xZePwin92cI): When call originator (A) connects to call recipient (B), the switch train (i.e., the path created with each digit) typically follows a "both party release" system, which means that when either party hangs up, only the final selector (as opposed to the entire switch train) remains. With the help of "malicious trace plugs"—diodes inserted into every final selector that could

potentially connect to B—an earth could be maintained on the switch train all the way back to caller A, even after A hangs up. In other words, the diode allows caller A to keep caller B "on the line" as far as the trace is concerned, regardless of A's actions. In *Black Christmas*, both caller and receiver are connected to the same exchange, so the process would have been fairly simple.

30. Shaviro, 52.
31. Sterne, 3.
32. Ibid., 45.
33. Ibid., 90.
34. Ibid.
35. Epstein and Liebman, 15.
36. Ibid.
37. Ibid.
38. *Eyes without a Face* (*Les yeux sans visage*, 1960) has an almost identical moment, with masked Christiane making a call but saying nothing.
39. Flusser, 138.
40. Ibid., 139.
41. Ibid.
42. Ibid.
43. Folklorist Jan Harold Brunvand dates "The Babysitter and the Man Upstairs" legend to the early 1970s in *Encyclopedia of Urban Legends*.
44. For many households in the 1970s with only one phone line but two phones, the prank of calling your own line was not only possible but indeed common.
45. See Kearney for a study of the conflicting uses of the telephone as a tool for independence or as a mechanism for containment in midcentury media texts. For an extension of those themes into babysitter media texts of the 1970s and 1980s, see Forman-Brunell, 139–58.
46. Steve Feke and Fred Walton, *When a Stranger Calls*, undated shooting draft, n.p., accessed July 28, 2015, http://www.imsdb.com/scripts/When-a-Stranger-Calls.html.
47. Jill's telephones are all push-button except her bedside phone, which, significantly, is the phone she picks up the night the killer attacks. The reversion to the earlier dial phone thus accompanies the return of the killer and his revocation of her phone privileges by cutting the line.
48. Joel, 342.
49. Ibid., 335.
50. Ibid., 354.
51. Ibid., 355.
52. Mario Bava's "The Telephone" ("Il telefono") in *Black Sabbath* (*I tre volti della paura*, 1963) features a telephonic stalker with similar voyeuristic claims, but the caller's comments about the recipient's appearance and various states of (un)dress are later revealed to be educated guesses.
53. See Sconce, 170–71.
54. Landlines, too, had their fair share of hauntings, but slashers such as *Black Christmas* and *Halloween* demonstrate a material grounding that mobile phone horror has largely ignored.
55. "No Signal (and Other Cellular Drama)," YouTube video, 4:55, posted by Richfoto's Channel, September 22, 2009, https://www.youtube.com/watch?v=XIZVcRccCxo.

56. See, for example, Cingular's ghostly Go Phone commercial and Phones 4U's television spots with a ghost girl. "Cingular Go Phone Commercial Horror," YouTube video, 0:33, posted by CommercialCriticBlog, June 24, 2009, https://www.youtube.com/watch?v=jqWYxT6oDog. The Phones 4U advertisements (which also include a zombie) were the most complained about ads in the United Kingdom in 2011 according to the *Guardian*. Mark Sweney, "Horror-Themed Phones 4U Advert Cleared by Regulator," *Guardian*, December 21, 2011, http://www.theguardian.com/media/2011/dec/21/horror-themed-phones-4u-ad-cleared.

4

DINING TABLE

The Family Circle at the Dining Table

For the first time in two years, Tetsuzō (Mitsuishi Ken) sees his two runaway daughters at the family dinner table—a happy family reunion.[1] "Father, it wasn't the same without you," say the daughters, hugging the man while their mother looks on tenderly. Tetsuzō holds his breath to keep silent, for he is not the recipient of the affection. He is watching the scene through a crack in the closet doors. The "father" receiving the hugs is working undercover for Tetsuzō as a client of the "Family Circle"—a Tokyo-based rent-a-family service where the daughters now work. In an elaborate scheme to mend his broken family, Tetsuzō has created a replica of his house, placing each object exactly as it was before he lost his seventeen-year-old daughter, Noriko (Fukiishi Kazue), and then her younger sister, Yuka (Yoshitaka Yuriko), to connections made through a mysterious website called Haikyo.com. The most poignant of the nostalgic furnishings is the low dining table (*chabudai*) with the word *daddy* etched in Noriko's childhood writing on the side. "Corny acting," thinks Tetsuzō. "Was this what their lonely, desperate clients wanted? But here I was, lonely and hiding in a closet." How did it come to this—a father paying for the vicarious experience of a family dinner with his own daughters?

Tetsuzō's staged version of the "happy family get-together around the dining table" (an approximate translation of *kazoku danran*[2]) is number eighteen of twenty "table events" in Sono Shion's low-budget family horror drama *Noriko's Dinner Table* (*Noriko no shokutaku*, 2006), a companion piece to *Suicide Club/Suicide Circle* (*Jisatsu Sākuru*, 2001), the better-known shocker about mass suicides tied to the same website that draws Noriko and Yuka into the rent-a-family business. I use *table event* as an adaptation of the anthropological term *food event* popularized by Mary Douglas and

Jonathan Gross to designate "an occasion when food is taken."[3] Although food events often overlap with table events, not all table activity is about food. Moreover, while food scholarship is a booming field and classic works such as *The Civilizing Process* by Norbert Elias call attention to elements of a table setting (the fork, the napkin, the tablecloth), the table itself is too often overshadowed by what sits on top of it.[4] Tables structure the family circle and limit the number of people that can enjoy the communion of its space. Tables express hierarchy (the head of a table) or equality (a round table); they bolster traditions and promote family unity (think Thanksgiving dinner) or create an arena to express tension and ideological divides (again, Thanksgiving dinner). Tables are educational spaces where children learn manners, hear adult speech and vocabulary, practice control of appetite, learn nutrition, and expand tastes, but tables are also spaces of interrogation, detention, boredom, and subjection to unwanted food or unwelcome demonstrations of authority.[5]

Historian Jordan Sand remarks, "Dining tables in Japan possessed a significance without counterpart in the West."[6] In Japan, observes Sand, "the ideology of modern domesticity was recognized from the beginning as foreign."[7] The table has less recently receded into the background in Japan, where its presence was ideologically fraught from the beginning. For the Westerner, floor dining at a low Japanese table defamiliarizes an essential piece of furniture by making the user aware (painfully aware, if braving the traditional kneeling posture) of how height and seating can structure a table event. In Japan, table height has historical ties to Western and Eastern traditions in flux during the nineteenth century, although today the strong political resonance once attached to the furniture no longer holds sway over the mind of the average diner.[8] Even less on the forefront of the imagination is the fundamental foreignness of dining tables of whatever height, not to mention the constructed nature of family dinner and of the nuclear family expected to partake in the ritual of a nightly shared meal. *Noriko's Dinner Table* foregrounds that artificiality with the absurdity and the eventual horrors of the Family Circle business. Oddly enough, real-life family rentals exist in Japan, as shown in the documentary *Rent a Family, Inc.* (2012), and similar companies are on the rise, or so claims a 2017 CBS fluff piece.[9] However bizarre the concept, a rent-a-family business becomes highly significant when contextualized within frameworks that have enabled domesticity to emerge as a marketable good. As Sand writes, "'Home' in Japan thus struggled into existence, consciously cobbled together from a variety of native and foreign models."[10] And unfailingly, a key participant in constructing models of harmonious modern family life is the dinner table. The table is the stage where we act out what it means to be a family. The history of the table in Japan appears exceptional, but only because it does not follow the same "civilizing process" (a problematic term in a cross-cultural context) traced by Norbert Elias as a trickle-down effect from medieval European aristocratic conduct through bourgeois dining practices of the nineteenth and twentieth centuries. European bourgeoisification and influence on manners in Japan is complicated by the fact that the country was not a blank slate when tables suddenly became a must-have furnishing for the modern Japanese home. Japan already had highly codified systems of manners and dining in place when the introduction of Western practices became a matter of political urgency.

The transition from the Tokugawa (or Edo) period (1600–1867) to the Meiji period (1868–1912) shaped the definition of the family and its relation to the nation-state in ways that remain relevant in the twenty-first century. After the failure of the shogunate and the death of Emperor Kōmei in 1867, political upheaval resulted in a regime change in 1868. Under the new Meiji ("enlightened") regime, Kōmei's second son, Mitsuhito, took on the name Meiji, and centuries of feudal rule gave way to an empire infused with the influence of European monarchies.[11] Unlike his father, Meiji embraced Western models of government, economics, and culture, especially insofar as imitating those models might lead to better trade deals and full acceptance of Japan's nascent nation-state. Considering how much diplomacy occurs over shared meals, it should come as no surprise that a reform in dining practices became essential to the strategic push toward Western-inflected modernization. As the influential reformer Fukuzawa Yukichi wrote in one of the many editorials of his newspaper (*Jiji-Shinpō*), "The whole world is dominated by Western Civilization today, and anyone who opposes it will be ostracized from the human society; a nation, too, will find itself outside the world circle of nations."[12] A seat at the table in the "circle of nations" and a seat at the table in the family circle were part of the same political project in the minds of Meiji reformers. Consequently, as the government took to constructing lavish Western banquet halls for entertaining foreign dignitaries, the ideology of the table spread to the private world of the home.[13] The revolutionary reform was not simply about getting Mom, Dad, and the kids together at the table; it was about getting a table, reinventing what counts as family, and beginning a new ritual that would redefine home life. The table thus shapes the architecture of both home and family.

The chabudai, or low table that we might imagine as the quintessential dining surface in Japan since time immemorial, came into use as a result of Meiji propaganda and reached widespread adoption during the Taishō (1912–1926) and early Shōwa (1926–1989) periods. Before the Meiji era, families did not share tables, nor did they typically eat together. Traditional dining of the Japanese aristocracy involved the use of individual tables with food served on trays perched on raised legs. By the fourteenth century, that serving practice gave birth to the tray table (*zen*), which began to gain widespread popularity in the seventeenth century.[14] The tray table made possible a clear expression of hierarchy through variables such as individually customized portions or variety of dishes, numbers of trays, and tray leg height. A common table, in contrast, is a democratic free-for-all. In China, a custom of dining at low tables while seated on the floor was popular until the eighth century and was imitated by the Japanese court for certain feasts during the Heian period (794–1185). Chinese "table dining" (*shippoku ry ri*) also appeared on some occasions during the Tokugawa period (1603–1868) and in Nagasaki Chinese-Japanese fusion (*shippoku*) restaurants, but trays were the norm and for many households remained so beyond the Meiji promotion of shared tables. Some rural holdouts continued to use trays instead of tables well into the twentieth century.[15]

The influential thinker Fukuzawa published the first Japanese book on Western dining in 1867, *Seiyō ishokujū* (*Western Clothing, Food, and Homes*), but before the average family could entertain the idea of a family dinner around a table as described by Fukuzawa, the notion of family had to be redefined.[16] Legally, the national family register system in 1871 initiated the process, and the 1898 Civil Code formalized a patriarchal system and marriage and inheritance laws to create what became known as the "Japanese family system."[17] Ideologically, the construct bound the private family to the state, as Sand explains, "by claiming it to be a unique and timeless native institution based on the ancestral cult, while linking it anew to the state myth of the emperor as national patriarch."[18] And if the emperor's new clothes were Western, logic dictated that the rest of the national family should follow his lead. More than ever (or "for the first time" according to Sand), houses became "nodes of intellectual concern" for the production of bourgeois culture and the "inculcation and performance of class dispositions."[19] Emergent daily newspapers, state-compiled textbooks, and a burgeoning publication industry dedicated to home life defined the new incarnation of home and gave birth to the concept of the modern family circle.

A rhetorical battle during the 1880s illustrates the debates around the Meiji reengineering of domesticity. Protestant social reformers introduced the Anglicism *hōmu* (home) in opposition to the hierarchical household system, *ie sei*. As anthropologist Sonia Ryang notes, *ie* can mean "household, the building itself, and family" as well as "one's people, boundaries, and something like 'inside,' depending on how it is positioned in usage."[20] The ie system describes the centuries-old model of a kinship household that resembles less a modern family than a business or, in the words of journalist Michael Zielenziger, "a vast tribal corporation with multiple subsidiaries."[21] In the ie system, family assets pass from father to oldest son, but if a father has no son, he can simply adopt one from another family. Likewise, servants and other nonblood persons become part of the ie through adoption, tenancy, or work.[22] Sand explains that although *ie* and *hōmu* appear antithetical—"indigenous and foreign, feudal and modern"—both terms proved sufficiently malleable to coexist.[23] Even so, a new home-related term, *katei*, overtook *hōmu* in importance because the word served not only as a spatial concept but also as a modifier for all things domestic. "*Katei* as a modifier feminized," writes Sand. "It also implied half of an equation, in which new public institutions and the nascent public space of society formed the other half."[24] Thus, home education (*katei kyōku*) and home hygiene (*katei eisei*), two *katei*-as-modifier examples, become terms with one foot in the space of the physical home and the other in the public space of society.[25] Publications with the word *katei* in the title flourished and, along with textbooks, stressed a new set of family values.

Wealthy bourgeois households had the luxury of creating a space consecrated to Westernized dining and its requisite furnishings. The homes of early European Americans had just recently gone through a similar process of remodeling for the sake of dining furniture. At the time of the American Revolution, only the wealthy had a space dedicated to eating. The average American family assembled a few boards on trestles as an eating surface and then disassembled the makeshift table at the end of a meal. More often than not, women and children ate quickly while standing, and only men took their meals seated.[26] The iconic, seated American family meal taken in the dining room coincided with the diffusion of clocks in the 1840s–1860s and with the more rigorous standardization of work and school schedules.[27] Historian Simone Cinotto locates the 1850s as the period by which the dining room became the de rigueur marker of middle-class respectability, noting that the furnishings for this sacred refuge were "chosen with special care, as they were designed to set the stage for the most important family ritual and demonstrate the wealth and the taste of the family."[28] The average American family, therefore, was aspiring to the new respectable standard for family mealtime and dining furniture not more than a few decades before the Japanese middle class began to synchronize schedules and reorganize space to accommodate a dining table.

The chabudai, a low table with folding legs, allowed families to abandon their trays without the need to furnish a separate room with table and chairs. At first, only the homes of the wealthy, idealized families pictured in Meiji domestic texts had Western-style dining rooms. At the turn of the twentieth century, Anglo-Saxon restaurants and teashops exposed Japanese diners to Western tables and chairs. Most department stores had at least two restaurants and a teashop by the 1920s.[29] Urban homes were switching from tray to chabudai during that period, while in rural areas, the peak changeover to the new folding tables occurred around 1934, according to Japanese sociologist Omote Mami.[30] Omote's study of government-authorized home economics textbooks printed between 1912 and 1943 reveals a state-driven emphasis on the virtues of family time at the dinner table. Textbook sections on living space and diet include instructions for outfitting a proper dining room, the importance of the dining table, information on dual-purpose living-dining rooms, and counsel regarding the education of children.[31] Textbooks of that period recommend that the family eat at least one meal a day together, promising that a regular family dinner schedule improves household discipline and yields positive psychological, educational, and digestive benefits.[32] Eating meals together nurtures love between family members, teaches manners, and unifies minds, say the textbooks. To that end, tasteful conversation is a must, although carefree small talk is a big adjustment for families accustomed to polite silence at the table.[33] By 1929, the basic descriptions of family meals and dining tables disappear from textbooks, presumably because they have been internalized.[34] By that point, the ritual of the happy family get-together presupposes a table as its most indispensable prop.

Noriko's Twenty Table Events

Just as the eleven beds and twenty-eight bed scenes of *The Exorcist* (see chap. 9) offer noteworthy insight into that film's domestic stakes, the twenty table events of *Noriko's Dinner Table* structure an object-driven method of reading that gets to the heart of the furniture-titled family horror-drama.[35]

Fig. 4.1. The reunited "family" at the chabudai for sukiyaki after a cathartic killing spree in *Noriko's Dinner Table* (2006).

Interwoven polyphonic inner monologues, dialogue, flashbacks, imagined realities, and an occasional scene from *Suicide Club* all packaged within five chapters ("Noriko," "Yuka," "Kumiko," "Tetsuzō," and "Last Chapter: The Knife in My Pocket") make *Noriko*'s 159 minutes an interpretive challenge, but the table events grasp the essential stakes of the film with more clarity than the film's chapter divisions. In order of appearance, the table events structure the film as follows:

1. A family dinner at the chabudai frames a seventeen-minute sequence at the beginning of the "Noriko" chapter. "I had a father, a mother, and a sister named Yuka," says Noriko's voice-over. A shot of each character establishes the place settings at the four sides of the table, concluding with Noriko, hands in her lap, head down, not eating. Food refusal is a powerful form of self-expression in the context of family dinner because a child's unwillingness to partake resonates as a rejection not only of food but also of the family circle. An overhead shot of the meal shows that Noriko's mother has prepared a typical family favorite: miso soup, rice, a salad, and a main plate with green beans, potatoes, pumpkin, and *hanbāgu*—a hamburger patty covered in brown sauce. The *hanbāgu*, a Japanized form of hamburger distinct from the fast-food *hanbāga*, "exemplifies the issue of food adoption and adaptation in Japan," according to food historians.[36] Given the hamburger's popularity as a top food choice among Japanese fifteen- to nineteen-year-olds (followed by spaghetti), we can assume that Noriko's refusal to eat has nothing

to do with her taste buds.[37] This lengthy opening food event leaves Noriko alone at the table with her father, all of the plates cleared except her own. As the father lectures, Noriko stares at her full plate while her mind wanders, her mental resistance to fatherly wisdom a rejection of another type of table nourishment. Noriko's dinner table has now become a detention center for the recalcitrant child.

2. Another family dinner at the Shimabara house, this one without Noriko, who has now run away to Tokyo. Yuka's voice-over expresses a desire to adopt the pseudonym Yōko and follow in the footsteps of her older sister.
3. Yuka (now Yōko) narrates her imagined version of her father's reaction to her departure, including a scene in which Tetsuzō has spread papers on the surface of the dining table in an attempt to find clues to the disappearance of his two daughters. He breaks down crying, lies on his side, and sees the carved "daddy" on the side of the table.
4. The same establishing shot used in events one and two, a family dinner, now shows only the two parents eating in silence at the table.
5. Tetsuzō, alone at a Western-style café table, takes notes on his investigation to locate his daughters. Table event five completes a subtractive narrative of the family circle from four (event 1) to three (event 2), two (event 4), and now one.
6. In the first in a series of staged, for-hire table events, Noriko (now "Mitsuko"[38]), her new friend Kumiko (or "Ueno Station 54" to her online friends), and with Kumiko's kid brother, mother, and father visit their grandmother. Noriko is not yet aware that Kumiko's supposed family members are actors in the Family Circle and that "Grandma" is a client. The grandmother wears a traditional kimono and serves tea and cakes from the low table in her living room. Noriko sees the family as "the epitome of happiness," with stronger bonds and more warmth than her own.
7. On the heels of the first "grandma" visit, the troupe visits a second grandmother. Noriko still assumes she is witnessing genuine family unity. The second grandmother wears westernized clothes and has a dine-in kitchen where the family enjoys an informal cup of tea and friendly conversation seated at a Western-style table.
8. The afternoon has passed, the family has prepared dinner together in Grandma's dine-in kitchen, and now the group sits around the table like the perfect family that Noriko believes them to be.
9. Now a member of the Family Circle, Noriko visits a middle-aged man (their client-father) in the Suginami ward of Tokyo, with Kumiko as her sister. The father yells at the girls to sit down, spouting his disapproval of their short skirts and studded leather jackets. The chabudai is small and littered with garbage and an overflowing ashtray. Kumiko acts like a brat, the father reaches across the table and slaps her, they argue, and the girls exit.

10. After a reconciliation with their "father" outside, Noriko and Kumiko sit down for a harmonious dinner at the now-clean table.
11. Tetsuzō meets a representative of the Family Circle at a Tokyo café. The mystery man gives a moralizing speech about connectedness to oneself and about societal failures to play family roles convincingly. "They fail as husbands, wives, fathers, mothers, children, et cetera. So the only way we can figure out what we can be is to lie openly and pursue emptiness. Feel the desert. Experience loneliness. Feel it. Survive the desert. That is your role," says the man. Suddenly, the entire café gives a standing ovation, as if every customer were an eavesdropping employee of the Family Circle.
12. The film flashes back to the two parents hunting for clues, papers spread across the home dining table.
13. Tetsuzō and his friend Ikeda sit at a hotel room coffee table and go over their plan.
14. Ikeda, as client, sits at the coffee table with Kumiko to pick out the girls for hire. As planned, he chooses Tetsuzō's daughters and asks Kumiko to play the role of mother.
15. The film flashes back to a Western-style restaurant table, five years earlier, where Kumiko meets her birth mother, who expresses profound regret for having abandoned her. "God. You suck at acting," says Kumiko. "You wanna switch? If you want, I can play your mother, you bitch." This sends the mother into a fit of tears. Kumiko's voice-over explains, "I thought about showing her how to play the role properly." The scene ends with members of the Family Circle taking the mother away to be trained as an employee. Kumiko tells them to train the father as well.
16. The film flashes back to a coffee table meeting with a realtor, during which Tetsuzō finds a suitable house to replicate his own.
17. Tetsuzō and his friend Ikeda meet at the staged house and sit at the chabudai to discuss the plan for the imminent rent-a-family visit that will reunite him with Noriko and Yuka.
18. Tetsuzō watches through the closet doors as Ikeda, posing as the client, sits at the table with Kumiko playing his wife and Noriko and Yuka as daughters. Ikeda announces that they will be having sukiyaki, but then he takes Kumiko aside to say that he forgot to buy meat. Kumiko runs to the store, which allows Tetsuzō to emerge from the closet and talk to his daughters (still at the table), who insist on using their aliases and pretend not to know him.
19. After a conflict that leaves Ikeda and four men in black suits dead, Kumiko continues her role as if nothing had happened and directs the family to prepare the sukiyaki. Yuka suggests they extend "the session," and the family settles down at the table for a three-hour meal. "Home-cooked meals are the best!" exclaims Noriko. "You have to eat your vegetables, too," says Kumiko with a smile. "Mom, can I have some meat?" says Yuka to Kumiko.

Then she asks her real father, "Want some meat, Dad?" Tetsuzō expresses remorse and a desire to start over. Tetsuzō's daughters are now using their real names, and Kumiko is playing their mother.
20. The daughters have bathed and gone to bed. Tetsuzō and his "wife" share tea at the table.

Told through table events, *Noriko's Dinner Table* has a circular structure: it begins and ends with the same table—the Shimabara family chabudai, personalized with an acknowledgment of patriarchal authority by the word *daddy* scratched into its veneer. The first set of events (one through five) establishes the dysfunctionality of the family circle, which erodes as each daughter runs away and shrinks to one person after the suicide of the mother. With table event six begins a commercialized alternative to the nuclear family dinner—something that looks like the Meiji-era textbook ideal until we learn that the "family" event is transactional and that the kinship is a construct. The two grandmother visits (events six through eight) depict equally successful versions of a family gathering around the table in a traditional and then a Western style. At the first grandmother's house, Noriko observes, "I wasn't related to them, but there I was, and it was cozy." At the second she thinks, "Could there be any more family-like family anywhere in the world?" When Noriko joins the Family Circle and visits the middle-aged man as his prodigal daughter (events nine and ten), she is genuinely moved to tears. The next set of events (eleven through sixteen, except twelve) occurs in nondomestic settings such as cafés, restaurants, hotels, and offices. Those public tables are all spaces where relationships and deals are negotiated, whether it be Kumiko's meeting with her birth mother, Tetsuzō's coffee shop encounter with a Family Circle representative, or business transactions with the realtor or Kumiko. Finally, the last set of table events (seventeen through twenty) returns to the home, or rather to a simulacrum thereof. In the replica home, at the same chabudai of the first table events, Tetsuzō reconstructs a relationship with his daughters that is at once a business deal and a blood bond.

The historical logic behind the refashioning of the happy family get-together around the table is found in the ie tradition that precedes the Meiji promotion of Westernized home life. To be clear, the ie system did not vanish with the discursive construct of "home" or even with family laws meant to dismantle feudal traditions, but it did begin to shrink or to take on new forms. Family law after World War II dissolved the ie by circumscribing family to the bonds formed by marriage rather than as a "house" (in the sense of organization) that could exist in perpetuity.[39] Industrialization, urbanization, and increased mobility did their part in the proliferation of nuclear families, as did the tight quarters of postwar housing complexes built in the 1950s and 1960s, which concretized Meiji-era ideas by insisting on a separate space for dining, no matter how small.[40] Some people, such as eminent Japanese psychologist Kawai Hayao, believe that ie has transferred into corporate culture. Kawai blames the collapse of traditional ie for the dysfunction of alienated, rootless young adults who lack strong family bonds (often because their parents are too busy with their corporate jobs), are uninterested in the corporate manifestation of ie, and struggle with an underdeveloped sense of their individuality.[41] In *Noriko's Dinner Table*, the rent-a-family business solves the broken family problem in a novel yet historically grounded way by reengineering the Meiji-era ideal of the family circle according to a capitalist version of ie logic. In other words, the notion of family returns to ie, not in opposition to hōmu but rather to save the family as an institution, for a price. The solution is as perverse as it is brilliant: the spectacle and experience of the family circle on demand, a capitalist construct better than the real thing. Family life had already been choreographed in the twentieth century by the Ministry of Education, from meal suggestions to recommended family tea gatherings for shared conversation and activities.[42] The Family Circle business simply reanimates, complete with "corny acting" (as Tetsuzō observes), the failed ideal thanks to the efficiency of the internet and a loyal family of employees.

The Family Circle business is built on the ruins of the blood-related family circle. Just as the notion of modern domesticity was cobbled together by the government, the rental business patches up the broken Meiji ideal with the disaffected victims of its failures. The disrepair of the modern household is reflected in the name of the website that draws away so many teenagers: Haikyo.com, or translated, Ruin.com. *Haikyo*, from *hai* (useless, obsolete) and *kyo* (hill), explains the urban exploration blog *Abandoned Kansai*, has become "a synonym for both urban exploration and abandoned places."[43] Because it connotes abandoned architectural structures, *haikyo* resonates with Gothic traditions of crumbling buildings and haunted houses. Although *Noriko's Dinner Table* is not Gothic in the supernatural sense (not a single long-haired ghost with a grudge in sight), the return-of-the-repressed haunting manifests itself in the film through the reinsertion of ie into the crumbling architecture of the modern family. Lifeblood spills into Haikyo.com through suicides and runaways, but the

Family Circle business returns that blood in another form. And where one might see only loss and death, the Family Circle sees the circle of life.

The circular theme of the film (and its companion piece, *Suicide Club/Suicide Circle*) posits conflicting images of circles as closed forms that represent either isolation or freedom, as symbols of inclusion or exclusion, and finally as figures of eternal return that paradoxically serve as the wheels of progress. The circular formations created by Haikyo.com are forever reconfiguring as dots detaching from one circle, free floating, and reattaching to other circles. A teenager using the site becomes a dot (color-coded by gender), a singular circle defining an identity apart from the family but connected to a new tribe online. Through this detachment, the teenager gains a stronger sense of self. The teenagers become strays, like the cats Noriko and Kumiko notice in the back alleys of Tokyo on Noriko's first real visit (table events nine and ten) as a worker in the Family Circle business. "Stray cats form families instantly," says Kumiko. "We have to relate to each other like stray cats do." Noriko observes, "Stray cats roamed the back alleys like blood flows through a vein." Blood ties, a defining principle of the family in Japanese civil law, are reimagined in the Family Circle metaphorically as blood transfusions. That is, the runaways from Haikyo.com supplement and replace the lack of those who, for one reason or another, have lost their blood relatives—stray cat blood to the rescue. The poetic horror of Haikyo.com resides in the abstract dots—the graphic representation of individuals whose path may include suicide (whence, *Suicide Circle*) or reinsertion into family networks (i.e., the Family Circle). In context, Haikyo.com reads as a compound unit: *ruin* (of domestic space) *dot* (the individual broken from a failed family) *com* (the commercial enterprise into which the runaway is inserted). In a sense, Haikyo.com and the Family Circle are following the time-honored capitalist sales strategy of creating both the problem and the solution. Every runaway or suicide creates a potential client. As Noriko and Kumiko's visit to the middle-aged man makes clear, the blood relatives whose roles they assume have been lost to suicide, one of the paths taken by Haikyo.com users. Tetsuzō's journey to despair and back begins with the detachment of his daughters and ends with the dot-com reacquisition of his lost family. Dead bodies notwithstanding, the family rental is perhaps the most perfect dinner of his life.

While Tetsuzō tries to talk sense into his daughter during table event one, Noriko stares at a tangerine, and her mind wanders to a recent unexpected encounter with childhood classmate nicknamed Tangerine. Now seventeen, Tangerine has traded in her school uniform for a schoolgirl costume of the "All-Girl Fantasy School" where she is employed as a sex worker. Noriko finds Tangerine's story inspiring, not tragic as one might expect. Tangerine prefers "Fantasy School" over the real thing. Noriko admires Tangerine's freedom and independence. She is unfazed by the nature of her former classmate's work and seems not to realize that the girl has swapped one uniform for another. Then again, even Tangerine is aware of a crucial difference. "Recognize this uniform?" asks Tangerine with a smile. "Of course you wouldn't. It's actually a costume!" Costumes are valued over uniforms in *Noriko's Dinner Table*. The schoolgirl uniform belongs to the institution of the state, whereas the schoolgirl costume belongs to the institution of capitalism; the former is part of the state family, and the latter harbors the spirit of ie. The preference of costume over uniform comes from wanting to be part of a house (in the sense of ie) rather than a home. Noriko, too, finds liberation in becoming a different sort of costumed rent girl. She visits a large costume store owned by the Family Circle and stares in amazement at a giant medicine cabinet packed with toothbrushes of all varieties that can be changed to suit each client. This is method acting at its most thorough.

Tetsuzō's harsh assessment of their "corny" acting during table event eighteen changes once he gets out of the closet as onlooker and into his role as father. No dinner theater has ever reached the level of catharsis achieved by the Family Circle at Tetsuzō's chabudai. With five murders, a tearful reunion, and to-die-for sukiyaki, the scene is theatrical perfection right down to the one-pot meat dish that owes its existence to carnivorous late nineteenth-century Europeans but is now prized as "traditional" Japanese fare.[44] Nothing could be less, or rather, more, Japanese. *Noriko's Dinner Table* begins with a Japanese take on the hamburger and ends with a common-pot meat dish—family favorites that would have been scorned as vulgar and unclean back in the days of the tray table. From the outside, the spectacular family reconciliation at the table is all a lie, all corny acting. The film's climactic dinner event almost begs the viewer to reach the conclusion of so many modern guidebooks to Japan, their condescension summarized excoriatingly by historian Gavin James Campbell as follows: "As the guidebooks suggest, there *are* no real Japanese people. They are simply actors in a never-ending performance who have forgotten that the proscenium, the props, and the lines are all fantasy. Japan is a flim-flam society."[45] Too easily we might confuse the overacted, costumed world that Noriko finds so appealing with the affectless irony of postmodern pastiche, when in fact the performance is profoundly sincere in its motives and honest in its acknowledgment of the theatricality at the heart of modern domesticity. As the mysterious man in table event eleven explains (to a standing ovation, no less), families do not play their roles convincingly. Therein lies the problem. The Family Circle is the solution to a century of bad acting. If the rent-a-family's style seems corny, blame the scripts of late nineteenth and early twentieth-century textbooks, magazines, and other media. The actors are being faithful to period conventions.

Twentieth-century literary critic and scholar Isoda Kōichi describes the transformation of the Japanese domestic space as a desire to imitate the nobility of European characters such as the ones in Racine's tragedies. The Japanese welcomed the Western-style high-rise, Isoda argues, because they aspired to multistoried dwellings evocative of European mansions. "The emotional underpinning of this process was a consciousness of 'shame' toward agricultural life, or, in a reverse expression of this, none other than a longing for the world of Racine's stage."[46] Although Japanese housing was not westernized entirely, it was gradually transformed "into spaces habitable by Racine's fictional characters."[47] Appropriately, Isoda's emblematic figures are tragic ones. With the accoutrements of the tragic hero comes the tragic fate. With the dining room comes the tragic family drama. *Noriko's Dinner Table* identifies the most important prop in the theater of family life and stages not tragedies exactly but cathartic table events where all's well that ends well.

The horror of *Noriko's Dinner Table* is the reminder of alternative family structures, some of them older and stronger than the norm manufactured by the Victorian middle class. The table—the fetishized prop of Victorian domesticity—becomes a monument to the failure of family unity in *Noriko's Dinner Table*, reparable, perhaps, by performances taken as seriously as a corporate job. A study of family mealtime in the United States concludes that the ideal "has historically been more the exception than the rule" and that with the possible exception of the 1950s, most American families have been unsuccessful in meeting it.[48] With the invention of frozen dinners in 1954 and the popularization of the TV tray table not long after the ideal of family dinner had reached its zenith, the props of American eating started to move away from the common dining surface. Trays might be better props for lives less obsessed with a Victorian ideal. Tables remain central to the image of the family, even if in practice, table events are more likely to involve less food-centric activities such as homework, board games, or craft projects. The dining room has already fallen out of favor in the age of "open concept" layouts. A *New York Times* article announced the disappearance of the dining room in 1991.[49] More recent articles call the dining room an "endangered real estate species," a largely irrelevant catch-all, the least-used room in the house.[50] The days when a table deserved its own room are drawing to a close. The Gothic McMansions of today are not crumbling; they are remodeling, knocking out walls to open up space for entertaining. Guests are the new family.

Noriko's Dinner Table is less a horror film than a *mono no aware* film, or it would be if "pathos of things" were a genre. The poignant and translation-resistant term *mono no aware* signifies a profound sense of empathy for things, an awareness, often melancholic, of transience. The table events of the film are built around acknowledging the loss of the family circle, and depending on one's point of view, the attempt to repair that loss with the Family Circle is either sad, a good marketing scheme, or as frightening as Norman Bates's solution to the loss of his mother. Above all, a melancholic *mono no aware* emotion flows throughout the film and through every character. Clients, runaways, ringleaders, abandoned family members—all feel a loss that is experienced most acutely through a sensitivity to the dining table. The film ends on a bittersweet note that comes the morning after the postmassacre three-hour sukiyaki family dinner. Yuka begins the cycle of breaking off from the happy family circle just hours after its reconstitution. No longer Yuka, no longer Yōko, she is "just some nameless girl." Back at home, Noriko wakes up. A tear runs down her cheek. Her final voice-over shows that she has come full circle. "Goodbye, adolescence. Goodbye, Haikyo.com. Goodbye, Mitsuko. I am Noriko." The subtractive cycle begins again, but if Noriko's newly cobbled-together family has learned one thing, surely it is that everyone becomes family at the dinner table.

Notes

1. I am respecting the standard word order (family name first) for all Japanese names in this chapter.
2. Omote, 5.
3. Douglas and Gross, 5. Douglas and Gross adopt the term from an unpublished master's thesis by Michael Nicod.

4. "The fork is nothing other than the embodiment of a specific standard of emotions and a specific level of revulsion," writes Elias, 107.

5. See Larson, Wiley, and Branscomb for the effect of mealtime on childhood development.

6. Sand, 54.

7. Ibid., 5–6.

8. See Sand, 377. Sand notes that the dichotomy of chair-sitting and floor-sitting has "melted into insignificance," though at the expense of the now "widely-dreaded" formal floor posture (*seiza*).

9. Adriana Diaz, "In Japan, 'Rental Family' Companies on the Rise," *CBS News* video, 2:54, May 6, 2017, https://www.cbsnews.com/videos/in-japan-rental-family-companies-on-the-rise/. The report mentions the same man featured in the documentary, a man who rents himself to give advice, and a puppy rental business—dubious support of a supposed trend.

10. Sand, 6.

11. See Cwiertka, 16–17; Redfern, 157.

12. Quoted in Hastings, 108.

13. On the Deer Cry Pavilion dinner parties, see Hastings.

14. See Yoshida, 110.

15. See Sand, 36; see also Cwiertka, 94–95.

16. Published under the name Katayama Jun'nosuke.

17. See Sand, 21. For a more nuanced look at the household registration system, see the edited volume by Krogness and Chapman.

18. Sand, 21.

19. Ibid., 2–3.

20. Ryang, 142.

21. Zielenziger, 67.

22. See Ryang, 102.

23. Sand, 22.

24. Ibid., 25.

25. Ibid.

26. Cinotto, 19.

27. Ibid., 20.

28. Ibid., 21.

29. Cwiertka, 51.

30. Omote, 6.

31. Ibid., 7.

32. Ibid.

33. Ibid., 10.

34. Ibid., 13.

35. I am defining as table event any time a character or characters sit at a table. A table event begins when a character sits at a table and ends when all characters leave the table. If a family gathers for tea, finishes, and goes about preparing dinner for the next hour before returning to the table for the meal, that counts as two discrete events. If all characters leave the table except for a child who must stay at the table until she has finished, that counts as only one event.

36. Ashkenazi and Jacob, 179.

37. Ibid., 54.

38. Noriko says that she chose the name Mitsuko after the name of the French perfume (Mitsouko). She has therefore reappropriated a commercialized, Europeanized form of Japanese identity.

39. Ashkenazi and Jacob, 52.

40. See Zielenziger, 68–69. See Sand, 376, for comments on the nDK (number + Dining Kitchen) plan as a perpetuation of the Meiji-era "family circle."

41. See Zielenziger, 69–70.

42. See Sand, 31.

43. "What Does Haikyo Mean?," *Abandoned Kansai* (blog), November 13, 2012, https://abandonedkansai.com/what-does-haikyo-mean/.

44. Tobin, 26–27.

45. Campbell, 95.

46. Isoda, 52.

47. Ibid., 55.

48. Cinotto, 32.

49. Carol Vogel, "Design: The Disappearing Dining Room," *New York Times*, February 10, 1991, http://www.nytimes.com/1991/02/10/magazine/design-the-disappearing-dining-room.html?mcubz=3.

50. Rapti Gupta, "Dining Rooms: The Endangered Real Estate Species," *Realty Today*, May 27, 2014, http://www.realtytoday.com/articles/5865/20140527/dining-rooms-endangered-real-estate-species.htm.

PART II
LIVING ROOM

5

(SLEEPER) SOFA

The Sofa Setup

Sofas are trouble. They are notorious pickpockets, as dramatized by the based-on-a-true-story *The Amityville Horror* (1979), in which a couch sabotages a wedding by stealing $1,500 meant for the caterer. There is no need to point the finger at unholy spirits; sofas are natural-born thieves, wily, unscrupulous, and slippery by any disciplinary standard. Centuries before "Netflix and chill" entered the vernacular, moralists remarked on the sofa's tendency to invite relaxed postures and behaviors. Art critics and bumper-sticker aficionados have decried the sofa's dubious taste and tyrannical grip on its surrounding environment with the credo "Art does not have to match your couch!"[1] Mathematicians, meanwhile, have canonized the unwieldy piece of furniture as the bane of combinatorial geometry in the furniture-moving puzzler known as "the sofa problem," leaving the "sofa constant" an unresolved mathematical problem to this day.[2] Philosophers, in turn, have twisted their minds around sofa-based thought experiments that only become more complex once a foldout mattress enters the equation (*Does the sofa cease to be a sofa when it's a bed? Is it one object or two?*).[3] And then there are the health risks. If sitting is the new smoking, then surely the sofa (rivaled only by the recliner) is Big Furniture's most insidious achievement. Little wonder Brian De Palma makes the sleeper sofa an accomplice to murder in his split-personality horror film *Sisters* (1973).

De Palma puts the sofa in play from the very beginning of *Sisters*, although its presence is not immediately apparent. The film opens with a close-up of a black man in white boxers pulling on his pants. The camera pulls back to reveal a locker room with a framed partition not yet covered by drywall. Enter an attractive blind woman who begins to disrobe on the other side of the open wall. The man approaches the divide and casually grips the wood framing as he considers his voyeuristic opportunity. As the woman undoes the last few buttons of her blouse, the camera zooms to a close-up of the man's face, the picture freezes, and the image crops twofold: a cartoonish blue keyhole frames the man's face, and at the same time, a black matte in the shape of a television screen imposes itself over the cinema screen. "It's *Peeping Toms*! Starring Ted Craft!" exclaims the announcer as the camera pans across the live studio audience. Ted welcomes the contestants, the audience, and those of us "peeking in at home" to "New York's newest and grooviest game"—a show in which contestants must guess the outcome of a *Candid Camera*-style stunt.[4] The blind woman, Ted explains, is not really blind. She is Danielle Breton (Margot Kidder)—a model who "has agreed to be our decoy" to test the reactions of newspaper advertising manager Phillip Wood (Lisle Wilson). As we watch the remainder of the game show, the television-shaped crop remains, reminding us that we too are victims of a setup: a surprise reveal that seats us at home rather than at the movies. De Palma has effectively moved us from the theater seat to the sofa.

De Palma fans know better than to trust the opening point of view in his films. As film scholar Chris Dumas has observed, the film that "opens inside another text" is one of De Palma's favorite tropes.[5] The director's sleight of hand often exchanges one type of voyeurism for another. The opening shower sequence of *Dressed to Kill* (1980), for example, makes us prurient voyeurs of Angie Dickenson's objectified nude body, but our relation to her changes to one of identification when the film reveals that what we are "seeing" is a woman's escapist fantasy as she endures her husband's uninspired lovemaking. *Blow Out* (1981) similarly toys with our point of view by starting behind the eyes of a killer only to reveal that we have been watching a teen slasher movie within De Palma's movie. We might be tempted here to have recourse to Russian nesting doll metaphors or French terms like *mise en abyme* to understand what De Palma is up to, but in *Sisters*, the sleeper sofa better accounts for the ways in which the film unfolds and folds back in on itself, for the facility with which it toys with positions of repose, and for the value of instability or duplicity as a defining design feature. With spring-loaded ease, De Palma's sleeper sofa repositions our gaze, consumes the object of that gaze (Phillip), and then becomes, in its own right, a fixed point of reference, frozen in the final shot of the film.

The trick in reading *Sisters* is not to be taken in by the decoy, the lovely aspiring model/actress Danielle. As soon as Danielle removes her coat and starts to unbutton her blouse on *Peeping Toms*, we take her to be the primary object of voyeurism, when in fact that object is Phillip. His is the first undressed body we see, even if that body is concealing rather than revealing itself. When Danielle enters the picture, the camera foregrounds the decoy and splits our voyeurism between complicity and judgment—complicity as our gaze mirrors and meets Phillip's at the center point occupied by the disrobing female body, and judgment as we look beyond Danielle to interpret Phillip's reactions. The moment of double cropping resolves the doubled voyeurism in favor of judgment by centering Phillip in the keyhole frame and leaving Danielle out of the picture. With twenty seconds on the clock, three choices to predict Phillip's behavior appear over the keyhole image: "Stop . . . Look . . . Listen," "Silence is Golden," and "This Way Out." Both contestants select "Stop . . . Look . . . Listen" (a logical conclusion for a show called *Peeping Toms*), but to their disappointment, the correct response—"Silence is Golden"—lies in the middle ground between concupiscence and chivalry, the only answer that hovers between stop and go. In the second half of the locker-room clip, Phillip turns his back on Danielle before she removes her blouse. "Silence is Golden" consequently refuses Phillip's face-to-face view of Danielle as well as our face-to-face view of Phillip. In the same way that the preguess segment forced our view away from the decoy to a keyhole frame of Phillip, the postguess segment ends with a shot of Danielle through the keyhole, now stripped down to her bra. We, the television audience, enact the "Stop . . . Look . . . Listen" response while Phillip remains out of view in golden silence. Two subjects and two reactions thereby anticipate two trajectories in the film: the first follows the decoy, and the second follows Phillip, or rather, the sofa that soon replaces him.

Outside the television studio, De Palma returns to the uncropped cinematic screen for a second round of voyeurism and bigger role for the sofa. A close-up from Phillip's point of view shows a gift certificate for dining and dancing for two at the African Room. Phillip shakes his head at the racial implications of the prize, and Danielle approaches to suggest that they use the certificate together. "I have brought my own cutlery," she says, referring to her equally patronizing parting gift. Phillip laughs, and the two have a pleasant dinner, interrupted briefly by the intrusion of Danielle's crazed ex-husband, Emil Breton (William Finley), who had been sitting in the front row at the television studio. After dinner, Phillip and Danielle take the ferry to Danielle's Staten Island apartment, where the inebriated model stumbles into her bedroom and strips in view of Phillip, who, this time, does not turn away. Phillip walks to the window to close the shades; noticing Emil lurking outside, he proposes to get rid of the snooping ex by pretending to leave. In essence, Phillip fakes the "This Way Out" option in order to remove the last member of the studio audience. After the successful decoy maneuver, Phillip returns to the apartment, where Danielle awaits him in a seductive pose on the couch. She opens the top of her robe, and seconds later, the sofa is supporting the couple's horizontal activity, its cushions, like Danielle's robe, already slipping off in the heat of passion.

The sofa has been enabling illicit behavior almost from the moment it entered polite society in late seventeenth-century France. Unlike the chaste armchair, the sofa invites dangerously relaxed postures and tempting proximity. "Every time you read that a female character is positioned on a sofa, well, you just know that her virtue will be eminently reproachable," writes French literary scholar Joan DeJean, noting the stunning frequency with which French novelists choose the sofa over the bed as "the ideal piece of furniture for seduction."[6] Indeed, women rarely sit on sofas in eighteenth-century French literature; rather, they fall into them, throw themselves upon them, or drape themselves nonchalantly across them, usually en déshabillé. Like Danielle in her robe, women on sofas in French engravings tend to forego sartorial decorum. A seventeenth-century engraving of Marie Anne Mancini, a patron of the arts famously accused of conspiring to poison her husband in order to marry her nephew, portrays the duchess in a negligee and open robe, hand across her breast.[7] Another engraving depicts an unnamed noblewoman "en Magdelaine," the figure of promiscuity followed by remorse, hands clasped in prayer and jewels thrown to the floor, suggesting, according to DeJean, "that her sofa has been her undoing."[8]

How a Man Becomes a Couch

Le sofa, corrupter of feminine propriety, is a masculine noun, but anthropomorphically speaking, "he" is more of a wingman or a harem eunuch. The word *sofa* derives from Arabic (*ṣoffah*), an etymological trend repeated in subsequent pieces of furniture associated with exoticism and comfort such as the divan and the ottoman. Historian Steven Parissien argues that the East became a suitable subject for home decor only once it had become "politically neutered" by the failure of the Turks' siege in Vienna in 1683.[9] Ottoman furniture invades Europe only after Europeans feel that the

Ottoman Empire can no longer do so. Upholstery effectively transforms the castrated other and its symbols of power into consumables. Men become furniture. The definitions of the word *sofa* in French dictionaries during the final two decades of the seventeenth century demonstrate that metamorphosis. A 1680 dictionary defines the sofa as "a platform on which the Turks place cushions and seat themselves," referring to the fixed architectural feature in the center of a Turkish home.[10] Ten years later, the sofa appears in Furetière's dictionary as both a built-in structure and a politically charged "term of relations" or "place of honor" for important guests. Furetière's explanatory sentence describes a drama in which French ambassadors refuse to meet with the grand vizier unless accorded a place of honor on the sofa, which the reluctant vizier ultimately grants.[11] The seventeenth-century reader of Furetière's definition would have instantly recognized that entry as a summary of the real-life diplomatic seating crisis and political scandal known as *la querelle du sofa*.[12] The reference to the sofa affair reappears in the first *Dictionnaire de l'Académie française* in 1694, this time emptied of any implied resistance from the vizier. From that point forward, dictionary entries retain only the victorious outcome of the seating scandal, asserting unequivocally that when the vizier receives the French ambassadors, they are given the "honors of the sofa."

Having claimed the sofa from their politically neutered rivals, the French freely adapt the seat of honor for their own homes. The 1694 dictionary thus also marks the appearance of a secondary definition, the sofa as "a sort of double backed daybed that has only recently been used in France."[13] By the mid-eighteenth century, the "double backed" definition had expanded to seating for three, the sofa had become a common feature of French bourgeois households, and French furniture upholsterers had reached unparalleled levels of skill.[14] The French set the trends for fashionable seating as well as the tone for its reception in other countries. The word *sofa*, like the furniture it came to represent, reached England with a delay of about two decades (1717, according to the *Oxford English Dictionary*), along with its associations with luxury, comfort, and the perils of less rigid postures. A letter from Lord Rokeby to his sister in 1740 confesses the appeal of the "idleness of the couch" and its "eastern manner of taking rest, by lolling at length" as opposed to the "uncouth practice of sitting upright."[15] Horace Walpole, always attuned to the sinister underbelly of the domestic, joked in 1745 that sitting on a sofa was tantamount to "*lolling in a péché-mortel!*"[16] Harriet Martineau, often considered the first female sociologist, once warned a family member, "Never indulge with the Sofa: believe me it is bad for you: as soon as you lie down your sad thoughts come again, and it is *excitement* instead of rest to lie and think on the Sofa."[17] Martineau understood that the sofa is a stimulant, a place where the mind races, a place that generates daydreams and thoughts that are not always healthy. The type of "lolling" or idleness encouraged by a sofa is as sinfully active as it is slothful. The mind tends to wander on a sofa, and not infrequently, so does the hand.

To the French, the sofa's influence on the body merited the coining of the adjective *sofalesque* to describe the sense of "abandon and nonchalance that a sofa invites."[18] A sofalesque pose, not surprisingly, leads to sofalesque behavior. No other household object better supports licentious lapses in conduct than the plush cushions of a couch. Mythologist Marina Warner has noted that the sofa so epitomized hedonistic orientalism to the English and French that some translations of *Arabian Nights* framed the stories not as tales told in bed but rather as tales told on a flying sofa.[19] Eighteenth-century author Claude Crébillon's "it-narrative" *Le Sopha* (1742), a sort of furniture-based sequel to *Arabian Nights*, shows to what degree the object functioned as a site of eroticism.[20] Crébillon imagines the inner being of a couch with the story of a soul condemned to drift through life as a series of sofas, never to be released until a virgin couple consummates their love on his cushions. Voyeurism meets furniture as the courtier who was once a sofa recounts his experiences to none other than the grandson of Scheherazade and Shahryar of *Arabian Nights*. Each of seven tales told through an object-oriented framework provides new opportunities for erotic vignettes and political satire, but equally important, *Le Sopha* suggests what it might be like to be a thing.[21] Crébillon's sofa, anthropomorphized as it is, by no means exists in the kind of inaccessible thingness of new object-oriented ontology, but it does point to an eighteenth-century willingness to acknowledge the entanglement of humans with the objects that push against them. Crébillon gives his reader a sofa that needs release as much as any of the lovers whose bodies press against it.

When Danielle leans back against the arm of her plush white couch, the outcome is as inevitable as it would have been in any erotic French novel, which is perhaps why De Palma (never one to shy away from carnal pleasure) omits the sex scene. Instead, he gives a high-angle view of the still-clothed Phillip on top of Danielle on the couch, followed by a shot of the couple from the side, which leaves just enough disrobing to allow us to see what Phillip misses: a grotesque scar on Danielle's hip from the traumatic operation at the origin of her psychosis. What ensues the next morning is less the stuff of boudoir fiction than a reimagining of the works of Hitchcock—specifically, the films *Psycho* (1960), *Rope* (1948), and *Rear Window* (1954). In De Palma's film, the homicidal alter ego of *Psycho*, the body hidden in plain sight of *Rope*, and the voyeuristic amateur sleuthing by a journalist of *Rear Window* coalesce around the sleeper sofa.

Danielle has an ill-tempered twin named Dominique who disapproves of her sister's sleepover guest. Still half-asleep on the foldout bed, Phillip hears but does not understand the sisters arguing in French in the bedroom:

"I got home really late, and I didn't want to bother you, so I slept on the couch."
"I think *I'll* go lie down on the couch."
"No. Stay here. I don't want you to go into the living room!"

Phillip gets dressed, and Danielle keeps him away from the bedroom by explaining that her twin sister gets upset when she is with another man. Normally, Dominique wouldn't be there, says Danielle, but today is their birthday. Danielle asks Phillip to pick up a refill on an empty prescription, and gentleman that he is, Phillip decides to surprise the twins with a birthday cake. Upon his return, Phillip unboxes the cake, retrieves a large chef's knife from Danielle's new cutlery set, and brings it to her on the sleeper sofa, where she lies facedown. Phillip puts the knife in her hand, and she thrusts it twice in his groin, once in his mouth, and three times in his back. As Danielle convulses in a posthomicidal fit, Phillip drags himself to the window and reaches up to write *help* in his own blood. As Phillip dies, De Palma splits the screen into the point of view from inside the apartment on one half and the point of view of witness Grace Collier (Jennifer Salt) from the window of a neighboring building.

As luck would have it, Grace is a conscientious journalist, a columnist for the *Staten Island Panorama*, proud enough of her work to have framed her own press clippings such as "Staten Islanders, Who Are We?" and "Why We Call Them Pigs." To the cops, she is "Miss Civil Liberties," an annoyance whose call merits a cursory investigation if only to avoid the prospect of a story with the title "Police Refuse to Investigate Brutal Race Murder." While Grace races outside to meet the police, Emil arrives at Danielle's apartment and helps clean up the scene. Together, Emil and Danielle lift the murder victim onto the sleeper sofa's metal wire support, which has been stripped of its mattress. With great effort, they fold up the caged corpse

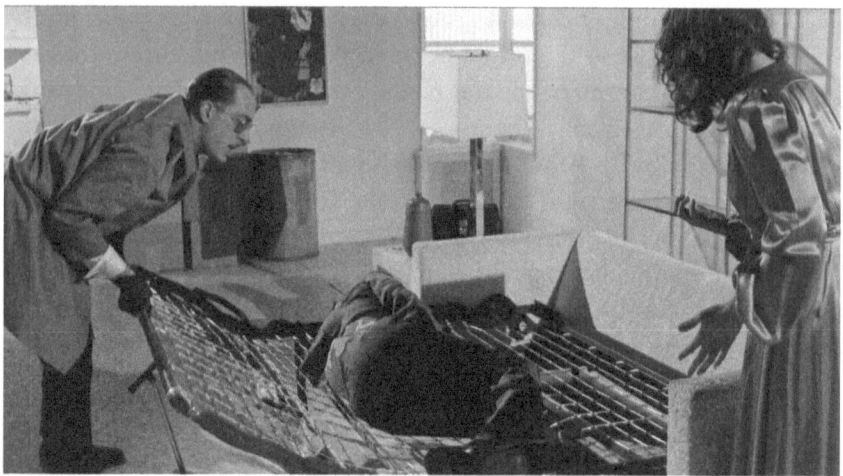

Fig. 5.1. Phillip is folded into the sleeper sofa in *Sisters* (1973).

into its sofa position, replace the cushions, and continue the cleanup. Emil scrubs the linoleum while Danielle puts on her makeup for the appearance of normalcy. Emil exits just in time for Danielle to invite the investigators in and seat herself (nonchalantly, of course) on the sofa for questioning, the picture of sexy innocence in her loosely tied pink satin robe. Danielle once again serves as decoy, and Phillip, the castrated other, is permanently shut out of view in the couch beneath her. The racial implications of the dead black man trapped in the white sofa are indisputable and have been brilliantly developed by Chris Dumas in *Un-American Psycho*. Had De Palma been able to land bigger stars, he would have cast Sidney Poitier in the role of Phillip, which would have made the murder resonate more strongly both as a parallel to Janet Leigh's death in *Psycho* and as a critique of race relations.[22] If we read the film through the sofa, we can see that De Palma's castrated African American other doubles the already-present castrated Turkish other in the furniture itself.

The Hitchcockian antecedents in De Palma's work have been noted without fail by every movie critic and picked apart by nearly every academic work ever written on De Palma, either to dismiss De Palma as a derivative hack or to celebrate him as a visionary.[23] Whichever side one favors, the mention of Hitchcock is unavoidable because De Palma has consistently discussed his deployment of Hitchcock's cinematic vocabulary in interviews. Critics and scholars have become less dismissive of De

Palma's work over time, and polemics pitting Hitchcock against De Palma are largely passé. Rather than enter into a "who wore it better" discussion of the two auteurs, an object-driven reading of *Sisters* might instead look at the sofalesque transmutation of familiar Hitchcockian elements. Those who have seen Hitchcock's *Rope*, in which two college students stash the body of their murdered classmate in an old chest used as a buffet table for a dinner party, will recognize the suspense created by furniture as a blind spot (and those who have read Žižek will recognize in the term *blind spot* a potentially circuitous Lacanian line of inquiry best left to works longer than this chapter).[24] Both Hitchcock's chest and De Palma's sleeper sofa derive their value from their ability to conceal. A hinged Jacobean chest such as the one in *Rope* makes an ideal storage space for linens, books, household goods, murder victims—anything that needs to be locked up or kept out of sight. The flat top of the chest provides a surface that can double as seating, a table, or even a bed when needed.[25] A sleeper sofa, in contrast, hides only one thing and is therefore less a receptacle than a split-personality object whose dark side springs to life when activated, like a sleeper agent or a sleeper cell. A sleeper sofa is a bedroom hidden in a living room. The chest's job is to consume objects, while the sleeper sofa's job is to change the nature of a room, to move between day and night, to transform public space into private space, to be Jekyll and Hyde.

De Palma and Hitchcock both use furniture to hide a body in plain sight, and both find methods to keep us looking at the furniture when the characters do not. De Palma constructed the entire apartment set of *Sisters* in order to track through the space in the same manner that Hitchcock did in *Rope*. His greatest disappointment was having to abandon a long tracking shot that would have followed the police around Danielle's apartment and repeatedly returned to the couch, each time showing a spot of leaking blood as it gets bigger and bigger.[26] Technical limitations failed to capture in a continuous shot the radical shifts in perspective required by the couch. The higher human-level shots of the search consequently took precedence over the lower couch-level shots, which instead had to be replaced with close-ups and television-style coverage. The result of the failed tracking shot is a loss of fluidity between two perspectives, which, more than a missed opportunity for an exercise in style, represents an imbalance between the decoy search (that is, the search executed by the police and Grace as Danielle tags along) and the competing draw of the sofa. Nevertheless, despite the missing visual seesaw ride between the decoy and the one object in the apartment that is overlooked, De Palma tracks the sofa counterpoint well beyond the confines of the living room.

After the apartment search fails and the police leave the scene, De Palma splits the next round of searching into human and sofa halves in a manner that makes the sofa search seems ridiculous. Amateur sleuth-journalist Grace Collier continues her quest to prove Danielle's guilt despite the dismissal of the case by the police.[27] With the help of private detective Joseph Larch (Charles Durning), she gains access to a file about Danielle and Dominique and also learns that the body is most likely hidden inside the unusually heavy sofa that two moving men are loading into a truck. Preoccupied with Danielle, Grace decides to follow the lead in the folder while the dogged PI trails the sofa. With this investigative split, De Palma tracks the human on the one hand and the object on the other. And while Grace's search is a thrill ride that dives into the head of the deranged Danielle, Larch's pursuit of the sofa comes across as comedic and absurd, completely emptied of human psychology or intrigue. Even the men driving the truck do not qualify as characters, let alone menacing coconspirators. Neither is the couch a character in the anthropomorphic fashion of Crébillon's *Le Sopha*, for although De Palma, too, has constructed a narrative about a man in a sofa, this couch is dead silent. If we are looking to understand the inner life of an object or want to know what it's like to become a couch, Phillip once again disappoints with the answer "Silence is Golden."

The Decoy on the Couch

Grace, meanwhile, makes rapid progress in her sleuthing. The file that Larch found in Danielle's apartment contains medical records that identify Dominique and Danielle as the Blanchion twins, "Siamese twins" (another term of orientalist objectification) whose story Grace remembers from an article in *Life* magazine. Grace visits the *Life* reporter and gets access to a video titled "Blanchion Twins Separated." The documentary about "Canada's first Siamese twins" states that orphans Dominique and Danielle grew up at the Loisel Institute. A photo appears of the two young girls on a high-backed sofa, followed by a photo of the girls now grown, with Emil lurking behind them in a lab coat. "That's Danielle's husband!" cries Grace. The director of the Loisel Institute speaks: "It seems the older they become, the more precarious is their psychological balance, both within themselves and between one another." The video ends with the news that Dominique and Danielle were "forced by nature" to undergo a surgical separation. The Loisel Institute claimed that the surgery was a success, but the reporter tells Grace that a nurse he bribed confirmed Dominique's death.

De Palma's inspiration for *Sisters* came from a real 1966 *Life* article about Russian conjoined twins Masha and Dasha, as did the actual photo used as the younger Dominique and Danielle in the documentary. The photo of Masha and Dasha encapsulates the key elements of the story: the twins, the sofa, and the psychological problems. The photo caption in the original article reads, "At age 11, Masha and Dasha, slouched on a couch, their third leg tucked behind them. When they were younger they enjoyed special attention. As they matured they came to comprehend the full meaning of their deformity. Doctors now predict they will need psychiatric help."[28] In an interview about the making of *Sisters*, De Palma recalls his reaction to the photo: "One of the twins had a very surly, disturbing look on her face and the other looked perfectly healthy and smiling. And this strong visual image started the whole idea off in my mind."[29] De Palma's incarnation of the twins omits some of the physical complexities of the Russian twins, such as the third leg and the shared reproductive system mentioned in the magazine article, but what the Blanchion twins lose in physical deformity they more than make up for in psychiatric problems. Like Mrs. Bates in *Psycho*, deceased Dominique lives on as an alter ego prepared to punish arousal with death, to kill any threat to the family bond. Danielle's convulsions, her blackout, and her argument with her sister are all manifestations of the repressed, dead sister. "Dominique" did, in fact, go lie down on the sleeper sofa mattress while Phillip was out buying the birthday cake, and Dominique killed Phillip.

As Grace soon learns, Emil's role is more complicated than that of the jealous ex-husband. He is the lover, the psychiatrist, and the surgeon responsible for the schism between the sisters. Pregnancy was the "act of nature" that led to the twins' surgical separation, hastened by Dominique's attack on the unborn child with garden shears. Emil himself gives Grace the sordid details of the tragic story, but only after drugging and hypnotizing her so that she will remember nothing once she awakes. The revelation occurs in a room of a psychiatric residence that Emil directs. Grace trails Emil to the in-patient clinic and watches through the window as the psychiatrist throws Danielle onto a black couch and injects her with something to make her sleep. Not long thereafter, Grace too finds herself drugged and hypnotized, placed next to Danielle as if she were Dominique, both women forced through hypnosis to (re)live the traumatic events of the separation. The sequence uses Grace's pupil to iris-in and iris-out of black-and-white surrealistic vignettes that reveal the twins' persecution, Danielle's relationship with Emil, Dominique's attack on the unborn child, and the surgery that resulted in Dominique's death. For Grace, the hypnotic sequence provides answers that Emil has preprogrammed her to repress once the session has ended, while for Danielle, the hypnosis reverses repression to exorcise the specter of Dominique once and for all. Emil thus operates simultaneously as the agent of repression and of remembrance. He is at once the mad doctor and the helpful therapist.

In the struggle that Grace witnesses through the window of the psychiatric residence, De Palma literally portrays a psychiatrist pushing his patient onto the couch, like an evil Sigmund Freud working in tandem with his favorite piece of furniture. Thanks to Freud, psychoanalysis is barely conceivable without the couch as a companion to induce various states of consciousness. And yet the sofa escapes scrutiny such that when an interviewer asks De Palma to explain his fascination with violence, for example, and the filmmaker responds, "I'd have to be on the couch a long time to figure it out," no one doubts what he means or thinks to ask, "Why the couch?"[30] No follow-up is required. The couch disappears into figurative language as a metonym for the psychoanalytic process. Again, the human distracts us from the material object. We fall for the decoy. As sofa-aware scholar Andreas Mayer states, "The social and historical conditions and the deep historicity of the Freudian enterprise have been neglected in favor of human-centered, psychological readings."[31] After all, what kind of fool follows the couch? But in *Sisters*, given Emil's proclivity to push people *onto* and *into* sofas, and given De Palma's tendency to make his viewers look *from* and *at* sofas, we must acknowledge that the furniture functions as something more than shorthand for therapy.

Like Crébillon's *sopha*, Freud's couch invests itself in an eroticized game of eavesdropping and attachment. Draped with an oriental rug and amply cushioned, the iconic couch in Freud's consultation room sets a scene both homey and exotic, calculated to put domestic surroundings and sofalesque lolling in the service of medical systems of control. The sofa, the bed, and adjustable patent furniture generate a culture of compulsory comfort without which modern in-patient facilities such as the one in *Sisters* would be inconceivable.[32] When Freud was still a toddler, an upholsterer in Paris had already patented the first convertible sofa beds (*canapé-lit* and *canapé-sopha-lit*) and was selling them to doctors alongside articulated furniture such as recliners for dentists and chaises for invalids.[33] Patents in the United States from the 1870s reveal a quest to make ever more elegant foldout sofa beds for the home, and by the 1880s, the sofa bed had clearly become a "class of furniture."[34] Freud did not own a sleeper sofa, but the fact that he called his couch an "examination bed" points to a fluidity of boundaries between homey seating and unhomey medical furniture.[35] In his arrangement of furniture, Freud placed the analyst behind the head of the reclining patient, disrupting the conversational dynamic of domestic seating in favor of a framework that Warner has compared to the Sultan listening to stories in *Arabian Nights*.[36] Freud's couch makes the analyst more Peeping Tom than interlocutor.

For the patient, the sofa enables a release of repressed memory, an unbridled emission of narrative. As a result of the vulnerability and ease procured by the sofa's cushiony repose, the patient becomes more likely to develop the attachment known as "transference love," which the analyst can exploit to good or bad ends.[37] De Palma takes that attachment to the extreme in the figure of Emil, who impregnates one patient and kills her sister in a botched surgery. Furthermore, Emil's abusive deployment of the sofa suppresses evidence and represses memory. Once he has pushed Danielle onto the couch and has her under sedation, Emil moves her to the bed, followed by Grace. There, Emil pushes the women into a deeper state of unconsciousness for his hypnotic dream narrative revelation. "Watch," he tells Grace. "Remember," he commands Danielle, fusing the voyeurism of film to the recuperation of memory. Yet Grace's spectatorship leads to complete repression once she awakes, and Danielle's recuperated memory leads to the castration and murder of Emil with his own scalpel. Once the police arrive, the murder that Grace worked so hard to solve has been excised from her memory, and Danielle can only assert that Dominique is dead and that she has never hurt anyone in her life. Before dying, Emil has metaphorically folded the bed back into the sofa. He has repressed the crime. The human search has reached the dissatisfying conclusion that "Silence is Golden."

But that was the decoy. In an ending that frustrates or puzzles most viewers, De Palma refuses to abandon the sleeper sofa. As Grace, who has reverted to a state of childhood in her bedroom, repeats the denial of the crime planted in her head by Emil, the picture dissolves to the sofa. The dissolve has the momentary effect of superimposing Grace onto the couch, which sits by an REA Express station somewhere in rural Canada, next

108 | Household Horror

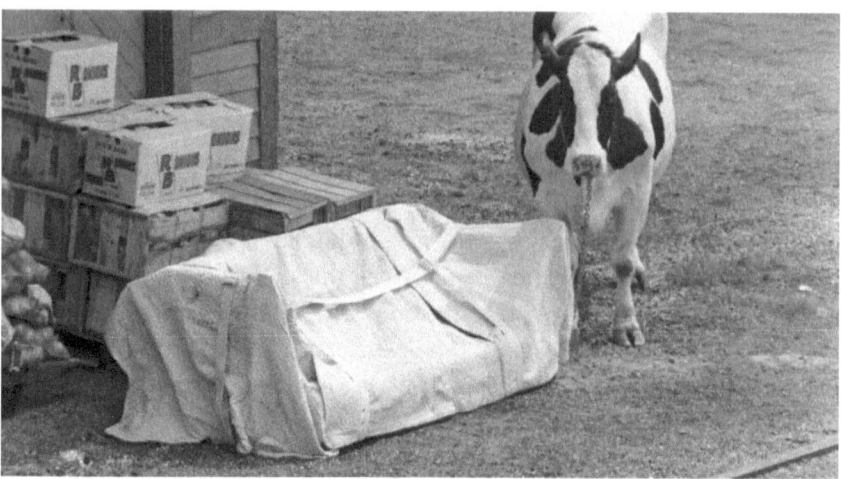

Fig. 5.2. The "straitjacketed" sofa in rural Canada in *Sisters* (1973).

to a cow. The sleeper sofa is locked down tight, straitjacketed in its white moving blankets, bound up into its couch form. De Palma has moved us from the psychodrama of Danielle to a train stop in the middle of nowhere, from *Psycho* to a furniture version of *Waiting for Godot*. Perched high on a telephone pole disguised as a line repairman, Larch stares at the sofa through binoculars—the voyeur in a spectacle nowhere near as engaging as Danielle's blind girl striptease on *Peeping Toms*. A crane shot pulls back. A farmer picks up the cow. Nothing happens. The picture freezes on Larch watching the couch, just as Phillip's face was suspended in that moment of voyeuristic uncertainty in *Peeping Toms*. The words *The End* appear over the frozen image, frustrating any hope of a resolution. Larch is suspended waiting for a person that will never come, and De Palma has made us voyeurs of a couch whose cushions hide more than spare change.

Notes

1. On the maligned tradition of "sofa art," see Reed.
2. See Wagner.
3. On the sleeper sofa and the argument for intermittent existence, see Burke. See also Arnold.
4. The title *Peeping Toms* pays homage to Michael Powell's *Peeping Tom* (1960), which intertwines psychiatry, psychopathy, and voyeurism and includes a blind character.
5. Dumas, 182.

6. DeJean, 118.
7. Unknown, "Madame la Duchesse de Bouillon en deshabillé negligé sur un sopha," 17th century, engraving, 30 × 20 cm, Bibliothèque nationale de France, département Arsenal, ARS EST-368 (268).
8. DeJean, 117.
9. Parissien, 59–60.
10. Pierre Richelet, *Dictionnaire françois* (Genève: Jean Herman Widerhold, 1680), s.v. "sofa." All translations mine.
11. Antoine Furetière, *Dictionnaire universel* (La Haye: A. and R. Leers, 1690), s.v. "sofa."
12. On the "querelle du sofa," see Colin.
13. *Le dictionnaire de l'Académie françoise, dédié au Roy, Tome Second M–Z* (Paris: Jean-Baptiste Coignard, 1694), s.v. "sofa."
14. The "high point of competence" was reached in France in 1770, according to furniture expert and curator Peter Thornton. Thornton, 58.
15. Robinson-Morris.
16. Quoted in DeJean, 118.
17. Martineau.
18. *Trésor de la Langue française informatisé* (Paris: CNRS, 2002), s.v. "sofa," http://atilf.atilf.fr/.
19. Warner, 146.
20. For other examples of eighteenth-century "it-narratives," see Park.
21. For an analysis that takes seriously the thingness of Crébillon's sofa, see Shoemaker.
22. De Palma mentions his casting wish list in Rubinstein, 8.
23. For the most complete philosophical theorization of De Palma-as-visionary, see Peretz.
24. Both Peretz and Dumas have deployed the notion of internal blindness in a Žižekian-Lacanian sense.
25. Ireland, 381.
26. Rubinstein, 7.
27. The name Collier is no doubt a nod to Constance Collier, who played Mrs. Atwater in *Rope*, while Grace is likely an homage to Grace Kelly, who does some sleuthing for her wheelchair-bound photojournalist boyfriend (Jimmy Stewart).
28. "Masha and Dasha: Rare Study of Russia's Siamese Twins," *Life*, April 8, 1966, 70.
29. Rubinstein, 3.
30. Pally, 98.
31. Mayer, 222.
32. Former Freud Museum curator Lydia Marinelli pioneered this material study of Freud with the exhibition and book *Die Couch*. Freud's use of a couch is directly influenced by Dr. Silas Weir Mitchell's advocacy of comfort in the service of medicine. Marinelli 18.
33. Roubaux, 15.
34. See for example, Benjamin F. Farbar, sofa-bed, US Patent 278004 A, May 22, 1883.
35. I use *unhomey* here as a literal translation of Freud's *unheimlich*, or uncanny.
36. Warner, 158.
37. See Mayer, 218.

6

REMOTE

Zap

Some call it zapping; others call it grazing, channel surfing, or channel hopping. The act of using the remote to flip through television channels to watch everything and nothing at the same time confirms Marshall McLuhan's famous dictum that the medium is the message. Channel surfing approaches the degree zero of television, the medium in its purest form. To advertisers, working the remote is a subversive act, a dreaded practice of "selective avoidance" that undermines commercials, the engine of classic TV content.[1] For Umberto Eco, each individual uses the "plurality of messages" to make a "composition with the remote-control switch."[2] Perhaps we are all armchair Picassos making cubist art, each click a new angle in a portrait of media presence. Is it a coincidence that the word *intertextuality* emerges for the first time (1973) just as the remote control market was recovering from 1960s stagnation and was habituating the masses to zapping through media texts? If you are thinking "Correlation does not equal causation," I say, fine—zap—let's change channels. After all, this chapter is not about television; it is about remote control and the object we now call the remote. Specifically, it's about the remote(s) in *Poltergeist* (1982)—the Tobe Hooper film that most people think of as a Steven Spielberg film (and for good reason, since Spielberg wrote, produced, and remote-controlled the entire project). *Poltergeist* is the movie with the iconic poster of a little girl communing with her parents' television, her hands raised to the medium at its true degree zero—the static of those bygone days when dead air was still a thing, when TV media had a bedtime and a patriotic sign-off lullaby to signal its imminent shift into snowy slumber. *Poltergeist* and the remote are the content, and this chapter will access them through an unstitched, fragmentary form of content zapping that—although no Picasso—adds up to a form of engagement befitting the object of study.

Spooky Action at a Distance

What happens when neighborhoods are affected by spooky action at a distance? That's roughly the question behind both quantum mechanics and the film *Poltergeist*. Or maybe not, depending on concepts such as locality and nonlocality. Locality, as George Musser explains, "is a slightly pretentious word for a neighborhood, town, or other place"—say, for example, Cuesta Verde Estates, home of Steve (Craig T. Nelson) and Diane (JoBeth Williams) Freeling and their dog and three kids.[3] Local action (as opposed to spooky action at a distance) means that objects are influenced only by their direct surroundings. During the sequence that establishes the charm of the Spielbergian suburb and the theme of remote control, a man pedals an undersized bike while struggling to keep a twenty-four-pack of beer under his arm, his efforts thwarted by mischievous kids with remote-control (a.k.a. radio-control or RC) toy race cars. The kids' remotes send the RC cars on a wild chase that causes the man to drop his beer. Local action means that cause and effect can be explained locally by things touching. The man's foot pushes the bike pedal, which powers the drive train, which moves the bike—visible local action at work. The RC cars also demonstrate locality, even though not every step in the causal chain is visible. When the kid operates the control, a circuit is formed that tells the device to transmit radio waves up the antenna in pulses detected by a receiver in the toy car and interpreted as driving instructions. This is remote action but not "action at a distance" in a quantum sense because we can trace the chain of events. Locality is also what undergirds media theorist Marshall McLuhan's contention that media are extensions of ourselves. As much as McLuhan likes the revolutionary qualities of quantum mechanics (which he calls "physics minus the connections") his media theory is very touchy-feely: "The wheel is an extension of the foot, the book is an extension of the eye, clothing, an extension of the skin, electric circuitry, an extension of the central nervous system."[4] Nonlocality, in contrast, is spooky because it means two things can happen simultaneously light-years apart as if one affected the other but without any apparent communication or medium of transmission, all thanks to quantum entanglement. And that kind of spooky action is simply not needed to explain *Poltergeist*. Not yet.

Figs. 6.1 and 6.2. Steve and Ben have a remote shootout in *Poltergeist* (1982).

This Town Ain't Big Enough for the Two of Us

Steve Freeling and six of his buddies are in the living room yelling at the television and drinking beer when suddenly the football game changes to Mister Rogers crooning about neighborly friendship. "I apologize," says Steve. "My neighbor's on the same remote." Steve leans out of his window to confront his neighbor, Ben (Michael McManus), who has stepped out of the side door of his own house. A wooden fence divides their property line. The houses are not more than fifteen feet apart. A remote showdown is about to begin. Each man clutches an identical Zenith Space Command 600 remote control in his hand. "My kids wanna watch *Mister Rogers*," says Ben, his clenched teeth holding a cigar. "I don't care what you're watching, Ben, just show a little mercy with that thing," says Steve. Ben stretches his arm up toward the top of the fence, aims, and clicks. The scene cuts back to Steve's living room TV, where the football game once again changes to the soft-spoken man in the cardigan. "Move your set," says Ben. Steve extends his arm, steadies his Space Command 600, and returns fire. *Click*. "Move yours, Ben." Negotiations have failed. Them's fightin' words. *Click. Click*. The television changes between the two channels. The men exchange rapid remote fire while backing into their homes. *Click. Click. Click. Click. Click. Click. Click.*

Television Electronics: Theory and Servicing

A textbook written around the time of *Poltergeist* explains that the two most popular schemes for remote-control signaling to the television are "1. Ultrasonic waves (34 to 54 kHz range), mechanically or electronically generated"

and "2. Infrared wave transmission and reception, using an infrared transmitting LED and a receiving sensor."[5] The book illustrates the function of an ultrasonic system with internal and external photos of a Zenith Space Commander 400 remote. Inside the remote sit four aluminum tubes of slightly different lengths (like tiny wind chimes or the resonators of a marimba) and four actuating hammers, one to strike each tube. When a button is pressed, the associated hammer strikes and plays what we would call a note, if we could hear it. The note is a frequency just outside of a dog's hearing range. The manufacturer determines which frequencies to generate and what function to assign to those frequencies. For example, a 2.5-inch tube will emit a frequency of 50 kHz. When a hammer strikes that tube, a microphone pickup in the television receiver hears that frequency and converts it to an equivalent electronic signal assigned to perform a function such as channel up or channel down. The remote gives an acoustic musical performance that the television hears electronically through a transducer. The television dances to its tune by hopping around channels, adjusting volume, turning on and off, and muting or unmuting—basic actions limited by the number of tubes. Because the action is generated mechanically, the Zenith remote does not use batteries. The same effect can be produced electronically, but the sound needs amplification (like an electric guitar) and therefore requires batteries. Electronically generated ultrasonic waves provide more control frequencies, and therefore more functions, without the tubes used by Zenith.

Meanwhile, Back at the Saloon . . .

With the football game on TV, Steve's living room becomes a modern-day saloon where riled-up men drink and swear while two remote-slinging enemies have a shootout just outside. It's a man's world. In the universe of male-gendered technological devices, the remote is as virile as a chainsaw. Study after study has confirmed that the man of the house controls the remote most of the time.[6] Data from 1982 (the year of *Poltergeist*'s release) show not only that fathers were the least likely to ask permission before changing channels but also that 90 percent of the time, the father acted alone in making decisions with the remote.[7] Diane Freeling steers clear of the living room during the football game. She makes the children's beds upstairs while singing the catchy Miller beer commercial jingle that's stuck in her head—an ad executive's dream come true.

Space: The Final Frontier

Midcentury technology loves space as much as it loves cowboys, which, if *Star Trek* has taught us anything, makes perfect sense. In 1955, before the successful Space Command series, Zenith launched the Flash-Matic—a space-gun-shaped remote that was basically a fancy flashlight made to be aimed at one of the four corners of a Zenith TV screen. The Flash-Matic user mirrors the gunshot action of the television's cathode ray picture tube, where an electron gun fires a beam at the fluorescent screen that produces the points of light interpreted by the observer's eye as the picture. With the Flash-Matic, the living room becomes a firing range with photoelectric cells as targets hidden in the four corners of the Zenith television. Hit one corner with a beam of light to turn the TV off and on; hit another to mute the sound or to change channels. As the thirty thousand unlucky purchasers of the Flash-Matic discovered, sunlight from the window or any other wayward light source can also participate in the action, giving the effect of poltergeists controlling the screen.[8] In 1956, Zenith's Space Command remote put the failed flashlight gun to rest and introduced the ultrasonic control that would stick for two decades. One popular print ad from 1960 shows a man's hand working the Space Command while watching a Western—cowboys at one end of the living room and a space commander in his armchair, the all-American future-nostalgia combo.[9]

Layer Cake

Most people think that *Poltergeist* is a movie about a house built on an ancient Indian burial ground.[10] It is not. The unscrupulous developer who built the Cuesta Verde estates, although untrustworthy, explicitly states as much, and as the coffins unearth themselves in the climax of the film, we have proof. *Poltergeist II: The Other Side* (1986) includes an Indian shaman character and develops a backstory about a cult leader who sealed his followers in a cave below the Freelings' home, but there is still no Indian burial ground. Why, then, does the Indian burial ground trope stick to *Poltergeist* despite the denial within the film? *The Amityville Horror* (1979), *Wolfen* (1981), *The Shining* (1980), and other films, novels, and television shows are, of course, part of the answer, but more importantly, the pervasive burial ground dread comes from the fact that all American real estate is essentially built on Indian ground. To quote little Carol Anne Freeling (Heather O'Rourke), "They're heeeere!" Or rather, were, until Andrew Jackson and many others drove them from their lands. *Poltergeist* is a layer cake of hauntings. And below every American haunting lurks the specter of a history repressed by the immaculate birth story of America, the blank-slate nation.

Political Action at a Distance

Media scholar Caetlin Benson-Allott remarks that the first use of *remote control* in English dates to the 1794 trial of political reformer Thomas Hardy for high treason. Solicitor general Sir John Milford coined the term to describe "control of people or institutions exercised at a distance"—indirect or "remote control" as opposed to Hardy's call for direct democracy by a sovereign people with perpetual authority.[11] In 1903, the term once coined to describe a political power imbalance was now applied to the control of electrical equipment. To a television, a remote is a scepter of electronic despotism. TV operations leave little room for democracy.

Layer Cake Sequel

Poltergeist's fictitious Cuesta Verde Estates has a believable Southern Californian name that evokes the linguistic imprint of Spanish colonization. A cuesta is a hill with a gentle slope and a steep slope made of alternating beds of strata such as limestone, shale, sandstone, and mudstone—a geological layer cake. The establishing shots for Cuesta Verde were taken in Agoura Hills, an area settled by Chumash tribes about ten thousand years ago. The first recorded contact with the Chumash Indians began in 1541, with the expedition led by Juan Rodríguez Cabrillo, but contact remained minimal until the late 1700s when the Spanish missionaries invited the natives to either change their ways or move. By 1850, the tribe was dispersed.[12]

Tribes and Neighborhoods

Click. Steve and his friends cheer on the Rams. A pass is thrown. "Now he's got a receiver, Jim Youngblood!" *Click.* "Please won't you be my neighbor?" Remote interference has zapped away from the warring tribal ritual of American football to the invitation to join a remote neighborhood that exists on PBS, where children are citizens of *Mister Rogers' Neighborhood.* Carol Anne is not the only person who speaks to "TV people." Steve and his friends yell at Jim Youngblood, and Ben's children are in dialogue with Fred Rogers as participants in his neighborhood-building project. Steve and Ben fight with their remotes on behalf of their house for access to their television tribe. The fence makes property boundaries clear, but the forty-foot range of the Zenith remote challenges those boundaries and turns ultrasonic space into the new Wild West.

McLuhan's essay "Television: The Timid Giant" contrasts the "lowly" status of the movie western with the thriving business of the televised western. The new importance of the western in television, he contends, stems from the (then) low resolution of the medium, whose pointillist low-fi aesthetic of light and dark dots requires the viewer's sensory cooperation and participation to close its gaps. "With TV, the western acquired new importance," writes McLuhan, "since its theme is always 'Let's make a town.' The audience participates in the shaping and processing of a community from meager and unpromising components."[13] *Mister Rogers' Neighborhood* shares the town-building agenda of the televised western as read through McLuhan. Moreover, the subtitle of McLuhan's essay—"The Timid Giant"—is a good description not only of television but also of Mr. Rogers in the recurring "Neighborhood of Make-Believe" segments in which he looms over his puppet land like a kindly Godzilla in a cardigan.

An Excavation

In 1969, the Agoura Meadows shopping center was approved for construction. Work was halted and an excavation commenced when human remains from hundreds of bodies were discovered, all buried between 1600 and 1785. The land approved for the shopping center was discovered to be an ancient Chumash burial ground. After six months of excavation, the bodies were sent to a remote, undisclosed location where, according to a Chumash elder, they received traditional burial rites.[14] The original burial site is now a supermarket parking lot.[15] For a remote God's-eye view, type

"Vons, 5671 Kanan Rd, Agoura Hills, CA 91301" into Google maps, switch to satellite view, and zoom in until the similarities between a parking lot and a cemetery begin to emerge. At maximum zoom, stitching errors (visual errors caused by the way that Google combines images) deform the cars as if they have melted into asphalt or are rising like coffins from Cuesta Verde Estates.

Remote Advertising

From the very beginning, television remotes were sold as tools for advertising avoidance. The popular 1950s "Blab-Off" remote was not much more than twenty feet of lamp cord and an on/off switch made to perform one function: mute.[16] Remotes can be credited with pushing advertisers to make more interesting commercials, but remotes must also take part of the blame for the growth of product placement strategies within entertainment—strategies that also exist in films like *Poltergeist*, where the Freeling household virtually doubles as a Sony showroom. When it launched in 1979, the Sony Trinitron KV-2643R owned by the Freelings boasted the biggest television screen in America—a whopping twenty-six inches at a cost of $1,349.95.[17] The Freelings also have a Sony Trinitron in their bedroom, a nine-inch Sony KV-9400 in the kitchen, and a Sony Studio 7080 hi-fi sound system with turntable, cassette deck, integrated amp, tuner, audio timer, and a remote. The video and cassette recorders used by the paranormal investigators are also Sony products. One of the only non-Sony devices in the house is the early 1970s Zenith Space Command 600 remote, which is incompatible with all of the televisions owned by the Freelings. A Sony Trinitron remote, which uses infrared light rather than ultrasonic waves, would not have had the problems of neighborly interference required for the conflict, but more importantly, the Sony remote lacks the satisfying *click* that adds drama to the shootout between Steve and Ben.

Poltergeist, Noun

Poltergeist comes from the German *poltern* (to make a loud noise or uproar, to rumble, to thud) and *geist* (ghost). It means "a ghost or other supernatural being supposedly responsible for unexplained physical disturbances such as loud noises and the movement of objects."[18] A poltergeist is a noisy ghost.

YouTube Video: "TV Static Noise 10 Hours, HD 1080p"

On December 10, 2013, NemArt uploaded a ten-hour video of static in high definition with audio and a separate MP3 file for download to audio devices.[19] As of January 17, 2018, the video has 1,310,681 views. "I liked the part where the static was on the TV," says SnarkieVlogs in the top of 1,494 comments. "Can you link the time?" asks Jonathan Simen. "If you look carefully at 3:08:46 you'll see it," replies SnarkieVlogs. "Oh hey I see it now, that part is pretty good. IMO the best part is 7:59:32," writes Simen, launching a debate among scores of YouTube users as to which second of the ten-hour static video is the best. Burnt Bacon, whose typing can barely keep up with his enthusiasm, writes, "bro bro bro . . . . . . but di you we the part at 8:45:21 when the screen was like zzzzzzzzzzzzzzzzzzzzzz?" Meanwhile, WhoKnownsAndWhoCares? waxes nostalgic: "Reminds me of the days when a tv was a giant box." Some commenters associate static with Sadako, the vengeful ghost who climbs out of televisions in the *Ring* film cycle beginning with *Ringu* (1998), but NemArt and dozens of other YouTubers consider the static a sleep aid or a tool for concentration. The description of SleepDroid Studios' ten-hour static video says, "Some believe that white noise simulates being back inside the womb."[20] As a matter of personal preference, I consume static in smaller doses by binge-watching HBO, which has bookended every show with the fuzzy stuff since 1993.[21]

A Different Controller

Another non-Sony device in the Freelings' home sits on top of their bedroom television, and unlike the Space Command 600, this device is compatible with their television: an Atari 2600 video computer system. The Atari brings the arcade experience of a joystick controller to the home and alters the user experience of interacting with a television screen. The joysticks are tethered controllers. A wireless version, the Atari 2700, was scheduled for release in 1981 but never shipped.

You're Gonna Ruin Your Eyes

Before her transdimensional trip through the closet (a mystical use of storage space normally reserved for armoires in fantasy and horror), Carol Anne watches television static on three separate occasions. First, Carol Anne communicates through the static with the "TV people" after her father has dozed off in the living room. The scene follows the opening of *Poltergeist*, which begins with a black screen and an orchestral rendition of "The Star-Spangled Banner." If you are inclined to stand up and sing along, you will be reaching the part about rockets and bombs bursting in air just as movement appears on screen—dark shadows and hundreds of oblong flickering dots in shades of blue and green. The extreme close-up shows grids of dots that the viewer, with the help of the score, can vaguely piece together as fragments of patriotic imagery. McLuhan's assertion that television is a mosaic and that the viewer "unconsciously reconfigures the dots into an abstract work of art on the pattern of a Seurat or Rouault" now has the opening of *Poltergeist* as a case in point.[22] The camera pulls back just as the Iwo Jima Memorial (Marine Corps War Memorial) closes out another broadcasting day and signs off. When Carol Anne makes her way downstairs, the television is playing static, the electromagnetic noise often called snow. The following night, Carol Anne watches the snow on her parents' bedroom TV at 2:37 a.m.—a nod to Room 237 in another movie with a tuned-in kid and a lot of television watching. The next morning, Carol Anne leans up to the kitchen TV, changes to a channel with no signal, and watches the static. Her mother notices the static and says, "Oh, honey, you're gonna ruin your eyes. This is not good for you." She flips the channel to an old war movie just as a soldier lobs a grenade amid heavy gunfire.

Big Bang Afterglow

Cosmic microwave background radiation is widely recognized as "the afterglow of the Big Bang."[23] Competing cosmological theories suggest that electromagnetic currents from billions of galaxies are "whispering through the cosmos" or that gravitational waves might be causing the distortion.[24] Explorer satellites such as the COBE (1989–93), the NASA WMAP (2001–10), and the ESA Planck (2009–13) revolutionized knowledge about the origin of the universe. While "Big Bang Afterglow" might sound like a pay-per-view offering, Carol Anne watches the cosmic broadcast three times on her favorite eyesore nonprogram. In the words of Bill Bryson, "Tune your television to any channel it doesn't receive, and about 1 percent of the static you see is accounted for by this ancient remnant of the Big Bang. The next time you complain there is nothing on, remember that you can always watch the birth of the universe."[25]

Some Atari 2600 Games

Adventure (Atari, 1980)—rescue an enchanted chalice stolen by an evil magician. Use the joystick to move in any one of eight directions across a labyrinthine series of screens. The manual explains the foreign concept of navigating space beyond the boundaries of one screen: "To move from one area to an adjacent area, move 'off' the television screen through one of the openings, the adjacent area will be shown on your television screen."[26] Today, a tile-based game space (à la *Zelda*) no longer needs an explanation. We expect an adventure game to travel beyond the constraints of one screen.[27]

Missile Command (Atari, 1981)—protect your peaceful planet Zardon against the attacking Krytolians by deploying antiballistic missiles (ABM). Beware of cruise missiles that look like satellites. Use the joystick controller to aim and the button to fire your ABMs.

Yars' Revenge (Atari, 1981)—you control a "fly simulator" called a Yar. Destroy a laser base called a Qotile by breaking through a shield and blasting the base with a Zorlon Cannon. "The Yar will move in whatever direction the joystick is pushed. The screen 'wraps' from top to bottom, bottom to top. This means that if you fly the Yar off the top of the screen, it will appear at the bottom, and vice versa," explains the game manual.[28] *Yars' Revenge* scored high in sales to adult women, which makes it not implausible to suggest that Diane Freeling might occasionally get lit and play the game.[29]

Haunted House (Atari, 1982)—explore a mysterious mansion once inhabited by an old man named Zachary Graves. Work your way through twenty-four rooms in search of pieces of a magic urn, and an ancient scepter that scares off evil spirits. Light your way with matches by pressing the red button on the joystick controller.

Six Types of Gratification

A study conducted back when MTV was still a music video station identifies "six types of gratification" that people get from remotes:

1. The selective avoidance of unpleasant stimuli
2. Getting "more" from television
3. Annoying others
4. Controlling family viewing/accessing television news
5. Accessing music videos
6. Finding out what's on television[30]

Playing the TV

Consider the number of remotes that litter a TV room: DVD remotes, remotes provided by cable and satellite companies, universal remotes that we never quite get around to programming as complete replacements for other remotes, remote apps on smartphones, remotes for Apple TV or similar devices, voice command remotes, and game controllers. We do more than watch TV; we play it. Media scholar Sheila Murphy explains, "Seen in conjunction with another device one uses to 'play' the TV set, the remote control, the dynamics of user agency, interactivity, and 'control' over the television emerge as key ways that television sets, remotes, and controllers all provide new, 'alternative' modes of using TV."[31] The Wiimote by Nintendo suggests that the distinction between "controller" and "remote" is unnecessary. Instead, we might think of controllers and remotes as devices that play the TV.

Alexa, Play Carol Anne

Remotes play televisions, games, music, locks, heating systems, and security, but above all, remotes play space. As Benson-Allott observes, "the 'remote' of remote control stresses the space between the user and the machine, a space that the remote occupies in a peculiar way."[32] A remote interpellates space as media. When philosopher Louis Althusser wrote that "individuals are always-already interpellated by ideology as subjects," he was not talking about nonhumans.[33] He was explaining how ideology interpellates (i.e., forms, or brings into being) human subjects through acts of hailing and recognition such as a knock on the door or a handshake. Althusser was not thinking of computer handshakes as ideological protocols, nor was he imagining a world populated by digital assistants, but the same bringing-into-being occurs in all machine-to-machine, person-to-machine, and object-to-object communication. Ask Alexa to play a song, and you have become a human version of the Zenith Space Command 600, the emitter of frequencies to which Alexa responds. The mutual interpellation positions Alexa as a subject and the human as a remote device. Voice-controlled assistants reclaim remote control as a sonic event. Increasingly, we play the air.

This Sky Ain't Big Enough for the Thirteen Hundred of Us

There are more than thirteen hundred active satellites and an estimated five hundred thousand pieces of "space junk" orbiting the earth.[34] Lisa Parks and James Schwoch define satellites as "part of an assemblage of technologies of remote control that at once can be organized to observe, communicate about, and target sites on Earth."[35] Satellites redraw boundaries as they make footprints on the earth's surface. Parks and Schwoch note that there are more than twice as many communication satellites in geostationary orbit as there are countries in the world. In other words, "Satellite operators have carved up the planet and staked out new territories in ways reminiscent of European political leaders during the Treaty of Westphalia centuries ago."[36] Sometimes these orbit boundaries impinge on national boundaries. One such event occurred on January 24, 1978, when the Cosmos 954—a Soviet radar satellite designed to track US nuclear submarines—crashed into the Great Slave Lake area of Canada's Northern Territories. The forty-six-foot-long, five-thousand-ton device became a huge media story. "Seemingly overnight," observes Parks, "a satellite the public had never known to exist became the object of urgent searching, scrutiny, and media spectacle." Particularly impacted were the "Inuit and Chippewa communities living in the vicinity of the crash, whose water and food supplies were in danger of exposure to radiation."[37]

Spooky Action at a Distance Sequel

Guided by Dr. Lesh (Beatrice Straight) and Tangina (Zelda Rubinstein), the Freelings issue gamelike commands to Carol Anne: "Stay away from the light!" "Run to the light!" "Do not go into the light!" The Freelings' older daughter, Dana, tilts her head toward the ceiling to speak, her back to the paranormal team, who monitor Carol Anne's favorite static channel. Carol Anne's voice bounces around, adding a sense of spatial disorientation. Suddenly, a bright spot opens in the ceiling, and in a gesture that symbolically rejects time while defying space, the portal spews old timepieces onto the carpet. Although the television participates in this and other scenes, its function is as a receiver, not a container. On that point, my reading differs somewhat from that of Jeffrey Sconce, who positions *Poltergeist* within the context of television shows such as *The Twilight Zone* (1959–64) and *The Outer Limits* (1963–65), in which the television contains a liminal zone, an "occult space within television itself."[38] For Sconce, the television in *Poltergeist* is a "gateway to oblivion."[39] I agree that Steve Freeling no doubt feels the same way as he pushes the TV out the hotel room in the final shot of the film. Nonetheless, even more than a film about television, *Poltergeist* is about action at a distance. Carol Anne is swallowed up into the vortex in her closet, not into the Sony Trinitron TV set, and she returns through a portal in the ceiling. The television is a piece of the picture, but remote-control phenomena are everywhere.

I said at the beginning of this chapter that we do not need "spooky action at a distance" to explain *Poltergeist*. Einstein's famous "spooky" characterization of nonlocality refers to objects that are moved or changed without touch, without respect for classical notions of time and space, without separation between cause and effect. A remote control is not a good example of those spooky phenomena. On the contrary, we can trace the action of a remote-control event as a line of things that touch each other. The user of the Space Command clicks a button, and a hammer strikes a note that sends ultrasonic waves to the microphone in the TV, where the sound is translated into a command. And yet "spooky action at a distance" is too irresistible to pass up because it describes metaphorically an aesthetic truth about the objects within and without *Poltergeist*. English revolutionaries, ancient Chumash settlements, a supermarket parking lot, the Cosmos 954 satellite, Atari Missile Command, a Rams game, *Mister Rogers' Neighborhood*, TV static YouTube videos, the big bang, and a fictitious suburban lot are nonlocal objects as separate from each other as the dawn of the universe is from a voice-controlled digital assistant named Alexa. Those objects are entangled in a profound aesthetic sense that I have alluded to through this chapter's version of channel hopping.

Nonlocality, for object-oriented philosopher Timothy Morton, "implies that the notion of being located at all is only epiphenomenal to a deeper, atemporal implicate order."[40] That order, here, is suggested by objects that act on one another without touching in space or time. The satellite view of a Vons parking lot that is in fact multiple aerial views poorly stitched together is a deformed aesthetic trace whose descriptive failure on one front is an allusion to something deeper on another, something Morton calls "interobjective reality" or "the sum total of all these footprints crisscrossing everywhere."[41] In that way, a Chumash burial ground crisscrosses with *Poltergeist* after all, and people are not wrong to think that the film is about an Indian burial ground. Likewise, the antiballistic missiles on an Atari game are entangled with a downed Russian satellite. Like a Zenith Space Command 600 firing at a Sony Trinitron TV, these are not causal connections in the sense of local action but allusions to other types of connections, nonlocal ones for which "remote" is simultaneously a prerequisite and a meaningless concept. *Poltergeist* may in fact have something to say about what happens to neighborhoods affected by spooky action at a distance, but what it says happens not only in the film but also in supermarket parking lots, in *Mister Rogers' Neighborhood*, on YouTube, and in mismatched remote controls.

Notes

1. Avoidance behavior includes anything judged unpleasant: ads, news reports, politicians, etc. See Walker and Bellamy, 9.
2. Eco, 148.
3. Musser, 3.
4. McLuhan and Fiore, 31–40. For the "physics minus the connections" quote, see "Wave-Particle Wonder—Marshall McLuhan," YouTube video, 4:29, accessed January 7, 2018, https://www.youtube.com/watch?v=ZRk0Bux3mvU.
5. Kiver and Kaufman, 300.
6. See a comparison of four studies in Bellamy and Walker, 140.
7. Copeland and Schweitzer, 157.
8. Thirty thousand Flash-Matics sold in a year when 5.7 million TV sets were sold—hardly a great success story. See Benson-Allott, 54.
9. See Benson-Allott, 61–62.
10. My assertion "most people" is based on online comments, satires, and asking my own students to tell me what the original *Poltergeist* is about. A note on *Indian*: I use the term here rather than *First Peoples* to evoke the popular language associated with the trope (e.g., "Indian burial ground").
11. See Benson-Allott, xiv.
12. Pascal, 11.
13. McLuhan, 279.
14. Pascal, 11.
15. Ibid., 20.
16. See Laura Alpern, "The Story of Blab-Off," *Early Television Museum*, accessed January 7, 2018, http://www.earlytelevision.org/blab_off.html.
17. *Wired* tracked down many of the devices. Bryan Gardiner, "The Gadgets from *Poltergeist* That Fueled Our Nightmares," *Wired*, March 11, 2015, https://www.wired.com/2015/03/poltergeist-gadgets-and-gear/. If the Freelings had purchased their TV in 1981, they might have paid $879, which in 2017 is equivalent to about $2,400.
18. *Oxford English Dictionary*, 3rd ed. (2006), s.v. "poltergeist."
19. "TV Static Noise 10 Hours, HD 1080p," YouTube video, 10:00:37, posted by NemArt, December 10, 2013, https://www.youtube.com/watch?v=toI4mTEdAf8.
20. "10 Hours of Static White Noise," YouTube video, posted by SleepDroid Studios, May 11, 2015, https://www.youtube.com/watch?v=uUOHpxNlOow. Video no longer available.
21. On HBO and its static branding, see Johnson, 8–11.
22. McLuhan, 273.
23. Mather and Boslough, xviii.

24. Ibid., xx.
25. Bryson, 12.
26. *Adventure* Game Program Instructions, Atari, 1980, 2.
27. For a detailed look at *Adventure*, see Montfort and Bogost, 43–63.
28. *Yars' Revenge* Game Atari Game Program Instructions, Atari, 1982, 3.
29. See Montfort and Bogost for a discussion of *Yars' Revenge*, 81–97.
30. See Bellamy and Walker, 3.
31. Murphy, 104.
32. Benson-Allott, xvi.
33. Althusser, 176.
34. See Quartz Media's visualization. David Yanofsky and Tim Fernholz, "The World Above Us," December 21, 2015, https://qz.com/296941/interactive-graphic-every-active-satellite-orbiting-earth/.
35. Parks and Schwoch, 4.
36. Ibid.
37. Parks, 223–24.
38. Sconce, 133.
39. Ibid., 166.
40. Morton, *Hyperobjects*, 47.
41. Morton, *Realist Magic*, 71.

7

SEWING MACHINE

A Good, Christian Machine Gone Bad

When hunky all-star athlete Tommy Ross (William Katt) approaches telekinetic high school pariah Carrie White (Sissy Spacek) to ask her to the senior prom, he finds her browsing the library stacks, her arms loaded with books. "What are you doing?" he asks. "Reading," she responds, pulling the books closely to her chest to conceal the titles. "Yeah, what are you reading?" She hesitates. Her card catalog search has led her to books such as *The Secret Science behind Miracles* and *Cosmic Consciousness*. "It's about... uh... sewing." Just the kind of answer one might expect from a mousy introvert. "Sewing... that's good." For Tommy, the conversation starter has hit a dead end. Better move directly to the prom request. For us, however, Carrie's knee-jerk attempt at normalcy marks the perfect starting point for a meaningful encounter with the machine responsible for stitching both Carrie's lackluster school attire and the stunning pale blush satin dress that is famously soaked in pig's blood in a cruel prank, the moment of her prom queen coronation: Margaret White's sewing machine—the instrument the religious zealot operates ecstatically while her daughter does penance in a locked closet and makeshift shrine for having had the audacity to menstruate. To be precise, the device is a 1930s White Family Rotary electric crinkle embossed black iron sewing machine. It sits prominently in the main living area of the White home, not far from the tapestry wall hanging of Da Vinci's *Last Supper*. And even without dwelling on the fact that the White brand shares Carrie's surname, an object-focused analysis inevitably leads to the conclusion that the sewing machine is as burdened with religious baggage as Carrie herself.

The fact that Mrs. White (Piper Laurie) would allow a sewing machine into the heart of her home testifies to the success of more than a century of proselytism by sewing machine manufacturers. Early inventors found their machines far less welcomed. Barthélemy Thimonnier, credited with inventing the first workable sewing machine sometime in the 1830s, lost his shop to an angry mob of two hundred tailors.[1] Walter Hunt, another inventor, was dissuaded from his pursuit by the pleadings of clergy, who claimed that the machine would force thousands of women to seek alternative—even illegal and licentious—sources of revenue.[2] But by the 1860s, manufacturers had developed brilliant rhetorical strategies for socializing the disruptive threat. In a moral rebranding, a catalogue published in 1864 calls the invention an "honest machine" and a "Christian institution."[3] Testimonials written by ministers and missionaries commend the civilizing influence of the new technology, and an "Eminent Lawyer" praises the "moral and social advantages" gained by adopting into one's family the "easily domesticated, and very inoffensive" device.[4]

The Singer Sewing Machine Company took the Christian civilizing mission to a new level of imperialistic zeal. "On every sea are floating the Singer machines," boasts the company's account of its unprecedented corporate dominion.[5] With the title *Genius Rewarded* emblazoned on the cover in gilded letters befitting a medieval Bible, the book conflates capitalist expansion with divine recompense. Despite a "paltry and inauspicious beginning," the sewing machine had become an exalted instrument of unification:[6] "Its cheering tune is understood no less by the sturdy German matron than by the slender Japanese maiden; it sings as intelligibly to the flaxen-haired Russian peasant girl as to the dark-eyed Mexican Señorita."[7] Eighty-four years before Disney's animatronic dolls piped out "It's a small world" for the first time, Singer had already flattened the world with stories of Paraguayan pampas, fair-skinned Irish lasses, and "China's tawny daughter" united by the "self-same stitch."[8] For the 1893 Columbian Exposition World's Fair, Singer published an expanded set of an already popular trade card series featuring people around the world brought into "universal kinship and sisterhood" through machine sewing.[9] Singer's narrative of Algerian history, in a typical tone of condescension, asserts that the country was dominated by "pirate bands" committing "outrages against Christian people" until the civilizing forces of education, the railway, and the Singer sewing machine tamed their barbarism.[10]

Although Singer was by far the most successful among its corporate peers, every American manufacturer worth its salt employed similarly zealous rhetoric. The White Sewing Machine Company's trade cards from the

Fig. 7.1. Margaret White sews piously at her White sewing machine in *Carrie* (1976).

same period feature bucolic landscapes with humble churches, little girls with prayer books, doves, winged angels ringing church bells, and other imagery calculated to appeal to good Christian consumers. Among the more striking images of White's Christian branding is a trade card featuring a crucifix and a white rose, with the caption "The White. King of all Sewing Machines. 500,000 Now in Use."[11] The white rose harmoniously intertwined with the symbol of crucifixion implicates the ascension of the White brand with the biblical narrative of redemption. Through skillful manipulation of iconography, the White Sewing Machine Company symbolically coopts the "King of kings" as an implicit endorser of the "King of all Sewing Machines." Consequently, sales statistics take on an evangelical fervor as capitalism and Christianity find common cause in their missions to civilize the world and ease the burdens of the heavy laden.

When Margaret White sits at her sewing machine, she is the picture of piety, her face aglow in the Rembrandt lighting cast by the machine's bulb. She hums nineteenth-century hymns as she feeds fabric through White's signature vibrating shuttle. A tomato pincushion attached to the front of the iron arm punctuates the predominantly blue and black hues that blanket the scene. Only Margaret's red hair rivals the chromatic draw of the plush object. Like Margaret, the pincushion is a throwback to Victorian-era superstitions. According to Victorian lore, a tomato placed on the mantel of a new home brings luck and wards off evil spirits.[12] Outside of tomato season, some red fabric sewn into a ball and filled with sand or sawdust offered a suitable substitute that, unlike a real tomato, could double as a convenient pin storage device. Thus we could argue that Margaret's sewing machine bears the fruit of Victorian beliefs. A less chaste but perhaps more relevant reading might note that the pin-pricked tomato cushion recalls the figurative association Mediterranean cultures have made between the tomato and female genitalia since the plant's arrival in Italy from the New World in the sixteenth century.[13] Names such as *pomo d'oro* (associated with the golden apples of the Hesperides), *pomme d'amour*, and "love apple" indicate the tomato's symbolic charge in relation to mythologies involving women and forbidden fruit. Indeed, here, the argument that ended with Carrie being banished to the broom-closet shrine and Margaret finding solace at her sewing machine most fittingly ties the red fruit back to the Bible.

Having learned that Carrie has begun to menstruate, Margaret opts to recite the perverse catechisms of a book chapter devoted to "The Sins of Women" in lieu of a more conventional mother-daughter chat. "Why didn't you tell me, Mama?" asks Carrie, while her mother expounds on Eve's culpability in the fall of man through sexual intercourse. "And Eve was weak. Say it! Eve was weak!" yells Margaret. "Eve was weak! Eve was weak! Say it!" Once Carrie affirms Eve's flawed nature, Margaret continues from memory, "And the Lord visited Eve with a curse. And the curse was the curse of blood." Striking Carrie like a revival preacher banishing the devil, Margaret pleads with the Lord to show her iniquitous child "that if she had remained sinless the curse of blood would never have come on her." Finally, Margaret drags Carrie to the closet shrine while quoting Genesis 3:16 in support of her belief that childbearing is God's second curse. Contrary to her namesake (Saint Margaret, the patron saint of pregnant women), Mrs. White has little compassion for a woman's reproductive power. She can only view Carrie's period as the first in a series of curses visited on women by a wrathful God.

Margaret characterizes her own maternal status as the result of sexual weakness. Like Eve, she has succumbed to the sins of the flesh and has endured the pains of a fallen woman. Thus, when Margaret toils away, illuminated by the glow of her sewing machine's bulb, she is as much a picture of postlapsarian shame seeking to clothe its nakedness as she is a woman redeemed by God's grace. Her red hair recalls the hues of Michelangelo's *Temptation and Expulsion of Adam and Eve*, and the vivid red pincushion attached to the arm of her sewing machine calls to mind the forbidden fruit inextricably tied to the invention of sewing itself. Margaret sings of holy blood as she sews: "There is pow'r, pow'r, wonder-working pow'r in the blood of the Lamb." Behind her, Carrie emerges from the broom-closet shrine to the arrow-pierced Saint Sebastian (a top contender, were pincushions to elect a patron saint) to utter a penitent, "Thank you, Mama."

As the White household soon demonstrates, even the most virtuous sewing machine harbors the potential for sinful abuse. Nineteenth-century doctors identified links between sewing machine work and "venereal excitement," tension, and menstrual problems.[14] Studies on autoeroticism describe factories where one can hear the telltale sounds of sewing machines increasing in velocity and then dying back down many times a day as factory seamstresses enjoy the stimulating side effects of the dual treadle movement.[15] Mrs. White's electric sewing machine requires no such action. Nevertheless, Carrie turns the machine against her mother's values. Once Carrie has acknowledged her telekinetic gifts, she begins to fashion a prom dress, which is not, to her mother's chagrin, the sackcloth jokingly envisioned by the popular girls at school. Instead, Carrie has chosen a decadent satin in a shade of pink so pale it approaches white. One among many changes made in adapting Stephen King's novel for the screen, the choice of pale satin over thick crushed red velvet connotes intimate apparel and evening wear. The sleek, spaghetti-strap style, meant to be worn braless, is the sartorial antithesis of sexual repression. To quote Margaret, this dress will make everyone see Carrie's "dirtypillows."[16]

Brian De Palma's love of split-focus diopters allows for unsettling visual reinforcement of the sewing machine's murky status once Carrie takes control of the needle. A split diopter makes one half of the lens nearsighted so that the right and left halves of the picture can be on radically different planes with each half maintaining its focus. This schizophrenic approach to depth of field allows De Palma to create a close shot of Margaret kneeling in prayer, foregrounded on the left half of the frame, while keeping Carrie in equally sharp focus on the right half of the frame in the background as she tailors her dress. Unlike traditional deep focus, which (to use sewing metaphors) has a seamless depth of field, the split-focus diopter has a visible seam between the right and left halves in the form of a blurred vertical patch between the two sides of the frame. In the split-focus tableau of the prayerful mother close-up on the left and the sinful daughter medium-long distance on the right, De Palma has placed the sewing machine in the "seam" between the two competing focal lengths.

At the moment of Carrie's psychotic break, De Palma rips the seam of the film through the use of his signature split-screen technique. The catalyst for the break is the iconic dumping of pig's blood from a bucket tenuously perched above the stage where Carrie and her date stand for their coronation as high school prom royalty. De Palma fixes our gaze on the long rope that runs from under the stage, up along the curtain, and to the bucket in the rafters. From the wings, mean-girl-turned-ally Sue (Amy Irving) watches Carrie's big moment and then notices the rope jiggling at the edge of the curtain. As Sue's eyes follow the line up the fabric, across the stage, and back down, De Palma traces the rope's path back to the hands that will tear the fairy-tale moment apart with a simple tug. Once the thread is pulled and Carrie unravels, so too does our point of view, first in a kaleidoscopic montage of laughing prom attendees and then in a series of shots that alternately split and sew back together our vision of the massacre. Douglas Keesey (whose book on De Palma adopts the split screen as its central metaphor) remarks that Carrie's stare on one side of the screen often cues "violent cuts to the suffering of characters on the screen's other side."[17] She slides from one side of the diptych to the other as her vengeful telekinetic gaze slams doors shut, topples gym fixtures, and wields a fire hose. The split-screen view accomplishes a moral function, according to Keesey, as it allows us to look *with* but also *at* Carrie, thereby countering sympathetic identification with moral repudiation.[18] One might say that Brian De Palma is showing us that, like the White sewing machine, he can tailor just as effortlessly to our most pious or salacious instincts.

When Carrie returns home, drenched in pig's blood, ready to admit that her mother was right, she finds the house filled with enough red and white candles to stock a cathedral. The dress form and ironing board have been overturned like moneychangers' tables in Herod's temple. The sewing box is on the floor, and as the camera pans to the sewing machine, we see that the device now holds liturgical candles. A Bible sits next to the machine on the sewing table, and religious imagery adorns the wall behind it. A spool of red thread matching the current state of Carrie's dress sits at the base of the sewing machine in a triangular grouping with the red pincushion and a red candle. Whether the result of careful planning or of pure chance, these three visual drops of red grouped around the sewing machine echo a long literary and folk tradition of three blood drops tied to womanhood.

Folklorist Francisco Vaz da Silva notes that Chrétien de Troyes was already using the "three drops of blood" trope in the twelfth-century

Conte du Graal, when Perceval is reminded of his beloved at the sight of three drops of blood on white snow.[19] In literature written five centuries later, Vaz da Silva locates once again three drops—this time in ricotta cheese—in Giambattista Basile's tale "The Three Citrons." The Grimms' "Snow White" queen similarly beholds three drops of her own blood on the snow as she wishes for the birth of a beautiful daughter.[20] Sleeping Beauty, or "Briar-Rose" in the Grimms' version of the tale, famously pricks her finger on a needle at the age of fifteen and falls into a deep sleep surrounded by a thicket of thorns to await a worthy husband. Vaz da Silva explains, "Both the pricked finger and the subsequent defloration entail bleeding." The three drops correspond to "three bleedings punctuating a woman's destiny at puberty, defloration, and birth giving."[21] *Carrie* (1976) begins with menstrual blood, moves to a blood-soaked prom dress, and ends in the shedding of a mother's blood. A good fairy-tale mother "passes on her blood drops and takes briars as they come, the bad one clings to rosebuds out of season."[22] Margaret White, in contrast, seeks to suppress feminine blood altogether, and her daughter's enchanting flirtation with the sewing needle leads not merely to three drops but to a bloodbath.

Serial Stiches

Among the numerous cinematic progeny of real-life cannibal couturier Ed Gein, serial killer "Buffalo Bill" of *The Silence of the Lambs* (1991) has the most intimate relationship with mechanized sewing. Norman Bates (*Psycho*, 1960) has his taxidermy, and Leatherface (*The Texas Chainsaw Massacre*, 1974) his mask, but Buffalo Bill's construction of a bespoke suit of female human skin wins the prize for morbidly aspirational sewing project. Jame Gumb (Ted Levine), nicknamed "Buffalo Bill" by the FBI, targets women as if shopping for fabric. We first see him in action when he enlists a kindhearted young woman into helping him load an oversized easy chair into his van. His fake cast gains the sympathy of Catherine Martin (Brooke Smith), who has just pulled up to her apartment with a bag of groceries. Gumb grabs one side of the chair, and Catherine pulls the other until she has been wedged backward into the van, hidden from the viewer. Only Gumb's backside is visible when we hear him ask, "Say, are you about a size fourteen?" Her response—"Sorry?"—gives way to screams as Gumb brutally knocks her out. Inside the van, Gumb drapes Catherine's unconscious body facedown across the chair. A close-up shot of the blouse tag confirms

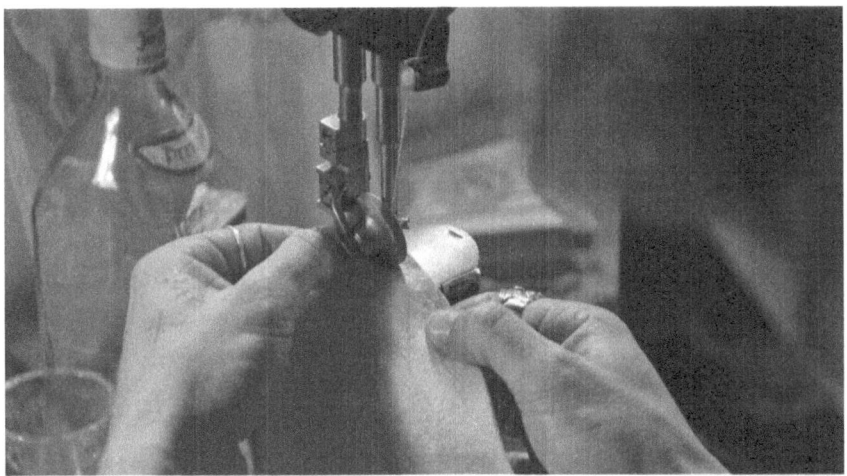

Fig. 7.2. Jame Gumb works on his disturbing sewing project in *The Silence of the Lambs* (1991).

the accuracy of Gumb's guess: size 14. The shot then cuts to a close-up of scissors cutting a thin-whale corduroy fabric counter to its large-scale horizontal pattern of bright fruit on a black background. We follow the path of the scissors as they move up and then halt momentarily before cutting through what we now discern to be the collar of Catherine's blouse, still on her body. Gumb's hands part the fabric to each side, like a surgeon opening a patient. He strokes the bare skin of his victim's back and murmurs his approval. "Oh, good. Good," he repeats, before tossing the fabric out the van window and driving away.

From the viewer's perspective, Clarice Starling (Jodie Foster) takes a surprisingly long time to piece together the motive behind Buffalo Bill's habit of removing geometric patches of skin from his victims. Hannibal Lecter (Anthony Hopkins), in contrast, understands the killer well before he asks Clarice to bring him the FBI case files. "Why do you think he removes their skins, Agent Starling? Enthrall me with your acumen," he asks during their first meeting. Clarice posits, "It excites him. Most serial killers keep some sort of trophies from their victims." Hannibal corrects her textbook response (but not her grammar) in a way that reinforces his own exceptionalism and hints at a more corporeally bonded killer-victim relation. "*I* didn't," he replies. Clarice retorts, "No. No, you ate yours." Hannibal incorporates his victims' bodies into his own. Ingestion subsumes the subject-object separation of trophy collecting. Gumb, too, seeks fusion, albeit at the epidermal layer. Like Hannibal, Gumb is not in the business of collecting souvenir objects. Hannibal knows that Clarice and the FBI are off track, that they are thinking in terms of slashing, cutting, and dissecting rather than fusing or stitching. He has not been enthralled by Clarice's acumen so much as amused by her quick retort about his cannibalism. In that light, Hannibal's sudden willingness to look at the FBI questionnaire that Clarice has brought seems to be a reward for a good verbal spar, just as, seconds later, his rejection of the "blunt little tool" reads as a volatile response from an easily bruised ego. But that assumption is worth questioning. Had Lecter truly believed that a standardized government questionnaire would exhibit the degree of perspicacity and nuance required to probe his psyche? Not likely. Instead, we must consider the plausible alternative explanation that Hannibal's outburst is, in fact, a bit of theater for the benefit of his fledgling criminal profiler. Hannibal's refusal of "dissection" pushes the discussion back to the surface of things, back to a train of thought that hints at perverse distortions of the fashion dictum "The clothes make the man."

Consider Hannibal's calculated attack on Clarice as he rejects the questionnaire: "You know what you look like to me with your good bag and your cheap shoes? You look like a rube. A well-scrubbed hustling rube with a little taste. Good nutrition has given you some length of bone, but you're not more than one generation from poor white trash, are you, Agent Starling?" Countering the FBI's "blunt tool" with his own cruel precision, Hannibal has cut Clarice to the core while remaining focused on her clothing. The spectator has likely paid little attention to Agent Starling's attire until Hannibal uses it to strip away her facade. Her clothing is, after all, fairly unremarkable. She wears a brown tweed, menswear-style jacket with large shoulder pads; a sheer, white top with a modest neckline layered over a camisole and tucked into a belted knee-length dark-brown wool skirt; dark stockings to match; and classic, closed-toe, low-heeled brown leather pumps. Had Hannibal so desired, he could have psychoanalyzed Clarice's jacket: tweed (educated, vaguely Holmesian), oversized (form concealing, defeminizing), ample shoulder pads (a tailor's trick to compensate for the inadequacies of the narrow-shouldered man, long since adopted by women to fabricate a more powerful silhouette). Or her top: just sheer enough to suggest the femininity otherwise concealed by the jacket, but without the buttons of a blouse, and cut with a neckline that sits high on the collarbone. Or the camisole: a deep V-shape that subtly shows through the top, simultaneously serving the function of modesty and alluding to the décolletage that the conservative neckline of the top negates. Each element of her ensemble plays out a gender struggle in which certain expectations of femininity are both met and suppressed in a complex balance appropriate to Clarice's ambitions to compete in a male-dominated field.[23]

In Hannibal's estimation, Clarice hopes to clothe her way out of the identity into which she was born. As does Gumb. Her approach is conventional and his psychopathically criminal, but each relies on a "woman suit." More importantly, each involves skin. Hannibal's deconstruction of Clarice begins with the perfume she is not wearing but that lingers on her skin ("Sometimes you wear L'air du Temps, but not today") and ends by calling attention to the two parts of her ensemble made of skin: her "good bag" and her "cheap shoes." Hannibal "the Cannibal" Lecter makes no moral distinction between the flaying of human and animal skin or the consumption of their flesh. Hannibal is an aesthete, not a moralist. Yet his attention to Clarice's "good" leather bag and her "cheap" leather shoes subtly introduces the commodification of skin as a key marker of social identity. Catherine, a senator's daughter, held in a dried-up well while her (or "its," to use Gumb's language) skin is conditioned for slaughter, has the full resources of the FBI working to save her. The animal that gave its life for Clarice's bag or her shoes did not. The difference between a well-heeled fashionista with a shoe fetish and a psychotic killer tailoring a human skin suit matters little, if at all, to Hannibal. More important to him is getting into Clarice's head and fostering a relationship with her by slowly feeding her clues. The best way to achieve both goals is to criticize her uninteresting, overly practical shoes—shoes that are certainly not made of fine lambskin.

Hannibal's most triumphant moment in getting underneath Clarice's skin comes much later in the film. Locked in a temporary holding cage, Hannibal moves beyond the topic of clothing and tutors Clarice in the first principles of Stoicism. "Of each particular thing ask: what is it in itself?" The killing is incidental, he explains. Covetousness is the killer's manner of relating to the world. In return for his insight, Hannibal demands that Clarice share a clue to her own actions as a runaway orphan under the care of a distant relative. Why did she flee the ranch? Hannibal is convinced that the childhood trauma that sparked her flight continues to inform Clarice's actions even now. She explains that it began with a sound like children's screams coming from the barn. She crept up to the barn and saw the spring slaughter of the lambs. "They were screaming." She tried to free them, but they wouldn't run, so she took one lamb and carried it for miles until the sheriff found her. "What became of your lamb, Clarice?" asks Hannibal. "He killed him," she replies. Hannibal has now found the thing "in itself" that Clarice is doing. "And you think if you save poor Catherine, you can make them stop, don't you? You think if Catherine lives, you won't wake up in the dark ever again to that awful screaming of the lambs." Clarice answers, "I don't know . . . I don't know." Hannibal visibly relishes the uncertainty of the response. Her troubled reaction confirms the value of the Catherine/lamb metaphor as well as the fear that figurative thinking is inherently limited.

The titular lambs that Clarice wants to silence connect her to both Hannibal and Gumb, because as human/animal metaphors, the screaming lambs provide a model for the ontological flattening in which all three characters participate. More simply put, if human beings are coequal with "lamb beings" in the depths of Clarice's psyche, then Clarice has already removed a tendency to privilege one over the other (leather handbag and shoes notwithstanding). Clarice's failed childhood foray into animal rights activism has led her to a career path that offers variations on the theme of rescuing mammals from slaughter. For Gumb, the only hierarchical difference between a lambskin coat and a woman-skin suit is that Gumb doesn't covet lambs. For his part, Hannibal feeds equally on animals and humans. More importantly, Hannibal's quid pro quo exchanges with Clarice, which alternate between her childhood memories and narratives about the killer, build an economy that allows Hannibal to trade up to a more delicious psychological meal. Without question, aesthetics is the "in itself" of Hannibal's cannibalism. At heart, Hannibal sees the world in terms of stylistic difference rather than sheer essence. His Stoicism is comparable to what Gilles Deleuze calls "Stoic mannerism," wherein manners of being exceed classical Aristotelian essentialism.[24] Or, as Steven Shaviro's Whiteheadian-inflected reading of speculative realism asserts, "Aesthetics involves feeling an object *for its own sake*, beyond those aspects of it that can be understood or used."[25]

We might say that Hannibal rejects "Buffalo Bill's" utilitarianism as an ontologically misguided mind-set. As he tells Clarice, "Billy is not a real transsexual. But he thinks he is. He's tried to be. He's tried to be a lot of things, I expect." Clarice, too, falls under attack for trying to be something through her clothes. Hannibal, in contrast, prides himself on being inscrutable with or without masks. His prison jumpsuit has done nothing to diminish the status of his being, because his being is attached to the slippery and transcendent notion of taste. After his last session with Clarice, Hannibal enjoys a nice lamb chop, extra rare, to literalize through taste the delicious tale of the screaming lambs. He then immediately interrupts his meal to perform a transformative guise à la Buffalo Bill by killing a guard and then wearing the guard's face over his own to exit the building in plain sight. Neither of those actions means that Hannibal wants to "be" something that he is not. The dramatic skin-mask escape is a stylistic flourish, another bread crumb for Clarice, but not an attempt at identity construction.

Feminist critic Judith Halberstam labels *The Silence of the Lambs* "a postmodern horror movie" and argues that Jonathan Demme's film "no longer assumes a depth/surface model" because horror "resides at the level of skin itself."[26] Her postmodern interpretation cites Demme's references to films by Hitchcock, De Palma, and Wyler as evidence that the film "has cannibalized its genre."[27] One could infer that Demme has made the film that Hannibal might have made. Whether cannibalism—even of the postmodern variety—eschews depth/surface models remains debatable nonetheless. Hannibal's treatment of Clarice suggests his faith in surfaces as a means of indirect and limited access to depths that exceed his full grasp. When Hannibal tells Clarice, "I think it would be quite something to know you in private life," he is acknowledging the limits of his surface understanding. Yet the dialogue concerning Clarice's childhood trauma relies on the psychologist-patient dynamic in which deep truth is ferreted out of a subject by a professional through narrative interpretation. The psychologist-patient model posits that one's own subjectivity is no guarantor of self-understanding. In similar fashion, Hannibal claims for himself, as well as for the medical professionals at any of the three major gender reassignment surgical centers, a better understanding of "Billy" than the would-be transsexual has of himself.

Gender identity has been as problematic to critics of the film as it is for Gumb. Clashes over whether *The Silence of the Lambs* should be scorned for perpetuating homophobia and demonizing transgender identities, praised for its depiction of a strong female lead, or characterized as retrogressive on all accounts have made the film an interpretive minefield.[28] For her part, Halberstam resists "the temptation to submit Demme's film to a feminist analysis" about the dangers of aestheticizing the serial killing of women, and she resists "the temptation to brand the film as homophobic" or to read the film in any way that would "puncture the surface and enter the misogynist and homophobic unconscious of Buffalo Bill, Hannibal the Cannibal and Clarice Starling."[29] Instead, she makes Buffalo Bill into a figure of posthuman gender. In Halberstam's retelling, "Lecter points out that Buffalo Bill hates identity, he is simply at odds with any identity whatsoever; no body, no gender will do and so he has to sit at home with his skins and fashion a completely new one."[30] The argument has its appeal, but the contention that Buffalo Bill has a generalized disdain for "any identity whatsoever" comes from Halberstam, not Hannibal. Billy hates *his* identity, not any identity, and the depths of his own psychopathy have been repressed and sublimated through sewing. In Hannibal's own words, "Billy hates his own identity, you see, and he thinks that makes him a transsexual. But his pathology is a thousand times more savage, and more terrifying." Whether or not we label the entire film a reinforcement of retrogressive gender tropes, this much is clear: the chill we are meant to feel when Hannibal characterizes Billy's pathology in such superlative terms relies on a baseline fear of gender identity disorder (a medical classification that many people view as prejudicial). In essence, the rhetorical move says, "You think *that's* bad? Well, *this* is a thousand times worse." Surface modification cannot solve Gumb's pathology. Sewing will not save him.

By the time Clarice and Hannibal discuss Billy's pathology—roughly the halfway mark in the film—more than enough clues have been provided to piece together Billy's sewing project: Hannibal has asked Clarice to speculate on why the killer removes the skins; he has sent Clarice to the storage locker of "Hester Mofet," where she discovers, in the back seat of a car, a headless mannequin with a decoupage scrapbook to one side and a jar containing a man's head with crudely applied women's makeup to the other; he has discussed the "fledgling killer's pathetic attempt at transformation"; he has explained that the killer has probably been refused gender reassignment surgery; and he has asked if the victims were large, "roomy." In addition, Clarice has participated in an autopsy of a victim from whom two large diamond-shaped patches of skin had been removed. Hannibal tells Clarice that she is so close, but Clarice cannot see the answer. Clarice does not make the connection between the skin removal and the killer's desire for transformation until she visits the sewing room of the killer's first victim and notices two large diamond-shaped paper sewing patterns pinned to a dress. There, in Fredericka's sewing room, it finally hits her. She calls her boss. "He's making himself a woman suit, Mr. Crawford, out of real women!" The camera pulls in to a close-up of the pinned fabric. Clarice stutters with excitement, "And he, and he can sew, this guy. He . . . he's very skilled. He's a tailor, or a dressmaker, or . . ." She can't quite decide on a label.

Gendered assumptions about sewing may have been one of the mental roadblocks to investigators seeking to understand Gumb. A correlation between masculine aggression (let alone serial killing) and sewing is as counterintuitive to Clarice as the thought that the killer might be transgender. In most Western cultures, home sewing had been an art handed down from mother to daughter. The place of mechanized sewing in the home, the factory, or the tailor's workshop, however, was unclear at the time of its birth. "In its infancy," notes historian Judith Coffin, "the sewing machine was polymorphous."[31] But Coffin is quick to add that in advertising, "those polymorphous tendencies were quickly repressed in favor of a more gendered identity."[32] Indeed, British and American nineteenth-century newspapers treat the sewing machine differently depending on whether its surrogacy is intended for the female seamstress or the male tailor. As early as 1834, the *Preston Chronicle* reports that an "ingenious mechanic" (possibly Thimonnier) is making a machine for sewing. The projected use implicates men's clothing and male needle workers: "Should the plan succeed generally, a suit of clothes, after they are cut out, may be put together in one hour by one man, with the exception of working the button-holes, and putting buttons on!"[33] In the mid-1840s, when articles about sewing machines begin to appear with frequency on both sides of the Atlantic, the narrative splits into at least three strands, which bear summarizing before considering their relevance to Gumb's serial stitching.

The first narrative, more common in Europe than in the United States, is that of the machine as mechanical foe to the "knights of the needle."[34] Tailors did not take kindly to the prospect of mechanizing their craft. The *Dundee Courier* announced in 1846 that Elias Howe's newly invented sewing machine had received the nickname "The Devil among the Tailors."[35] Headlines such as "Tailors Superseded by the Sewing Machine" did nothing to allay the fears of craft guilds and unions.[36] In Belfast, assault charges were filed against tailors with enough frequency to merit the somewhat blasé criminal report headline, "The Tailors Again."[37] News of strikes and protests related to sewing appeared regularly in British headlines during the 1850s. A lengthy appraisal of the Belfast manufactures in 1860 explains that sewing machines came late to the linen capital because tailors were jealous of "the iron sartor" and "did not recognize it as a legitimate member of their body."[38] Due to consistent opposition by tailors, the narrative of the male-gendered machine found no traction.

The second narrative, widely diffused in trade literature, newspapers, and magazines during the nineteenth century, is that of the Promethean genius male inventor come to bestow upon womankind a divine technology.[39] The hyperbole and melodrama of these accounts reaches extremes limited only by the imagination. Bad poetry abounds. Panegyric verse gives way to Messianic speech when the machine is personified. By 1874, sewing machines had been around long enough that references to older models could elicit nostalgia for maximum pathos, as seen in the story "Saved by a Sewing Machine," published in the *Boston Investigator*. The tale begins at a church raffle, where a "man-of-war's man," a sailor, wins a sewing machine. That night, the reluctant recipient of the machine rescues Rosa, a young woman of "not more than sixteen summers," from the clutches of the same "destroyer of womanhood" who raped and murdered his only sister. The sailor gives Rosa the machine, thanks to which she earns a savings, clothes herself properly, and marries into high society. Years later, the old-fashioned machine sits in Mrs. Rosa C.'s parlor, covered in purple velvet on a solid silver plate encircled by a wreath of flowers. The story ends, "When the curious ask why she keeps that old-fashioned machine so choice, she answers reverently—'It is my Saviour!'"[40] The narrative of the sewing machine as boon to womankind posed no threat to artisan tailors, since their work was sharply divided from the degraded labor of seamstresses. From the point of view of the factory owner, an "Iron Needle-Woman, born to toil and not to feel" had a drawing power of less altruistic aims than elevating the status of the human needle-woman.[41]

The third narrative also characterizes the machine as inherently feminine. Equally suited to a work-from-home scenario as to the female duties of family sewing, the sewing machine promised to boost domestic productivity with the help of a mechanical servant as dutiful as a French maid and far less likely to disrupt one's marriage.[42] A catalogue for Grover and Baker's Family Sewing Machine describes children "silent with curiosity" and a baby lulled "into a sweet slumber" by the "gentle murmuring sound" of the machine."[43] Decorative elements, rather than functional ones, adapted the machine for the boudoir to address those anxious to counteract its industrial qualities. Wilson's catalogue calls attention to the fact that even its base model is "ornamented with elegant designing in gold leaf, with silver plated Trimmings."[44] The machine argued for a rightful place in the well-appointed bourgeois household alongside the piano: "In America, a sewing machine is far more common than a piano, and immensely more useful."[45] The *Glasgow Herald* claims that in the United Kingdom, "a sewing machine will be as essential an article of household furniture as a piano-forte."[46]

As companies competed for a share of the fast-rising "family machine" market, the gender of the sewing machine came to exclude the masculine subject, the two main exceptions being the foreigner (usually one under colonial rule) and the military man during wartime, forced to use the machine for wont of women. Judith Coffin writes, "By the late nineteenth century, a man at a sewing machine became a kind of anthropological flash card; instantly recognizable as foreign"[47]—not merely foreign but also docile and feminized. Of the various narratives constructed to describe the nature of machine sewing and of the person participating in it, that of the male machine as a replacement for the tailor was the shortest lived. The inventor-genius savior to womankind narrative persists in attenuated form in biographies to this day, and the gender identity of machine sewing remains largely female.

Gumb's sewing machine, like that of Margaret White, is out of step with modern times. His machine sits on an old-fashioned sewing table with a wrought-iron base, probably made by Singer. The machine is an electric industrial model, iron, coated in black Japan, the most prevalent durable surface for industrial and domestic models from the nineteenth century until the introduction of plastic casings. Where a typical machine might have varnished gold leafing and floral cutouts to varying degrees as a decorative flourish, Gumb has customized his plain black machine with decals of pin-up girls—a look more in keeping with the aesthetic of World War II bomber planes or truckers' mud flaps. Pin-up decals on a plain black industrial device suggest a regendering of the machine in the masculine "iron sartor" role that failed to gain acceptance among the social narratives of sewing.

The first shot of Gumb at his machine comes after a traveling shot through his basement workspace: first his gloomy moth and butterfly habitat, then the cold stainless steel dissection table where he skins his victims, with a tray of knives nearby. The space contains nothing remotely homey or feminine. Next, the camera moves uneasily down the dark hallway and into a room with lavishly costumed mannequins. A buzzing sound mixes with music and Catherine's screams off camera. As the camera pulls in and pans left, we see Gumb from behind, nude on the chair facing his sewing table. The workspace is cluttered. To his right, the attentive viewer might notice a piece of skin stretched on a board, partially covered with a diamond paper pattern tacked on top. To his left, an ironing board leans against a wall covered by a large American flag that serves as an inspiration board. As the camera moves closer, the sound of the machine grows louder, and we see more clearly the items pinned to the flag: a pin-up of a girl provocatively posed by a motorcycle, a clock, images of butterflies, drawings of winged figures resembling fairies or superheroes, and some polaroid photos. His space has markers of femininity and masculinity, as if the iconography stereotypically associated with an auto shop had combined with the bedroom pin board of a teenage girl.

Roughly thirty-five minutes later, we see Gumb sewing close-up. The camera moves in from just behind his shoulder to show hands stretching his fabric taut under the needle. An extreme close-up of the violent piercing action reduces the needle to a relentless assault weapon, abstracted from the rest of the machine. Corresponding to the close-up, a heightened sound of rapid, industrial pounding from the mechanism's movement shatters any association between this device and the lulling hum touted in early domestic advertisements. Instead of the familiar presser foot of domestic machines, used to gently hold fabric in place as it feeds under the needle, Gumb's machine uses a textured roller—a sort of metal wheel that holds down difficult or "sticky" fabrics such as vinyl or leather. The needle, the roller foot, and Gumb's hands occupy the full frame, working in complicity to control the peachy-tan fabric whose texture has become all-too-identifiable and horrific. How does one speak of Gumb or his machine, both equally monstrous? Like Clarice, we must leave Gumb midstitch, lost in the seam of an ellipsis. "And he, and he can sew, this guy. He . . . he's very skilled. He's a tailor, or a dressmaker, or . . ."

Sutures and Seams

Lucky McKee's *May* (2002), like *Carrie*, features a misfit whose sewing talents outmatch her social skills. May (Angela Bettis) is a young, single paraveterinary worker with a lazy eye and no social life. Since childhood, her only friend has been Suzie, a doll with the mournful eyes of a Margaret Keane painting. A flashback to a lonely childhood birthday party shows May's mother reluctantly offering her the handcrafted substitute best friend

Fig. 7.3. Craft supplies and surgical supplies are equally at home in May's sewing room. *May* (2002).

with the instruction that the doll is too special to take out of its case. The hand-me-down companion embodies her mother's dictum, "If you can't find a friend, make one." Now in her twenties but still alone, May tells her encased confidante that she craves a genuine human relationship. May fixates on Adam (Jeremy Sisto), a mechanic and horror cinephile with beautiful hands. At work, May entertains the advances of her flirtatious coworker, Polly (Anna Faris), whose neck she finds particularly alluring. Then, there are those people whose admirable qualities are restricted to body parts, such as the sexy legs of Polly's lover, Ambrosia (Nichole Hiltz); the arms (and Frankenstein tattoo) of Blank (James Duval), a friendly punk at the bus stop; and the ears of Adam's new fling, Hoop (Nora Zehetner). Disappointed by her real-world encounters with humans, May decides to literalize her mother's counsel and build herself a best friend from all of the best parts. She lays out surgical tools stolen from the animal hospital alongside her sewing notions, and in a frenzied montage during the final minutes of the film, her hands alternately cut, piece, stitch, and suture until she has created Amy, a patchwork best friend made of flesh, fabric, and a cat fur pelt.

May is part seamstress, part surgeon. Like Buffalo Bill, whose workspace includes both a dissection table and a sewing room, May operates in the ambiguous gender divide between surgery and sewing. At home, she makes all of her own clothing without patterns. At work, she assists in animal surgery. When a distraught man approaches the reception desk with the mangled, severed leg of his pet dog, May responds with a matter-of-fact confidence that she can reattach the limb. Stitching is simply what May does. "I work at the animal hospital, and I sew," she tells Adam, who, in his own way, also works with body repair and crafts. Adam repairs cars at an auto body shop, and at home, he creates morbid collage art inspired by his cinematic hero, Dario Argento. May informs Adam that some people think her work is "kind of gross," to which he responds, "I love gross. Disgust me, please." Adam, in turn, wonders if May will be freaked out by his decor, to which May replies, "Nothing freaks me out." The match looks promising, like the kind of couple Tim Burton might bring together if he managed an online dating service.

After a romantic dinner of mac and cheese, paired with lime Gatorade served in May's best stemware, Adam and May move to the couch for a private screening of his student film, *Jack and Jill*. The black-and-white Romeroesque short, set to the music of Tommy James and the Shondells' "Hanky Panky," starts with a retro couple on a romantic picnic and ends in deliriously sexualized acts of mutual cannibalism. Adam looks at May for a reaction as Jill bites off Jack's finger. May smiles and scoots closer to Adam as the on-screen violence escalates. Jack feasts on Jill's inner thigh. Jill's teeth rip through Jack's chest. May snuggles against Adam. The film ends with the credit "Reggia di Adam Stubbs," and then Adam turns to May. "So . . . what did you think?" May smiles. "It was sweet." Adam pauses. "Sweet?" May adds one point of critique: "I don't think she could have gotten his whole finger in one bite, though. That part was kind of far-fetched."

The *Jack and Jill* film within a film is the work of the editor, Rian Johnson, who has since become a successful writer and director of indie and Hollywood films including *Brick* (2005), *Looper* (2012), and *Star Wars: Episode VIII—The Last Jedi* (2017). Rian Johnson's horror pastiche, stitched into Lucky McKee's updated *Frankenstein*, draws attention to filmmaking as patchwork. At its most basic level, *May* has entered a familiar postmodern "meta" register in which the spectator of *May* is watching two characters on a date as they watch a VHS movie about two characters on a date. After the viewing of the movie, Adam lies on top of May, replicating the eroticism of the picnic. May then doubles the film in her own manner by biting Adam's lip and smearing his blood on her face with his finger. "It was just like your movie," she explains after Adam recoils and puts on his shirt to leave. May's inability to view Adam's film with the proper degree of detachment leads to their separation. This will be their last date.

The spectator of Lucky McKee's film—and Rian Johnson's film within McKee's film—has no difficulty separating Jack and Jill's eroto-cannibalism from Adam and May's date nor any trouble drawing parallels between the two narratives. The editing of the movie-viewing sequence is calibrated to maintain our attachment to May in her world without overinvesting in the connection between May's world and that of Jack and Jill. McKee's success in attaching us to his film hinges, in part, on Johnson's failure to do the same. That is, if we disproportionately notice in *Jack and Jill* the quick edits, the "artsy" shots, the ironic soundtrack, the use of monochrome, the retro setting, the absurdity, the pretentious Italian credits, and so on, there is little chance we will put the two couples on the same plane. Instead, by the time May tells Adam, "It was just like your movie," we will cringe empathetically in anticipation of the moment when her understanding of Adam's film catches up to ours. In so doing, we get caught between two films; we are tied into *May* through its difference from and similarity to *Jack and Jill*. If the McKee-Johnson stitching act is successful, we invest in *May* at the very moment when cinematic artifice is at its most exposed. We may find ourselves saying, as the credits roll, "I don't think she could have fit those legs into that cooler, though. That part was kind of far-fetched."

Although comparisons between film and sewing-machine technology may at first glance seem forced, they are well warranted. The standard stitch of the average sewing machine—the lockstitch—might serve as a metaphor for the *Jack and Jill* viewing sequence. A lockstitch employs two threads, an upper thread that feeds from the main spool and through the needle and a lower thread wound in the smaller bobbin. The needle punctures the fabric vertically and brings the top thread down through the hole and into contact with a hook mechanism, which loops the needle's thread around the bobbin thread. A take-up arm then pulls up on the entwined thread so that the stitch occupies the hole in the middle of the joined fabric. The small metal teeth of "feed dogs" guide the fabric through intermittent advance before the needle plunges once again to create the next stitch. By analogy, we might say that in the pivotal scene where McKee's film (the top thread) and Johnson's film (the bobbin thread) entwine, the edited sequence loops our point of view right into the hole opened between the two films. Our gaze invests in each puncture, or edit, thereby stitching us into the work. The comparison has its limits, but the relation between sewing and cinema is far from arbitrary. Sewing and filmmaking are, in fact, linked historically at a technological level, and theoretically in psychoanalytic discourse of film "suture."

Film scholar Jacques Aumont, who prefers the term *intervention* to *invention* when it comes to the Lumière brothers' place in the history of modern cinema, notes that of all the technical elements that had to come together for modern motion pictures to exist, Louis Lumière's only moment of pure invention was his solution for the intermittent advance of film through the adaptation of a technology commonly used by sewing machines.[48] In a 1935 statement, Auguste Lumière proclaimed his brother to be the sole inventor of the machine, explaining that during a feverish and sleepless night, Louis solved the missing piece of the puzzle by envisaging a tooth-and-claw mechanism that would produce "a movement analogous to that of a sewing machine presser foot."[49] Lumière used perforations at either side of each frame (one pair of round holes per frame as opposed to Edison's four rectangular pairs) whereby prongs or teeth could grab and advance the film. Louis Lumière adapted for his Cinématographe the same kind of eccentric system that drives the feed of a sewing machine.[50] In a sewing machine, one eccentric (i.e., off-center ring on a drive shaft) moves the teeth of the feed dogs, which pull the fabric along, while another moves the needle up and down, synchronized so the advance of the fabric pauses for each needle puncture and then moves on to complete each stitch. Similarly, Lumière used an eccentric to move a framework with two prongs to engage the film. Like fabric running through a sewing machine, the film stopped just long enough to be pierced, not with a needle but with light for exposure (a pause of approximately 1/48 second) and later for projection (sixteen frames per second).[51] Cinema, therefore, has a deep kinship with sewing at its origins.

At a theoretical level, the operations of sewing and film intertwine with editing and spectatorship in the divergent and much-contended strands of "suture theory." Inspired initially by the work of Jacques Lacan, suture theory proposes a psycholinguistic model for the relationship between the viewer and the language of cinema. Kaja Silverman's synthesis of suture theory finds the following common thread: "Theoreticians of cinematic suture agree that films are articulated and the viewing subject spoken by means of interlocking shots."[52] That is, in the language of cinema, meaning emerges from the relationship between shots, not uniquely from the content of those shots. Of all the syntactic structures in the grammar of film, the shot/reverse shot is the most beloved among suture theorists because it lends itself to a narrative of subject identification (similar to Lacan's mirror stage) in which the viewing subject experiences both pleasure and lack, which feed a desire to repair a perceived absence by inscribing the self into the very cinematic discourse that brought about the psychic wound. Accordingly, the move from shot (one character's speaking position) to reverse shot (their interlocutor's position) upsets the viewer by revealing the arbitrary nature of the frame. Silverman explains that in the classic suture theory of Jean-Pierre Oudart, the shot/reverse shot "alerts the spectator to that other field whose absence is experienced as unpleasurable while at the same time linking it to the gaze of a fictional character."[53] Thus, the cut (between shots) is a wound, an absence inflicted by an "other" (i.e., the filmmaker, or more accurately, the medium of film), which the viewing subject repairs after each new cut by retreating into a position of identification with the fictional character subject. Cutting permits stitching. Like two threads, the viewing subject outside the film and the viewing subject inside the film interlock with each cut.

Applied to the *Jack and Jill* patchwork sequence in *May*, suture theory demands an interpretation beyond the simple labeling of the scene as an instance of postmodern self-referentiality. A suture-inspired reading of the scene requires a careful consideration of the seams, the patterns of shots into which we are stitched. The *Jack and Jill* viewing scene opens with Adam and May on the couch facing the television in a medium shot that is not quite head-on but slightly angled to privilege May. Adam begins the scene with the words "You ready?" as he points the remote, and May, referencing classic cinema projection, replies, "Roll 'em." McKee has sandwiched the scene between the dinner and the make-out session gone awry. The cuts between Adam and May on the couch and Jack and Jill on the television function as a sequence of shot/reverse shots between the two couples, between the two films, and even between the couch and the television. I distinguish the shots as TV POV (the point of view that shows Adam and May on the couch from roughly the place of May's television set) and Couch POV (the point of view, also slightly askew, that shows the *Jack and Jill* video on the TV screen in the darkened room). In the complete sequence, ten TV POV shots alternate with nine Couch POV shots to form what I have described earlier as a "lockstitch" between the two films.

The *Jack and Jill* viewing puts us on the couch with May and Adam to watch the film (Couch POV) but rips us away from that shared couch space each time the shot cuts to a view of May and Adam (but not us!) on the couch reacting to the film (TV POV). For us, the continuity of the *Jack and Jill* film is maintained only at the level of the "Hanky Panky" soundtrack. Our own visual lack is thus signaled through audio continuity. Visually, our Couch POV is interrupted nine times by the TV POV that allows us to observe the reactions of May and Adam. If May and Adam were sitting on the couch having a conversation, then the shot that includes both of them would be the master shot that provides the context for a shot/reverse shot sequence of their conversation. Instead, the screening of *Jack and Jill* moves the conversation visually between two movie couples (from our perspective) or between a real couple and a fictional couple (from the perspective of Adam and May). According to the psychology of suture theory, the sudden cut from the Couch POV to the TV POV inflicts a wound that generates cinematic meaning. In sewing, the violence-and-reparation process is comparable to cutting and then stitching fabric in order to turn a few yards of cloth into a pair of pants or a shirt—something we might slip into, identify with, and wear as an extension of ourselves. The editor offers one viewpoint and then deprives the viewer of it in order to give the reverse point of view, thereby creating the conditions of cinematic language, stitched together under the complicit gaze of the viewer. Fabric piece one: Jill bites off Jack's finger. Fabric piece two: May smiles lovingly at Adam. The viewer finds meaning, according to the logic of suture, by investing in the space of absence provided by the cut. The narrative thread thus moves through the holes, and the viewer is entwined in the lockstitch movement by getting wrapped up in the fabric(s) of the story.

Each of the nine Couch POV shots takes the viewer into a series of quick edits in *Jack and Jill*, the majority of which are shot/reverse shots between the two characters. The first Couch POV shot includes its own sequence of eight shots in eleven seconds. After a cut to TV POV of Adam and May smiling, the film cuts back to Couch POV for five more shots of *Jack and Jill*, then back to TV POV to see Adam and May, then back again to Couch POV for nine more shots, and so on. In less than two minutes, the cuts in *Jack and Jill* alone (i.e., the Couch POV) total sixty-six shots, making the film as violent in form as it is in content, if one accepts Oudart's Lacanian reading of a shot/reverse shot as the infliction of a psychic wound. Of course, whether the rapid-fire edits of *Jack and Jill* magnify the wound-and-stitch effect or diminish (or even deny) it depends on one's assumptions about the length of time required to psychically invest in a point of view. In other words, is there a temporal/spatial threshold for suture? The Lumière brothers' Cinématographe deployed sixteen frames per second as an acceptable rate for creating the illusion of motion to the human eye. Similarly, we might ask the suture theorist whether there is a minimum number of frames that must pass for a psychic stitch to occur.

More often than not, a shot/reverse shot involves two characters, as in a dialogue where the POV alternates between two speaking subjects. Psychoanalytic models, which are inherently anthropocentric, favor a human-to-human shot/reverse shot. In the rare cases where suture theorists acknowledge POV emanating from objects, the shots ostensibly represent a denial of suture, such as the shot/reverse shot between Marion in *Psycho* (1960) and her showerhead, which Kaja Silverman refers to as "obtrusive and disorienting."[54] Silverman points to the showerhead shot as a rare example of a director deftly exposing the lethality of the cinematic machine by denying the comfort of suture. According to that logic, suture can occur only between sentient, presumably human, subjects. In the *Jack and Jill* sequence, I have opted for the terms *Couch POV* and *TV POV* to suggest that shots can be as much about stitching the viewer into the (discursive) positions of televisions and couches as they are about connecting the viewer psychologically to characters, perhaps even more so for a film such as *May*, whose limited theatrical release but strong presence in home video rental chains (and later iTunes and Netflix) all but guarantees an at-home viewing on the couch in front of the television.

In theory, a series of 180-degree countershots, such as those where we look directly into Jill's eyes as Jack, and vice versa, creates the conditions of suture between the viewer and the characters. We identify with Jack as we stare into Jill's eyes and then with Jill as we fix a psychopathically amorous gaze on Jack. In McKee's film, however, the darkness of the surrounding room emphasizes the 4:3 aspect ratio of May's television cabinet, and the slightly skewed angle of viewing corresponds roughly to Adam's side of the couch. McKee's framing ensures that we remember that we are watching Adam's film on a TV screen. Far from seamless, the setup neither denies suture nor hides the stitches.

May's climactic construction of Amy, an amalgamation of flesh, fabric, and fur, embodies a literal synthesis of human and nonhuman material that extends suture beyond classic notions of human consciousness. In a montage that intercuts stitching and suturing, the sewing room becomes the production studio where May's editorial skills reach their apotheosis.

Adam's hands, Polly's neck, Ambrosia's legs, Hoop's ears, Blank's arms, her pet cat's fur, and an ample supply of fabric and sewing notions make an anagrammatic companion whose seams are as obvious as those of Frankenstein's monster but whose materials reposition horror beyond soulless reanimated flesh. Amy, May's monstrous DIY BFF, is a posthuman and postgender monstrosity, but not the kind of self-as-other creature commonly associated with the body horror of, say, Cronenberg's *The Fly* (1986) or Tsukamoto's *Tetsuo: The Iron Man* (1989). Instead, we might more accurately describe *May* as *sewing horror* or *suture horror*, due to the film's preoccupation with the nature and limits of stitching.

One of May's final steps in creating Amy is the sewing of the fabric head onto the neck of human flesh. As May stitches the head onto the neck, she merges her two sewing-based identities (the surgeon and the seamstress) and negates any formal distinction between a suture and a stitch. Her project disturbs us almost as much for its lack of human flesh as it does for its inclusion of human body parts. The faceless, machine-sewn burgundy fabric makes a feeble simulacrum, at best, of the human head. It resembles no one. The muscled arms fastened to a patchwork fabric torso amplify the uncanny experience one might feel when undressing a doll with porcelain limbs and witnessing for the first time the abrupt and disquieting discontinuity of its stuffed-cloth body. The sight of stitched material of such dissimilar natures turns sewing into a form of betrayal—the kind of disruption to internal verisimilitude scorned by Aristotle as a design flaw, an obstacle to the suspension of disbelief. Had the writer of *Poetics* been addressing toy manufacturers instead of poets, he would no doubt have advocated for unity of material as the most efficacious route to immersive play. Reanimated flesh, however monstrous, requires less imaginative investment than a patchwork of flesh and upholstery fabric. May's project is therefore arguably more difficult than that of Dr. Frankenstein, for May demands the kind of thoroughgoing materialism that allows life to suffuse fabric as well as flesh.

Horror at its most fundamental level is what philosopher Emmanuel Levinas calls "the menace of pure and simple presence."[55] We fear the pure presence of matter. The thought that objects watch us, the suspicion that objects have lives and wills of their own, the alien presence of things—that fear of matter is enough to paralyze the child who wakes up and sees the unfamiliar shapes of toys in the dark. Who can see the impassive gaze of doll eyes in a dimly lit room and not shudder? As a horror trope, doll eyes typically tap into the fear of inanimate presence, the dread of being watched by something not quite human. In *May*, the inanimate eye conveys the equally distressing, and more tragic fear of not being seen. "See me!" May cries out as she looks into the blank eyes of her creation. "See me!" she yells, but Amy remains lifeless and unseeing. The scene has an unexpected poignancy as we witness May's horror at her failure to create an object that will look back. That's the problem with dolls—and films. They don't look back.

But what if they could? How can vision be stitched into the thing? For May, whose inability to fit in has always been tied to her vision problems (we have seen her move from eye patch to glasses to contacts as her social prospects improve), the trial-and-error process leads to a retreat from the three-dimensional world. She seeks Amy's gaze as a substitute for her failed human connections. May puts her glasses over the doll eyes, as if to correct Amy's vision, but nothing happens. Then, in a last-ditch, almost Oedipal attempt at clarity, May runs to her vanity, grips a pair of scissors, and gouges out her right eye for Amy. May places her sacrificed eye on the left eye of her creation, facing it like a mirror. "See me!" She lies next to Amy and sobs. "See me." The eye tumbles to the side toward one of the hands that formerly belonged to Adam. The hand reaches up and strokes May's face tenderly. Her gift has been reciprocated. May's willingness to invest her vision in the thing that cannot look back at her is rewarded by the caress of the filmmaker's hand. This is suture: the investment of vision that brings the dismembered, stitched-up creation to life. An eye for an eye.

May's eye gouging functions as suture's counterpart to Luis Buñuel's straightedge razor to the eye in *Un chien andalou* (1929). The surrealist's film asserts the power of montage over vision through the razor-wielding hand of another, whereas May punctures her own vision in order to bring sight to the inanimate stitched body. Buñuel's film resists the repose of symbolism and metaphor, but as film scholar James Lastra has observed, "*Un chien andalou* is structured around the formal permutation of a few central objects."[56] Chief among those objects are the eye and the hand. "Starting with the eye, and moving through a series of graphic matches and chains of substitutions, we find ourselves back at the image of the hand," notes Lastra.[57] Likewise, *May* starts with the eye and ends with the hand. *May* begins with the young girl socially outcast because of her eye patch and ends with the grown girl sacrificing her good eye for the stroke of a reanimated hand—a hand May has both severed and stitched. Cutting works in tandem with assembling, as May well knows, but the final operation that brings reciprocity (or its illusion) to the assemblage is suture. Film does not exist without the stitch.

Notes

1. See Coffin, *The Politics of Women's Work*, 47–48.
2. See Lubar, 22.
3. Willcox and Gibbs, 11.
4. Ibid.
5. Singer Sewing Machine Company, 43.
6. Ibid., 74.
7. Ibid., 43.
8. Ibid., 44.
9. Ibid., 44. The 1881 set had twelve cards, the 1882 set had twenty-four, and the 1883 set had thirty-six. Thirty more countries were added during the early twentieth century. See Domosh, 465n5.
10. "Algeria" trade card in Singer Manufacturing Company, *Singer International Trade Cards* (set of 32), 1892. The "costume series" images and accompanying narratives also ran as advertisements for several years in popular magazines.
11. One of several variations of the crucifix with flowers the White used in its trade cards.
12. Alexandra Churchill, "The Mystery of the Tomato Pincushion Has Been Solved," *Martha Stewart Living*, September 3, 2014, http://www.marthastewart.com/1082584/mystery-tomato-pincushion.
13. The connection was particularly strong in the case of the tomatillo, with its splitting husk that reveals a "venereal and lascivious" inner fruit. See Gentilcore, 10.
14. See Coffin, "Credit, Consumption, and Images of Women's Desires," 774–75.
15. Ibid., 777.
16. King, *Carrie*, 98.
17. Keesey, 102.
18. Ibid., 103.
19. Vaz da Silva, 242.
20. Ibid., 243.
21. Ibid., 245.
22. Ibid.
23. On the historical negotiations of women's clothing in the workplace, see Steele. On broad shoulders in women's wear, see Kidwell.
24. See Deleuze, 60–61.
25. Shaviro, 53.
26. Halberstam, 38.
27. Ibid.
28. A good example can be seen in the clash between gay and feminist critics in the *Village Voice*. See Phillips. On monstrosity, see Tharp. For an interpretation of the film as "deeply retrograde," see Young.
29. Halberstam, 40–41.
30. Ibid., 39.
31. Coffin, "Credit, Consumption, and Images of Women's Desires," 758.
32. Ibid.
33. "Sewing Machine," *Preston Chronicle* (Preston, England), May 31, 1834.
34. "The Tailors Again—Charge of Conspiracy and Assault," *Belfast News-Letter* (Belfast, Ireland), April 8, 1853. The *Manchester Times* refers to tailors as "knights of the

thimble." "The Lancashire Sewing Machine," *Manchester Times* (Manchester, England), June 11, 1853.

35. "The Devil among the Tailors," *Dundee Courier* (Dundee, Scotland), July 21, 1846.

36. "Tailors Superseded by the Sewing Machine," *Huddersfield Chronicle and West Yorkshire Advertiser* (West Yorkshire, England), February 24, 1855, 3.

37. "The Tailors Again."

38. "Belfast Manufactures," *Belfast News-Letter* (Belfast, Ireland), September 13, 1860.

39. See Fernandez, 158.

40. Susan H. Wixon, "An Original Story: Saved by a Sewing Machine," *Boston Investigator*, April 29, 1874, col. A, 3.

41. George P. Morris, "Song of the Sewing Machine," *Boston Investigator*, June 3, 1858, col. A, n.p.

42. Fernandez, 162.

43. Grover and Baker Sewing Machine Company, 3.

44. Wilson Sewing Machine Company, 1.

45. "Sewing Machines," *Sheffield and Rotherham Independent Supplement* (Sheffield, England), June 9, 1860, 6.

46. "The British Sewing Machine," *Glasgow Herald* (Glasgow, Scotland), September 6, 1859, n.p.

47. Coffin, "Credit, Consumption, and Images of Women's Desires," 759.

48. Aumont, 417.

49. August Lumière, quoted in Sadoul, 11 (translation mine).

50. Sadoul notes that the circular eccentric of the February 13, 1895, patent was soon replaced by a "Hornblower eccentric," also commonly used in sewing machines. See Sadoul, 14.

51. Borgé and Borgé, 57. As a cautionary note, it is worth mentioning that many otherwise useful sources, such as this one, attribute the illusion of movement to the debunked "persistence of vision" theory of Plateau. The following description of the device with the triangular version of the eccentric is given by Louis Lumière in 1936:

> The device consisted of a sliding block driven with a reciprocating vertical motion by means of a triangular eccentric, which stopped the motion of the block completely at the top and at the bottom of its travel during one-sixth of the total time. When the block was stationary, the tines or claws of a kind of fork located at the side sank into the perforations of the film, under the control of a helical cam. These pins described a rectangular path and carried the film along during their downward motion and left it motionless during their withdrawal, their upward course, and their sinking in. A pressure member, acting upon the film as a light brake, was sufficient to hold the film in perfect alignment with the gate behind which the image appeared, thus absorbing any play in the apparatus. (Lumière, 49)

52. Silverman, 201.
53. Ibid., 204.
54. Ibid., 211.
55. Quoted in Trigg, *The Thing*, 50.
56. Lastra, 29.
57. Ibid., 29–31.

8

HOUSEPLANT

Invasion of *The Secret Life of Plants*

Lava gushes and swirls in an infernal pool of magma below an apocalyptic red sky. Under the howl of wind and the crash of thunder, three deep, synthesized notes form a taunting loop: a diminished fifth (nicknamed the "devil's interval") that resolves momentarily to a perfect fifth only to return to the bombastic root note and repeat again the cyclic struggle between dissonance and harmony. Clouds loom overhead and then float below like waves, disorienting the viewer's perspective, pushing the eye to cling to land when it appears. The overture reaches a fever pitch as the jagged, barren surfaces of a desolate planet now dominate the frame. Then blue. An enormous wave rolls and crashes from the right to the left side of the screen. A second wave responds, roaring from left to right, as if the ocean were arguing with itself. A dissolve transports us to a deep blue expanse in which floats a mysterious semitransparent sphere dotted with glowing yellow specks. Other spheres of its kind join the scene, then dozens more. The darkness teems with floating specks of life. All the while, the march of the synthesized score indicates the unfolding of something epic and sublime, otherworldly and terrifying, a mise-en-scène befitting the awakening of Godzilla from the briny depths. Then, more calmly, bioluminescent jellyfish propel themselves through the blue. Below the crashing waves, lush green seaweed mimics the grace of the jellyfish. The overture subsides, and now, seven minutes into the film, an authoritative male voice narrates: "Birth and rebirth in endless rounds of procreation. In shock from the trauma of awakening, the planet is bleak, arid, uninhabitable. But a new arrival will transform the scene." That new arrival is a plant.

The Secret Life of Plants (1978), the film adaptation of the eponymous 1973 runaway best seller by Peter Tompkins and Christopher Bird, is as much a horror film as it is a documentary. Consider the film's tagline: "An incredible world of beauty and terror with a haunting music score by Stevie Wonder." Or consider its scenes of torture: a CIA interrogator hooks electrodes to his subject, who must witness the grim fate of creatures as they "fall to their deaths in boiling water." A Soviet scientist slices a head with a butcher's knife for no reason other than to watch her captive "feel the mutilation of its comrade." Never mind the fact that the chopped head is a head of cabbage (as is its "comrade") or that the CIA interrogator is recording the reaction of a philodendron to the death of brine shrimp—according to the central premise that plants are rational beings with rich emotional lives and a profound capacity for empathy, the film is nothing less than vegecidal snuff.

I propose that *The Secret Life of Plants* be read as a companion piece to the 1978 version of *Invasion of the Body Snatchers*. The two films reconceptualize what it means to be a plant and what it means to coexist with plants. Both films use time-lapse imagery to question human and plant notions of temporality in ways that elevate the status of plants and privilege their graceful beauty. Both films evoke pity and paranoia in equal parts, imagining the human race as plant caretakers but also as potential victims of their uncanny sentience, their intuition, and their construction of the ecosphere both inside and outside the home. Plants are simultaneously victims and builders of their environments. Thanks to the preoccupation with acid rain during the 1970s, plants become key figures in political and cultural interventions, while in the home, the humble houseplant influences architecture, decor, and human behavior. *The Secret Life of Plants* and *Invasion of the Body Snatchers* make the perfect double feature to grasp the elevation of plant being and sentience even amid the fading of 1960s flower power.

Violence is the empathy-generating machine of the documentary *The Secret Life of Plants* and the preferred experimental arena of its science. Through their humanlike reaction to violence, plants demonstrate their capacity to feel, and thanks to their spectacular suffering, we humans consume a leafy green variety of fear that will be good for us and for the planet. A scene in which a Soviet man follows orders to destroy a live cabbage with his bare hands in front of another live cabbage resonates not only with the fellow plant witness but also with the human viewer. The anthropomorphic form of the potted cabbage heightens the drama as the Soviet executioner brutally breaks the necklike stalk and rips chunks of leaves from the cabbage head. In an American experiment reminiscent of the psychological

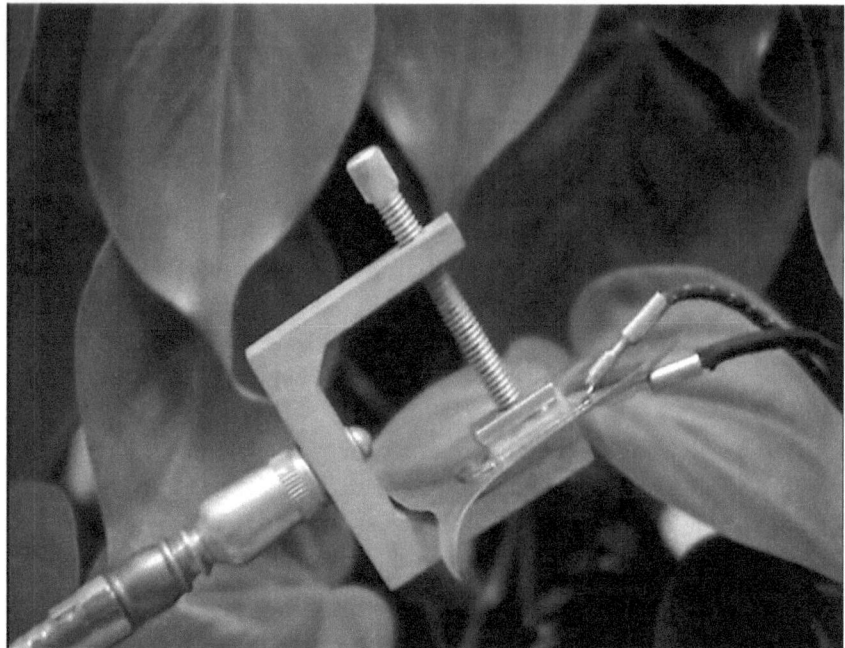

Fig. 8.1. Plant interrogation by Cleve Backster in *The Secret Life of Plants* (1978).

conditioning in *A Clockwork Orange* (1971), a parapsychology expert measures the galvanic response of a man and a plant to a stream of disjunctive images—trees, shrubs, flowers, children riding bikes, a showering woman lathering her bare breasts, a nuclear explosion, and so on—ostensibly proving the plant's telepathic connection to the man's reactions of arousal and distress. In the former experiment, the scene of cabbage torture gives the human viewer of *The Secret Life of Plants* a chance to empathize with imminent danger to plants, and in the latter *Clockwork Orange*-style experiment, the plant gets a chance to demonstrate that it too can ride the emotional roller coaster of a movie in sync with its human counterparts. And if a dose of Cold War anxiety can serve to establish an interspecies bond, so much the better.

Beauty, eroticism, and terror intermingle in *The Secret Life of Plants*, as they often do in horror films. The cinematographic manipulation of time and space entice the human gaze to process the spectacle of nature according to familiar sociosexual roles. Thanks to time-lapse imagery, the upward motions of sprouting seeds and erect flower stems burst into bloom and spring to life as objects of potent phallic elongation. On the heels of the time-warped vitality, the film returns to human time, allowing the camera to zoom slowly into the passive petals of orchids and deep into the undulating curves of their blossoms. For the first time in the film, a female narrator interjects a sentence: "Since the dawn of human creation, we have looked to plants to nourish us with their flesh, shelter us with their fiber, and enrich our world with their beauty." A male narrator continues, "Plants, yielding themselves to man, share in his spiritual flowering." Plants invite sex by design. Certain orchids, we are told, grow "into an exact replica of the female bee" in order to lure the male bee into an act of pollination. Plants are alluring and deceptive, even deadly. A return to time-lapse imagery gives a close-up view of a fly in the grips of a verdant *vagina dentata*—the Venus flytrap—one of more than five hundred varieties of "flesh eaters," according to the film.

The documentary fosters a sense of awe in which vegetal alterity exceeds and precedes human life. Plants yield themselves to us, but we also depend on them. The very air we breathe is "given to us by plants," says the speaker at a garden party of the Plant Communication Society. "We are the absurd appendages of an ongoing nature and nothing more. The plants alone prepared the earth for all life." The garden club members—wealthy, predominantly white, clad in light-colored linen—sublimate the colonial impulse as they collect houseplants from across the globe ("a pepper plant direct from Venezuela, a candlestick plant direct from the West Indies, a Jacob's ladder from Malaysia, and from China, a strawberry begonia!") and listen with rapt attention as their Hindu guest invites them to participate in the following thought experiment: "Imagine receiving from plants, locked in their own dimension of time and space, a view of our own chaotic world." A cut to a time-lapse blooming flower dissolves to time-lapse imagery of mechanized human activity, as if to suggest a temporal shift to plant point of view. Thus, even as the speaker asserts that plants are locked in their own dimension, the film overcomes those temporal restrictions with a result that demonstrates the graceful vitality of plants and the stuttering dysfunction of mechanized humanity.

As media scholars Allan Cameron and Richard Misek have observed, slow motion usually poeticizes the human figure, whereas time-lapse denies it "physical presence and narrative gravity."[1] For the plant body, time-lapse performs the same rhetorical gesture that slow motion accomplishes for the human. The condensation of hours or days in the life of a flower into mere seconds of cinematic time has inspired wonder in moviegoers ever since F. Percy Smith's *The Birth of a Flower* set the tone for the time-lapse bloom in 1910. Thanks to popular science films in that tradition, we have come to expect from time-lapse blossoming sequences a certain balletic grace that belies the rapidity of the technique's temporal elisions: a pace we might associate with slow motion were the subject an animal or a human. Like slow motion, time-lapse celebrates the temporal elasticity of the still frame forced to submit to a projection speed to which the capture does not conform. Slow motion represents a surplus of frames in relation to the playback speed, whereas time-lapse refuses to capture the number of frames per second (whether it be sixteen, twenty-four, thirty, forty-eight, or some other standard) required for the playback's measure of "real" time. Through a strategic rate of capture, time-lapse makes the imperceptible movements of plants legible with the same romanticized visual rhetoric that would have us believe that two lovers running toward each other across a meadow must do so in slow motion.

Oliver Gaycken's work on early time-lapse science films shows how accelerated plant movement "provided evidence for an argument for a kinship previously posited but never before apprehended."[2] Charles Darwin's dot-to-dot tracings of plant circumnutating movements published in 1880 in *The Power of Movement in Plants* had attempted to demonstrate that kinship, but German plant physiologist Wilhelm Pfeffer's sensational time-lapse documentation of eleven days of bean plant growth in 1898 produced an affective response far more impactful than static scribbling.[3] The cinematic decomposition of movement unlocks the very psychology of plants, according to Germaine Dulac: "We feel, visually, the painful effort a stalk expends in coming out of the ground and blooming."[4] Time-lapse satisfies what Cameron and Misek refer to as "the demands of anthropocentric time."[5] The time-lapse blossom elevates the status of plants without disrupting human chronocentrism. *The Secret Life of Plants*, like the garden party speaker, takes for granted a reciprocal fascination between humanity and the silent plant-other, whose concern with human affairs is intense, flattering, and disconcerting. For if plants can think, what do they think of us? If plants can talk, what are they saying about us? "Spread across the land, what message do they send from this to other worlds?" The film dares not answer.

The Secret Life of Plants portrays an earth entwined with greenery that feels what we feel and registers our emotions more deeply and accurately than do our fellow humans. In contrast, we humans have little or no idea what plants feel. We may talk to our houseplants, but we have forgotten how to listen to them. Exceptions to the rule are non-Westerners celebrated by the film such as the Dogon tribe in Africa, the renowned polymath Jagadish Chandra Bose (described strategically as an "obscure Indian scientist"), and a chosen few Westerners operating outside of mainstream science. George Washington Carver, another figure scorned "for his communion with the fairyland of plants," receives, along with Bose, special acknowledgment in the form of Stevie Wonder's "Same Old Story"—a hagiographic pop ballad that combines religious fervor with disappointed resignation. Wonder throws his hands in the air at those who will not accept the truth.

The wildest claims are thus conscripted into the familiar narrative pattern of a prophet on a daunting mission to convert the unbeliever. Faith must step in where science falters, preferably a faith that supports the ethos of communion with the vegetal kingdom, such as Hinduism. Hence, like a voice from the dust, an old recording of Bose leads to the film's conclusion: "I understood for the first time that ancient message proclaimed by my ancestors on the banks of the Ganges thirty centuries ago: They who see but one in all the teeming manifoldness of the universe, unto them alone belongs eternal truth, unto no one else." Finally, a film that began with swirling lava and a sinister overture ends with Wonder singing in paradisiacal settings about the "inevitable being" and secret life of plants. The message is clear: Inevitability trumps doubt. Resistance is futile. *The Secret Life of Plants* has no place for unbelievers. Time-lapse is on our side. Welcome to the world of beauty and terror; wipe your Birkenstocks on the coir doormat on the way in. On second thought, don't. The plants are watching.

Pseudoscience notwithstanding, the argument for brain-like behavior in plants has a legitimate pedigree and a thriving posterity. Charles Darwin demonstrated electrical signals in carnivorous plants such as sundews (*Drosera*), the Venus flytrap (*Dionaea muscipula*), and the butterwort (*Pinguicula vulgaris*) in *Insectivorous Plants* in 1875. Then in 1880, Darwin's *The Power of Movement in Plants* overshadowed his earlier work with its demonstration of chemical signals in plants, according to plant physiologist Eric Davies.[6] "For some reason," explains Davies, the chemical evidence "was so compelling that others soon forgot about plant electrical activity and focused on chemical signals."[7] Animals, in contrast, had been shown to have electrical activity as early as 1791 but had not been known to use chemical signals until the early 1900s. Consequently, for more than a century, discussion tended toward a neat but erroneous distinction between plants and animals based on their characteristic signaling mechanisms: electrical signals for animals and chemical signals for plants. That division underwent revisions with the discovery of chemical signals in animals. More than ever, animals possessed "a more 'lively' status" than plants.[8] Meanwhile, electrical signals in the vegetal world remained, for the most part, either unacknowledged or ignored due to a lack of interest.[9] Among the exceptions, plant physiologist Barbara Pickard produced compelling evidence of electrical signals in noninsectivorous plants in 1973. Had Pickard's published review gained better traction, perhaps plant science would have reclaimed for the vegetal world a level of signaling vitality accorded only to animals. Pickard's timing, however, could not have been more ill-fated. That same year, Tompkins and Bird's book, *The Secret Life of Plants*, captured the public imagination with wild claims built on pseudoscience. For a scientist, *The Secret Life of Plants* made the worst possible ally.

So despised was *The Secret Life of Plants* among the scientific community that two years after its publication, the annual conference for the American Association for the Advancement of Science (AAAS) hosted special sessions to denounce the work. Cleve Backster, whose research was featured prominently in the book, was invited to the conference to serve as a punching bag in this revenge-of-the-nerds spectacle. A report on the conference by the American Institute of Biological Sciences makes no effort to hide the bemused disdain that typified professional reception of Backster's experiments. "First came 'The Secret Life of Plants.' Perhaps we can now expect 'The Secret Life of Yogurt,'" begins the report, referencing Backster's new foray into "inter-yogurt communication."[10] Nonetheless, Backster stood firm in his claim to have measured, via electrodes, the emotional reactions of plants as witnesses to the killing of brine shrimp, and he remained steadfast in that claim despite the fact that no scientist had been able to reproduce his results. In attendance were respected scientists Edgar L. Gasteiger (of Cornell University) and John M. Kmetz (of the Science Unlimited Research Foundation), each of whom had attempted to replicate the Backster plant experiment; the latter consulted with Backster himself in the setup. Backster objected that Kmetz had not followed his instructions to the letter. "Fortunately," observes the report, "Kmetz and Backster were seated at opposite ends of the table."[11]

Four years after the scientific smackdown and six months after the release of the film adaptation of *The Secret Life of Plants*, Arthur Galston copublished an article with the aspirational title "The Not-So-Secret Life of Plants: In Which the Historical and Experimental Myths about Emotional Communication between Animal and Vegetable Are Put to Rest." The article begins with an indictment of 1960s anti-intellectualism and antiscientism and accuses Tompkins and Bird of exploiting the general malaise "about pollution, overpopulation, unemployment, growing crime" and war.[12] Supported by uncontrolled experiments and anecdotal observations, the book asserts that plants communicate with each other, respond to trauma experienced by other beings, transmit and receive signals from other life forms in the distant universe, transmute elements, exhibit musical taste, and predict the weather. By promoting the outlandish findings of one-man laboratories, Tompkins and Bird had fueled public distrust toward professional scientists.

The critique of the Tompkins-Bird narrative focuses on two of its heroes: Indian scientist J. C. Bose and would-be scientist Cleve Backster, who by this point had enjoyed fame in print, film, and television. In the case of Bose, who died in 1937, the issue was the book's mischaracterization of Bose as an obscure Indian outcast and misinterpretation of his findings on the functional similarities between plant and animal tissues.[13] The real target of the article is "polygraph expert" Cleve Backster.[14] Backster makes a good poster boy for *The Secret Life of Plants* because he is a true believer with a dramatic born-again story. A former counterintelligence specialist in the United States Army and later a CIA polygraph expert, Backster makes an unlikely plant apologist. Founder of a lie-detection training facility for FBI and police interrogators, Backster better fits the role of villainous plant torturer than that of new-age eco-apologist. And indeed his story begins with plant interrogation and torture. The events strain credulity: Alone in his Manhattan office, at 7:00 a.m., on February 2, 1966, Backster decides to hook galvanic skin response (GSR) sensors to his *Dracaena* plant. He attaches the sensors with some rubber bands, waters the plant, and tests his hypothesis that the plant's electrical resistance will decrease as it draws in moisture. Chart readings fail to support his hypothesis, but he notices a reaction during the first minute of recording that resembles that of fear in a human subject. Backster explains the motives behind his next move: "So I thought, 'well, if this plant wants to show me some people-like reactions, I've got to use some people-like rules on it and see if I can get this to happen again.'"[15] Backster turns to the familiar territory of provoking fear. Will a plant react to threats? Probably not verbal threats, he assumes, but what about bodily harm? "I wasn't into talking to plants, not at that time. So as a substitute threat, I immersed the end of a leaf, that was neighboring the electroded leaf, into a cup of hot coffee."[16] But nothing happens. On the contrary, the stoic houseplant's readout indicates boredom. Undeterred, Backster decides to get a match and burn the very same leaf hooked up to the electrode. Suddenly, just as the image of burning the leaf passes through Backster's mind, the polygraph needle jumps to the top of the chart. "Gee," thinks Backster, "it's as though this plant read my mind!"[17] At that moment, his whole consciousness changes.

That same year, Backster pays membership dues to the AAAS, but his research finds ears only in the *International Journal of Parapsychology* and in the popular press.[18] In 1968, the journal publishes his methods, which clash with mainstream scientific practice. "Mother Nature doesn't appear to jump through a hoop ten times in a row merely because someone wants her to," says Backster to his critics.[19] He espouses instead a process best described as intuitive and free-associative. When plants at his lie-detection school exhibit reactions for no apparent reason, Backster intuits that that plants are responding empathically to the lethal effects of flush-activated disinfectant on cells in urine in the men's room several floors above his office.[20] Like a puppy, Backster's plant gets excited whenever he returns to the lab. A plant in New York City reacts to a surprise party in New Jersey due to its bond with an employee at the school.[21] Plants in Lebanon worry about the escalation of tension in the Middle East.[22] Two months after the fact, Backster claims to find proof that plants feared for the lives of microscopic bacteria in the office sink when boiling water was poured down the drain.

The problem with Galston's desire to "put to rest" the myth of secret plant powers is Backster's popular appeal as a medium of sorts—one of a select few attuned to the terror and beauty of the vegetable realm. Davies's 2004 article on electrical signaling in plants asserts that Tompkins and Bird "extinguished any prestige on the topic of electrical signals," making it "essentially untouchable in the eyes and minds of funding agencies."[23] Plant scientists, "wittingly or unwittingly, practiced a form of self-censorship in thought, discussion, and research that inhibited asking relevant questions of possible homologies between neurobiology and phytobiology," according to advocates of plant neurobiology as an emerging field of research.[24] Biologist and author Daniel Chamovitz says the work "stymied important research on plant behavior." His popular book *What a Plant Knows* warns the general reader, "My book is not *The Secret Life of Plants*; if you're looking for an argument that plants are just like us, you won't find it here."[25] What you will find, however, is a willingness to anthropomorphize plant intelligence in terms similar to the Tompkins-Bird narrative. You will find in *What a Plant Knows* plants that see you, that know what color shirt you are wearing, that know if you have repainted your house, that use your sense of smell to their own benefit, that communicate or eavesdrop, and that feel your touch but do not like it. Chamovitz may not be thrilled at seeing *The Secret Life of Plants* appear under the "Customers Who Bought This Item Also Bought" results on Amazon, but the algorithmic compatibility of the two books highlights a certain kind of narrative buy-in by the public, enabled by a shift in rhetoric among scientists.

The emergence of plant neuroscience suggests a newfound willingness to adopt or reclaim anthropomorphic language in the service of legitimate science. "I am not claiming that plants have eyes or noses (or a brain that colors all sensory input with emotion)," writes Chamovitz. "But I believe this terminology will help challenge us to think in new ways about sight, smell, what a plant is, and ultimately what we are."[26] In other words, Chamovitz is willing to make plants a little more human in order to make humans reconsider their own sense of exceptionalism. Chamovitz (and the very notion of plant neuroscience) embraces an approach favored by many speculative realists: the employment of "a certain cautious anthropomorphism" in order to avoid anthropocentrism.[27] Although a hotly contested term, especially due to the Backster legacy, the adoption of the word *neuroscience* by plant physiologists is not about claiming that plants have brains but rather about asserting that thinking or intelligence does not require one.

Greenhouse Effect

We return to 1978 for another movie opening: December 20. Just one week after the release of *The Secret Life of Plants*, a sci-fi horror film makes the perfect companion piece to the documentary about the terror and beauty of plants. *The Invasion of the Body Snatchers* (1978) opens with a sequence eerily similar to the documentary: a desolate planet, a dissonant score, barren volcanic rock, a blue expanse in which jellyfish-like creatures drift and scintillate with bioluminescent sparks. In place of ocean tides, the translucent blobs ride currents of solar winds toward a world they will radically transform. The tranquil floating scene transitions to a vertiginous zooming effect that recalls the famous Charles and Ray Eames short, *Powers of Ten* (1977), in which the viewer is catapulted at exponential speed into far reaches of the universe and then back down to earth, to Chicago, to a lakeside picnic, and into the cells of a sleeping man. In our alien migration scene, the camera plunges from outer space toward the city of San Francisco, where the invaders land on unsuspecting plants during a rain shower. Not long thereafter, the aliens mutate into the form that will prey on sleeping humans. Globs of the alien substance coat the branches of trees, trickle along the soil, and take parasitic hold of leaves. At unnerving speed, tendrils emerge from the matter and form pods on the leaves of their green hosts. From each pod, a pink flower bursts into bloom at time-lapse speed. Were we to swap audio tracks, the opening narration of *The Secret Life of Plants* would make a near-perfect graft for the sci-fi horror film: "Birth and rebirth in endless rounds of procreation. In shock from the trauma of awakening, the planet is bleak, arid, uninhabitable. But a new arrival will transform the scene." Once again, the terrors and temptations of vegetal being take center stage.

Don Siegel's 1956 *Invasion of the Body Snatchers*, based on the Jack Finney novella, has received more critical attention than Philip Kaufman's 1978 reimagining. Most commonly, readings of the 1956 version address the themes of Cold War anxiety and McCarthyist paranoia.[28] More broadly, the story of alien seedpods that replace sleeping humans with emotionless doubles entertains paranoid fantasies tied to politics, consumerism, gender, immigration, and the concept of the human. As film scholar Barry Keith Grant remarks, the enduring popularity of the film "derives in large part from a central metaphor for the monstrous that, like the vampire or the zombie, is sufficiently flexible to accommodate multiple interpretations, with a style and structure that is admirably economical even as it is highly expressive."[29] Don Siegel's 1956 version takes place over the course of three days in the small town of Santa Mira, California, where town doctor, Miles Bennell (Kevin McCarthy), discovers that complaints by fellow townsfolk that people are changing overnight are indeed well founded. Bennell and his love interest, Becky Driscoll (Dana Wynter), resist the pod people takeover and head for the hills after discovering in the nick of time their own doubles freshly emerged from pods in the greenhouse. Amid the chaos, emotionally unavailable Miles rekindles his love for divorcée Becky, alas, too late. Having lost Becky to the pod people, Miles runs like a madman through the traffic yelling, "They're here already! You're next! You're next! You're next!" and ends up in a psychiatric hospital where he must convince the authorities of the alien takeover.

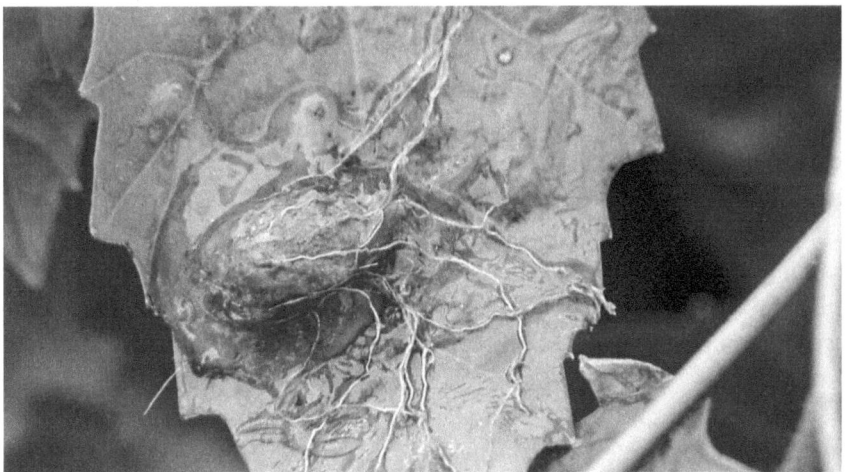

Fig. 8.2. Alien invaders perform a rhizomatic takeover of plant life in *Invasion of the Body Snatchers* (1978).

In Kaufman's film, San Francisco supplants the small-town setting of the original, and all of the main characters are health-care professionals of one kind or another. Matthew Bennell (Donald Sutherland) and Elizabeth Driscoll (Brooke Adams) work for the Department of Public Health (on Grove Street, naturally). Elizabeth's boyfriend, Geoffrey Howell, is a dentist (and the first to go, after Elizabeth puts a flowering pod on his bedside table). Dr. David Kibner (Leonard Nimoy) is a psychiatrist and best-selling pop psychology author. And Jack and Nancy Bellicec (Jeff Goldblum and Veronica Cartwright) are co-owners of a bathhouse spa. Together, Matthew, Elizabeth, Jack, and Nancy piece together the truth about the alien takeover and go on the run. Nancy seems to have read all the right books to intuit the hybridist displacement of humanity, and despite (or perhaps because of) her excessive emotionality, the touchy-feely supporting character becomes the last human standing.

In the memorable final scene, Nancy encounters her fellow resistant, Matthew, as he walks along a path lined with barren trees toward San Francisco's immense city hall. The camera follows Matthew from behind as he moves toward the looming government building. The low-angle tracking shot emphasizes the gnarled, empty branches of the trees that flank the walk. "Somehow, the only organic matter that seems to be really surviving are the pods," notes Kaufman.[30] Matthew pauses, turns, and looks down the path toward the patch of grass where Nancy stands and calls his name. She smiles and moves toward him, only to find her show of enthusiasm answered by a pointing finger, a gaping jaw, and a terrifying, otherworldly howl. As Nancy responds with her all-too-human screams of horror, the camera zooms into the pitch-black void of Matthew's open mouth.

Matthew's role frames the film with acts of surveillance. We first encounter him ferreting out a rat dropping from a pot of calf brain simmering in red wine at a French restaurant. As Matthew holds the suspect pellet in tweezers for closer inspection, the unscrupulous French restaurateur attempts to convince him that the object is a caper—a plant. Matthew knows better. "It's a rat turd," he says. In a similar vein, the final scene sets Matthew at the foot of city hall sounding the alarm at a human who had attempted to elude detection by masquerading as a pod person. Again, Matthew demonstrates expert consistency in his awareness of the treachery of images. His eye for difference adapts to whatever institutional structure or species he serves.

In Matthew's defense, literature professors Natania Meeker and Antónia Szabari argue that the health inspector's participation in the culture of management and surveillance is mitigated by his stir-fry home cooking and the "Chinese banner in his office," both of which qualify as "acts evoking ethnic and cultural multiplicity in theory particularly characteristic of San Francisco."[31] Indeed, Matthew knows his way around a wok, but the banner in his office deserves a second look, first because it is written in Japanese, not Chinese, but more importantly because its message—"Friends of the Earth"—is a proclamation equally suited to alien invasions and environmental activism. In fact, Friends of the Earth (whose antithetical acronym, FoE, aptly describes the arc of Matthew's character) is the name of an international environmental network founded in 1969 in response to an offshore oil spill in Santa Barbara, California.[32] FoE's mission statement could just as well be Matthew's before his replacement: "Friends of the Earth defends the environment and champions a healthy and just world."[33]

The friend-as-foe conundrum resides at the heart of the film and reveals the ambivalence of human-plant entanglement. Meeker and Szabari's comparison between the 1956 and 1978 versions of *Body Snatchers* brings well-deserved attention to the way in which the two films "make use of the figure of the plant to invoke a form of being that is both emotionless and productive, both shapeless and full of lively forms, both ancient and well suited to navigating the crises that modernity appears to carry in its wake."[34] Although portrayed as emotionless, the pod invasion engenders the "unearthly erotic appeal" of "vegetal agency that works better, longer, and harder" than human desire.[35] The very qualities that have traditionally relegated plants to an inferior status—their appearance of immobility, their slippery morphology, their lack of organs, their growth cycles—give plants an "ontological richness" that endows them with a "mystical excess" perfectly suited to invasion narratives.[36] Accordingly, the pod takeover injects humans with a "biological vitality" that reinvigorates an already-waning human affect and breaks down the barrier between vegetal being and human being.[37]

From an ontological point of view, the interplay between human and vegetal vitality presents a compelling framework for understanding the stakes of *Invasion of the Body Snatchers*. Nevertheless, in attempting to unravel the consequences of human-plant entanglement (especially as portrayed in the 1978 version), we must not elide the film's first victims: the plants. Like Nancy, who in the final scene assumes all too quickly and to her own detriment that the Matthew she sees is still the human she once knew, scholars often too hastily assume that they are encountering plants, when in fact, the pods are no more plants than the pod people are humans. We would do better to take a cue from Matthew's keen eye and not mistake a rat turd for a caper. Consider the opening sequence: The wispy spermatozoic strands that hover over the barren planet, detach into gelatinous blobs, and make their way to San Francisco are spores of an alien nature—seeds in a panspermic sense, but nothing that belongs in the same category as the trees and shrubs around Alamo Square Park. Rather than jump directly to the matter of alien spores as harbingers of vegetal ontology, we must first study the impact of the invasion on the local plants.

The amorphous alien matter arrives during a rainstorm. The arrival sequence features vegetation struck by the compromised raindrops and weighed down by the clear slime. A zoom aided by shallow depth of field isolates one of the many plant victims: a sickly stalk that drips with thick matter, its leaves brown and shriveled. A close-up reveals spent petals overcome by the gel. Meanwhile, the stop-and-start mechanical screech of a garbage truck and the noise of city traffic join with discordant synthesized tones to suggest anything but a pastoral ideal. A rain-blurred zoom angled toward the sky focuses on bare branches and the skeletal framework that once supported blossoms. As the downpour continues, streams of water and alien matter trickle along the dark soil. Another low-angle shot of withering branches reminds the viewer that the threat is coming from above. The drip-drop of rain one might normally associate with a soothing nature soundscape now becomes too loud for comfort, its tones a percussive reinforcement of Denny Zeitlin's disquieting score. There is another shot of the unnatural stream on bare earth; then the scene returns to a coated branch drooping with wilting flowers. The hum of traffic increases in volume, and in the blur behind the branch, we discern cars moving. If plants could speak, they would cry out, "They're already here. You're next!"

By 1978, images of threatening rain were well engraved in the public consciousness. Reports of acid rain in Norway caught American media attention in the beginning of the decade, and by 1974, tales of deadly rain creeping toward the eastern United States were making headlines. In June of that year, a front-page story in the *New York Times* reported an increase in the acidity of rainfall up to one thousand times the normal level: "In occasional extreme cases, rains have been found to be just as acidic as pure lemon juice."[38] Antipollution devices in smokestacks, whose filters targeted only visible particles, succeeded in giving the appearance of cleaner air but had done nothing to prevent sulfur dioxide and nitrogen oxides from entering the atmosphere. Experiments in which equivalent amounts of acid were sprayed onto trees recorded decreased growth, distorted shapes, dead spots, and decreased germination among the observable effects of exposure. In 1975, for the first time, major American scientific conferences had been devoted to the problem of acid rain. Evidence of damage to trees and plants had aggravated fears that "acidification of the soils may cause changes to the types of vegetation growing in affected areas" or, worse, that "acid runoff" from the soil could transport toxins to drinking-water reservoirs.[39]

Among the challenges brought to the fore by acid rain, the intrusion of the foreign into the domestic proved conceptually and politically treacherous. People seemed to be realizing for the first time that climate change is no respecter of national borders. The slippery boundaries of the "environment" put regulatory bodies in a state of crisis. In response, the Organization for Economic Co-operation and Development (OECD), an international group of countries founded in 1961 as an outgrowth of postwar efforts at economic reconstruction, formed an environmental committee in 1970, thereby creating "the first major international effort to curb air pollution."[40] Norway took charge of a fact-finding project to address the suspicion that sulfur emissions from the Ruhr industrial region in Germany and the English Midlands were the being carried across the sea by wind currents and "dumped on Norway in the rainfall."[41] An invisible, wind-borne foreign threat arriving in the rain—this was a new kind of postwar scare ripe for cinematic treatment.

By 1977, a year before the release of *Invasion of the Body Snatchers*, imperiled species of trout and salamander in the Adirondack Mountains had made acid rain a domestic concern in the United States.[42] Not surprising, then, is the environmental bent of the report on the Paris OECD meeting in June: "In environmental matters especially, the thoughtlessness of one may be the pollution of all. If a nation exports a radioactive cloud, contributes to other people's 'acid rain,' communicates a communicable disease, or transports poisonous chemicals or lethal organisms across national frontiers, a case for international action is arguable."[43] Globalization anxiety aligns increasingly with the brand of eco-horror in which a threat from the skies menaces the human race. The eco-invasion narrative affects the boundaries of domestic space at every level, from home ecosystems, where macramé hanging gardens complement lounge chairs and lava lamps, to planetary systems explored in the 1970s by the unmanned spacecraft of NASA's Viking Project. And if national borders fail to circumscribe or protect ecosystems, it stands to reason that planetary borders are no less at risk.

"We still talk of 'the' world, as if there were no others, just as we talk about 'the' Sun and 'the' Moon," writes astronomer and science popularizer Carl Sagan in 1977, "but there are many others."[44] Sagan invites his readers to marvel at "the wild and eerie landscape of our nearest planetary neighbor, Venus, where the clouds precipitate an acid rain that falls continuously."[45] Torrential acid rain falls on Venus, our neighbor, the Norway of our solar system.[46] "You're next! You're next!" It's just a matter of time—four and a half eons, give or take, according to a paper on the atmospheres of Earth and Mars in which Sagan and his coauthor predict a "runaway greenhouse effect" beyond human control. "Earth will resemble contemporary Venus," foretells the article.[47] A horrifying picture, but the prognostication is not entirely grim for those not averse to space travel. At the same time that our planet lapses into runaway greenhouse eco-horror, "the global temperature of Mars will become similar to that of present-day Earth."[48] The paper concludes with a wry word of advice for our planet's posthuman posterity: "If there are any organisms left on our planet in that remote epoch, they may wish to take advantage of this coincidence."[49]

In contrast to the 1956 *Invasion of the Body Snatchers*, which depicts neither outer space nor the first steps of the invasion, the opening sequence

Fig. 8.3. A pod person luxuriates in mud and reads Velikovsky.

of Kaufman's film traces the journey of foreign matter from a ravaged planet to our own and, amid an invasive downpour, follows the mutations forced on the neighborhood plants around Alamo Square Park. After the rainy shots of the sinister matter dripping on dead leaves, covering wilting flowers, or running along soaked soil, a postrainfall series of close-ups reveals globs of the alien gel taking a tentacular grip on leaves. For the first time, plantlike characteristics emerge from the substance. Something akin to tendrils or creeping rootstalks enacts a rhizomatic takeover of the surroundings. The roots grip their host-leaf and then form small green pods that bloom at the tip with a single pink flower. At the end of the gel-to-pod sequence, a medium shot of a shrub pans across to a human hand that picks one of the flowering pods from its host. The flower makes a perfect Trojan horse for aliens because plants have already invaded our homes. Elizabeth Driscoll instinctively moves her hand to her nose, reminding us that blossoms seduce the senses with their scent as well as their beauty. Flowering pod in hand, Elizabeth heads home to a domestic ecosystem already replete with greenery.

Elizabeth and Geoffrey live at 720 Steiner Street, in one of the Victorian-style "painted ladies" that make up "Postcard Row." Their home is nothing if not accommodating to houseplants. Plants occupy space in every room: they hang at eye level and sit in pots on shelves, on side tables, on kitchen counters, on the floor, and in an indoor greenhouse that adjoins a bedroom suite. The ample bay windows festooned with hanging ferns (the sine qua non of Victorian houseplants) recall the degree to which homes in the nineteenth century had adapted to serve the needs of their verdant occupants. By the 1890s, when the houses on Steiner Street were under construction, the display of plants in the home had become a moral imperative, an antidote to the ethical impoverishment of life away from the inherent virtues of the countryside. Early modern households had used plants for cooking, medicine, and other practical purposes such as pest and odor control, but the potted ornamental plant did not thrive as a common household object until much later, achieving unparalleled impact on the home environment during the nineteenth century.[50]

By the beginning of the seventeenth century, gardening books began to include sections on indoor gardening.[51] By the early eighteenth century, plants were available in Britain in nurseries.[52] At the century's end, as many as ten thousand new plant species had made their way into Britain.[53] The popularization of forced bulbs during the nineteenth century echoed the legendary, if exaggerated, seventeenth-century fascination with exotic flowers known as tulipomania.[54] Now indoors with their bulbs rather than as cut flowers, the hyacinth, the narcissus, the lily, the tulip, and other imported flowers took an honored place on the mantelpiece where they flanked the parlor clock or enjoyed prominence next to family portraits.[55] A taste for the exotic continued to bolster the floral industry. The orchid craze during the first half of the nineteenth century led to the plundering of rain forests in an attempt to bring ever more rare specimens into the home. The Hackney Botanic Nursery, the first commercial cultivator of orchids, put eighty-four species on the market in 1825 and by 1839 had increased its offerings to more than sixteen hundred species.[56] Potted flowers and cultivars spread from the mantel to other parts of the front parlor and then to the back parlor and deeper into the house, though less frequently to the bedroom, where what we might now call an "urban legend" held that plants posed a potentially mortal threat to sleeping humans—a warning our *Body Snatchers* victims would have done well to heed. A story published in *Gentlemen's Magazine* in 1764 claimed that a young German woman had died from carbonic acid emitted from the pot of violets on her bedside table.[57] Superstitions about the dangers of sleeping next to plants persisted well into the nineteenth century despite expert attempts to debunk the myth.

For the most part, North Americans followed British trends in houseplants and gardening, usually with a delay of a decade or more. Gentleman landscape designer and architect Andrew Jackson Downing relentlessly promoted the incorporation of pastoral values into rural and urban homes in America. Downing partnered with New York architect Alexander Jackson Davis, who introduced the bay window as part of the Gothic Revival style.[58] The bay window breaks up the boxlike architecture of the house, giving the front wall a plant-friendly protuberance perfectly suited to ever-growing collections of flowers and foliage. The elaborate display of plants from across the globe was turning homes into ark-like ecosystems for alien species, many of them engineered in nurseries. Wardian cases (the precursor to the terrarium) allowed finicky ferns to thrive in their own microclimates. In Britain, the fern and palm craze of the 1860s and 1870s saw citizens tearing up their own countryside in an attempt to recreate the forest indoors. In America, pteridomania led to one of the earliest plant-protection laws for fear of losing the *Lygodium palmatum*, or climbing fern, to the ravages of interior decorators and florists.[59]

By the end of the Victorian era, ornate installations of houseplants began to fall out of favor. Modernists of the interwar period preferred the architectural qualities of cacti and other succulents. Flower arranging superseded indoor plants until the 1950s, when Scandinavian style began to revive the interest in living interior greenery.[60] The 1960s and 1970s saw houseplants come full circle, replicating the Victorian taste for ferns, exotic plants, and junglelike glass-enclosed groupings. A newfound willingness to cohabit with and care for needy plants made Victorian homes such as those on Steiner Street the ideal domestic ecosystem. Like the 1870s, the 1970s was a high point for the houseplant.

The *Body Snatchers* films reflect the dominant trends of their time. The 1956 original includes cut flowers; windowsill kitchen gardens; plants as office, restaurant, and home decor; and a large greenhouse. The original film may have as many houseplants as the 1978 version, but with a crucial difference in their role. Other than the mention of a failed vegetable stand, Siegel's original shows no particular negative impact on domestic plants, whereas Kaufman's version opens with the impact of the invaders on plant life and shows houseplants not merely as decorative objects but also as beings with which humans interact. Abel Ferrara's *Body Snatchers* (1993), in contrast, takes place on a military base where the closest thing to a houseplant is one simple flower arrangement at the general's house. Other than a swampy gestational pod pond, the world of Ferrara's film is one of concrete and metal. Even more allergic to greenery is Joel Silver's *The*

Invasion (2007), which removes plants and pods entirely from the equation, focusing instead on a flu-like pandemic. Apart from the orchid in psychologist Carol Bennell's (Nicole Kidman) office, not a single houseplant appears in any character's home until after the threat has been contained. In the final scene, potted plants and a cheery kitchen herb garden now grace Carol Bennell's picture-perfect home.

Kaufman's 1978 film takes place during a period of houseplant enthusiasm unmatched since the Victorian era. Once again, horticulture, botany, and home decor found common interest. Garden clubs thrived. How-to books and magazines flooded the market.[61] So when Elizabeth comes home from the park and exclaims, "Look at this flower!" to her boyfriend, Geoffrey, who vegetates in front of a televised basketball game, the fact that her fascination is both aesthetic and taxonomic is not unusual. "You know, I think I've actually found something rare," she tells Geoffrey. "This plant. I think it's a grex." The conversation is framed by the open door of the bedroom/garden room suite, with the two humans mostly off camera and the greenhouse plants center frame. A grex, explains Elizabeth, is "when two different species cross-pollinate and produce a third, completely unique one." Jostled by Elizabeth during her search for a vase for the flowering pod, two hanging plants swing and rotate with agitation, as if quivering in fear. Elizabeth continues to read aloud as Geoffrey enters the frame in a green bathrobe that blends with the hues of the plants behind him. "Many of the species are dangerous weeds and should be avoided."[62]

Indeed, the plants have reason to fear, for they too are victims of the invasion. Imagery suggesting their impending demise not only bookends the film but also is present obliquely: a brown, dried stalk on a side table, a leaf from a hanging plant tracked as it falls in an empty bedroom while a phone rings in alarm, and significantly, the gray-brown husks of the pods themselves, piled in garbage trucks throughout the film in a manner that resonates as a disturbingly genocidal gesture. The pods are not, of course, conventional plants but rather the manifestation of the initial pairing. They represent the first level of "grex" cross-pollination and ultimately the instrumentalization of the vegetal in favor of the humanoid. Discarded en masse, the once-green vehicles of gestation highlight the supremely flattering anthropocentrism of the alien takeover. Ben Burtt's sound design for the "pod people" birthing scene, appropriately, includes samples of ripping, stomping, and popping of fruits and vegetables mixed with audio recorded during his pregnant wife's sonogram[63]—the sounds of embryonic human life mixed with plant death. Not unlike the Soviet scientists of *The Secret Life of Plants*, who rip heads of cabbage to prove the profound sentience of their victims, *Invasion of the Body Snatchers* promotes through visual and aural violence the thesis that plants can be both subjects and objects of horror.

The last survivor of the human protagonists, Nancy Bellicec, may as well be an emissary from *The Secret Life of Plants*. The bathhouse she runs with her husband blasts classical music, not for the clients who luxuriate in tubs of mud but for the plants. "It's wonderful for my plants," she tells a disgruntled client. "They just love it. Plants have feelings, you know, just like people. It's fascinating. This type of music stimulates the growth of the plants. They've done tons of experiments on it." Clearly, Nancy has read Tompkins and Bird. She has read other scientifically dubious popular works as well, such as Immanuel Velikovsky's *Worlds in Collision* and Olaf Stapledon's influential 1937 science fiction novel, *Star Maker*. A client who had previously given Nancy a plant (the alien grex) recommends Velikovsky as "must reading." Nancy replies that she has read the book several times already, and in turn, she suggests *Star Maker* (which includes a chapter on alien plant-animal hybrids) as another must-read.

Velikovsky shares with Backster the dubious honor of having received special attention from the American Association for the Advancement of Science. In 1974, a year before their public lambasting of Backster, the AAAS invited Velikovsky to San Francisco for the sole purpose of arguing that his theories did not merit their attention. Worse than a heretic, Velikovsky was, in the words of Isaac Asimov, an "exoheretic," that is, one of "those who arise from outside the professional world of science and who are immune to direct punishment by the orthodoxy."[64] Historian Michael D. Gordin has described Velikovsky as "ground zero" in the pseudoscience wars.[65] Velikovsky's *Worlds in Collision*, first published in 1950, claims that a series of catastrophic events recorded in sources as varied as the Old Testament, Greek and Roman mythology, and the Hindu Vedas supports a view of the cosmos that challenges the scientific orthodoxy. According to Velikovsky, the orbit of planets once intersected, leading to universe-altering collisions from which comets emerged. Venus, he claims, originated from a comet, which, having been expelled from Jupiter and having lost its tail in a run-in with Mars, transformed into the celestial body as we know it.[66]

Velikovsky uses scriptural accounts of catastrophic events to corroborate his cosmology. He argues that manna—the heavenly carbohydrate that sustained the Israelite exodus—was flammable liquid hydrocarbon from the tail of a comet. "The descent of sticky fluid which came earthward" is common to the traditions of both hemispheres, says Velikovsky.[67] Carl Sagan, who helped organize the AAAS panel against Velikovsky, chides in response, "No manna at all has been detected in comets."[68] Furthermore, notes Sagan, the hydrogen cyanide and methyl cyanide found in comets do not make for good eating.[69] Scientific disputes notwithstanding, Nancy Bellicec and her pod-person client are fans of Velikovsky. To a pod person, Velikovsky's claim that sticky fluid from heaven fed the Israelites or the notion that comet-riding critters caused the plagues of Exodus (flies, crop-destroying parasites, and possibly cosmic frogs) does not seem the least bit far-fetched. For the pods, the catastrophe narrative is autobiographical.

"We came here from a dying world. We drift through the universe from planet to planet, pushed on by the solar winds. We adapt. We survive. The function of life is survival," explain the replacements for Jack Bellicec and Dr. David Kibner as they corner Matthew and Elizabeth in the health department office. Theirs is a world "without fear, anxiety, and other emotions." As Kibner approaches with a syringe, he adds, "There's no need for hate now. Or love." These are adaptive beings that use plant life and then human life in their takeover of Earth, but they are neither plant nor human. In the era of *The Secret Life of Plants*, the vegetal world, in contrast, exhibits profound empathy and emotional responsiveness, even to its own detriment. A fern that loves classical music, a ficus that enjoys compliments, a philodendron that shudders each time the toilet is flushed—these are not the invaders of worlds; they are our domestic partners.

What, then, are the invaders if not plants, and what does the "grex" invasion say about human and plant beings? The central characters consider possible answers to those questions earlier in the film as they contemplate one of the pod flowers. Elizabeth warns, "It could be toxic." She explains that she has seen them growing on plants like parasites. Nancy proposes that the invaders are coming from outer space. "What are you talking about, a 'space flower'?" asks Jack. Nancy retorts, "Well, *why not* a space flower? Why do we always expect metal ships?" There are "other ways they can get into our system," she argues. "I mean, we eat junk, and we breathe junk!" Elizabeth picks up on the idea, albeit in a manner more in keeping with her position at the city health department. "Look, I don't know where they're coming from, but I know I feel as though I've been poisoned today." Encouraged by Elizabeth's support, Nancy continues, "Yeah, they could start getting into our systems and screwing up our genes, like DNA, recombining us, changing us."

Fear of toxins plays an integral role in the professions of all four main characters—Matthew and Elizabeth at the health office, Jack and Nancy at the spa. In turning their attention to the pod as a plant parasite that has taken hold of public and household green spaces, and in seeing themselves as equally susceptible to that invasive threat, Nancy and Elizabeth demonstrate the interspecies binding power of shared toxins. Vegetal and animal distinctions quickly lose relevance when both are threatened by a powerful atmospheric breach. Like acid rain, which transcends national boundaries and alters biological and institutional structures alike, the "space flower" points to vulnerabilities in the taxonomic gaps and other artificial boundaries where the invader thrives. The invasion puts the human and the vegetal on common ground but without a feel-good Stevie Wonder soundtrack or interpretive dance by a human dressed as an orchid. Instead, the communion with the vegetal in the face of catastrophe results in a hybrid citizenry emptied of its flower power.

Elizabeth's response to the group's discussion of the grex is to take the flowering pod to work for testing. There she encounters bewilderment and resistance from her colleague, Allen. "I can't understand why you've become so emotional about a little flower," he says. He continues, "We're not supposed to test flowers. They go to the Department of Agriculture." Elizabeth's frustration highlights disciplinary and institutional failures to address ecosystems as a whole. "I know where they go!" she objects. "I think it is affecting people!" Elizabeth's need to understand the invasion puts her in line with Tompkins and Bird's argument that institutional systems "divided and sub-divided into specialized cubby-holes" are not equipped to deal with the natural world.[70] Her insistence on the jurisdictional relevance of her office in an agricultural matter echoes the international regulatory impulse behind the OECD Environmental Committee. In the case of the OECD, the argument for broadening the scope of global regulation relies on a rapprochement between plants and humans as victims in the face of a shared crisis. Yet the constructed subject of institutionalized environmentalism is the pod person, not the flower child. The fight to protect the earth leads to a politicization of the natural world through the proliferation of regulatory bodies. Thus, the dire environmentalism of *Invasion of the Body Snatchers* turns friends of the earth into its foes. The main characters of the film are already sharing their respective domestic and business spaces with enough plants to fill a greenhouse. They are already living in harmony with many of the tenants of *The Secret Life of Plants*. What flourishes amid the invasion is not a greater love of the environment but rather a desperate attempt to save it by appeal to systems capable only of generating affectless pod citizens. The transcendence plants once offered or represented to the flower children of the 1960s erodes in this dystopian horror film of the 1970s like leaves in acid rain.

Strikingly similar in their opening sequences, *The Secret Life of Plants* and *The Invasion of the Body Snatchers* likewise share final shots worth comparing. The first ends in a manner congruent with its tagline about "beauty and terror." On the heels of the final quote by Bose about the "teeming manifoldness of the universe," one seed appears in an extreme close-up that zooms out to suggest a majestic presence hovering in space like the monolith from Kubrick's *2001: A Space Odyssey* (1968). Next, a fade-in to a misty volcanic landscape moves to a crane shot that reveals Stevie Wonder singing the film's titular theme song. A series of dissolves and crane shots shows Wonder alone in sublime settings where greenery sways with his music, waterfalls dwarf his presence, and trees tower above him. He sings about plant leaves as antennas that communicate beyond our galaxy. Finally, Wonder walks through a field of sunflowers as high as his chest. A crane shot tilts upward and zooms out to reveal an endless expanse of the homogeneous flowers, with not another human in sight. The music and imagery accompanying the end credits complete the eclipse of humanity. Syreeta's voice wistfully expresses her desire to come back as a flower in a future life, and time-lapse photography by Ken Middleham isolates rapid plant growth against a black void.

Like Stevie Wonder, Nancy stands alone at the end of *Invasion of the Body Snatchers*, though not in a field of flowers. She is the anachronistic holdout of humanity in a city overrun by pod hybrids. Of all the characters, Nancy is the most emotionally in tune with her plants, the most likely to imagine coming back as a flower as a good thing. But unlike Syreeta's romanticized floral reincarnation, which reflects a desire "to spread the sweetness of love," the threat to Nancy's human form comes at the cost of emotional and spiritual bonds. Both films negate the human through interspecies entanglement even while imagining humanity as an object of fixation for plants and aliens alike. Both films display anxiety about the potential loss of emotional connection between organisms. In both films, flower children are an endangered species. The solitary romantic figure in nature—Stevie Wonder as lone believer in a field of sunflowers (emphasized by a crane shot)—reinforces the "Same Old Story" of failed idealism. Although the beauty of the sunflowers contrasts sharply with the barren trees at the end of *Invasion of the Body Snatchers*, the horror of being swallowed up (a zoom into the black void of Matthew's howl) by a dehumanized bureaucrat in front of city hall puts Nancy in the same lone-believer position as Stevie Wonder in *The Secret Life of Plants*. Sole human in an endless field of flowers or sole survivor in a city of pod people, propagandistic documentary or sci-fi horror dystopia—it's the same story of beauty and terror told two ways.

Notes

1. Cameron and Misek, 39.
2. Gaycken, "The Secret Life of Plants," 55. See also Gaycken, *Devices of Curiosity*.
3. For an overview of Darwin's plant studies, see Whippo and Hangarter.
4. Quoted in Lavery, 5.
5. Cameron and Misek, 39.
6. E. Davies, 607.
7. Ibid.
8. Ibid.
9. Bose, featured in *The Secret Life of Plants*, is one of the more notable exceptions.
10. C. Russell, 217.
11. Ibid., 218.
12. Galston and Slayman, 337.
13. Ibid., 338.
14. Ibid., 337.
15. Backster, 23.
16. Ibid., 24.
17. Ibid., 25.
18. Backster's first popular press coverage was in *National Wildlife* in March 1968. He was featured again in a follow-up article in the February/March 1969 issue. Magazines such as *Reader's Digest*, the *Saturday Evening Post*, and *McCall's* published articles on Backster, as did newspapers such as the *Wall Street Journal* and the *Christian Science Monitor*. Backster made an entertaining guest on radio and television, including the *Tonight Show* with Johnny Carson.
19. Backster, 49.
20. Ibid., 35.
21. Ibid., 32.
22. Ibid., 27.
23. E. Davies, 607.
24. Brenner et al., 414–15.
25. Chamovitz, 5.

26. Ibid.
27. Shaviro, 61.
28. For a representative example of the McCarthyist reading, see Biskind. For a critique of the Cold War reading, see Sanders. An overview of the Cold War reading can be found in Grant, 63–76.
29. Grant, 8–9.
30. Philip Kaufman, DVD director's commentary, *Invasion of the Body Snatchers*, MGM, 2007.
31. Meeker and Szabari, 45.
32. The oil spill also inspired the creation of the first Earth Day on April 22, 1970.
33. "What We Stand For," Friends of the Earth website, accessed March 9, 2016, http://www.foe.org/about-us/what-we-stand-for. Page no longer available.
34. Meeker and Szabari, 33.
35. Ibid., 43.
36. Ibid., 34.
37. Ibid., 49.
38. Boyce Rensberger, "Acid in Rain Found Up Sharply in East; Smoke Curb Cited," *New York Times*, June 13, 1974, 1, 9.
39. Boyce Rensberger, "Acid Rain and Snow Regarded by Scientists as a Potential Hazard in Eastern U.S.," *New York Times*, May 23, 1975, 76.
40. Clyde H. Farnsworth, "Norse Seek Curb on Acid Rainfall," *New York Times*, November 26, 1970, 65–66.
41. Ibid., 65.
42. Harold Faber, "Deadly Rain Imperils 2 Adirondacks Species," *New York Times*, March 28, 1977, 62.
43. Harlan Cleveland, "In International Affairs, One Thing Leads to Another," *New York Times*, June 11, 1977, 15.
44. Carl Sagan, "The Next Great Leap into Space," *New York Times Magazine*, July 10, 1977, 13.
45. Ibid.
46. "Venus is very much like hell," writes Sagan in a popular anthology that features scientific and literary treatments of the planet. Sagan, "Life in the Universe," 147.
47. Sagan and Mullen, 55.
48. Ibid.
49. Ibid.
50. Horwood, 13.
51. Ibid., 7.
52. Ibid., 45.
53. Ibid., 57.
54. On historical myths surrounding the bulb trade, see Goldgar.
55. T. Martin, 88–90.
56. Horwood, 91.
57. Ibid., 104.
58. T. Martin, 13.
59. Ibid., 197.
60. Horwood, 161.
61. Ibid., 169.

62. The script makes a nod to the Cold War anxiety readings of the 1956 film here as Elizabeth reads, "Their characteristic and widespread growth pattern was even observed in many of the large war-torn cities of Europe. Indeed, some of these plants may thrive on devastated ground." Clearly, a case can be made for the grex as a metaphor for Soviet expansion. One could equally argue that the OECD demonstrates its own brand of global takeover on the devastated ground of war-torn Europe.

63. See "Practical Magic: The Special Effects Pod," bonus disc material from the 2007 DVD.

64. Asimov, 8. For a polemical rebuttal, see Greenberg. See also Mage. Also firmly on the side of Velikovsky were the editors of *Pensée*, who beat *Scientists Confront Velikovsky* to the punch by one year with *Velikovsky Reconsidered*. For a critique of both sides, see Bauer.

65. Gordin, 4.

66. In the opening sequence, the spores glide past the eye of Jupiter as if retracing the steps of the earlier catastrophe.

67. Velikovsky, 54.

68. Sagan, "An Analysis of *Worlds in Collision*," 73.

69. Ibid., 72.

70. Tompkins and Bird, 116.

PART III

BEDROOM

9

BED

Frame

Regan MacNeil has a problem with her bed. Most children do. In many households, bedtime avoidance insinuates itself into the nightly routine. *One more story. I just got up to get a glass of water. I'm not tired. It's too dark. It's too loud. It's too quiet. Can I sleep in your bed tonight?* Elaborate rituals, specialized lighting, curated music, blankets and plush toys that remain companions well beyond infancy, and myriad other accommodations in the name of nocturnal comfort suggest that a bed frame demarcates a zone of anxiety as much as a space for repose. Absent sleep disorders, a person tends to appreciate the charms of a bed more with age. One might therefore judge a twelve-year-old girl like Regan (Linda Blair) too old to be crawling into Mom's bed in the middle of the night. Yet she has good reason to do so: her bed shakes—not with the therapeutic vibrations of an expensive mattress or the twenty-five-cent tremors once offered by cheap motels but with the fitful convulsions of a demonic force for which her mother, Chris (Ellen Burstyn), seeks a rational, medical explanation. "The shaking of the bed, that's doubtless due to muscular spasms," says Dr. Klein (Barton Heyman) at the hospital. Unconvinced, Chris objects, "Look, I got on the bed. The whole bed was thumping and rising off the floor and shaking, *the whole thing!*" The doctor reasserts his authority: "Mrs. MacNeil, the problem with your daughter is not her bed. It's her brain." Out of confusion or in deference to medical expertise, Mrs. MacNeil backs down, and the focus shifts from furniture behaving badly to the inner workings of a child who suffers from either brain lesions, psychological disorders, or demonic possession. By the time *The Exorcist* (1973) rules out the first two options, a shaking bed is the least of Regan's troubles. Nonetheless, the problem with Regan is very much her bed, and that problem extends beyond the MacNeil household.

Consider a brief inventory of the film's beds. The original theatrical cut of *The Exorcist* includes eleven beds with meaningful ties to the characters—five domestic and six hospital beds. In order of appearance, they include the following:

1. Chris MacNeil's bed, a fashionably upholstered double bed headed by a regal quarter-tester canopy valance that matches the wallpaper. In spite of its comfort, the bed functions primarily as a workspace or a proscenium for drama. Chris makes her first appearance in the film on her stately bed, wide-awake and annotating a script for her latest movie role. Her second appearance in bed shows her rest interrupted at ungodly hours by the competing demands of acting and parenting: a movie set wakeup call to her right, and to her left a visit from Regan, who has crept into the space left empty by Chris's estranged husband.
2. Regan MacNeil's bed, a low-post colonial-style double that lacks luxurious upholstery but offers a surplus of space for a child. Once the possession is in full swing, the bed transforms along with Regan. Makeshift upholstering pads and straitjackets the wooden frame, and wrist straps complete the metamorphosis toward institutional control. Regan's bed has its own character arc as the forces of medicine, religion, domesticity, and demonic infestation compete for dominance of the space. A tally of the bed scenes reveals that Regan's bed steals the show, with sixteen appearances compared to three appearances for Chris's bed and one appearance each for beds three through eleven.[1]
3–4. The Karras home beds, notable only for their lack of use. When angst-ridden priest Damien Karras enters his mother Mary's house, he tosses his coat on the twin bed that serves as no more than a relic of his underprivileged upbringing. After talking briefly with his mother, who prefers to rest in her chair, Damien exits through her room and passes her empty bed, whose simple metal frame has more in common with care facilities where hygienic, pest-resistant materials replace cozy but less practical wood and upholstery.
5. The first of the sick beds that soon dominate the film. Karras learns that his mother has been hospitalized in the overcrowded psychiatric ward at Bellevue among rows of impersonal, metal, clinical beds. Side rails and wrist straps make this bed a prison for Mrs. Karras. Damien vows to free his mother from her pitiful confinement, but his well-intentioned decision leaves Mrs. Karras back home without proper supervision. The infirm woman dies alone in her bed not long thereafter, her body discovered days later by neighbors. The film thus suggests that an unsupervised bed can have deadly consequences.
6. Damien's dorm-room bed. With a colonial style similar to Regan's but humbler in size (a twin), height (a low base), and framing (shorter posts, no footboard), Damien's bed combines the institutional context of a dormitory, the

childhood nostalgia and monastic austerity of a twin, and the same traditional style as Regan's bed. Additionally, his bed is the site of the only dream sequence in the film, another bed-related amalgamation that compresses into one space elements connected to Regan, to Damien's struggle with his mother, and to larger institutional and religious issues.[2]

7–11. A series of hospital beds including an examination table used for a shot; a gurney; an examination table used for an arteriogram (a scene that notoriously induced vomiting and fainting in theater audiences); a tilting examination table used for an encephalogram, complete with head clamps and straps evocative of a medieval torture device; and finally, a hospital bed at the Barringer Clinic. The institutional beds are the foil to the home bed just as the excruciating medical tests are the foil to the exorcism. Were Chris MacNeil to strap her daughter to her home bed and subject her to a medieval religious ceremony from the outset, the viewer would likely reject the actions as abusive, but as one critic observed, "the leap from the agonies of modern medicine to those of ancient religion becomes, in the mind of the audience, more than just believable: it becomes desirable."[3]

Bed problems related to both poverty and excess plague the characters in *The Exorcist*. Damien Karras suffers from intense guilt over his inability to find a proper bed for his mother. His uncle is quick to point out that if Damien had become a Park Avenue psychiatrist instead of a priest, Mary could be living in a penthouse rather than recovering from injury in the depressing communal room of a psych ward. Chris MacNeil, in contrast, gives Regan the best care money can buy only to find that each new institutional bed does no more than add pain to the ordeal. Regan's home bed is larger than Damien's, and her bedroom not much smaller than the Karras home, but yet again, superior sleeping quarters fail to protect the girl from harm. Regan would prefer the refuge of her mother's bed, and rightly so, because Chris MacNeil's bed never shakes or levitates. But staying in Mom's bed is out of the question as per the dictates of authoritative parenting guides such as those of Dr. Benjamin Spock.

Would it be unfair to blame Dr. Spock for Regan's possession? Probably, since his book appears neither in William Blatty's 1971 novel nor in the movie adaptation. Nevertheless, the degree to which Spock's advice had permeated society justifies indulging in a hypothetical blame game for the sake of a broader argument about the nature of a child's bed in postindustrial society. And since critics have blamed Spock for nothing less than destroying America, this thought experiment is relatively tame. By the 1970s, Spock's *Baby and Child Care* (or *The Common Sense Book of Baby* and Child Care in its first edition in 1946) had already reached its second generation of parents, and if soaring sales figures are any indication of influence, Baby and Child Care was fast approaching the moral authority of the Bible.[4] By pitching medically inflected child-rearing advice as common sense, Dr. Spock gave a modern, reassuring alternative to grandmotherly wisdom at a time when extended families were moving farther apart. Coincidentally (or not, for the blame-Spock crowd), the "me" generation of baby boomers begins the same year as first edition of Spock's book. Although Chris MacNeil precedes the baby boomer generation by five years (or seven in the chronology of the novel), her status as a celebrity with a broken marriage and no visible extended family fits the profile maligned by conservative critics as the ethos of Spock's permissive, narcissistic regime.[5] Whether raised on Spock or not, Chris is of the perfect age and temperament to apply his teachings to her own daughter.

Spock's supposed overindulgence notwithstanding, when it comes to bedtime, the book's advice comes across as unduly strict and dogmatic, as if the doctor had meant to establish a catechism of the bed. Consider how his numbered rules, often in the question-response format favored by the catechism, indoctrinate parents on every point of proper childcare:[6] "255. How much should my baby sleep?" is followed by a three-paragraph answer. "257. On back or stomach?" gets five paragraphs. Point 259 insists that by six months, if not from birth, a baby needs to be out of the parents' room. Point 260, "Better not let the child in your bed," warns against allowing a child to cling to the security of a parent's bed for any reason, for "there is the devil to pay to getting him out again."[7] Spock's guide to parenting scripts and directs a parent's actions right down to the proper tone for delivery (acting experience would certainly be a plus when attempting to pull off "friendly, firm, and breezy" when denying a bed-fearing child a drink of water or a second trip to the bathroom). The frame of the bed, in Spock's domestic drama, thus participates in the moral and psychological well-being of a child. Nothing less than the development of the child's emerging self is at stake. Little wonder the battle over Regan's autonomy is so explicitly tied to her bed.

In the context of the history of sleeping, Spock's advice is anything but common sense. Only in the recent past has the bed become an individual space. From an evolutionary standpoint, sleeping huddled in groups makes better sense as a source of heating and protection. The skeptic need only watch an episode of the reality show *Survivor* to see how quickly people revert to communal sleeping when stripped of modern luxuries. Paleoanthropologist Daniel Lieberman points to a compilation of reports on the sleeping customs of hunter-gatherers, pastoralists, and subsistence farmers to show that humans have very rarely slept in isolation.[8] The environment we have come to think of as desirable or beneficial to sleep hygiene may have done more harm than good. "Industrialized sleep," to use Lieberman's term, has deprived children of the rich sensory experience of earlier times and has contributed to the steady decline in the number of hours the average American sleeps each night (two to three hours fewer today than in 1900), not to mention the corresponding rise in insomnia. Electricity rightly deserves much of the blame for altering sleep habits, but so too does the space dedicated to sleep. The invention of separate rooms for the bed (first known as "*la chambre à coucher*" in thirteenth-century France and the "bedchamber" in fourteenth-century England), the eventual democratization of the bedroom, and the increasing isolation of the bed have changed the nature of sleep from a cooperative social contract into a solitary battle with the dark.

"The worst thing you can threaten a child with is sending him to bed," says author Anthony Burgess.[9] Burgess singles out the bed of early adolescence as a breeding ground for fear: "The terrors come when the child is too old to sleep with his mother and too young to sleep with a lover or mistress."[10] Obvious Freudian implications aside, Burgess's observation highlights temporary lack, and therefore liminality, as the defining feature of a childhood bed. The "big boy" or "big girl" bed, to use a favorite parental euphemism, reframes the move to a less enclosed sleeping climate as a rewarding rite of passage. And indeed, the exit from a crib's prison-cell structure represents newfound freedom. In fact, a toddler's jailbreak skills often determine the timeline of the move from crib to bed. If all goes well, the new minimum-security space creates a healthy transition to greater independence. Surveillance tends to decrease, baby monitors disappear, and the bedroom belongs less and less to the parent.

Fear of communicable diseases, including syphilis and tuberculosis, and moral concerns regarding sexual activity spurred on the shift from communal to solitary sleeping in the mid-nineteenth century.[11] A solitary bed, however, presented its own possibilities for temptations—chief among them, masturbation. A radical deterrent devised by Daniel Schreber (a German judge best known for having inspired Freud's work on paranoia) prevented self-stimulation by means of a bed harness strapped across the child's chest and arms to keep the sleeper in the morally correct faceup posture and to make touching oneself impossible.[12] *The Exorcist* plays out that moral anxiety in the extreme when possessed Regan masturbates on her bed with a crucifix. From that point on, religious, medical, and parental authority figures keep Regan's body strapped to her bed frame in a manner even less comfortable and efficient than Schreber's bed harness. Due to the invading demonic forces, surveillance and discipline return to the adolescent girl's bedroom. Likewise, Damien's mother loses her own bedstead autonomy and must forcibly submit to the disciplinary bed frame equipped with straps when hospitalized at Bellevue after a cerebral edema. Regan MacNeil and Mary Karras thus remind us that from cradle to grave, control over one's bed is not a given. Clearly, no other piece of furniture represents as contested a space as the bed.

The true story behind *The Exorcist* marks the bed as a figure of equal if not greater significance than those in the novel or film. The 1949 *Washington Post* article detailing the exorcism of an unnamed fourteen-year-old boy mentions a shaking bed as evidence of demonic infestation. Robbie Mannheim (a.k.a. Roland Doe, both pseudonyms) complained of a shaking bed and strange noises in his bedroom. His family talked to their Lutheran minister, who expressed skepticism. A month later, the minister asked Robbie to stay in his own home, where he witnessed the shaking bed for himself. Neighbors reportedly invited Robbie to stay over in their homes, where they claimed to have seen the same violent, involuntary movement of the boy's bed. A Catholic priest took up the task of the exorcism and stayed with Robbie for two months, during which, according to the article, "he said he personally witnessed such manifestations as the bed in which the boy was sleeping suddenly moving across the room."[13] Director William Friedkin, who did research of his own about the case in preparation for the film, taped a phone interview with a relative who saw Robbie's mattress "raised up in the air, up and down, up and down," after which she ran to the bed, where "that mattress raised both of us right up in the air."[14]

During the months of Robbie's possession, his symptoms occurred only at night, after he had changed and gone to bed.[15] Moreover, the fact that the paranormal activity was not limited to any one bed suggests that the general category of bed was more at issue than a particular haunted space. The most logical explanation for the selective behavior is that beds functioned as a trigger for Robbie, possibly due to past sexual trauma. Although the church had authorized the exorcism, a Jesuit examiner later reviewed and discredited Robbie's case as "a psychosomatic disorder with some kinesis action that we do not understand," or in the words of film critic Mark Kermode, "a text-book case of hysteria with mild, associative telekinetic side-effects."[16] Of course, no medical textbook includes telekinesis as a side effect of conversion hysteria, but the logic behind the two ideas is similar in that any acceptance of the mind influencing matter without a demonstrable organic cause requires a leap of faith. The inherent physiological problem posed by the now defunct diagnosis of hysteria is the assumption that an immaterial force can generate material phenomena. If medical tests find no organic cause (e.g., brain lesions, nerve damage, etc.) for symptoms that are nevertheless real, and if the doctor can rule out malingering (i.e., faking it), the diagnosis moves to the etiologically problematic space between neurology and psychiatry, to that netherworld where a mysterious process called "conversion" transforms something not measurable into something diagnostically legitimized. The problem with conversion disorder or hysterical neurosis is that nobody can explain how that "conversion" happens physiologically.[17]

By some estimates, as many as one-third of new patients at neurology clinics exhibit medically unexplained symptoms.[18] In medieval and early modern times, unexplainable behavior might have been relegated to the domain of religion, where possession offered a plausible explanation. In *The Exorcist*, the MacNeil family passes from neurology to psychiatry to religion—a move that William Blatty wanted audiences to view as a pathway to truth rather than a regression toward superstition. When Chris MacNeil's doctor so quickly dismisses the bed in favor of the brain, Blatty wants to prove him wrong. The excruciating battery of invasive tests by neurologists and psychiatrists leads the audience to conclude that science is operating on inside-out assumptions, whereas the shaking bed, or the notion of possession in general, operates from an outside-in premise. This is not to say that medicine as a whole ignores external factors any more than religion ignores the internal—indeed, exorcism is the religious cousin of excision—but the problem with Regan MacNeil comes from the outside (her bed), not from the inside (her brain).

As both a Harvard-educated psychiatrist and a priest, Damien Karras is better equipped than any other character in *The Exorcist* to serve as a link between science and religion, and he does so by changing from the skeptic who offers to help in his capacity as a psychiatrist to the believer who saves Regan by embracing his calling as a priest. Karras visits Regan in her room

190 | Household Horror

Fig. 9.1. Regan's possessed bed in *The Exorcist* (1973).

three times before requesting permission for the exorcism, and during each visit, the veil of doubt persists. Projectile vomiting, speaking in tongues, reactions to (fake) holy water (a big setback), frigid room temperatures, and the message "help me" embossed on Regan's skin all fail to erase Damien's skepticism. Even when requesting the exorcism after the third visit, Damien expresses uncertainty to his superiors. Then, during the fourth visit, while assisting exorcist Father Merrin, Damien sees the bed shake and levitate. Only then does belief take hold. As in the real case of Robbie Mannheim, the moving bed generates conversion. As the footboard levitates as high as Damien's chin, a close-up registers his expression of unquestioning belief. Father Merrin prods Damien to continue his reply in the exorcism ceremony, and slowly, the bed returns to the floor: first possessed, first exorcised. Now Regan must follow suit. The straps rip from Regan's wrists, her blanket flies off, and Regan's body levitates just as her bed did earlier. The priests chant "The power of Christ compels you" several times in unison, and Regan descends. End of round one.

The demon has not yet left Regan, but the most important object has been stabilized. During Regan's levitation, both priests grab the bedposts to steady themselves. The frame acts as an altar from behind which the men of God chant and fling holy water at Regan's floating body. The bed stays in place even as a sudden quake throws the priests to the floor. For a few seconds, the silhouetted demon appears, as if in a vision, while Regan kneels up on her mattress, raises her hands, and sways in gestures of tortured worship. The illusion of the bed as demon-altar quickly returns to a shot of Regan, still supine, wrists tied together. Father Merrin crawls toward her and kneels, elbows resting in prayer against the mattress. His genuflection reclaims the Christian function of the bedside as a domestic altar. Merrin remains kneeling in bedside prayer while Damien retrieves the blanket from the floor and wraps it around Regan like a parent tucking in a child at bedtime. The two "father" figures then sit on the edge of Regan's mattress, one to each side, slumped in exhaustion. Damien sits quietly on the mattress for about forty seconds before the scene changes.

The final synthesis of the film's many beds occurs when Damien wanders back into the room and sees his mother sitting up in bed in place of Regan. He approaches the apparition, and the shot returns to Regan. Damien sits on the edge of the mattress and pats Regan's brow with a cloth while Regan, in the voice and imperfect English of Mary Karras, asks, "Damien, why you do this to me?" At that moment, Damien is simultaneously father and son, doctor and priest. The beds have converged: the sickbed, the deathbed, the mother's bed, the child's bed, the defiled bed, the sacred bed, the communal bed, the solitary bed. Regan's bed embodies all of the qualities and contradictions inherent in a piece of furniture that frames a space for birth, sex, death, dreams, nightmares, the sacred, and the profane. If, as French theorist Jean Baudrillard contends, certain pieces of furniture (bed, buffet, and armoire) constitute domestic monuments (*meubles-monuments*) that fight for traditional values in the home, the bed stands at the head of that trinity.[19] Regan's bed is the battlefield where forces of moral order compete for power with the winds of change.

The Exorcist tames the bed at great cost, first through the martyrdom of Father Merrin, who dies in a posture of prayer at Regan's bedside, and then through the self-sacrifice of Damien, who sends the evil spirits back out the window by taking them into his own body and jumping to his death. Significantly, Damien instigates the final fight with Regan's possessors by knocking her off of the bed and onto the floor. Once Damien has cleansed Regan (and her bed) of evil by offering up his body as host, putting himself into the role of the biblical swine into which Jesus cast Legion, the girl returns to her innocent state. She cries for her mother, who comes running. As Chris later tells Father Dyer, despite the ordeal, Regan remembers nothing. The beatifically amnesic girl thus regains innocence, ready to move to a new home and a new bed. As a cautionary tale, Regan's possession and subsequent exorcism reaffirm religious control over the bed, even if post-traumatic amnesia means that the lessons learned are for the benefit of everyone but Regan herself.[20] Three dead bodies and a boarded-up bedroom window make the happy ending of *The Exorcist* cold comfort to all surviving adults. The best Chris can hope for is to prolong the renewed innocence of her daughter and to create an environment less susceptible to problems of the bed.

Mattress

The Exorcist and other bedroom-centric horror movies figure into a long-standing tradition of morality tales that pit girl against bed. The repertoire of folklore and fairy tales canonized as bedtime stories is replete with girls both common and noble who encounter trouble in bed in the form of too much sleep, too little sleep, or uninvited guests. Regan's near-fatal consumption by a demon and her last-minute rescue by a patriarchal figure echoes the bed terror of Little Red Riding Hood, the foolhardy girl devoured by the wolf hiding in bed and saved by the deus ex machina arrival of a hunter. In other tales, a girl tests the bed as much as she is tested by it. Goldilocks, for one, is a famously obsessive mattress tester, though easily satisfied compared to the titular princess of Hans Christian Andersen's "The Princess and the Pea." The latter proves her suitability for royal marriage by sensing a pea hidden under twenty mattresses and twenty featherbeds, proving that discriminating taste in beds has its advantages as well as its perils.

Once upon a time, many of those tales had more bite: Little Red wound up dead, and Goldilocks, in an earlier iteration as an old hag, ended her break-in days impaled on St Paul's Cathedral. Over time, folkloric beds have become relatively safe spaces, and picky Goldilocks has enjoyed a second life in motivational speaking and marketing consultation, where her three-tiered approach to achieving "just right" has become a foundational pricing principle. Her image has also undergone makeovers for the sake of mattress endorsements. Beautyrest magazine ads in the 1970s dressed Goldilocks as a sexy vixen in a naughty baby doll nightie cuddled up to three stuffed bears.[21] More recently, she has ditched the plunging neckline and has deployed sassy wit to attract more than 166 million YouTube views for the Purple Mattress "raw egg test."[22] The sense of danger once associated with the compulsion to try out beds is long gone. In horror films, however, the bed remains a vital testing ground for adolescent girls, their boyfriends, and the occasional parent.

According to Casper, the millennial-friendly mail-order mattress company, the ideal sleep surface has "just the right amount of sink and bounce" thanks to the perfect combination of "springy latex foam" and "supportive memory foam."[23] Horror movie mattresses, in contrast, have entirely the wrong degree of sink and bounce. A case in point is Regan MacNeil's restless bed in *The Exorcist*. Or, for a possessed bed with too much sink, see the cult classic *Death Bed: The Bed That Eats* (1977). When not snoring, Death Bed devours young couples, fried chicken, sundry snacks, and Pepto-Bismol by absorbing them into an acidic liquid core that bears a strong resemblance to Mountain Dew soda. Depictions of unwanted "sink" with a higher degree of realism occur in the slashers *Pieces* (1982) and *The House on Sorority Row* (1983), in which knife attacks gut waterbeds and leave young co-eds flopping like vulnerable fish in a bucket.

In less aqueous scenarios, too much sink stems from too much memory, as in *Psycho* (1960), where the fetal-shaped indent of Mrs. Bates on an empty mattress hints at something deeply amiss. When Lila Crane snoops in the Bateses' home and spots the sunken mattress, we cannot help but wonder how long a body must lie immobile to fossilize its impression so deeply. The mattress that remembers in spite of a body's absence is the antithesis of high-tech memory foam, whose real virtue is its ability to forget. The perfect mattress erases as quickly as possible any evidence of use, just as the perfect hotel does day after day with each room. When an old mattress remembers too much, when it sags with the trace of its human occupant to the point where the past imposes itself onto the present, comfort gives way to confinement. A mattress that has lost its resilience haunts us with poses forged in unconsciousness. Past behavior inscribed in the surface traps the sleeper in the same way a temporal loop traps a ghost in the residue of history. The tabula rasa of so-called memory foam is what dreams are made of; the mattress that remembers is the stuff of nightmares.

Among the many films that exploit mattress horror, Wes Craven's *A Nightmare on Elm Street* (1984) stands out for its mattresses with too much sink, too much bounce, and a vicious excess of repressed memory. Freddy Kreuger, the iconic serial killer–turned–dream demon who deploys claw-like knives on his gloved right hand to murder the teen children of his vigilante executioners, owes a debt of gratitude to his pillow-topped partners in crime. *Nightmare*'s mattresses are the unheralded accomplices that lull victims into the dormant state required for Freddy to access their bodies. Mattresses participate in every death in the film, not merely as passive enablers of sleep but also as consumptive forces that can ingest or expel victims at will, or as membranous portals between realities. Bedding, too, works alongside the mattress in every death scene in the original film. In Rod's jail cell hanging, the sheet is clearly the star. But here, Rod's death will be set aside, deferring the question of sheet horror to the next section. For now, we will push the sheet to a secondary role and focus on three cases where excess sink and bounce turn the mattress into a zone of terror.

The first death occurs during a postcoital dream sequence at the house of high school student Tina Gray (Amanda Wyss). Tina has been having nightmares about a disfigured man in a dirty red-and-green-striped sweater whose "fingerknives" have slashed her nightgown and left their mark in the real world. While her mother is out of town, Tina invites boyfriend Rod (Jsu Garcia) and friends Nancy (Heather Langenkamp) and Glen (Johnny Depp) to stay the night. Glen and Nancy endure the boredom of their chaste vigil downstairs while Tina and Rod emit orgasmic cries from the upstairs bedroom and then let sleep take its course. Tina finds herself once again in a nightmare where violence has real-life consequences for her but not for her tormenter. Freddy delights in his own indestructability in the dream world. He stretches and retracts his arms like giant accordions. He cuts off his own fingers and laughs as green goo and insects spurt from the severed stumps. When Tina grabs his face, his skin slips off as easily as a sheet yanked off a bed. One layer of horror gives way to the next.

If Tina's nightmare has a theme beyond that of a deadly game of cat-and-mouse, that theme is without question the "rubber reality" (as critics have called it) behind Freddy's power.[24] The confusion of waking and sleeping life within Freddy's realm exploits the metamorphic possibilities of dream logic. In nightmares, Freddy terrorizes his victims with his ability to mutilate and mutate himself without harm to his body or identity. Film scholar Anna Powell's Deleuzian interpretation of *Nightmare* calls Freddy's collusion with inanimate objects a flamboyant display of "becoming-anything" and a "rejection of the barriers we draw between worlds."[25] Indeed, the reciprocal relation between Freddy and the objects he permeates, animates, or becomes presents a form of object horror based on plasticity. In fact, the 1940s comic book superhero Plastic Man inspired the shape-shifting of Craven's horror villain as well as the color-coded technique for identifying him no matter the form he adopts. Says Craven in a

2008 interview, "[Plastic Man] used to change shape, but you could always tell it was him because the couch would be red with a green stripe down it—or yellow?"[26] Borrowing the technique, Craven puts the red and green of Kreuger's signature striped sweater on the Cadillac at the end of *Nightmare* to mark the vehicle as the shape-shifting Freddy. The striped sweater effect strengthens Freddy's identity but weakens the horror of the object in itself by dressing up its thingness in the garb of ego. A Freddy-mobile is never really a car. Like all possessed or haunted object narratives that maintain an anthropocentric hierarchy (*Death Bed*, *The Exorcist*, every horror movie ever made about a doll, etc.), *Nightmare*'s Freddy upstages the objects he interacts with or becomes. In other words, when the sweater effect is in play, Freddy's rubber reality, at best, only hints at the reality of rubber.

There are, however, no red-and-green-striped mattresses in *Nightmare*. Freddy colludes with rather than becomes mattresses in the deaths of Tina, Glen, and Nancy's mother, Marge (Ronee Blakley). In the first death, Tina defends herself against Freddy underneath the sheet, but from Rod's point of view, she is overreacting to an invisible foe, as a sleeper tends to do during a bad dream. Rod pulls off the sheet and watches in horror as Tina's shirt rips open and knife wounds appear on her skin. Tina's body bounces upward, levitates, flips to a supine position, and spins, knocking Rod off the bed and splattering blood across the room. The unseen force drags Tina's hemorrhaging body to the ceiling; she succumbs and tumbles, dead, onto the blood-soaked mattress and then to the floor. Tina's death scene moves through three visual stages that make explicit the porosity of the bed: first, complete immersion in the nightmare alley; second, the view of Tina and Freddy in the real bed, both visible only as long as the shot lingers between the membrane of the two sheets; third, the point of view that excludes Freddy as a visible entity once Rod pulls off the sheet. The three steps move from dream reality to bedroom reality with the mediating in-between of the sheets.

Glen's death equally imagines the mattress more as a membranous portal than as a Plastic Man–style permutation of Freddy. The scene begins with Glen watching TV in bed while simultaneously listening to music through headphones plugged into his stereo. As the station (KRGR) goes off air, we see that Glen has fallen asleep with the portable television on his lap. A high-angle shot captures the sudden emergence of Freddy's arm as it shoots up through the mattress and grabs Glen's exposed midriff. The arm pulls Glen down into the hole that has appeared in the middle of the bed.

Fig. 9.2. A geyser of blood bursts from Glen's mattress in *A Nightmare on Elm Street* (1984).

Glen reaches for his pillow and comforter, searching in vain for a stable hold as his body, bedding, and television sink into the mattress. Glen disappears into the pit, capped off by his stereo. Seconds later, a geyser of blood (220 gallons, or enough for approximately 183 Glens) bursts from the hole up to the ceiling. Again, Freddy bounces in and out of limited visibility in a way that allows the object to participate in horror in its own right, unlike the striped sweater effect of the car-shaped Freddy at the end of the film.

Marge's death, like the murders of Glen and Tina, draws attention to the mattress as a permeable membrane in a rubber reality. Marge falls victim to Freddy as a consequence of Nancy's scheme to draw the villain from the dream world into her booby-trapped home. Nancy believes that if she falls asleep, finds Freddy, and manages to hold on to him at the moment when her alarm rings, she can pull him into the physical realm and kill him. As planned, Nancy gets Freddy out of the dream, smashes him over the head with a coffee pot (an appropriate weapon against a sleep monster), lures him to the basement, and sets him on fire. Still ablaze, Freddy makes his way back up to the second floor, where he throws himself on top of Marge in her bed. Nancy's father tries to snuff out the fire with a blanket, but too late: Freddy has vanished from under the blanket, and Marge is now a charred skeleton. As Nancy and her dad look on, the mattress becomes a pool of luminescent blue fluid. Marge's skeleton sinks into the glowing pool, a light flashes, and the mattress returns to its normal springy state, complete with a fresh fitted sheet and two pillows.

In response to the sudden erasure of her mother, Nancy jumps onto the mattress and pounds its springy surface with her hands. The barrier refuses to give. As she turns her back and moves toward the door, a mist begins to drift across the bed. With the atmospheric shift, movement returns to the mattress. The sheet begins to distend. A head-sized protrusion stretches up from the tensile fabric, and then knife claws rip through the cotton cocoon, completing a sequence evocative of uterine fluidity followed by a monstrous birth. From there, the film moves toward its unhappy ending: Nancy enjoys a moment of illusory triumph over Freddy. She reclaims all of the power she has given him and demands that she be reunited with her dead friends and mother. Her empowerment is like that of the lucid dreamer, awake within the dream: "I know the secret now—this whole thing is just a dream." She turns her back on Freddy and grasps the doorknob to exit the bedroom. Freddy lunges but then disappears into her back as a flash of blue static. As Nancy exits the threshold of the bedroom, she enters a world of bright light and heavy fog where friends and family reemerge unscathed and where Marge, who has quit drinking, declares, "Oh, I believe anything is possible."

Nancy has exited straight into the utopic image of Reaganite suburbia.[27] Her house is restored, the smashed trellis that once neighbored her bedroom window is back up, and the bars installed by her parents no longer block the windows. Her friends pull up in a 1959 Cadillac convertible, and her mother waves goodbye. Nancy seems to have regained control. Then, without warning, the convertible closes its red-and-green-striped top, and the windows trap the friends inside. Pounding on the car window just as she pounded on the mattress earlier, Nancy screams for her mother, but the Freddy-car drives away. As Marge waves and smiles on the doorstep, Freddy's arm bursts through the small glass panel of the front door and pulls her body into the house. The porosity of dream and waking spaces thus ends with the victims trapped in the two cells that dominate life in 1980s American suburbia: the car and the home.

As Freddy's rubber reality pits the Sturm und Drang of sleep against the rationality of waking life, the mattress emerges as the most important contact point between those two spheres. The frightful moments of excess sink or bounce in the death scenes unleash a metaphorical and physical tension inherent to the inner life of a mattress. Normally, mattress anatomy lessons are reserved for furniture showroom floors, where salespeople educate the consumer with cross sections enclosed in clear plastic. Only then do we see that the fabric epidermis, with its absurd floral patterns or cloud-like quilting, belies a hidden industrial interior fraught with tense coils and foams. Mattress guts, feats of human engineering to combat the discomfort of solid ground, embody a reality that may be literally more rubber than Freddy. Sapped from rubber trees, whipped into froth, and vulcanized to increase elasticity, springy latex foams or their synthetic cousins inhabit the mattress core, often in concert with spun steel, to provide a balance between hard and soft, between stability and instability.

Foam mattresses have been produced since 1931, two years after E. A. Murphy whipped bubbles into latex rubber with a kitchen mixer and stabilized the milky froth with a gelling agent.[28] Synthetic latex replaces or dilutes rubber latex in many products. Formulations and production formats vary, but all mattress foams result from a physical process of entrapping bubbles (bubble entrainment) followed by some degree of bubble expansion that transforms the spheres into polyhedral cells.[29] The mattress maker Savvy Rest uses a cake analogy to explain the look and feel of two varieties of molded foam: Dunlop foam (the one cooked up by Murphy) is compared to a dense pound cake, while the complex flash-freezing and baking process known as Talalay produces foams more comparable to the soft, springy texture of angel food cake.[30] The Goldilocks principle applied to foam requires cell walls that are neither too open nor too closed. The perfect balance between linkage and detachment prevents cell walls from breaking down too quickly.

The metaphorical value of foam is such that German philosopher Peter Sloterdijk has developed a massive "spherology" trilogy whose final volume uses foams to define the qualities and structures of contemporary life. Foams subject "that which is dense, continuous and massive" to "an invasion by the hollow."[31] Mixing and agitation hollow out substance, if only temporarily, "as if in some nocturnal coup."[32] Dreams are foams, according to a popular German expression (*Träume sind Schäume*); they are an "undermining of the solid by the untenable—a ghost light, a superfluity, a mood, a swamp gas, inhabited by a dubious subjectivity."[33] A more idiomatic cognate for *Träume sind Schäume* might be "dreams are but shadows."[34] Hamlet says as much—a fact that did not escape Wes Craven, who taught college English before becoming a filmmaker. Fittingly, Craven quotes twice from *Hamlet* as a background to Nancy's battle with sleep during English class. As Nancy drifts in and out of consciousness, a student described only as "surfer" in

Craven's script recites passages from two acts of *Hamlet*—first as Horatio, "The graves stood tenantless and the sheeted dead did squeak"(act 1, scene 1), and later as Hamlet, "O God, I could be bounded in a nutshell and count myself a king of infinite space were it not that I have bad dreams" (act 2, scene 2). Refracted through "spherology," both quotes describe the foaming of structures typically valued for solidity. In the first, the graves release the dead from their cellular confinement beneath the ground, shrouded in just enough membrane (the sheet) to define their hollow reality. The spectral disruption by "the sheeted dead" portends a threat to the political order, according to Horatio. In the second quote, Hamlet points to the consequences of a domestic bubble that fails to function as a protective space where one can have good dreams.

A house, according to philosopher Gaston Bachelard, is a space that allows us to dream in peace. Without the protective bubble of the home ("the nonself that protects the self"), we become dispersed beings.[35] The sheeted dead have more power than the living when the shell of the home cracks. Drawing on Bachelard, Heidegger envisions a dwelling as a constructed space that shelters and protects us from the outside world, a space that lets us be (*be-lassen*), that frees us to construct the bubble of the self within the bubble of the home.[36] Similarly, for Sloterdijk, the human impulse to build an immunity bubble, or "egosphere," derives from a longing to recreate the uterine bubble—the protective walls of another being within which the self emerges. Nations, cities, and other communal structures reimagine or attempt to replicate the dyadic mother-child relationship, but those bubbles pop, implode, and explode, especially when they push against one another. In like manner, modernity and its perpetual revolutions are analogous to the sound and fury of bubble entrainment giving way to foam. Counter to Heidegger, Sloterdijk cannot accept the bubble of the home as a "gift of Being." Rather, he contends that whatever success humans achieve in creating structures of immunity comes only through "great efforts of formal design, technical production, legal support, and political molding."[37]

The foaming of the twentieth century might be seen as a proliferation of heroic (or tragic) attempts to control the atmosphere—the age of air-conditioning. For Sloterdijk, a confluence of terrorism, product design, and environmental awareness generates twentieth-century foam.[38] Architecture foregrounds the environment even as it wages war against it. Our machines for living (to borrow Le Corbusier's phrase) are, above all, environmental containers. The isolated bubble and the global sphere remain powerful totems, but the most accurate metaphor for our epoch, in Sloterdijk's phenomenological account, is foam. We do not live on a globe; we coexist in cofragile, coisolated, centerless conglomerations in which "the great majority of surrounding co-bubbles are simultaneously adjacent and inaccessible, both connected and removed."[39] The suburban houses in *Nightmare* present a clear picture of that foamed world, where children in each two-story bubble are dreaming the same dreams. In each house, there are multiple cells, and in each bedroom, a mattress—foams nested in foams.

A Nightmare on Elm Street seethes with the frothy wreckage of untenable spheres thanks to its chief foaming agent, Freddy Kreuger. Freddy penetrates, agitates, and alters the atmosphere of home, school, and jail. His presence foregrounds the coexisting cells within cells, as in the English class dream, in which he lures Nancy out of the bubble of the classroom and into the hallway, where he adopts the form of hall monitor—the regulatory figure in a space lined with endless cells of student lockers. Where one door opens, another door closes in Freddy's game of foams. When Freddy is not slashing his way through closed spaces (a mattress, a mirror, a door, a bathtub), he is taunting people with the barriers of their own immunological bubbles. In scene after scene, characters pound on or attempt to break through doors, windows, and mattresses with varying degrees of success: Glen breaks down the door after Tina's death, Nancy pounds on windows before Rod's and Glen's deaths, Marge pounds on the bathroom door and breaks in with a wire hanger, Glen's mother bursts into his room after his death, Nancy pounds on her front door, her father breaks down the front door, Nancy pounds on the mattress, and so on. Dreams are foams in *Nightmare*, and so are the spaces of waking life.

The foaming effect of Freddy's violence is comparable to a child splashing in a freshly drawn bubble bath: the agitation pops bubbles and produces foam. Nothing, therefore, could be a more appropriate synthesis of Freddy's role than the Excalibur-like emergence of his fingerknives in Nancy's bubble bath. The iconic scene calls attention to the bath as a waterbed where those who sleep risk death. A bath, by nature, is a failed replication of the bubble-bed of the womb. Our inability to sleep fully immersed in water recalls the primal trauma to the mother-child dyadic bubble. As warm and welcoming as it may feel, a bath can only feign uterine security and can only pretend to be a bed. With that understanding, we must recognize the blow-up bath pillow as one of the cruelest ironies of product design—a pillow that is not a pillow for a bed that is not a bed. Nancy's inflatable bath pillow is like those found even today at stores that understand the perverse logic of a bath pillow—stores such as Bed Bath & Beyond, whose name, incidentally, summarizes the most important locales of Craven's film. When Nancy nods off under a sheet of bubbly foam, her head against her bath pillow, and Freddy's bladed hand moves between her spread legs, we fear for the exceptional vulnerability of a posture associated with sex and childbirth. When the bathtub turns into a bottomless expanse of water—a bed with too much sink—and Nancy finds herself pulled into the deep, we also gasp. And in both cases, that fear is augmented by a primal connection between bubbles, beds, and a woman's body. Bed slashing, bath slashing, and body slashing are all forms of calling attention to the permeability or porosity of our spheres.

As immunity bubbles, the houses on Elm Street fail. The house, or the "shell of sleep," to use Sloterdijk's term, cannot protect its inhabitants from bad dreams. Even if the house is a place where "the skin-self is expanded into the bed-self—surrounded by a room-self in a house-self," the nesting-bubble myth must pop.[40] Freddy cuts through the house-self, the room-self, the bed-self, and the skin-self until all is foam. *A Nightmare on Elm Street* is a story about a crisis between bubbles and foams, a search for equilibrium as old structures pop. The reaction of Reaganite yuppies to the foaming of America is the adoption of antimattress mantras that could easily double as slogans to fight Freddy Kreuger: *Sleep is for the weak! The best don't rest! Sleep is the enemy of success!* According to the ethos of Generation Kreuger, the mattress is the enemy. A certain set of immunity sphere values (some might call them "family values") in the 1980s entwine with the mattress and the activities that do or do not take place on its foamy liminal padding. Sleep, like foam, undermines the solid, and the mattress embodies the fragility of foam both materially and metaphorically. After decades of sleep deprivation and an accompanying franchise of *Nightmare on Elm Street* films, Goldilocks is back with the promise of a perfect compromise, the sheeted dead are replaced by Casper the friendly mattress, and media mogul Arianna Huffington is fighting for *The Sleep Revolution*. Coexistence in cofragile, coisolated, centerless conglomerations is less frightening when the play of open and closed forms is seen no longer as the horror of bursting bubbles but rather as the flexible give and take of foam.

Sheet

Bubbles and foam describe essential qualities of a bed, whether the mattress hides layers of latex, steel coils, ill-gotten cash, hay, feathers, water, cotton, or user-regulated quantities of air. As a bubble, the bed forms an immunological sphere. As foam, a bed aerates the space allotted to sleep. Even a hammock shares the mission of injecting air into (or "foaming") our nocturnal hours. Humans have softened their contact with the solid ground since time immemorial. Germanic peoples slept on furs until the Romans invaded along with their beds. The Celts filled holes with leaves. For reasons unknown, the state bed in the Venetian Ambassador's Room at Knole is stuffed with lawyers' wigs.[41] Thanks to a 2011 dig in South Africa, we know that seventy thousand years ago, our ancestors slept on mats made of branches, sedges, rushes, and insect-repellant laurel leaves.[42] The geoarcheological discovery illustrates a quality of the bed beyond the protective bubble—namely, that a bed is sedimentary, that it is composed of strata, and that it interacts with the ground as much as it does with the air. The nesting-bubble image of skin-self to bed-self to room-self to house-self accounts for the atmospheric half of the picture but ignores the fact that a bed also interacts with the lithosphere, or in more current terms, the archaeosphere—the distinctive new layer of the planet generated by human activity. When we go to bed, we anticipate our inescapably embedded future in the archaeosphere, interred or cremated—earth to earth, ashes to ashes, dust to dust. Expressions such as sleeping "like a rock" or even "like the dead" draw the act of slumber toward the ground, while the compliment "it was like sleeping on a cloud" demonstrates a preference for atmospheric imagery when speaking of the sleep surface. In contemporary Western society, the prevalence of puffy white satin upholstery in caskets maintains an allusion to heavenly clouds, even if those clouds are destined to foam the earth from six feet under.

Horror conceptualizes the bed geospherically, always disrupting the balance between bounce and sink, always straining toward uncomfortable heights and depths. This chapter only begins to touch on the variations of strata that make a bed, and it could just as well have included pillows, quilts, duvets, non-Western beds, sleeping bags, cots, and other objects. The sleeper sofa chapter adds a split-personality bed to the mix but ignores many other devices designed for sleep. A lengthier consideration of the bed might treat the horrors of the space under a raised bed, but here, I will conclude with one very thin but highly significant layer of the bed: the sheet. *A Nightmare on Elm Street*, with its death by sheet and its Shakespearian references to the "sheeted dead," could have served just as well as sheet or as mattress horror, and indeed, the two components are intimately

Fig. 9.3. Michael Myers immobile among windblown sheets in *Halloween* (1978).

connected. For the sake of escaping Elm Street, however, I will close with the sleepy town settings in John Carpenter's *Halloween* (1978) and Alejandro Amenábar's *The Others* (2001).

Michael Myers unequivocally conflates the domestic bed and our final resting place in *Halloween* when he stages the body of murdered babysitter Annie Brackett in a cruciform pose on top of a bed, complete with a stolen headstone from his sister's grave as a grim stand-in for a headboard. Michael understands the world of the sheeted dead because he belongs there. As Murray Leeder has observed, Michael is a paradox not easily explained through the conventions of a single genre. He is an embodied entity, a psychopath mental asylum escapee, a serial killer, yet his behavior seems, at times, to defy the laws of the natural world. When Laurie (Jamie Lee Curtis) looks out her bedroom window and sees Michael standing motionless in the garden below between clotheslines of windblown sheets, he behaves like a ghostly apparition—there one moment, gone the next. The logic of the shot sequence is Gothic, directly modeled on the appearance and disappearance of Miss Jessel's ghost in *The Innocents* (1961).[43] Laurie stands frozen, her unbroken gaze fixed on the equally immobile figure of the there/not there Michael. Nothing moves but the sheets.

The supernatural aura of the film has sent some scholars searching for labels within Tzvetan Todorov's literary theories of the fantastic genre, which may, as Leeder remarks, be inadequate for discussing the film.[44] That inadequacy comes through in the recent reassessment of Todorov by French literature scholar Corry Cropper. The fantastic, argues Cropper, relies heavily on objects as significant actors, from animated statues to chairs, wigs, paperweights, and coffee pots, but Todorov's theory of the fantastic filters those objects uniquely through human subjects. Influenced by Immanuel Kant's belief that objects have no meaning outside of a perceiving human subject, Todorov takes one of the most object-centered literary genres and theorizes it in a way that minimizes any object-to-object interaction that does not include a human.[45] If Todorov fails to provide an adequate theoretical framework for horror films such as *Halloween*, it is because of his theory's insistence on privileging the human subject above all else. Films, of course, are made by and for humans, but that fact should not blind us to the nonhuman object actors in a film, even when those objects are not stealing the scene, even when they fall into the category that object-oriented philosopher Graham Harman calls "dormant objects," or objects that do not seem to be affecting anything.[46]

As still and as silent as a statue, Michael Myers lets objects speak in many of his appearances on screen. In the telephone chapter, for example, I argue that Michael allows telephony to speak for itself when he holds the receiver to his face and yet says nothing. In the scene where Michael stands among the clotheslines, the wind and the sheets animate each other, while the human figures maintain photographic stillness. Sheets (and elsewhere, curtains) allow the wind to express embodiment, to exist as an object, while the wind, in return, allows the sheet to exist as a thing that creates embodiment. Wind and sheet speak to the most fundamental elements of cinema: movement and screen.[47] These are moments when the psychology of the characters takes a secondary position or disappears altogether. Film loves fabric pushed by the wind just as it loves a thin sheet of cloth draped over a nude. Undulating fabric draws out the eroticism and sometimes the terror of loosely defined shapes.

Michael Myers has another name, as Leeder points out, one that appears separately in the closing credits: "The Shape." When Leeder asks Carpenter to explain the insistence on distinguishing Michael from the Shape, the director replies, "I wanted to bleach the humanity out of him. I wanted him to be nothing, just like a vessel onto which we could project things."[48] Michael, then, is not so different from the white sheets on the clothesline or the screen of a movie theater. He is at once form and absence. As such, Michael embodies a paradox that can never fully satisfy a psychological reading of the film. He has a bare-bones backstory (fleshed out in later films), limited to the opening scene in which, at age six, he murders his older sister. Otherwise, Sam Loomis (Donald Pleasance), Michael's psychologist and hence the most authoritative source of insight into his psyche, provides scant information, which, if anything, serves to "bleach" the humanity from Michael rather than provide psychological depth. Loomis informs a nurse that Michael has not spoken in fifteen years. Tellingly, Loomis refers to his patient as "it" rather than "him." Loomis explains to Sheriff Bracket that Michael has "no reason, no conscience, no understanding," not even "the most rudimentary sense of life or death." He describes the young Michael's face as "pale, blank, emotionless," with the blackest of eyes. Michael is already the sheeted dead.

In the scene of Lynda's murder, Michael enters the bedroom draped in a sheet with holes cut out for eyes, like a trick-or-treater from the 1966 television special, *It's the Great Pumpkin, Charlie Brown*.[49] Having just killed Lynda's boyfriend downstairs, Michael, or the Shape, appears in the doorway of the upstairs bedroom in his sheet-ghost disguise, minimalist to the point of excluding a mouth hole, but with the stylistic flourish of his victim's glasses. Lynda files her nails in bed. The Shape stands on the threshold and says nothing. Unnerved and exasperated, Lynda moves out of bed and picks up the phone to call Laurie. As Lynda looks out the window, the Shape moves toward her and then strangles her from behind with the phone cord. Lynda struggles against her attacker and grabs at the sheet, finally pulling it off the Shape as her lifeless body slumps to the floor. The sheeted Shape is once again the masked Michael Myers.

Lynda's death scene presents what Leeder identifies as the master paradox of the film: "The veneer of a ghost, the most disembodied of horror archetypes, conceals one of the most embodied, the serial killer."[50] The scene efficiently conveys the sheet's power to regulate eroticism and identity. The sheet makes the ghost, but it does not make the man. The unsheeted dead have identities, important backstories that must be put to rest, whereas the sheeted dead are all shell and no substance. The sheet is a layer that flattens all hierarchies and performs the same service for all things (the wind, a psychopath, the undead, a piece of furniture) no matter their psychological depth. The sheet bleaches not only humanity but also human-centered subjectivity.

Alejandro Amenábar's *The Others* shows that a sheet's power to neutralize identity is strong enough to frighten even a ghost. Under a sheet, forms become less distinct and consequently hold more power. An object under a sheet is not a blank slate but rather a poorly erased one. Thrown over furniture, sheets create ambiguous outlines. A coat rack covered by a

Fig. 9.4. Room of sheets in *The Others* (2001).

sheet is not readily identifiable as a coat rack. A chair under a sheet gives a general appearance of chair-ness, but placed on top of a table, the shrouded chair-table mass becomes a monstrous composite. A full-length mirror hidden under a sheet takes on the form of a broad-shouldered intruder. A wooden statue, no matter how realistically carved and painted, is never more human than when it hides under an opaque veil of fabric.

Darkness tends to increase the otherness of a draped object, but darkness is no prerequisite to sheet horror, as *The Others* demonstrates when protagonist Grace Stewart (Nicole Kidman) comes unglued in broad daylight amid a room crowded with sheet-cloaked furniture. After hearing noises, Grace enters the "junk room" with apprehension. She walks into the sea of sheeted objects, her head barely raised above their white peaks. She senses the rustling of another presence and hears the sounds of voices that seem to come from something hiding under the sheets. Grace moves wildly from object to object, ripping the sheets from a statue, a coat rack, a chair on a table, and a mirror. Unlike Michael Myers, Grace cannot stand still and let the sheets speak, because if she does so, those voices will make her acknowledge her similarity to the ghostly furniture all around her.

The big spoiler in *The Others* is broadly comparable to the well-known twist at the end of M. Night Shyamalan's *The Sixth Sense* (1999): ghost has epiphany concerning its undead status. In Amenábar's film, however, the revelation exceeds the knowledge of which side of the veil one occupies.

The plot hinges on "others" as a concept that can pivot suddenly from its outward-facing direction back toward one's own self. Grace and her children, presumably haunted by ghosts, turn out to be the ghosts that have been unwittingly haunting the new owners. The sheeted furniture scene amplifies otherness as a haunting that emanates from strata both above and beneath a veil of presence. In other words, the haunting works both ways. The others haunt the Stewarts, and the Stewarts haunt the others. While all signs point to a classic haunted-house story—isolation, disrepair, servants that harbor secrets, dark spaces lit by candle, creaks and groans, immaterial apparitions—*The Others* explores the fear of living under the sheet, of being the sheeted dead. Amenábar accomplishes an inversion of light and dark through Grace's belief that her children suffer from a potentially fatal "allergy" to light (erythropoietic protoporphyria). With light as the enemy, the Stewarts' entire home becomes subject to a perpetual cloaking between locked doors, behind drawn curtains, and in dim rooms. Metaphorically, Grace's photophobia shows her resistance to the truth. Philosophically, the inversion shows the similarity between the horror of sheets and the horror of darkness.

Grace instinctively represses any evidence of her inhumanity. She avoids the memory of smothering her children to death with pillows. Equally unwelcome and more philosophically complex is the recognition of Grace's *un*humanity—a term I adopt from philosopher Dylan Trigg.[51] The *un* in Trigg's *unhuman* alludes to the uncanny, described by Freud as "that class of the terrifying which leads back to something long known to us, once very familiar."[52] The "unhuman," for Trigg, is not about a repressed memory but rather "something that comes back to haunt the human without it fully being integrated into humanity." It is the horror "of experiencing oneself as other."[53] Like many philosophers who want to get beyond the human, Trigg relies on the wonderfully creepy vagueness of the words "there is" (*il y a*), as French philosopher Emmanuel Levinas explains. The *il y a* presents, in the words of Levinas, "a menace of pure and simple presence"—a "*horror of darkness*" that invades and swallows up objects (including humans) yet does not annihilate them.[54] Trigg calls this a "nocturnal ontology," a metaphysics that acknowledges being in a way that moves beyond personal ownership. Thus, even our "own" beings include something alien. Levinas describes unsettling otherness in his explanation of insomnia, claiming, "I do not stay awake: 'it' stays awake."[55] Whatever "it" is, therefore, lies beyond consciousness and beyond the human.

For Levinas and Trigg, the indefinable presence that seems to invade in darkness is a plane of existence we do not usually notice. As twilight falls, the lowered contrast between objects and that "other" presence makes "it" more evident. Amenábar performs the same allegorical gesture, but he does so through a perpetual veil of fog and fabric. The fog thickens the atmosphere, and the fabric shuts out light and softens forms. Nocturnal ontology is sheet ontology. Whether by cloak of darkness or cloak of sheet, the otherness of being cannot be made manifest without a veil. A linen-wrapped mummy, a shrouded body, a satin-lined coffin, a sheet draped over furniture or fitted to a mattress—all participate in an unhumanity that emanates from both sides of the veil. The sheet protects the things it envelops, making them all the more thinglike in the process. A sheet protects a mattress from the secretions of our bodies, letting us bleach away whatever traces of our own otherness we would rather not encounter. Sheets, like darkness, make manifest the other that lives among and inside us.

Although this chapter has touched on only three parts of a (Western) bed, the ontological stakes of sandwiching the self between foamed and sheeted strata should now be clear. Between the dyadic immunity bubble of the womb and the death shroud lies a series of beds with their associated rituals and rites of passage. To go to bed is to succumb to ontological flattening, to bleach humanity, to acknowledge the body as an "it" or a "shape" that hovers between atmosphere and archaeosphere. Joining the community of objects each night can be both reassuring and frightening. As I note in the introduction to this book, bedtime stories such as *Goodnight Moon* have enduring appeal in part because they acknowledge objects at the very moment when even the most anthropocentric among us must give up human exceptionalism. To hail each object at bedtime ("Goodnight bears / Goodnight chairs . . .") is to join forces with other objects as separate beings as if to assure ourselves that the fuzzy borders of darkness (the Levinasian *il y a* of pure presence) will not dissolve us even if we do, each night, become foam.

Notes

1. I have counted as "bed scene" each time a bed appears, in the same way a character in a play might exit and reenter the stage. The total, twenty-eight, does not include extra hospital or dorm room beds not related to the main characters.

2. Friedkin says that in combining images and events linked to Father Merrin, Damien Karras, and Regan MacNeil, he wanted to show "the symbiosis of dreams." See Kermode, 49.

3. Westerbeck, 532.

4. Jane Brody writes that throughout its first 52 years, the book was "the second-best-selling book, next to the Bible." Brody, "Final Advice from Dr. Spock: Eat Only All Your Vegetables," *New York Times*, June 20, 1998.

5. For more on the attacks on Spock in the media, see Maier, 320–28. Conservative websites into the twenty-first century continue to blame Spock for ruining America.

6. The 1968 edition, which I am using to reflect the edition a woman Chris MacNeil's age might have read, has a total of 806 points.

7. See Spock, 166–69.

8. See Lieberman, 231.

9. Burgess, 19.

10. Ibid., 22.

11. Brunner, 115.

12. See Tourn, 184–85.

13. Quoted in Travers and Reiff, 18.

14. Ibid., 30.

15. See Kermode, 15. By this, I am referring to Robbie's behavioral symptoms, not the movement of objects. Items other than the bed moved, including a desk at school, an armchair, a rocking chair, a breadboard, a kitchen table, and flying objects including a Bible, a coat on a hanger, an orange, and a pear. See Allen, 7–9.

16. Allen, 208; Kermode, 15.

17. See Halligan, Bass, and Marshall's edited volume for a medical overview of the study of hysteria.

18. Stone and Zeman, in Halligan, Bass, and Marshall, 102.

19. Baudrillard, 23.

20. Insofar as *The Exorcist* is concerned, and not the film's sequels.

21. See *American Home*'s June 1971 issue, page 35, for example.

22. "How to Use a Raw Egg to Determine if Your Mattress Is Awful—Purple Mattress," YouTube video, 3:58, posted by Purple, April 26, 2016, accessed October 4, 2018, https://www.youtube.com/watch?v=4BvwpjaGZCQ&t=68s.

23. Alyse Borkan, "Why Is Casper Winning So Many Awards?," *Casper the Blog*, October 11, 2016, http://blog.casper.com/why-is-casper-winning-so-many-awards/.

24. See Muir, 114.

25. Powell, 103.

26. Steve Biodrowski, "Wes Craven on Dreaming Up Nightmares," *Cinefantastique*, October 15, 2008, http://cinefantastiqueonline.com/2008/10/wes-craven-on-dreaming-up-nightmares/.

27. In *Visions of the Night*, Kelly Bulkeley remarks that coincidentally, Reagan's reelection theme, "It's Morning in America," was airing successful television ads the same year the *Nightmare* was frightening Americans in the theater. See Bulkeley, 110.

28. See Loadman, 204.

29. See Ciesielski, 213–22.

30. Laura, "Different Latex, Different 'Feel,'" *Savvy Rest Blog*, October 22, 2009, https://savvyrest.com/blog/different-latex-different-feel.

31. Sloterdijk, 28.
32. Ibid.
33. Ibid., 30.
34. Ibid., 831n4.
35. "Le non-moi qui protège le moi" (translation mine). Bachelard, 26.
36. See Heidegger, 361.
37. Sloterdijk, 137.
38. Ibid., 85.
39. Sloterdijk, 54.
40. Ibid., 504–5.
41. Willes, 8.
42. Brunner, 79.
43. Leeder, 46.
44. Ibid., 40.
45. See Cropper, 27.
46. See Harman, "Time, Space, Essence, and Eidos," 15.
47. On cinema as wind, see Thomas.
48. Leeder, 90.
49. For a nonhorror ghost film that uses the sheeted Charlie Brown–style ghost to very poignant effect, see *A Ghost Story* (2017).
50. Leeder, 52.
51. Trigg, *The Thing*, 5.
52. Freud, 123.
53. Trigg, "Horror of Darkness," 116.
54. Quoted in Trigg, *The Thing*, 50 (emphasis in original).
55. Ibid.

10

TYPEWRITER

On Reading "All Work and No Play Makes Jack a Dull Boy"

No object in Stanley Kubrick's *The Shining* (1980) proves too insignificant to merit exegetical treatment by fans and critics. The documentary *Room 237* (2012) has given a platform to theories hatched from cans of Calumet Baking Powder, gaudy carpet patterns, ski lodge posters, a child's sweater, and of course, the Adler Universal 39 on which Jack Torrance (Jack Nicholson) types his tortured magnum opus, *All Work and No Play Makes Jack a Dull Boy*. History professor and *Room 237* interviewee Geoffrey Cocks points to the Adler brand name (*Adler* means "eagle" in German) as evidence that the typewriter "refers to the SS extermination bureaucracy," while the forty-two-character sentence typed by Jack ostensibly evokes the year of Nazi Germany's genocidal Final Solution, making *The Shining* Kubrick's Holocaust film.[1] Michael Wysmierski's YouTube video "The Shining Code 2.0" notes that because Eagle was the name of the Apollo 11 lunar module, we are to conclude that the moon-colored Adler affirms Kubrick's directorial role in NASA's fake footage of the moon landing.[2] I dismiss those and other crypto-kubrological endeavors not for their logical acrobatics but for their decoder-ring approach to objects, which uses the things themselves only as a portal to the mind of the tyrannical "Author-God" figure that Roland Barthes imagined overthrowing in his 1967 essay "The Death of the Author."[3] For *The Shining* is precisely a film about the death of the author, a film about the author reduced to the "scriptor," as Barthes would say, or the author reduced to the typist in the case of Jack Torrance. Kubrick certainly understood that all meaning does not derive from the fount of the author's mind, and so I will appeal to that same authority I seek to decenter so that objects can be recognized as something more than ciphers.

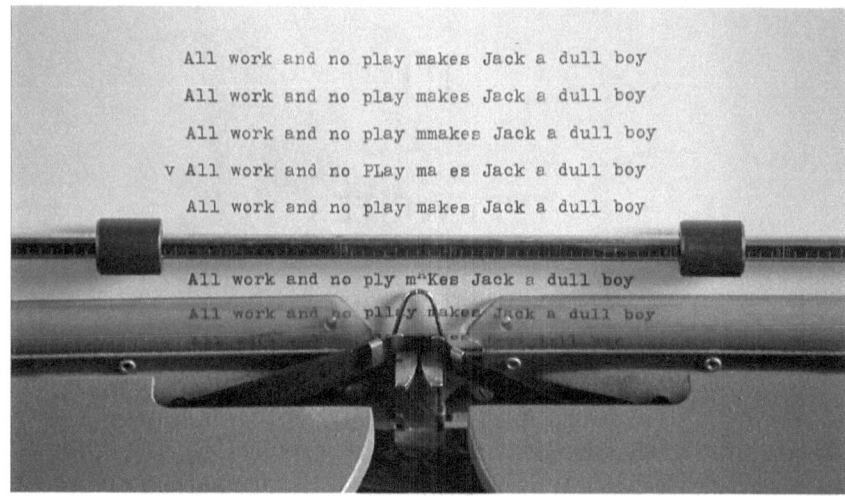

Fig. 10.1. Jack's work in progress in *The Shining* (1980).

One lesson that even the casual viewer can glean from Jack Torrance's favorite proverb is that one must be willing to engage in both work and play or else suffer the consequences. Therefore, I have playfully worked in preparing this chapter: I have pored over Jack's permutations of a single sentence, mapping out every typo as if piecing together the Da Vinci Code. I have reached out to a leading "typospherian" as my forensic oracle. I have performed and discarded experiments better left to high school English classes (prompt: interview a typewriter; prompt: pretend the poem "Paysage" by Guillaume Apollinaire inspired *The Shining*). Finally, I have flown to London to search the Kubrick Archive, not only to read Kubrick's notes, not only to stare blankly at the shorthand scrawled in June Randall's continuity notebooks, but most crucially to read thousands of pages of "All work and no play makes Jack a dull boy"—seven boxes and two loose envelopes, to be exact, including hundreds of pages in French, Spanish, German, and Italian—all in an effort to endure what Wendy Torrance (Shelley Duvall) could not: a thorough and ponderous reading of Jack Torrance's work taken on its own terms, as a coproduction of writer and typewriter, as a material recording of a series of typographic events whose meaning is not limited to conventional narrative. This approach will require a willingness to play along, to entertain meaning amid absurdity, to value form over content, and to consider shades of ink, alignment of letters, and depth of indentations, with attention to typographical error akin to Freudian appreciation of verbal slippage. Interpretive play facilitates appreciation for the work performed by a prop.

Assistant director Brian Cook recalls Kubrick's playful attitude toward the interpretive contributions of the film critic: "Stanley used to always say to me when we weren't sure what we were doing, 'We'll let the French critics tell us what this scene is supposed to be about.'"[4] And so we do the same for the famous typewriter scene, first with the help of Jean-Pierre Oudart, a critic for *Les cahiers du cinéma* at the time of *The Shining*'s release, and then through the work of Michel Ciment of the film magazine *Positif*. Ciment, the preeminent French Kubrick scholar, enjoyed access to Kubrick that the press-averse director granted to only a few, while Oudart is best known for his seminal work on suture theory (see chap. 7). Oudart's seven-page review fits the effusive cerebral *explication du texte* model that Kubrick expected from a French critic, and perhaps for that reason, it is rarely cited by Kubrick scholars. Those willing to navigate Oudart's labyrinthine prose will find the typewriter at its center. Unlike a conventional star-obsessed review, Oudart includes the performance of nonhuman characters. In the French critic's estimation, the film is about typewriters as weapons against language, as infernal machines that write characters—the monospaced characters of words that replace the musicality of language with machine-gun fire, and the human characters Jack and Wendy, torn apart by the machine's violence.

Oudart hyphenates the character names Jack and Wendy with the typewriter in subsections of his article: "*La machine à écrire-Jack*" and "*La machine à écrire-Wendy*"—hybrid formulations that convey a double meaning in French. *La machine à écrire-Jack* means "the typewriter-Jack" but also "the machine [designed] to write Jack."[5] Thus, Jack and Wendy are doubly implicated as participants in the machine's assault on language and as characters generated by the machine. For Oudart, Jack's nightmare about cutting his wife and son into pieces is an extension of the typewriter's "massacre of the sentence" (*massacre de la phrase*).[6] "The sentence" here can be taken both in the sense of the specific sentence that Jack types and in the general sense of "the sentence" as a set of words, or, for those familiar with Oudart's Lacanian leanings, as an enunciation that bifurcates the speaking (or in this case, typing) subject and reveals the inability of consciousness to control speech. "It is not the love of language that makes one write, but the terror of the murder perpetuated by writing," asserts the critic.[7] Jack's relentless assault on one sentence turns him into a "murderous paranoid machine, beyond the play [*jeu*] of words, beyond the sexual pleasure of language," while Wendy, too, is beyond words, hysterical and yet transfixed by the typewriter, by this "Other that kills her [*lui fait la peau*—literally, 'makes her skin' or 'skins' her] and angers her [*la met hors d'elle-même*—'puts her outside of herself']."[8] Oudart's choice of idiomatic expressions evokes destruction through separation brought on by the typed word. Wendy is beside herself as she stares at the machine that is tearing her family apart. Kubrick's genius, says Oudart, "consists of making writing, the machine of writing, into an object of terror" that functions as "the savage operator of the symbolic and sexual disjunctions of the couple."[9] Thus, the typewriter facilitates linguistic dismemberment and, taken to the extreme, threatens to extend that violence to the flesh. Jack's nightmare, after all, occurs when he falls asleep at his desk, his head at the base of his typewriter. The machine of writing is Jack's undoing.

Like Oudart, Michel Ciment puts language front and center in his reading of *The Shining*, or at least he seems to do so thanks to an epigraph by symbolist poet Arthur Rimbaud: "*Je est un autre*"—"I is someone else."[10] Rimbaud's famous subject-verb disagreement, as a concise expression of the conflict between the self and the written self-as-other, suggests an affinity between tortured writer Jack Torrance and the nineteenth-century poète maudit. Ciment does not pursue the relation between Rimbaud's declaration of split subjectivity and Jack's repeated typing of his own name but instead prefers to diagnose Jack in Freudian terms. He sees Jack's withdrawal from his family within the womb-like confines of the hotel as a "regressive involution" that cultivates narcissism.[11] Jack succumbs to violence because "he has proved incapable of sublimating his instincts by writing his novel."[12] Jack's failure, however, is Kubrick's success as it allows the director to reiterate at the elemental level of the nuclear family the breakdown of those who "live in closed, isolated worlds, like hermits in non-communicating cells"—the inherent problem of "air-tightness" that Ciment identifies in *Dr. Strangelove* (1964), *2001: A Space Odyssey* (1968), and *A Clockwork Orange* (1971).[13] Ciment calls *The Shining* one of Kubrick's most intimate works "because it's about an intellectual (a former teacher) who sees himself as an artist but can only type out one disturbing sentence *ad infinitum*."[14] One statement that Kubrick makes time and again, according to Ciment, is the expression of ambivalence toward technological mediation: "Kubrick's films reflect his perfectionism, his inordinate taste for technology, his fascination with diagrams and statistics, but also his fear of any flaw in a totally programmed system, of an excessive dependence on machines."[15] If we add *The Shining* to the likes of *Dr. Strangelove*, Jack's "All work and no play" suddenly makes sense as the "Yee-haw!" of the head of a nuclear family riding toward technologically facilitated annihilation.

As Kubrick might have expected, the French critics come through with a deeply theoretical explanation of what Jack and his typewriter mean, something that turns *The Shining* into the director's intensely personal reflection on the impulse to produce art through tools (the typewriter, language) that threaten to turn against those who wield them. Reading Ciment, in particular, one begins to see Kubrick as a double of Jack, as a man with a movie camera who has succeeded where Jack and his typewriter have failed. Kubrick's reputation for repeated takes of a single scene certainly invites comparison with Jack's approach to writing. Moreover, Kubrick's harsh treatment of Shelley Duvall doubles Jack's abuse of Wendy. The infamous Guinness World Record–setting 127 takes of a scene in which Duvall had to maintain a state of hysteria enacts on the performer the same traumatic encounter with repetition that terrifies Wendy upon discovering the "All work and no play" typescript. Coincidentally, that notorious scene follows Wendy's discovery of the stack of Jack's typed pages. And so Jack's repetition terrifies Wendy while Kubrick's repetition terrifies Shelley—twin horror that seems to play out forever and ever and ever. In a rather sad rationalization of the pitiless retakes, Duvall recalls, "I remember being yelled at a lot, but in the end he got my best performance!"[16] Wendy would not have said the same about Jack.

Kubrick scholar Catriona McAvoy has attempted to rehabilitate the director's reputation by demonstrating his flexibility and open-mindedness with cowriter Diane Johnson and other collaborators, but McAvoy's defense of his process faces the obstacle of daughter Vivian Kubrick's making-of documentary, which casts an unblinking eye on the director's unsympathetic treatment of an exhausted, demoralized Duvall.[17] Vivian's film provides cinema verité corroboration of the conflation of Jack and Stanley as cohort tormentors of Wendy/Shelley. Duvall therefore becomes the living embodiment of a split subject terrorized by typescripts. Filmed evidence notwithstanding, McAvoy is right to question the director-as-tyrant rhetoric, given Stanley Kubrick's own hand in fashioning his persona in the final edit of Vivian's film. Music supervisor and assistant editor Gordon Stainforth maintains that Kubrick himself insisted on cutting two sequences

Fig. 10.2. The Adler Universal 39 typewriter in *The Shining* (1980).

that showed him "in a rather warm light" instead of "that kind of aggressive light that has been rumored."[18]

Another point of convergence between Stanley Kubrick and Jack Torrance is the Adler typewriter, which may have been Kubrick's personal machine. Theories abound about the provenance and significance of the Adler Universal 39 seen in the film. Every detail fuels speculation about possible hidden messages from Kubrick. Close readings of *The Shining* argue that deep meaning lies in the Adler brand name, the typewriter's color change from lighter to darker gray, and various anomalies with the typed pages in the film, including nonsensical positioning of paper in the platen and pages that are there one moment and gone the next. Author Bev Vincent adopts the "near-heretical position" that the film is teeming with "continuity errors and mistakes in logic."[19] If one believes Kubrick infallible, argues Vincent, those errors are mistaken for hidden messages—a phenomenon director John August calls the "genius fallacy."[20] Vincent's fallibility argument makes sense in the same way that the proliferation of typos makes sense in Jack's numbing repetition of the same sentence. Excessive repetition breeds error. Or is it practice makes perfect?

Here, the paths diverge between Jack Torrance and Stanley Kubrick, for Jack had no second set of eyes, much less a team at his disposal. Stainforth argues that June Randall, who had worked on continuity with Kubrick for years, would never have overlooked so many errors. Therefore, Stainforth concludes, the supposed continuity errors were probably "Stanley having a bit of fun in the film."[21] Having attempted to read June Randall's seven notebooks of recorded shots ("attempted" because the notes are a mixture of longhand, shorthand, and the occasional doodle of a chrysanthemum), I am inclined to agree with Stainforth about Randall's competence even while endorsing Vincent's point that not every detail is part of a hidden code from a genius auteur to the discerning fan.[22] Intentional or not, disruptions to continuity have become integral to the media text. The same could be said of Jack's typos. If "all work and no play" changes to "all work and no lay," if "a dull boy" changes to "adult boy" or "Jack" to "Hack," "work" to "worm" or "boy" to "bot," those transmutations harbor meaning whether present by slip of the finger or by sly authorial intent.

While no one knows completely what Kubrick was thinking (or Jack, for that matter), the Adler Universal 39 typewriter's role on both sides of the camera is worth pursuing, both to clear up confusion in Kubrick scholarship and, more crucially, to consider the nuance that a prop brings to its performance. Vincent says the typewriter was "Kubrick's own personal machine," which, if true, makes it the perfect point of convergence for Jack Torrance and Stanley Kubrick as mirror images.[23] Kubrick's personal assistant, Leon Vitali, supports that claim in a *New York Times* interview but downplays any deeper meaning: "That was Stanley's typewriter . . . a lot of the decisions made on the set were about pragmatism."[24] Vivian Kubrick's making-of documentary shows her father typing, but on a bright-yellow portable Tippa-S (an Adler, but not remotely similar to the Universal 39 model). Further confusing matters, Kubrick's biographer, John Baxter, paints the director as a technophile and early adopter of machines far more advanced than either of the two manual Adler typewriters: "Fascinated as ever by new technology, Kubrick owned one of the first electric typewriters to include computer memory." According to Baxter, "Kubrick used the computerised typewriter to produce the five hundred pages of manuscript which fill the box on Jack's table."[25]

Faced with the conflicting reports, I asked Richard Polt, philosophy professor and author of *The Typewriter Revolution*, to hazard a guess as to what "computerised typewriter" Kubrick might have been using and whether that machine could have produced the "All work and no play" pages. Conceivably, Polt told me, Kubrick could have purchased one of the first electronic typewriters such as the Olivetti ET 101 or the Exxon Qyx, both released in 1978, but those machines could not have typed the pages in

The Shining. Telltale impression irregularities point to a manual typewriter, where the human hand determines the force with which the typeslug strikes the ribbon and pushes ink onto paper. Jack's typing is riddled with the traces of keys hit with too much or too little force. But why should we care? Arguably, this line of inquiry might seem better suited to a subreddit debate. I pursue it here nevertheless if for no other reason than to suggest that attention to the typewriter behind the "All work and no play" pages is no less warranted than attention to Kubrick's use of music by Bartók and Penderecki in the film. The details of a prop can say as much about a media text as the choice of lenses, film stock, actors, or music, especially when that prop has worked on both sides of the camera.

As an instrument, a manual typewriter is more musically expressive than an electric typewriter because it is sensitive to variation based on the user's touch. Author Kingsley Amis, a devoted user of "an Adler office model of the acoustic (i.e. non-electrical) sort" (the same used by Jack Torrance), eschewed word processors and stuck to his "alphabet piano" for decades because of its musicality.[26] Extending Amis's acoustic metaphor, we might consider how the sonic qualities of the audible strikes are recorded onto paper with each thrust of the typeslug that hits the inked ribbon. The effect of pressure applied to the keys of the "acoustic sort" of typewriter differs from identical pressure on the electric sort in a manner analogous to the dynamics of a piano compared to those of a harpsichord. The manual typewriter responds to harder and softer keystrokes with louder (darker) and quieter (lighter) and sometimes inaudible (blank) letter impressions. The electric typewriter, in contrast, either registers the strike or does not. There is no in between.[27] Jack's typescript bears the marks of his uncontrolled pressure. Considered as a recording of a musical performance, the "All work and no play" papers have the dynamic characteristics of a piano, not the rationality of a harpsichord—manual, not electric.

As to whether the Adler brand was merely a pragmatic choice, as Vitali suggests, or one harboring double meaning (as if both could not be true), those in the latter camp may gain vindication from Kubrick's handwritten notes during development. In all caps in the margins of chapter 26 of Stephen King's novel, Kubrick lists "JACK QUESTIONS" including "DOES HE HAVE A TYPE-WRITER? WHAT KIND"?[28] At minimum, "What kind?" suggests attentiveness to manual versus electric, possibly even brand. Kubrick's annotations also show that the director considered foregoing the typewriter altogether. On another page, Kubrick writes, "Could Jack write in long hand instead of typing. Writers in movies always type!!"[29] But Kubrick embraced the trope, turning Jack into a failed version of the heroic man-and-his-typewriter figure—Jack as a Hemingway manqué, drinking alongside the ghosts of the 1920s as if living in the glory days of Montparnasse, or Jack as a would-be Kerouac, were it not for domestic responsibilities and all that snow blocking the road. Instead, he types the same sentence over and over in the Colorado Lounge, his "acoustic" typewriter facing a piano—an instrument that loses concert-hall glory in a hotel-lounge setting where tip jars too often dictate a numbing repetition of the same old songs. *Play it again, Sam. Type it again, Jack.* Is that what the scene is about? Someone fetch a French film critic.

It's better to stick with the knowable answers to Kubrick's questions. First question: "Does Jack have a typewriter?" Answer: Yes. And that choice results in a particular percussive force. The typewriter does not inscribe; it pummels. It is, in the words of media scholar Friedrich Kittler, "a discursive machine-gun. A technology whose basic action not coincidentally consists of strikes and triggers proceeds in automated and discrete steps, as does ammunition transport in a revolver and a machine-gun, or celluloid transport in a film projector."[30] Hemingway praised the machine's "mechanical staccato" as a mitrailleuse in the "infantry of the mind."[31] Kubrick's choice to enlist the typewriter plays into a long-standing association between typing and weaponry—one, in fact, also present in the novel, where King describes Wendy listening to Jack work: "It was like listening to machine-gun fire from an isolated pillbox. The sound was music to her ears."[32] However violent the sound, there is pleasure in hearing thought exit the mind in open fire onto a blank page. Second question: "What kind?" Answer: Manual, with its accompanying acoustic qualities—the alphabet piano, not the alphabet harpsichord; Bartók, not Bach. Jack's mental breakdown registers more powerfully through the expressive qualities of a manual machine.

The fusion of mechanical assault and mental breakdown recorded on Jack's typed pages is instantly discernable. The printed pages are as jarring and dissonant to the eye as the overlapping pieces by Penderecki that Stainforth layered into the "All work and no play" scene are to the ear.[33] Jack's "massacre of the sentence," so to speak, is not an efficient, clinical execution but a case of overkill full of misfires, a sloppy, graphic butchering as disturbing as Grady's hatchet job on his family. Grady euphemizes infanticide as editing in the same way Faulkner famously euphemizes editing as infanticide with the injunction (taken up and amplified by Stephen King) "Kill your darlings." "But I *corrected* them, sir," says Grady to Jack, letting him understand that to do his job well, he will have to kill his darlings. Grady's "correction" of his family was, as Ullman tells it, both messy and neat: "He ran amok and, eh . . . killed his family with an axe" but then "stacked them neatly in the West Wing." Jack's massacre of the sentence is a disturbing combination of messy and neat. The mechanized action of typeslug striking paper that Oudart finds so destructive to poetic fluidity (all work and no play) is countered by Jack's unsteady hand. The horror of precision overlaps with the horror of imprecision in the pages that put Wendy in hysterics in front of the typewriter. Worth considering is how the scene would play using alternative writing technologies. Imagine instead a William Blake or Curt Cobain–style journal, or the mixed-media Mead notebooks of John Doe in David Fincher's *Se7en* (1995)—too much craft and no sense of Kubrick's beloved technological breakdown.[34] Or consider an electric typewriter, an electronic typewriter, or worse still, a computer—too little human touch.[35] *The Shining* is a manual typewriter film, a monospace film, a film full of typos.

Prolific film scholar Robert Kolker rightly argues that the voice of type is easily ignored in film criticism. He chastens critics of *2001: A Space Odyssey* for having noticed the film's minimal dialogue but having failed to see "just how much language, via print, computer graphics, mathematical formulas, and configurations, does in fact appear."[36] "2001 is a Helvetica film," says Kolker.[37] "Helvetica," he explains, "is the typeface of the modern age and has achieved the status of having a meaning beyond what the words formed by it have to say."[38] Kolker refers to the people on the space mission as "sans-serif figures" and goes so far as to call the monolith a "dark version of a Helvetica character."[39] Surprisingly, Kolker's remarks exemplify the blind spot they seek to address. *2001* is not a Helvetica film; it is a Gill Sans film, an Albertus film, a Eurostile (or Microgamma), Manifold, Spartan, Univers, and Futura film.[40] There is no Helvetica in *2001*. Unfortunately, Kolker's mistaken type identity seems to indicate that we are still at a stage of film scholarship where all sans serif typefaces look alike.

To find Helvetica—the typeface that Kolker sees as an "ideological event," an emblem of sanitized, orderly modernity—Kolker could have looked instead to *The Shining*, which he dismisses as a "broad, loud, perfectly unsubtle film" and an unfrightening "parody of the horror genre."[41] Just as silence distracted critics from type in *2001*, noise seems to have deafened Kolker's ears to its voice in *The Shining*, where Helvetica makes an effective counterpoint to the standard pica typeface of Jack's Adler. Helvetica, a clinical, neutral typographic voice associated with corporate and governmental identities, appears in the opening credits, the end credits, and the title cards that break *The Shining* into sections.[42] Helvetica hovers in God's-eye omniscience as it scrolls across the opening helicopter shots of the Torrance family Volkswagen's serpentine ascent toward the Overlook Hotel. With each subsequent appearance in the title cards, Helvetica asserts an external, neutral voice in opposition to Jack's tempestuous typing and skewed point of view. Not only do the Helvetica title cards ("The Interview," "Closing Day," "A Month Later," "Tuesday," "Thursday," "Saturday," "Monday," "Wednesday," "8 a.m.," and "4 p.m.") progressively compress and intensify time, they also reassert the same God's-eye view that lends an ominous sense of dread to the opening drive. The story of the Torrance family is not authored by Jack but rather overseen by external forces that toy with narrative and temporal logic. *The Shining* is a Helvetica film closing in on the man with a typewriter who thought that he could occupy the Author-God role, a man who seems poised to do so as he gazes above the model hedge maze inside the hotel but who dies frozen outside in the real one. The Helvetica type and Jack's type, like Stanley and Jack as authors, contrast views of what it means to overlook. Consider the first few definitions of "overlook" as a verb in the *Oxford English Dictionary*: "1. To look upon from above; to survey; to view openly. 2. To look down on; to despise; to treat with contempt, to slight. 3. To look (a thing) over or through; to examine, scrutinize, inspect; to peruse, read through. 4. To fail to see or observe; to pass over without noticing; to leave out of consideration, disregard, ignore."[43] Helvetica as used in *The Shining* surveys, reads through, flips through the story with increasing speed like Wendy viewing the typed pages. We might even see Helvetica's affective stance perhaps not as contempt but as indifference insofar as it depersonalizes the drama and denies intimacy. Jack and his typewriter "overlook" in the sense of disregard or failure to see. They specialize in manifesting error and malfunction.

We might be tempted to see Jack's repetitive writing as the equivalent of the HAL 9000 singing "Daisy Bell (Bicycle Built for Two)" in *2001: A Space Odyssey*, in which case Jack is the party heading toward breakdown and eventual deactivation, the loser in the battle of man and machine. After all, Jack, like HAL, decides that to murder the crew is the best way to fulfill his mission. The comparison works to a point, but while the sentient computer reverts to its first song as a dying breath, Jack's tireless typing produces text that accumulates meaning despite its limited lexicon. As Frederic Jameson observes, "Whether the Jack Nicholson character can write or not, he certainly *does* write, as the most electrifying moment of the film testifies; he unquestionably produces 'du texte,' as the post-structuralists put it (even if you are tempted to recall Truman Capote's comment about *On the Road*—'that's not writing, that's typing!')."[44] Jameson hints at an important proposition—that we read the work as text for its own sake—but he moves straight to the words themselves and concludes that this is "a text about *work*" and "the impossibility of cultural or literary production."[45] Jameson's interest in the conditions of late capitalism pulls focus away from the idea of "text" wherein the typed page, to repurpose Kolker's statement on Helvetica, achieves "the status of having a meaning beyond what the words formed by it have to say."[46] True, "All work and no play makes Jack a dull boy" is a statement about work (and its antithesis), but ad infinitum repetition turns the words into filler text like the *lorem ipsum* used by graphic designers to play with layout before inserting the real text. Jack is not a conventional author; he is a dummy-text generator who explicates the forms of typewritten language.

Kubrick's Jack Torrance is "outlining a new writing project," as Jack tells Ullman, but he never explains what that means. In King's novel, Jack writes a play called *The Little School* and gets angry at the direction the work is taking in act 5. Preproduction notes from October 1977 indicate that Kubrick's intent to follow the Jack-as-playwright path was short-lived. Scene treatments by Kubrick describe Wendy discovering page after page of "All work and no play makes Jack a dull boy" on scattered sheets of the manuscript that she has thrown on the floor in anger.[47] The short paragraph explaining the scene does not include details about the forms each page would take, and unfortunately, whatever instructions Kubrick gave to his secretary, Margaret Adams, who tirelessly typed the pages seen in the film, remain a mystery.[48] Second unit director Greg MacGillivray recalls, "I went up to [Adams] once and said, 'Why don't you just Xerox that?' She looked at me, 'Nope. Piece of paper #1 is different than paper #2. We'll never know when Jack has been working on it and when he's stopped for a break and then picked up and started working on it again. Stanley wants forty pages of this style.'"[49] The truth is, the reams of pages include both hand-typed and photocopied pages—a fact easily discerned in the archive by flipping the paper over to see the embossing caused by the force of the typeslug. Even so, Adams typed more than the ream seen in the film given the number of reams held in the archive and the number of sheets destroyed and replaced in the process of shooting. Based on MacGillivray's recollection, Kubrick had fairly specific ideas about the kinds of text Jack Torrance would produce.

The text Wendy sees begins with an already-complete page spooled in the platen—a double-spaced version of utmost simplicity, with one sentence per line and no punctuation. Atop the ream of paper on the desk lies a single-spaced page of six paragraphs of oppressively dense text that pushes uncomfortably into the margins. She begins to flip through the stack, which includes other pages similar to the first but with erratic punctuation and more typos. Spacing and indentation lose consistency; other pages appear formatted with indented, short, centered, stanza-like groupings that give the appearance of a research paper or a work of prose interspersed with poetry. The most striking variation is a subtractive version of the proverb where the removal of one word from the front with each successive line creates an axe-shape that can be read horizontally or diagonally downward, always leading toward the word *boy* at the opposite points and along the edge of the blade. Coincidentally, the form is identical to an early Greek figure poem (a form known as *technopaegina*) called "Axe."[50] The experimental form of Jack's "Axe" text also recalls the concrete poetry movement that flourished internationally in the 1950s–1970s, the "golden age of the typewriter," according to graphic designer Barrie Tullett.[51]

Pages not seen in the film include text with chevron zigzags, text formed into columns of one or multiple words, text that exploits tabs, text grouped into stanzas or paragraphs, text perfectly justified and neat, and text that overlaps and wavers as if the user had tugged at the paper rather than let the machine guide it. In addition to the English pages, versions with proverbs in French, German, Spanish, and Italian, likely typed by other people, were used in the theatrical releases for those languages (but not in foreign DVD copies, to my knowledge), each with idiosyncratic patterns and errors.[52] One of the Italian pages (*Il mattino ha l'oro in bocca*—"The morning has gold in its mouth") has the most whimsical variation, patterned into the form of an airplane or a bird in flight. The Italian also uses the highest number of exclamation marks. The French (*Un "Tiens" vaut mieux que deux "Tu l'auras"*—equivalent to "A bird in the hand is worth two in the bush"), because it contains dialogue within the proverb, plays extensively with quotation marks, sometimes stacking six to each side. The French also employs ellipses to create a stuttering effect (*v . . . v . . . vaut m . . . mieux que deux*

"Tu l . . . l . . . l'auras," etc.). The Spanish (*No por mucho madrugar amanece más temprano*—roughly, "No matter how early you get up, you can't make the sun rise any sooner") has a high percentage of stiflingly small margins and frequently mixes numbers with letters. The German (*Was du heute kannst besorgen, das verschiebe nicht auf morgen*—"Never put off until tomorrow what you can do today") has a very high amount of words overwritten with XXXXX, giving the text the appearance of a redacted document.

Jack's filler text communicates genre through layout and demands that the reader consider how visual authority operates within the typographic grid independently of the words on the page. The multiplicity of forms so overwhelms the redundancy of the content that the architecture of the typed page speaks instead. "All work and no play makes Jack a dull boy" alternately signals dense prose, scholarly research, tables, lists, and poetry—a chorus of voices. Jack's magnum opus shows what the urtext of the typed word as a musical score for horror might look like, how punctuation comes alive through typos, how the insertion of commas midword creates a sensation of panting, how quotes nested five pairs deep create a mise en abyme, or how the removal of space between words (allworkandnoplaymakesjackadullboy) makes one realize that the space bar, the largest key but the most overlooked figure of punctuation, governs the flow of air and grants or denies breath to the text at will. A look at the axe-shaped subtractive poem—which exists in the archives in two versions, one all lower case and one all caps—might be an entry point into a deeper discussion of hierarchical and relational status of the upper- and lowercase letters that appear in countless variations. Errors specific to slips of the hand, a light touch or a violent one; errors specific to mechanical malfunction, to keys that stick or refuse to respond, to paper that does not advance—all of those details are ways in which type and the typewriter communicate even when the author seems unable to say anything. The effect of so much typing with so little narrative is horrifying, overwhelming, too much and too little to read, an empty structure full of ghosts.

Misery's Typewriter

Another hack writer snowbound in Colorado with a woman he'd like to kill, another typewriter embroiled in violent conflict over a typescript without end—*Misery* (1990), directed by Rob Reiner and adapted by William Goldman from Stephen King's 1987 novel, has no haunted structure like *The Shining*'s Overlook Hotel, but the film shares a central preoccupation with typographic dysfunction and the problem of eternal return. *Misery*'s protagonist, Paul Sheldon (James Caan), is trapped by his own success as the creator of Misery Chastain, heroine of a Victorian-era series of bodice-ripper romance novels. Paul would like nothing more than to kill the woman who, as his literary agent reminds him, put braces on his daughter's teeth, is putting her through college, and bought him two houses and floor seats to the Knicks. And so he does. As he explains to his "number-one fan," Annie Wilkes (Kathy Bates), women often died in childbirth in 1871. Besides, "Misery's spirit is still alive"—a glib response that only enrages Annie. But all is not lost. As luck (or careful planning) would have it, Annie holds Paul captive in her remote country house. After prying Paul from his overturned car and breathing life into him during a snowstorm, Annie now has the power to do with Paul what she will. Unable to walk or call for help, Paul must type his way back to Annie's good graces on a defective Royal 10 typewriter—a sturdy "fifty-pound clunker" that Annie says she got for a great price "on account of it's missing an *n*." Paul's job is to resurrect the Victorian heroine by writing *Misery's Return*—a masterpiece that Annie proposes be dedicated to her for nursing Paul back to health. *Misery*, like *The Shining*, considers both the musicality and the violence of type through a writing project as torturously Sisyphean to Paul as "All work and no play" is to Jack or Wendy Torrance. *Misery*'s typewriter complicates the emancipatory narrative often associated with the machine's invention and dramatizes the paradoxical coexistence of feminine and masculine tropes associated with its use.

Given Annie's volatile nature and her oscillation between caring for and threatening Paul, it is not difficult to see the captor as a castrating mother figure.[53] "I feed you, I clean you, I dress you. And what thanks do I get?" yells Annie. "You just better start showing me a little more appreciation around here, Mister Man." In some way, all of the women in Paul's life, Misery Chastain included, make similar demands. As Paul's agent, Marcia Sindell (Lauren Bacall), says, Misery Chastain is responsible for caring for Paul's daughter, "and what thanks does she get? You go and kill her." Even though Marcia manipulates Paul with finesse, she is ultimately a surrogate for his fan base. Even when Paul has triumphed in the end, having killed Annie and Misery, at last having published a book without a picture on the cover, Marcia cannot help but ask Paul to bring Misery (and Annie) back to life. Over lunch, as Marcia proposes the idea of a book about the ordeal,

Annie reappears on the face of the woman pushing a dessert trolley toward their table—another number-one fan with a tray of food and a large knife in her hand. Better food, nicer digs, same story.

Not one for subtlety, King characterizes typing as autoerotic sublimation: "You beat a typewriter instead of your meat."[54] Paul's survival depends on his ability to channel his energies through the keyboard, to become Misery, to play the Scheherazade to Annie's Shahryar. King's novel makes that comparison explicit, as Paul reflects, "Yes, he supposed he had been his own Scheherazade, just as he was his own dream-woman," in his masturbatory fantasies.[55] Paul owes his success as a writer to his ability to transmute storytelling practices born of masturbation into something that endlessly defers climax. Scheherazade, who forestalls death through serial storytelling, is the prototype for the serial novelist or the screenwriters of Annie's beloved childhood cliffhangers (or "chapter plays" as she calls them). Paul's success has depended on his ability to maintain narrative stamina in order to please women, but he cannot do so without playing a woman whom he can never truly finish off, for Misery is Paul's Scheherazade. Thus, the painfully formulaic plot twist that resurrects Misery on the clunky Royal is inseparable from social advancement—just as Scheherazade becomes queen and saves her own life through seriality, *Misery's Return* begins, to Annie's delight, with the surprise revelation of Misery's nobility. Paul is king (Shahryar and Stephen) and queen. His life depends on the coexistence of the demanding reader and the seductive storyteller. Paul cannot "Jack (Torrance) off" alone in his room all day, for Annie will not abide so much uselessly spilled ink. Jack's typescript is type for type's sake, but Paul Sheldon serves at the pleasure of Annie Wilkes.

The typewriter complicates the pen-penis metaphor that has no doubt existed for as long as phallus-shaped writing implements have been placed in the hands of bored juvenile scribes. While the pen is naturally prone to comparisons with male genitalia, the typewriter, first marketed as the "machine to supersede the pen," does not so readily accommodate sexual euphemisms.[56] The pen maintained its totemic virility (and continues to do so, if the luxury pen industry is any indicator) while the typewriter became a machine to prevent "pen paralysis."[57] E. Remington and Sons, makers of both firearms and sewing machines, manufactured the Sholes and Glidden typewriter beginning in 1873 (later renamed the Remington No. 1) and aimed the machine initially at the male consumer, often exploiting the fear of "pen paralysis" in their advertising. Pen paralysis, a term that refers to both writer's cramp and writer's block, represented a threat to the chief measure of a man: his productivity. A Remington trade catalogue from 1875 boasts, "No fear of pen paralysis, loss of sight, or curvature of the spine from using the machine."[58] In 1878, *The Type-Writer Magazine* includes a scare piece about a lawyer who might have saved his hand, "now rendered nearly useless" by pen paralysis, if only he had adopted the typewriter years ago.[59] A letter recommending the typewriter as a gift claims the machine will help a man "lengthen his life of usefulness many years."[60] For what good is a man who can no longer wield his pen?

Pen paralysis was of sufficient concern to merit a paper at the New York State Stenographer's Association in 1881. Mr. Slocum, who reports on his three years studying the matter, paints a sad picture of the condition "when the arm refuses to mark the orders of the mind," a condition to which he, "as nearly a perfect specimen of ambidextrousness as you can find," has nevertheless fallen prey from time to time.[61] As late as 1915, advertisements aimed at men were still playing up the fear of pen paralysis: "Pen Paralysis! Have you got it?" asks Remington in the *Journal of the United States Artillery*. "No, we do not mean merely paralysis of the fingers. We mean another kind of paralysis far more serious, the kind that paralyzes the pen writer—not sometimes, but *always*." Pen writing, the ad copy continues, creates needless waste that handicaps a man's time and labor, "a handicap which means partial paralysis of all his energies."[62] The implication in pen paralysis fearmongering is never that the typewriter represents virility but rather that it helps preserve a manly grip by preventing pointless expenditure of a man's energy.

The typewriter does not supersede the pen in phallic potency. Despite the ballistic assault of typeslugs waging alphabetic war on the blank page, comparisons with the tame, domesticated sewing machine are more relevant than weaponry metaphors, at least initially. The typewriter emerged from the same production facilities as the sewing machine, and like the sewing machine, it promised speed and mechanization to protect tired hands. And yet the differences in reception of the two devices show that design and advertising alone cannot dictate the terms of our relationship with a technological product. As the sewing machine chapter in this book explains, the "iron sartor" was initially marketed to and opposed by the "knights of the needle"—male tailors who saw in the machine a competitor to their craft.[63] The bellicose medieval imagery adopted by the press makes the needle a lance and the sewing machine a formidable iron foe, more rival than asset. The sewing machine achieved success only after proposing itself instead as a replacement for women's work, either in the guise of the gallant companion to the overburdened seamstress or in the role of "Iron Needle-Woman," a sort of Stepford-wife mechanical servant that never complains and that outperforms and replaces its flesh-and-blood counterpart. On the surface, everything about the typewriter follows the same pattern as the sewing machine. The early mass-marketed typewriters even had the appearance of sewing machines, the same black Japan enamel with floral ornamentation, the same iron stands, and a treadle for the carriage return—a design analogy quickly abandoned. Typewriters, in other words, were poised to enter homes in the Trojan horse of the iron sartor. As the 1874 Sholes and Glidden sales pamphlet states, "The Type-Writer, in size and appearance, resembles the family sewing machine. Its appearance is graceful and ornamental, making it a beautiful piece of furniture for any office, study, or parlor."[64] And yet its socialization in the home was a failure compared to that of the sewing machine.

The office was a different story. There, the simultaneous acceptance of typewriters and women coincided to the point of a creating misleading conflation of woman and machine. No historian can resist mentioning that the word *typewriter* once referred to either the machine or the woman hired to use it—another mechanical bride for industrial man. Kittler is only slightly exaggerating when he writes, "Prior to the invention of the typewriter, all poets, secretaries, and typesetters were of the same sex."[65] The percentage of women stenographers and typists in the United States skyrocketed from 4.5 percent in 1870 to 95.6 percent in 1930.[66] By 1890, less than two decades after the early Sholes and Glidden machines, 60 percent of all typing and stenography jobs were held by women.[67] This had to have come as a shock to the fraternity of stenographers in New York who, just nine years earlier, had invited Miss Jeannette Ballantyne to present a paper (just before Slocum's report on pen paralysis) on "Ladies as Law Stenographers"—a novel idea at the time. After explaining to the men why she has taken the liberty to change "Ladies" to "Women" in her assigned title, Miss Ballantyne talks about the challenges faced by women in the workplace.[68] Nowhere does Ballantyne suggest that the typewriter was her gateway to the workplace. Instead, she credits persistence and access to education.[69]

The gender of secretaries underwent a radical shift after the invention of the typewriter, but the causal connection is often overstated. Historian Margery W. Davies's study of women and office work from 1870 to 1930 brings a broader context to that claim, one that includes changes in the structure of capitalism in the United States after the Civil War. The expansion of firms and increase in paperwork and correspondence resulted in more offices and a need for more clerical workers. Literacy was the basic skill required for clerical work, and more women than ever were graduating high school (more than men, in fact).[70] If anything, the typewriter facilitated the transition of women into the office due to the machine's lack of a gender. The argument that women were naturally suited to the typewriter thanks to superior dexterity came after women were already working as typists.[71] *The Story of the Typewriter*, published in 1923 for the fiftieth anniversary of the typewriter, includes a frontispiece entitled "Emancipation" and heralds (with angelic figures no less) Sholes as the man who changed women's lives, but the emancipatory narrative is best viewed as an attempt to co-opt social and economic change after the fact.[72] The truth is, typewriter or no typewriter, women were typically assigned the most routinized tasks in the office.[73]

Kittler, who is quick to repeat the cum hoc fallacy that the typewriter is behind gender diversification in writing, secretarial work, and typesetting, not long thereafter credits typeface with the disappearance of "bipolar sexual differentiation."[74] Simply put, typed words are desexualized words. "Mechanized and automatic writing refutes the phallocentrism of classical pens," says Kittler.[75] Type replaces the steady flow of ink from the tip of a pen with a depersonalized, fragmented orchestration of writing as a musical performance. Penmanship paints words; type plays them.[76] Each letter has its assigned part. No one has ever purchased a pen at a discount "on account of it's missing an *n*." And so that missing *n* is not only an opportunity to highlight the reader's role in supplementing the text (or Annie's role as an editor who volunteers to fill them in by hand); the missing *n* is also the malfunction that reveals, in the classic Heideggerian sense, the phenomenology of a tool that would have remained transparent were it not for the breakdown.

The missing key shows that the "alphabet piano" metaphor is a phenomenological reality and not just a figure of speech or a sales strategy. The arrangement of those letters also has impact, including, for example, how we think about punctuation. In reference to the QWERTY displacement of the period from its earlier location between the letters *t* and *e*, media scholar Jeff Scheible writes, "Imagine the subliminal ways in which we might have thought of punctuation differently if it had indeed occupied a place among other letters, rather than on their peripheries."[77] Early typewriter history is full of alternative keyboard layouts (and alternatives to the keyboard), various approaches to upper- and lowercase letters, and differing levels of visual engagement with the machine or with the type itself.[78] But the first tectonic shift of the modern typewriter is the fracturing of writing into keys, whatever their arrangement. That shift disrupts certain phallocentric associations (but by no means eradicates phallocentrism) and adds new musical gestures and rhythms similar to classical keyboard instruments. The Samuel W. Francis writing machine of 1857, a commercially unviable mechanism for typing made of wood, metal, and ivory keys, is the most piano-like typewriter ever built, but even the conventional four rows of black keys on the archetypal 1895 Underwood have never lost their connection to music.[79]

"The Typewriter," composed for typewriter and orchestra by Leroy Anderson (best known for the Christmas song "Sleigh Ride"), exemplifies the comical disjunction and uncanny correspondence between the typewriter and the piano. The piece features a soloist seated at a typewriter as if a concert pianist. The typist performs rapid keystrokes and rhythmic carriage returns accented by the "ding" of typewriter's bell in time to the orchestra's lively accompaniment. Although Martin Breinschmid's 2008 performance of the novelty piece is now the best known, with YouTube views fast approaching three million, the number was once associated with the flamboyant showman and pianist Liberace, who, fittingly, is the only man other than Paul Sheldon that Annie Wilkes honors with a shrine her living room.[80] "I'm going to put on my Liberace records!" exclaims Annie once Paul brings Misery back to life in the noble manner that satisfies her standards for verisimilitude. "You do like Liberace, don't you?" Paul forces a smile and lies. We know that Paul is a sports-arena kind of guy who would not be caught dead at a Liberace concert. Thus, the subsequent typing montage set to Liberace signals acquiescence (after a failed poisoning) to Annie—an oddball coupling of her two favorite men to parallel the "oddball situation" (as Paul calls it) of the collaboration. To Annie, the pairing makes perfect sense, while to the audience, the juxtaposition is as comical as "The Typewriter" novelty piece. The montage shows Paul typing chapter after chapter of *Misery's Return*, extreme close-ups of the hands and keyboard in profile and from above, arpeggio-like movements of the fingers across the keys, the occasional flourish of a raised hand, and matched shots of Paul at the machine in profile spanning days of labor, all performed in lockstep with Liberace's overwrought rendition of Tchaikovsky's Piano Concerto No. 1.

Fig. 10.3. Paul types like a pianist to the sounds of Liberace in *Misery* (1990).

The Liberace/Sheldon piano/typewriter montage moves from comical to something resembling harmony. Paul appears to be writing at record pace, Annie has nothing but positive feedback, and shots of the sheriff reading one of Paul's paperbacks complete a representation of writing, editing, publishing, and reading—acts that the typewriter brings into closer association, according to McLuhan.[81] All the while Paul is regaining strength. He and the typewriter are playing a double game. Paul lifts the typewriter above his head as if to smash it but then brings it back down, and then we realize that the old Royal 10 is rehabilitating the arm that he keeps in a sling. The device once marketed as a cure for pen paralysis is now secretly helping Paul shoulder-press his way back to full upper-body strength. After the concerto climaxes, accented by the "ding" of the typewriter bell and a clap of thunder, the mood shifts. Paul does a few shoulder presses before Annie walks in looking morose, suicidal, and probably homicidal. From this point to the end, the typewriter starts to resemble the entity that frightened Wendy Torrance with its intimate and exclusionary relationship with her husband, its endless expenditure, and its refusal to satisfy the curious reader with an anticipated narrative.

McLuhan's vision of typing as a liberating activity is only partially convincing because, despite all the talk of emancipation, typing as a (re)generative activity has historically privileged men over women, just as McLuhan does with his examples: "The poet at the typewriter can do Njinsky leaps or Chaplin-like shuffles and wiggles. Because he is an audience for his own mechanical audacities, he never ceases to react to his own performance. Composing on the typewriter is like flying a kite"[82]—or like masturbating. The book that Paul finished before his captivity, the one Annie hates and demands that he, an "old dirty birdie," burn in order to be cleansed, has no title and, by Paul's own admission, no discernable plot. "What's it about?" asks Annie. "It's crazy, but I don't really know," says Paul. Of course, we know the book is a gritty, semiautobiographical tale of life in the slum, but all Annie can see is profanity. Left to his own devices, Paul's dream project is to write about himself and about nothing, to produce untitled work for no one but himself. Not so different from Jack's book, *Untitled* triggers hysteria for Annie just as Jack's plotless reams of self-referential variations on a proverb trigger Wendy. Leaps, wiggles, and shuffles, the exuberant gestures of McLuhan's typophilia are allowed to Annie, Wendy, and many other women at best only vicariously. In the novel, *The Shining*, Wendy earns money as a typist for English professors while Jack pursues his dream of being a writer.[83] As for Annie, even when she pretends to be an aspiring writer to explain the presence of a typewriter in her house to the sheriff, she does so as a failure. Annie is a consumer of type. Annie's status as a serial killer is her one breakthrough into a male-dominated vocation, but the plight of the serial killer vis-à-vis publishing is to rely on the journalists to author the story. The serial killer is a maniacal scrapbooker, a collage artist, a clip-and-paste appropriator of memories written by others. Annie's only book is her *Memory Lane* scrapbook.

Misery's typewriter winds up Paul's accomplice in brutal acts orchestrated as poetic justice. Paul postpones Annie's murder-suicide pact by promising to finish the book in order to bring Misery back to the world for good. He teases Annie with the prospect of answering all the cliffhanger questions in Misery's story, but then he refuses satisfaction, not in the pleasurable manner of Scheherazade but as a definitive power reversal. "Remember how for all those years nobody knew who Misery's real father was, or if they'd ever be reunited? It's all here. Does she finally marry Ian or will it be Winthorne? It's all right here," says Paul as he lights a match and sets fire to the pages he has doused in lighter fluid. *Misery's Return* suffers the same fate as *Untitled*. Annie lunges toward the burning manuscript while Paul uses the opportunity to bludgeon her with the typewriter. As the fight continues, Paul grabs the smoldering pages and shoves them in her mouth. "You want it? Eat it!" In King's novel, Paul yells, "Suck my book," lest there be any doubt that this is an act of oral rape by text. Annie fights back but trips over Paul's leg and falls headfirst—"ding"—onto the typewriter. A couple more blows to the head with an iron pig and Annie is dead.

"To save time is to lengthen life," says the proverb adopted for the Remington typewriter seal. Typewriting thus imagined represents a promise to stave off death. And in a way, the typewriters in *Misery* and *The Shining* do just that: they forestall death for as long as the typing continues. The efficiency of type is nevertheless to be feared if the biblical statement "the letter kills" can be extended to describe the act of slugging out words onto a page.[84] Type accelerates writing compared to the pen, but more importantly, it performs writing in a way that differs from the pen. The typewriter fractures ink flow into a percussive symphonic score that adds new expression and new errors to the imprint of the extended hand. The unique qualities of type are not limited to the promise of saved time, for the twenty-first-century resurgence of typing is, as Richard Polt states, "a rebellion against efficiency."[85] As for saving tired hands, a computer keyboard supersedes a manual typewriter. Instead of looking at type through the narrative of progress, films such as *Misery* and *The Shining* allow us to sit uncomfortably with type that refuses narrative and with typewriters that record paralysis as much as they free the hand from it. Annie Wilkes is as much a victim of pen paralysis as she is a victim of the typewriter. Jack Torrance is more an explicator of type than an author. Typewriter horror allows the machine to help and to hinder, to function and to malfunction, to move fluidly between gender stereotypes, and finally to be more than a mechanical servant. A Royal 10 typewriter ad with a speech bubble coming out of the platen best expresses the sentiment of horror's typewriter: "I'll talk for myself."

Notes

1. See Cocks, 74.
2. "The Shining Code 2.0," accessed July 20, 2017, https://youtu.be/FBaAfl4SuI4. YouTube has since removed the channel for copyright violations. A new edit can be found at "The Shining Code 2.0," YouTube video, 1:19:12, posted by Through the Aether, August 17, 2017, https://www.youtube.com/watch?v=9BsjRlT-8fc.
3. Barthes, 53.
4. Bozung, "Interview with Brian Cook," 699.
5. The compound noun structure in French of noun + à + verb (*machine + à + écrire*) indicates the thing followed by what it is designed to do. Typewriter (*machine à écrire*) is

a machine designed to write. *La machine à écrire-Jack* thus can be read in one sense as a machine designed to write Jack.

6. Jean-Pierre Oudart, "Shining: Les inconnus dans la maison," *Cahiers du cinéma*, November 1980, 6. All translations are mine.

7. Ibid.

8. Oudart, 6, 8.

9. Ibid., 8.

10. Ciment, 135.

11. Ibid., 144.

12. Ibid., 146.

13. Ibid., 107.

14. Ibid., 146.

15. Ibid., 42.

16. Bozung, "Interview with Shelley Duvall," 373.

17. See McAvoy. Vivian Kubrick's "Making *The Shining*" is included as a bonus feature on the Blu-ray DVD.

18. Bozung, "Interview with Gordon Stainforth," 642. Hours of unseen footage taken by Vivian Kubrick (at the wrong speed) sit in the Kubrick Archive where they will remain unseen, even by the archivists, until the donors say otherwise—perfect fodder for pointless speculation.

19. Vincent, 296. Vincent debunks some of the hidden message claims.

20. John August, "Cinematic Geography and the Problem of Genius," *John August* (blog), July 26, 2011, https://johnaugust.com/2011/cinematic-geography-and-problem-of-genius.

21. Bozung, "Interview with Gordon Stainforth," 655.

22. As an example of her thoroughness, for each take (thirty-three total) of the ball rolling toward Danny while he plays on the carpet, June Randall has notes: "too far left," "too far away," "too fast," etc. Continuity notebook 3, Kubrick Archives.

23. Vincent, 304.

24. Thank you, Bev Vincent, for pointing me to the *Times* article. David Segal, "It's Back. But What Does It Mean?," *New York Times*, March 27, 2013, http://www.nytimes.com/2013/03/31/movies/aide-to-kubrick-on-shining-scoffs-at-room-237-theories.html.

25. Baxter, 35. Baxter may have been confusing the chronology with Kubrick's adoption of a computerized system while in the planning stages of *Full Metal Jacket* (1987). Kubrick invited Alan Bowker to his home office in late 1983 to early 1984 to install an IBM XT. In one of the photos Bowker took during his stay, the Adler Universal 39 can be seen on a cart next to a desk. It is not, however, painted dark gray. See Alan Bowker, "Stanley Kubrick," accessed August 8, 2019, https://bowkera.com/stanley-kubrick/.

26. Amis, 232.

27. For the purposes of this thought experiment, I am assuming the ribbon is well inked and the machine in proper working order. Electric typewriters are not error free.

28. Kubrick Archive, SK 15/1/3, 246.

29. Ibid. Kubrick's marginalia include writing in all caps and in upper- and lowercase script. With the help of Kubrick archivist Richard Daniels, I was able to verify that both styles of annotation are Kubrick's own.

30. Kittler, 191.

31. Hemingway, 18.

32. King, *The Shining*, 134.
33. Stainforth remarks that no one seems to have noticed that he has layered Penderecki on top of Penderecki. See Bozung, "Interview with Gordon Stainforth," 653.
34. Kubrick's notes indicate he had considered using "school loose-leaf books, pen, pencil, various inks."
35. With computers, horror invariably depicts breakdown through glitch. See Olivier, "Glitch Gothic."
36. Kolker, *A Cinema of Loneliness*, 131.
37. Ibid.
38. Ibid.
39. Ibid., 132.
40. I am still lacking precision here, ignoring the weights and variants. For a thorough analysis, see Dave Addey, "2001: A Space Odyssey," Typeset in the Future, January 31, 2014, https://typesetinthefuture.com/2014/01/31/2001-a-space-odyssey/.
41. Kolker, *A Cinema of Loneliness*, 100.
42. To be precise, the Helvetica has been slightly rounded but not quite as much as the Helvetica Rounded available as a computer font today.
43. *Oxford English Dictionary Online* (2017), s.v. "overlook," https://www.oed.com/.
44. Jameson, 93.
45. Ibid.
46. Kolker, *A Cinema of Loneliness*, 131.
47. Kubrick archives, SK/15/1/18.
48. Adams has been even more press averse than Kubrick.
49. Bozung, "Interview with Greg MacGillivray," 617–18.
50. See Kwapisz, 3.
51. Tullett, 33.
52. I base my belief on the fact that shapes not present in the English pages are found restricted to a single language.
53. For a Freudian reading of the novel, see Schroeder.
54. King, *Misery*, 226.
55. Ibid.
56. Sholes and Glidden.
57. On the lower end of the pen spectrum, the 2012 introduction of BIC "For Her" pens was as telling as it was ill advised.
58. E. Remington and Sons.
59. Wyckoff, 8.
60. Ibid., 9.
61. Slocum, 78, 83.
62. *Journal of the United States Artillery*, advertising section, vii.
63. "Iron sartor" and "knights of the needle" are terms used in the British press in the 1850s. See chap. 7.
64. Sholes and Glidden.
65. Kittler, 184.
66. From US census data cited in M. Davies, 10.
67. Lupton, 43.
68. Ballantyne, 76.

69. Ibid., 72.
70. See M. Davies, 55–56. See also Strom.
71. M. Davies, 55.
72. Herkimer County Historical Society, frontispiece.
73. See Strom, 187.
74. Kittler, 187.
75. Ibid., 206.
76. I am referring to the stereotypical iconic typewriter and not to variations of the many machines that paved the way. For thoughts on the phenomenology of some alternatives, see Polt, "Typology: A Phenomenology of Early Typewriters," Classic Typewriter Page, accessed July 22, 2017, http://site.xavier.edu/polt/typewriters/typology.html.
77. Scheible, 41–42. Coincidentally, *t* and *e* are the other two letters that stop working in King's novel.
78. See Polt, "Typology," for wonderfully defamiliarizing alternatives to the canonical machine.
79. The Herkimer County Historical Society's *Story of the Typewriter*, published to commemorate the fiftieth anniversary of the machine, includes other piano-like predecessors, including Beach's machine of 1856 for the blind and the 1868 Sholes, Glidden, and Soule patent model, which used six piano keys. See 25, 27, 47.
80. "The Typewriter Leroy Anderson Martin Breinschmid with Strauß Festival Orchestra Vienna," YouTube video, 2:10, posted by Martin Breinschmid, September 10, 2009, accessed July 22, 2017, https://youtube.com/watch?v=g2LJ1i7222c.
81. See McLuhan, 230.
82. Ibid.
83. See King, *The Shining*, 53.
84. 2 Corinthians 3:6.
85. Polt, *The Typewriter Revolution*, 32.

11

ARMOIRE

Memory Is an Armoire

Art director Cho Geun-hyun spent too much money to buy just the right armoire for the South Korean Gothic psychological horror film *A Tale of Two Sisters* (*Janghwa, Hongryeon*, 2003). He splurged at an antique shop. "It was expensive. It was over the limits of our budget," he confesses. "I didn't think of the consequences." Even so, he already knew what he would say if questioned about the extravagance. "What are you going to do now? Do you want a cheesy movie?"[1] He knew that would be enough to shut down objections. This film was meant to elevate the genre, to ride the Korean Wave that began in the late 1990s in Asia and take it all the way to international fame. And it worked: 2003 was a banner year for cinema in South Korea thanks to the crime drama *Memories of Murder* (*Salinui chueok*, 2003), the adaptation of French novel *Les liaisons dangereuses* as *Untold Scandal* (*Joseon namnyeo sangyeoljisa*, 2003), and *A Tale of Two Sisters*—three films in three different genres that garnered critical praise and commercial success.[2] As if the occasion required an English term, "well-made" became the industry buzzword for features with "a distinctive directorial style and commentary on social issues"[3]—in short, not cheesy. *A Tale of Two Sisters* broke the box office record for the horror genre in Korea and topped sales among the "Asia extreme" label/genre invented by UK distributor Tartan, although the film is not particularly graphic.[4] The poster, a formal family portrait with two girls in blood-soaked white dresses slumped on a sofa, is more gruesome than the actual film. In fact, *A Tale of Two Sisters* has more in common with *The Others* (2001) and *The Sixth Sense* (1999) than with other South Korean "Asia extreme" titles such as *Oldboy* (*Oldeuboi*, 2003), which sent Rex Reed into an infamously racist rant about the depravity of "a nation weaned on kimchi."[5] *A Tale of Two Sisters* differs in setting from the high school horror films in the vein of the popular *Whispering Corridors* (*Yeogo goedam*, 1998) series, and it does not focus on technology like *Phone* (*Pon*, 2002) or the Japanese-inspired *The Ring Virus* (*Hangul*, 1999), but it does engage themes common to many early twenty-first-century South Korean horror films such as the virgin ghost and the haunted object.[6] And in this case, getting the right haunted object meant going over budget to buy an antique armoire.

According to theorist Jean Baudrillard, an armoire is one of the three "furniture-monuments" (*meubles-monuments*) of the home, along with the bed and the buffet.[7] Baudrillard's trinity of furniture-monuments accords a special status to pieces that are not merely monumental in size but whose function is that of a monument to the continuity and persistence of traditional family structures. Baudrillard's furniture-monuments are wooden pieces often handed down from one generation to the next that exude a unique presence through their temporal, material, and symbolic relation to the home, its inhabitants, and its objects. A piece of wooden furniture has time inscribed into the very fibers of its being. "Wood has its own odor, it ages, it even has its own parasites, etc. In short, this material is a being," writes the theorist.[8] The purpose of objects, for Baudrillard, is to personify human relations, to inhabit space, and to have a soul.[9] That is not to say that Baudrillard believes in the innate being of objects in the manner expressed by more recent strains of speculative realism and object-oriented ontology. Humans invest objects with a soul, he contends. Nevertheless, that investment is reciprocated. Objects invest in us and are linked to us in a "collusion" that creates a density of affect that constitutes their "presence."[10] As a monument, an armoire carries memory and becomes a "family portrait," according to Baudrillard.[11] Taking the sentiment further, French philosopher Gaston Bachelard argues that an armoire is "something more than a family chronicle," something like memory itself.[12] Armoires, he says, are "veritable organs of the secret psychological life." They are "hybrid objects, subject objects. Like us, through us and for us, they have a quality of intimacy."[13] All armoires are haunted spaces in the sense that they are monuments to family, memory, and secrecy. In *A Tale of Two Sisters*, the armoire is a family chronicle, the site of tragedy and memory and a container of presences. The armoire is a womb, a grave, and a haunted house within a haunted house.

Technically, nothing is haunted in *A Tale of Two Sisters*—at least, not in the traditional sense of a supernatural haunting. The nature of the "ghosts" in the film is a point of confusion to many viewers, and in part,

Fig. 11.1. The armoire in *A Tale of Two Sisters* (2003).

that uncertainty is what director Kim Jee-woon intended. But for a Western audience, the film is doubly confusing because it deconstructs a folktale that is not part of a Western tradition. The Korean title, *Janghwa, Hongryeon*, names the familiar characters and establishes certain expectations in the same way that a horror film based on Sleeping Beauty or Snow White might activate background knowledge in Western audiences. The story of Janghwa and Hongryeon had been adapted five times in Korean cinema before Kim Jee-woon's retelling, with versions dating back to the silent era (one in 1924 and another in 1936) and a three-decade streak in 1956, 1962, and 1972. More recently, in 2009, a 150-episode television drama (*Janghwa Hongryeon*, a.k.a. *Love and Obsession*) proves the story's timeless appeal and adaptability. The familiarity means that Korean viewers will immediately recognize certain tropes but will also notice substantial deviations from the traditional plot, not the least of which is the relocation of the site of tragedy from a lake in the original to a piece of furniture not found in homes during most of the Joseon dynasty (1392–1897), the era that gave birth to the tale. The shift from water to furniture, from exterior to interior, from natural to constructed space must be understood in the context of Kim's restructuring of the tale. And for most Western viewers, that requires an extra step, a review of the story that Kim's adaptation changes so dramatically.[14]

The story of the two sisters, Janghwa (Rose) and Hongryeon (Lotus), begins with a childless couple and miraculous conception of a baby girl,

Janghwa. Three years later, a second daughter, Hongryeon, is born. All is well until the mother contracts a mysterious illness and dies. The father remarries, but his second wife is ill-tempered, favors her own sons, and is abusive to the two girls. Concerned about inheritance, the wicked stepmother devises a plan to bring shame to Janghwa. She skins a rat and places it in the girl's bed. Next, she tells her husband that Janghwa has dishonored the family. Pointing to the mass of bloody flesh in the bed, the woman accuses Janghwa of aborting a child conceived out of wedlock. The father sends the disgraced daughter away to live with her grandmother, which gives the stepmother an opportunity to plan the girl's disappearance. The stepmother instructs her favorite son to ride off with Janghwa and drown her in a lake. After a struggle by the lake, Janghwa manages to tear herself free, but her sorrow is so great that she plunges into to water to join her deceased mother in the afterlife. Hongryeon eventually learns the truth about what happened and decides to find the lake in order to reunite with her sister in death. After the two tragic deaths, local judges die one after the next—a pattern that indicates a need for justice. Finally, a high official is sent to investigate. Around midnight, a girl in a green jacket and red skirt appears to the brave official and tells him about her death and the fate of her older sister who was falsely accused of abortion. He investigates, examines the supposed fetus, and discovers it to be a rat. The wicked stepmother is sentenced to decapitation and dismemberment, and the son, to death by strangulation. The father is acquitted and released to give his daughters a proper burial. A few years later, the father remarries a kind woman who gives birth to twin girls, Janghwa and Hongryeon reincarnated.

The tale fits within the *gongan* or "public case" narrative tradition wherein heinous acts are ultimately punished by the judicial system.[15] The outcome restores patriarchal order, avenges the virgin ghosts, and punishes the "monstrous-feminine," to use Barbara Creed's term. The father is clueless if not negligent in his duties as a parent. He is responsible for putting his daughters in jeopardy, and yet he is acquitted and given a second chance with a new set of daughters and a gentler wife. Where the father fails, the law steps in. In Kim's adaptation, the father, Bae Su-yeon (Kim Kap-su), is equally feckless and equally absolved of any personal responsibility even though his relationship and probable infidelity with his wife's nurse likely aggravated his wife's depressive and suicidal state. Furthermore, his relationship with the nurse, Eun-ju (Yum Jung-ah), brings an unsympathetic future-stepmother figure into the house while the suffering mother is still alive. As for any institutional intervention to supplement the father's failings, Kim's version substitutes the medical system for the judicial system, but with a far less satisfying outcome. The film begins and ends at psychiatric facilities, where Su-mi (Im Soo-jung), the Janghwa figure, is admitted for inpatient care. While a convincing argument can be made that the bookended institutional setting represents a victory for the patriarchal system, there is nothing triumphant about the resolution, nor is there much hope that Su-mi will recover. Institutions neither save the day nor right wrongs in Kim's adaptation, but the shift from a legal to a medical system does constitute a meaningful deviation from the source material. The story is no longer a "public case" narrative but rather a private medical matter in which a father institutionalizes his daughter for lack of a better option.

For some viewers, the psychiatric denouement disqualifies the film as Gothic.[16] For others, the film deserves the Gothic label because the scientifically rationalized and demystified supernatural is undermined by ghostly occurrences not linked to Su-mi's warped perception.[17] Without belaboring the genre argument, I maintain that the film is an exploration of repressed memory and guilt personified as (imagined) ghosts. As support, statements from the director and from the character Eun-ju suffice. In an important moment, the "evil stepmother" personality of Su-mi's dissociative state makes a statement about scary hauntings: "Know what's really scary? You want to forget something, totally wipe it out of your mind. But you never can. It can't go away, you see. And it follows you around like a ghost." In the Tartan DVD commentary, Kim makes the same point at least three times: "This film presents [bad] memories as a ghost or a hateful spirit."[18] Regarding a ghostly attack on the real Eun-ju at the end of the film, Kim says, "This is not a didactic movie. But Eun-ju is also suffering. It's different from Su-mi's ritual. But she is also suffering. The ghost appearing in front of Eun-ju shows that she also has bad memories. That memory is haunting her in the form of a ghost. I wanted to show that."[19] Finally, in a "Behind the Scenes" featurette, Kim again states, "A ghost can be a visualization of fear in the mind."[20] Kim's adaptation, therefore, is neither about a triumphant judicial system nor about successful medical intervention; *A Tale of Two Sisters* is about being haunted by memory. And memory exists both inside and outside the mind, where it interacts with material forms. One of those forms, theorists like Bachelard and Baudrillard propose, is an armoire. Bad memories are ghosts for Kim, but for Bachelard, "memory is a wardrobe [*armoire*]."[21]

Containment Narratives

Another obstacle to understanding the film is its temporality. Media scholar Frances Gateward explains that regardless of genre, most Korean feature films "rely on narrational strategies that deviate from the paradigm of linear progression"—so much so that audiences have come to expect "parallel flashbacks, contradictory flashbacks, open-ended flashbacks, and sometimes even flashbacks within flashbacks."[22] According to media scholar Wing-Fai Leung, the flashback is commonly used in Asian ghost films "as a site of memory, in particular of traumatic recollection."[23] Thus, while the temporal structure of *A Tale of Two Sisters* is confusing to audiences accustomed to linear progression, to a Korean audience, the film follows the conventions of contemporary Korean horror. Layering temporal containers is but one aspect of a larger project of open and closed spatial and temporal structures. Kim's film might be best understood as a containment narrative in which the armoire as the central figure references the womb, architectural and organizational structures, and memory. The psychiatric hospital is one container in the film, the house another, and the armoire the nucleus of containment. The film is a nesting box of containers.

The story centers on a mind haunted by trauma and guilt over two deaths tied to an armoire. The armoire has become a taboo subject for Su-mi and her father. The two armoire deaths are, first, that of the depressive mother, who takes pills and hangs herself in the armoire in Su-yeon's (Moon Geun-young) bedroom, and, second, Su-yeon's death under the heavy armoire after it falls as a result of her attempt to pull out her mother's hanging body. The crash of the armoire appears to have been heard by everyone in the house, but Eun-ju is the only person to check the room. When Eun-ju sees the overturned armoire and then Su-yeon's hand underneath desperately reaching for help, she backs out of the room in shock but also to weigh her options. Just then, Su-mi emerges from her bedroom, reprimands Eun-ju for being upstairs, and tells her to stay out of their lives. Annoyed, Eun-ju warns Su-mi that she will regret this. "What can be worse than standing here with you?" replies Su-mi before running out of the house. Meanwhile, Su-yeon is dying, and the one person aware of the accident is now unwilling to intervene. The trauma of the two deaths causes a mental break in Su-mi, who alternately takes on the personalities of her dead sister and her stepmother to cope with her remorse. Over the course of three days, Su-mi plays three roles without realizing it until events unfold that force her to acknowledge her sister's death and to realize that the Eun-ju she has been seeing is her own invention infused with elements of the folktale. Because the director shows the three personalities as distinct characters who speak to one another and to the father, the viewer has no reason to believe that Su-mi suffers from dissociative identity disorder. Even when "Su-yeon" learns she is dead, we have the impression that she is an amnesic ghost, as in *The Sixth Sense* or *The Others*. Only when the real Eun-ju appears and effectively destroys Su-mi's illusion does the audience realize that both Su-yeon and the Eun-ju seen during the three-day period are fractured aspects of Su-mi's split psyche. Thus, the story externalizes Su-mi's inner demons and then pushes them back into the closed space of her mind. The two frightening ghosts—one a girl in Su-yeon's green dress and the other a woman with long, black hair who resembles the dead mother—are equally not supernatural if we accept the director's explanation; instead, they are visual manifestations of guilt that appear in different forms to different characters in the film. Notably, the only people who do not see ghosts in the film are the men, who, like the father in the original tale, are tormented more by having to deal with hysterical women than by any sense of personal culpability. Clearly, that gender difference alone supports K. K. Seet's argument that "the current Asian horror film is ultimately conservative and functions as a form of narrative containment."[24]

The plot structure of the film leaves so much opportunity for confusion that one scholar has made it a case study in unreliable narration.[25] Even when viewing the hospital scenes that bookend the three days, the viewer may not understand whether the two scenes are separate hospital visits or the same one with one long flashback in the middle. Leung favors the latter, although one could argue that a photograph shown in good condition in the opening hospital scene but then defaced and ripped during the three days at the house points to two different hospitalizations. The flashbacks at the end of the film while Su-mi is in her hospital room include a mixture of memories that belong to Su-mi and to Eun-ju and scenes witnessed by neither character. At one point, an audio cue of the mother's whistling seems to be heard simultaneously by Eun-ju and Su-mi, and when Eun-ju is attacked by the ghost in the armoire, a cut to the exterior of the house and then to Su-mi at the hospital with a tear rolling down her cheek implies a remote awareness of what is happening back at the home. After the armoire ghost attack, a new flashback shows the events that unfolded the day of the tragedy, clarifying Eun-ju's complicity in Su-yeon's death. As Su-mi runs from the house the fateful day after her argument with Eun-ju, a shot of Eun-ju closing the shutters signals her unwillingness to save Su-yeon and reinforces the horror of containment that pervades the film. A desaturated freeze-frame of Su-mi, her back to the house, suspends time in photographic stillness, like a moment of regret etched into memory. But that moment, too, changes to a sad and beautiful shot of Su-mi sitting at the end of a dock by the lake—a reference to the lake of the original tale. That final shot is also desaturated, but color begins to return to Su-mi's red sweater in defiance of the stasis suggested by the black and white.[26] The impression of sliding between photographic and cinematographic temporalities through static shots and chromatic manipulation emphasizes a fluidity between the fixed historical fact and memories that, however painful, can bring the dead back to life. The moving and the still image thus figure as containers endowed with a presence not unlike storage devices for cherished objects.

The film establishes an affinity between the armoire, smaller containers of valued objects, and photography in several important scenes. *A Tale of Two Sisters* supports Baudrillard's armoire-as-family-portrait and Bachelard's memory-armoire connection as family photos accumulate around the armoire, or rather as they migrate to the armoire from smaller storage containers. Su-mi retrieves a couple of small cases from storage, takes them to her room, opens a chest at the foot of the bed, places the smaller cases inside, and then begins to rifle through their contents, setting aside more containers (a glasses case and a purse) in the process. Containers nested in containers harbor cherished family memories and objects with synecdochic connections to the past. As Su-mi flips through a stack of photos in one of the cases, we sense that she might be digging into a past she is not prepared to confront. After all, in the preceding scene, Su-mi has just asked her father to get rid of the armoire, and his response was to remind her that they had agreed not to talk about it. Now, by opening small containers and a larger chest, Su-mi is taking steps toward the furniture-monument that houses the memories responsible for shattering her psyche and her family. In fact, she later moves the photos to a table near the armoire, as if the gravitational pull from the furniture-monument draws all mementos into its orbit. Further solidifying the armoire-portrait connection, the scene of the tragic armoire deaths features a close-up of a broken framed photo of Su-yeon in the same green dress in the armoire.[27]

In an act that anticipates the netherworld between still and moving images that Su-mi inhabits at the end of the film, Su-mi slowly contemplates the images and then wildly flips through them at an untenable speed. Su-yeon's sudden appearance makes Su-mi stop abruptly, shut the chest, and sit on it, thereby returning to stasis and containment. But then, with a flourish and a "ta-da," Su-mi reopens the small case and begins to show her sister the other relics housed inside—items such as their mother's shoes, jewelry, and a silver circular-framed photo. Su-yeon contemplates the framed image and chants, "Taritakoum, Taritakoum," which, she explains to Su-mi, is a spell to summon their mother. Su-yeon's chant is very likely a transliteration of "Talitha koum" (or "Talitha cumi") from Mark 5:41 in the New Testament account of Jesus commanding a twelve-year-old girl to rise from the dead. Thus, Su-mi's opening of the small case with "ta-da" followed by Su-yeon's incantation to raise the dead evokes the religious nature of opening and closing a container of valued objects. As Bachelard observes, "When a casket [*coffret* or small chest] is closed, it is returned to the general community of objects; it takes its place in exterior space. But it opens!"[28] The "ta-da" of the opened casket is, in essence, the feat on which Christianity hinges, and it is also the essence of chests and armoires. When opened, the double doors of an armoire create a triptych that recalls religious theatricality. Decorative reliquary cabinets are essentially of the same moral order as furniture-moments, or so suggests Bachelard's description of opening an armoire. "If we give objects the friendship they should have, we do not open a wardrobe without a slight start," says Bachelard.[29] Therefore, contingent on our "friendship" or recognition of the objects as having a presence or soul, Bachelard asserts that to open an armoire is to experience the sacred. He adds, "Beneath its russet wood, a wardrobe is a very white almond. To open it, is to experience an event of whiteness."[30] The almond comparison recalls the *mandoria* (almond) shape used in traditional Christian art to frame Christ or the Virgin Mary. The shape also clearly associates the armoire with the maternal. Such is the case in *A Tale of Two Sisters*, where the armoire is the space of the mother.

The Armoire-Womb

In an uncanny moment of research while writing this book, I happened upon *Psychology of the House*, written in the 1970s by French architect Olivier Marc. If Olivier Marc were to explain how I, Marc Olivier, should end up writing *Household Horror*, I imagine he would appeal to the Jungian collective unconscious, the concept that undergirds his own book about houses. Marc delights in assembling similarities between the forms of houses across cultures, with a particular fixation on the female form. He notes the vaginal shape of the entrances to the mihrab of the Cordova mosque and the entrance to a Massa hut in Africa. He expounds on the rounded curves of the structures, the adornments of the "thick-lipped slit" of the entryway to a Massa hut, and concludes, "I was then convinced that the interior model which had presided over the birth of the form had been a mother's womb, seen from the inside. These houses were wombs."[31] Marc further observes the natural tendency of children to climb inside cardboard boxes.[32] While I do not share Marc's enthusiasm for Jung, his point nevertheless applies perfectly to the armoire in *A Tale of Two Sisters*, where a tale of abortion is transmuted into a story of death within a constructed womb. Here, the child does not willingly crawl inside the armoire as do children with cardboard boxes. Instead, Su-yeon is trapped and killed by an armoire, or in the second-chance alternate reality that Su-mi constructs, Su-yeon is locked inside the armoire by the evil stepmother and then saved by Su-mi. In the tragic death that Su-mi has repressed, the mother is literally (almost umbilically) tied to the armoire in a death that enacts a return to the womb. Su-yeon, too, is trapped by the devouring space, the hybrid armoire-mother.

The armoire is a womb-grave for the three women in *A Tale of Two Sisters*: the mother suspended and strangled by a sheet in the intrauterine chamber of the furniture, the daughter trapped by the armoire-mother combination, and the stepmother, whose fate one is left to imagine, similarly consumed after what amounts to the armoire's delivery of a ghost. Eun-ju's final moments with the armoire evoke simultaneous birth and death as she participates in the delivery of the ghost from between the folds of linens in the armoire. First, one door of the armoire creaks open; then Eun-ju approaches and opens the other door. Noticing something like black hair between stacks of folded cloth, she reaches her hand forward to investigate. Suddenly, from between the folds, the long-haired ghost expels itself, its birth accompanied by a gush of ectoplasmic fluid. Distorted, digitally altered sounds of a baby crying heighten the impression that Eun-ju has become midwife to a monstrous birth. A cut to the exterior of the house and the sound of her screams emphasizes the containment of the womb-house. Barbara Creed's notion of the "all-devouring womb of the archaic mother" applies to the armoire in *A Tale of Two Sisters* just as it does to other figures of horror Creed discusses such as "the toothed vagina/womb of *Jaws*," "the fleshy, pulsating, womb of *The Thing* and *Poltergeist*" and the titular monster of *Alien* (1979), which she discusses at length.³³ In horror, Creed contends, the mythological figure of the Mother-Goddess who created heaven and earth alone (i.e., without a male partner) is constructed as a negative abyss, an "all-incorporating black hole which threatens to reabsorb what it once birthed."³⁴ The horror of the abyss should not be confused with castration anxiety, warns Creed, for the womb, contrary to the Freudian conception of female genitalia, "cannot be constructed as a 'lack' in relation to the penis."³⁵ In other words, the womb does not derive from the masculine; it "signifies 'fullness' or 'emptiness' but always it is its *own point of reference*."³⁶ With that in mind, a confessional moment between Su-mi and her father takes on new meaning. Bae says, "I know you're very angry with me. And I know I'm a bad father," to which Su-mi replies, "You're not even a bad father." That is, he is barely a father at all. According to DVD commentary by the actors, Korean audiences erupted into laughter at a moment when Bae meekly asks if he can enter his daughter's room. The reaction to his sheepish request for permission (which Su-mi refuses to grant) illustrates an assumption that the patriarchal figure, by right, can penetrate any space. Although Bae is a passive figure of competing feminine desires (including possibly incestuous desire), he remains largely outside of the story, a peripheral presence in an armoire-womb story.

"Every poet of furniture . . . knows that the inner space of an old wardrobe is deep," asserts Bachelard.³⁷ That imagined depth is a central paradox of the armoire as a space of containment that doubles as a portal to unfathomable secrets and hence to the occult. A monster might be hiding in a closet, but the space of an armoire opens up to something much larger, something Bachelard calls "the dimension of intimacy."³⁸ That dimension possesses conceptual interiority not restricted by the space of the house. This is what C. S. Lewis understood when writing *The Lion, the Witch and the Wardrobe*—essentially an armoire-womb fantasy in which an absent mother is replaced by the armoire as a dimension of imaginative fecundity. The doors to a closet simply close off a piece of a room, whereas the doors to an armoire say "ta-da" for better or worse. In *The Conjuring* (2013), for example, a blindfolded mother faces off with the armoire in a game of "hide and clap." As she stumbles into a room in search of audible clues to the location of her hiding daughter, the doors of an old armoire creak open, and ghostly hands reach out from behind the clothing to draw her near with two claps. The chilling "hide and clap" scene featured in the film's trailer evokes a sense of dread not merely because of the supernatural but also because it taps into fear of the armoire as an abject womb.

Other spaces in *A Tale of Two Sisters* also reinforce the womb theme at the heart of the original tale. The womb-like abject refrigerator discussed in the "Refrigerator" chapter of this book appears in Kim's film as a substitute for the faked abortion narrative of the folktale. When Su-mi goes to the refrigerator, she spies something on the refrigerator shelves wrapped in brown paper and dripping blood. Inside the wrapping is a mangled, fleshy mess—not a skinned rat but rather a fish head and guts. Like the rotting skinned rabbit in Roman Polanski's *Repulsion* (1965), the rotten fish emblematizes an abject version of a popular fertility symbol. In Korea, the fish was an exceptionally prevalent sign of fecundity and was often used in figural locks of the Joseon dynasty attached to gates and storage furniture as a talismanic object.[39] In another scene of bloody-wrapper womb imagery, a bloodstained sack in the armoire, presumably with Su-yeon inside, becomes the object of a showdown between Su-mi, who tries to open it, and Su-mi's Eun-ju personality, who tries to kill the person inside. Su-mi's ghost sighting after a nightmare also invokes uterine horror when the legs of the maternal ghost frame the terrified girl in her bed while Su-yeon sleeps. Blood runs down the ghost's spread legs, and a grown hand emerges from between the legs like Su-yeon's hand grasping for life from beneath the armoire. After the ghost incident, Su-mi discovers that Su-yeon has just had her first period—in sync, not surprisingly, with Su-mi and Eun-ju. Like the nine duplicates of clothing that hang in the closet, the triplicate period is a clue to Su-mi's multiple personalities but also a sign of multiplicity, seriality, and repetition linked to a woman's reproductive system.

The substitution of an armoire for the amniotic fluidity of the folktale lake adds a final ghost to *A Tale of Two Sisters* that was not lost on art director Cho Geun-hyun when he was shopping for furniture: the ghost of a painful colonial past and its fracturing of Korean identity under the guise of a civilizing project. The stunning set design of the film stands out to critics, who typically link the setting to the Victorian era.[40] Often unremarked, however, is the fact that the Victorian influence is largely by way of Japan. The colonial period (1910–45) of Japanese rule marks a trauma for Korean identity. As Gateward's study indicates, the memory of Japanese rule figures prominently in the cinema of young Korean directors with no firsthand experience of the period.[41] Narratives about trauma and memory, even if not directly referencing the attempted obliteration of Korean identity by the Japanese, often engage that past obliquely. A dissertation by Hunju Lee draws attention to the colonial haunting manifest in architecture that has gone unmentioned by most scholars. Noting the similarity between the houses in *A Tale of Two Sisters* and the one in the Japanese film *Ju-on: The Grudge* (*Ju-on*, 2002), Lee writes, "The house's allusions to Japanese architecture might remind Korean viewers of Japanese colonial times during which Japanese-style houses were first transplanted to Korea." Those settings, argues Lee, "awaken painful memories about the era's wounds that have never been cured, but rather, that have been forced to be 'forgotten' by the futuristic governments that led the country's modernization and economic development initiatives."[42] The armoire and other furniture chosen for *A Tale of Two Sisters* are not the traditional Korean pieces of the Joseon dynasty but rather European antiques. "Korea never had a 'standing-up' living style in the past," says Cho. "We didn't have tables or sofas. We needed old furniture for this old house. We weren't intentionally using European antique furniture. That was our only choice. And it looked good. That was it."[43] Baudrillard's characterization of armoires as a family portraits should be expanded to include national portraits, and in the case of the furniture chosen by Cho, those hauntings are as layered as the narrative flashbacks or other figurative and literal nested containers in the film. Perhaps it is best to end with the words of the evil Eun-ju, resurrected from the Joseon dynasty tale by Su-mi's damaged psyche. Cruel as she is, her commentary about the nature of ghosts coincides with that of the director. Similarly, her commentary while dragging the body of Su-mi toward the armoire sums up the problem that haunts modern domesticity: "This damn house won't leave me the hell alone."

Notes

1. "Production Design Featurette," Tartan DVD featurette, *A Tale of Two Sisters*, 2003.
2. See Choi, 119.
3. Sim So-hui, editor of *Cine21*, quoted in Paquet, 95.
4. Tartan calls "Asia Extreme" both a brand and a genre. See Shin, 98.
5. After protests, the review was removed from the *New York Observer* website. See Shin, 96.
6. On tropes such as the virgin ghost and haunted objects, see Seo, 166.
7. Baudrillard, 23. Unfortunately, the term *meubles-monuments* has been translated in English as "monumental furniture," which erases the fact that Baudrillard is coining a compound noun by hyphenating two nouns rather than simply modifying a noun with an adjective—an important difference. For that reason, I am referencing the original French with my own translations throughout.
8. Ibid., 52 (translation mine).
9. Ibid., 22.
10. Ibid.

11. Ibid., 106. "L'objet ancien, c'est toujours, au sens fort du mot, un 'portrait de famille.'"
12. Bachelard, 80.
13. Ibid., 78.
14. I base my summary on the classic version collected by Zŏng In-sŏb. See Zŏng, 201–7.
15. See Leung, 175.
16. Tim Lucas, "A Tale of Two Sisters," *Video Watchdog*, April, 2005, 42.
17. See Dupuy, 65.
18. Tartan DVD commentary with director and actors, *A Tale of Two Sisters*, 2003.
19. Ibid.
20. "Behind the Scenes," Tartan DVD featurette, *A Tale of Two Sisters*, 2003.
21. Bachelard, 79. The words *armoire* and *wardrobe* are used interchangeably throughout the chapter. The Tartan DVD subtitles use *wardrobe*, and translators of Baudrillard and Bachelard also often change *armoire* to *wardrobe*.
22. Gateward, 193.
23. See Leung, 176.
24. Seet, 143.
25. See Kriel.
26. On color in horror, see Cameron.
27. Robert Cagle identifies the dress as a traditional Korean *hanbok*. If true, the dress adds another layer of memory and history to the armoire. See Cagle, 168.
28. Bachelard, 85.
29. Ibid., 81.
30. Ibid.
31. Marc, 13.
32. Ibid., 18.
33. Creed, 27.
34. Ibid.
35. Ibid.
36. Ibid.
37. Bachelard, 78.
38. Ibid., 85.
39. Haruhara Yoko, "The Key to Joseon Times," *Japan Times*, November 6, 2008, https://www.japantimes.co.jp/culture/2008/11/06/arts/the-key-to-joseon-times/#.WffBLhNSzUI.
40. See Cagle, 158; Oh, 64.
41. Gateward, 193.
42. Lee, 170–71.
43. "Production Design," Tartan DVD featurette, *A Tale of Two Sisters*, 2003.

PART IV
BATHROOM

12

RADIATOR

"He Watches Things Very, Very Carefully"

In 1965, David Lynch, an art school dropout with big ideas, spent an entire day staring at a bathroom radiator. Disillusioned after aborting a planned three-year stay in Europe after only two weeks, Lynch returned to Alexandria, Virginia, where in exchange for room and board, he helped redecorate the home of high school friend Toby Keeler. He began with the second-floor bathroom. Lynch's choice of tools says as much about his attention to detail as it does about his tendency to view the world as a canvas. Toby recalls, "He used a paintbrush that had a one-inch head on it! A teeny little brush. He spent *three days* painting this bathroom, and probably a day alone painting the radiator! He got into every single nook and cranny and painted that thing probably better than when it was new. It took him *forever*."[1] Nearly a decade later, in 1974, Lynch found himself once again between homes and in the middle of another interminable project facing another radiator. This time, the job had already taken three years. The American Film Institute had approved David Lynch's first feature-length film, *Eraserhead* (1977), in 1971 based on a twenty-two-page script and had given Lynch and his small crew free rein of the empty stables, greenhouse, and servants' quarters of the Greystone Mansion in Beverley Hills under the assumption that the project would be finished within a year, if not weeks. There, Lynch and his team set up a makeshift studio and began filming in 1972. By the spring of 1973, production was halted, leaving Lynch wondering if he would have to finish the film on his own using Claymation as a substitute for actors. But in May 1974, Lynch was able to resume what would ultimately be more than a five-year project.[2] The first scene shot in 1974 featured a radiator with a tiny stage nested in its coils and a cheerful chanteuse with the reassuring message, "In heaven, everything is fine."

Fig. 12.1. Henry contemplates his radiator in *Eraserhead* (1977).

Halfway through the shoot, Lynch's life was a wreck. He and his wife, Peggy, had separated, and most nights, he secretly slept on the set, probably not far from the radiator that so fascinates *Eraserhead*'s protagonist, Henry Spencer (Jack Nance). To say that Lynch and Spencer share certain character traits and experiences is not a stretch. The autobiographical qualities of the film, however abstract, have been noted by nearly every critic and by Lynch himself. Although the script was conceived in Los Angeles, the material and psychological conditions of the work derive from Lynch's time in Philadelphia as a newlywed and first-time father. "Philadelphia is known as the City of Brotherly Love, but when I was there, it was a hellhole," writes Lynch in his 2006 book about creativity and transcendental meditation—a practice he picked up in California during the *Eraserhead* years.[3] *Hellhole* also happens to be the word Henry's future father-in-law employs to describe the unnamed urban wasteland setting of *Eraserhead*. "I've seen this neighborhood change from pastures to the hellhole it is now," says Bill X (Allen Joseph) at the dinner party where Henry learns that his epileptic girlfriend, Mary X (Charlotte Stewart), has given birth to his, well, for lack of a better word, offspring. "They're still not sure it is a baby," says Mary. Either way, Henry is now a father saddled with unexpected responsibilities and a one-room apartment with a wife and a mewling baby creature swaddled in hospital gauze. As far as autobiographies go, *Eraserhead* is less a realist portrait than an emotional meditation.

Understandably, Lynch has not commented on speculation by critics that the mutant baby draws from his experience as new father of a child born with severely clubbed feet.[4] As for similarities in living quarters, David, Peggy, and baby Jennifer shared a twelve-bedroom home purchased for $3,500—nothing like the dimensions of Henry's one-bedroom apartment, but as the price might indicate, the neighborhood was full of "violence and hate and filth" and teeming with "factories, smoke, railroads, diners, the strangest characters and the darkest nights."[5] In other words, "beautiful," says Lynch, "if you see it the right way."[6]

One of the strongest similarities between Lynch and Henry Spencer is their eye for the marvelous in the mundane: "Henry is very sure that something is happening, but he doesn't understand it at all. He watches things very, very carefully, because he's trying to figure them out," says Lynch. "Everything should be looked at."[7] Film curator Greg Olson describes Henry as "an early member of the Lynchian cluster of characters who are searching for meaning in an inhospitable, chaotic universe. The seriousness and intensity with which these characters pay attention to what seem on the surface to be mundane details of their world invests the regarded objects with an almost metaphysical gravity and presence."[8] More than "almost," for Lynch does indeed find metaphysical weight in objects as ordinary as radiators. As French philosopher Éric Dufour argues, all Lynchian cinema aims "to make strange everything that is mundane, and in a symmetrical manner, to make mundane everything that is strange."[9] Lynch's ability to defamiliarize common objects seems to align his aesthetic with the surrealists, but the director does not approach his art with the surrealist manifesto in mind. While his work might disturb bourgeois conventions and certainly does interrogate the relation between dream states and reality, Lynch's drive to produce a new state of consciousness is propelled by childlike earnestness.[10] Even in his dismal apartment amid chaos, Henry stretches across his mattress and stares at his radiator with the beatific expression of a child ready to watch a favorite television program. Anyone who has heard David Lynch speak about his work or rhapsodize about the bliss of meditation can see that when the director praises the beautiful textures of a dissected cat or a rusting bridge, he is not trying to be provocative. Consider the childlike quality of the following thought from his 2006 book: "I don't necessarily love rotting bodies, but there's a texture to a rotting body that is unbelievable. Have you ever seen a little rotted animal? I love looking at those things, just as much as I like to look at a close-up of some tree bark, or a small bug, or a cup of coffee, or a piece of pie. You get in close and the textures are wonderful."[11]

Film curator Dennis Lim calls Lynch "the primitive artist of our most modern art"—a sort of naive genius who, perhaps wisely, does not participate in excessive intellectualizing over his own work.[12] "When you talk about things—unless you're a poet—a big thing becomes smaller," says Lynch.[13] What the film means is for others to decide, thinks Lynch, or better yet, for others to feel. "I *felt Eraserhead*, I didn't think it," explains the director.[14] Above all, *Eraserhead* requires an immersive, sensory engagement rather than verbal articulation. In Lynch's world, sounds are more important than words. Lynch's first wife, Peggy, recalls, "I was with David in his pre-verbal days. He didn't talk the way a lot of artists do. He would make noises, open his arms wide and make a sound like the wind."[15] So too does *Eraserhead*. The film opens its arms, envelops the spectator, and makes sounds like the wind, many of them emanating from the steam of a radiator. The heart, lungs, and spiritual center of *Eraserhead* reside in a hissing, mundane heating device that most people would consider unsightly. The radiator provides the sonic atmosphere of the film and embodies Lynch's fascination with industry and the transcendent beauty of pressurized, enclosed spaces. As Lynch once said in an interview, "*Eraserhead* is my most spiritual film, and, uhm, so, that's all I'm going to say."[16] No matter. What *Eraserhead* and Lynch refuse to say with words, they say with sounds, with hissing and buzzing, with howling and whining, and with the strains of a pipe organ penetrating the vaulted cast-iron architecture of a radiator. Such is the heaven of a hellhole.

French film scholar Michel Chion, whose work has spurred on the study of sound in film, gives Lynch his highest praise: "Lynch can be said to have renewed the cinema by way of sound."[17] To be fair, the director had ample help from sound designer Alan Splet, with whom he had collaborated even before the two moved to California. "We concocted and made every single sound," Lynch says.[18] The pair went to great lengths to create and record a vast collection of sounds, even to the point of calling someone in the middle of the night to ask if they could jump off their radiator to capture the audible effect.[19] Chion writes, "The film bathes in an uninterrupted sound-atmosphere, with the constant rush of boiler sounds, whirlpools, electronic organ chords, and the like."[20] The uninterrupted sound reflects Lynch's fascination with what he calls "room tone," which he explains as "the sound that you hear when there's silence, in between words or sentences."[21]

The room tone of Henry's apartment has a continuous undercurrent of radiator steam. Lim contends that the "droning" soundscape "reinforces the impression of a literal head movie, one that might be taking place within someone's pressurized, traumatized skull."[22] Lim sees the constant radiator hiss as something taunting and inescapable. And yet given the radiator's role as a curiously sacred space of warmth and refuge inhabited by an angelic "Lady in the Radiator" (Laurel Near), we might instead consider that one person's droning soundscape might be another's reassuring white noise or the vibrations of a unified field of consciousness. Although the idea of a spiritual radiator occupied by a moon-faced singer with a Doris Day bouffant hairdo seems absurd, the solace that Henry finds in the radiator has a parallel in Lynch's practice of transcendental meditation (TM). In July 1973, months before the "Lady in the Radiator" scene came into being, Lynch went to a TM center in Los Angeles, where an instructor who "looked like Doris Day" gave him a "very specific sound-vibration-thought" to use as a mantra.[23] Ever since, Lynch has tapped into that sound-vibration-thought twice a day for twenty minutes and has found in it a state of consciousness and happiness that he characterizes as "a thick beauty."[24]

Lynch and Splet layer sound upon sound to make *Eraserhead* pulsate with textures at once unnerving, heavy, and hypnotic. Chion observes that sound propels the viewer through the film in a continuum "shot through with discontinuities."[25] Abrupt sound cuts create "islands of sound time" such as Henry dropping a needle onto different tracks of the Fats Waller record that spins on his Victrola.[26] Chion exalts Lynch as a demiurge whose control over sonic inscription amounts to the creation of time—an image that arguably makes Lynch part Henry and part Man in the Planet (Jack Fisk), the former a manipulator of sonic space who lifts a mechanical arm and places a needle into the grooves of a record, and the latter an extraterrestrial lever-puller who makes life itself emit from Henry's gaping mouth in the film's cosmic opening sequence. Sound in *Eraserhead* is production and reproduction, each metallic screech and thump the birth cry of industrial output churning somewhere just out of sight. The continuity and discontinuity of sound in the film correspond to an environment where assembly-line production has outstripped organic growth. A continuum of discreet products stamped out for human consumption promises only confusion and dysfunction, like the fist-sized hemorrhaging man-made chickens served for dinner at the Xs' house. While the characters themselves are intent on making the distinction between the natural and the artificial

("They're man-made!" says Bill X of the chickens, and earlier, "People think pipes grow in their home. Well, they sure as hell don't!"), the sound works to undermine the separation between the products of human industry and those of cosmic creation. Mary's seizure, Mrs. X's orgasmic spasms, the incessant crying of the baby—all manifest as sonic textures in an industrial soundscape that knows no difference between the mechanical and the organic.

Eraserhead is a film that breathes and wheezes like a sickly infant, a film that buzzes and sparks with electrical spikes, hums with feedback, rumbles with passing locomotives, hisses with escape valve steam, and warbles and pops with low-fi record playback. Even when the dominant sounds shift abruptly to form Chion's "islands of sound time," a continuum derives from the sense that the world of *Eraserhead* shares a giant, common respiratory system. The escaping vapor in front of the X family home and the hissing pipes inside the living space, the vaporizer perched near the wheezing baby and the steam inside and outside the radiator exemplify the mirroring of interior and exterior sounds that Lynch deploys to create a feeling that the world is a composite organism. Richard Martin's book on Lynch's architecture notes that the director is "ever alert to how a building breathes and sweats."[27] From the absurd pipes in the X family home to the bricked-up window in Henry's apartment, Lynch draws the viewer's attention toward the openings and the blockages of the architectural body and builds the impression of sympathies between human and architectural forms. Sound creates those sympathies, as do pipes and tubing.

Scholars and critics have noticed the film's conflation of piping and human reproduction. The exposed pipe in the X home, for example, frames a crucial scene in which Henry discovers that he has fathered a child.[28] One critic blames a puritanical mind-set for the imagery, suggesting that the film emanates from the mind of "the sort of person who would refer to reproductive organs as 'plumbing.'"[29] But in the words of Justus Nieland, whose material approach to Lynch aligns most closely with my own, "the film's meditation on 'plumbing' is more than a puerile metaphor."[30] Nieland sees the "magical plumbing" of *Eraserhead* as one of many Lynchian examples of cinema as interior design.[31] Counter to the assertion of Mr. X, who is a plumber, Nieland argues, "pipes do grow in people's homes in *Eraserhead*."[32] The frequent juxtaposition of botanical themes with bleak industrial settings positions humans as well as the tortured forms of plants as industrial entities rather than natural beings. The bygone pastoral era referenced by Mr. X is now the stuff of home decor. The lobby of Henry's building has wallpaper and chairs with a botanical motif. Similarly, the Xs' living room is outfitted with floral drapes, floral wallpaper, and a floral upholstered chair, and their dining room features a hopelessly out-of-place oversized artificial floral arrangement and a floral still-life painting. In stark contrast to those manufactured depictions of nature, the few examples of organic growth in the film resemble pipes. But even pipes possess their own form of beauty for Lynch, especially when in a state of decay: "When you see an aging building or a rusted bridge, you are seeing nature and man working together," writes Lynch. "It's so organic."[33] Decay and malfunction are nature's supplement to human creation. An epigraph Lynch takes from the ancient Sanskrit text of the Upanishads for one of his book chapters is very telling:

> Know that all of Nature is but a magic theater,
> that the great Mother is the master magician,
> and that this whole world is peopled by her many parts.[34]

Lynch's love of magical theater nested within film and his global view of a unified field that underlies the world's many disparate parts find place within Henry's magical radiator.

In a sense, Lynch's radiator recuperates the wonder and mystery of heating and ventilation technology as a warm-bodied occupant of a home. Illustrations from early twentieth-century engineering and architectural texts do nothing to dissuade the mind from seeing pipes and radiators as treelike structures. Typical diagrams make it easy to imagine the boiler in the basement as a large trunk from which branches of pipes reach up into every room of the house and run through nests of radiator coils. In engineering illustrations, the heating and ventilation systems of an apartment building resemble rhizomes creeping through a hidden ecosystem in defiance of the neat boundaries that give human inhabitants the illusion of rigidly compartmentalized space. Drawings of lancet arches in a transverse section of a radiator could just as well have been taken from a textbook on medieval cathedrals. Exterior ornaments augment the wonder of a radiator, although more than anything, the design is meant to cover an eyesore rather than to glorify technology. Myriad articles in early twentieth-century women's magazines with titles such as "Camouflaging the Radiator" suggest that David Lynch and Henry Spencer are atypical in their desire to stare at cast iron heating devices.[35] That type of wonder was reserved for children, such as the young boy in the Dorothy Aldis poem "Radiator Lions," who tames the "most awful roarings" of the wild creatures in the parlor of his apartment.[36] Even for adults, noise—especially bothersome in early steam heating systems—animates the beastly side of the radiator. Similarly, a short story about a man, a woman, their baby, and a radiator in the 1891 *Book O' Nine Tales* gives a slew of descriptors for the radiator and its sounds, including "the 'Anvil Chorus,'" a "clattering din, as if all the kettles and pans in the house were being thrown violently across the floor," a "thoroughly inebriated drum corps practising upon sheet-iron air-tight stoves," the "fusillade" of an artillery regiment, "the brays of a drove of brazen donkeys," the "noise of mighty rushing waters, the clanking of chains, the din of a political convention, the characteristic disturbances of a hundred factories and machine-shops, with the deafening whirr of all the elevated railways in the universe."[37] At the end of the tale, in response to the husband's misogynistic joke about nagging wives, the radiator "gives a chuckle so apt as to suggest the possession of a sinister consciousness on the part of that noisy instrument of torture."[38] Lynch's radiator is quite tame in comparison—that is, until it leads Henry to commit infanticide.

Stompin' the Bug

Before there was the "Lady in the Radiator," the radiator was already a center of focus in *Eraserhead*. Shots of the radiator and of Henry staring at the unremarkable fixture had already been filmed before Lynch was hit by inspiration one day during lunch and sketched out "this little lady, and little fetuses falling out of her." As Lynch explains, "I thought she would live in the radiator, where it's nice and warm, and this would be a real comfort for Henry."[39] It's hard to imagine *Eraserhead* without the Lady in the Radiator, without the repetitive song "In Heaven" (an instant cult cover song), without the disturbing fetus-stomping and without the final embrace in radiator paradise—the happy ending that Lynch sums up as "Henry goes to heaven."[40] Nevertheless, even without its occupant, the radiator represents a point of fixation for Henry that embodies both warmth and pressure. Henry first uses the radiator to dry a sock, wet from stepping in a puddle on his way home. He contemplates the unadorned cast-iron device, and the hissing becomes louder and louder, creating an island of sound time (to use Chion's term) during which the camera pans along the radiator and then the base, where a covering of moss and earth gives the impression that radiators are planted in homes. Henry's gaze moves toward the bricked window, and outside rumblings join the sonic mix until the hissing dies down to its normal, still prominent level.

Henry's next contemplation of the radiator happens once the baby is in his apartment. The record player is spinning, but the music has ended. The needle conveys the hum of noise in that space where the printed label meets the smooth inner ring of the record. Henry lets it continue to spin and lies facedown across the mattress. He smiles at the radiator while Mary feeds the baby. The camera tilts up from the organic pile to the radiator coils, now illuminated from within. Again, a loud hiss carves out an acoustic island for Henry and the radiator. Amid the noise, a creaking sound and a brighter light indicate the opening of the stage, which Henry sees only for a moment before the lights dim and the cry of the baby intrudes on his radiator refuge.

The third radiator sequence begins once Mary has left Henry to care for the suddenly ill baby. Drowning out the steady sigh of the vaporizer and the whines of the baby, the radiator hiss once again carves out a separate space. A new creaking sound layer indicates the opening of stage doors as the camera moves into the cast-iron structure. Now inside, the camera sweeps along the stage, and one by one, bulbs light up the checkered floor. "Stompin' the Bug" by Fats Waller accompanies the Lady in the Radiator, who smiles and shuffles side to side, hands clasped to her chest. Fetuses do not fall out of her as Lynch had first imagined in his sketch. Instead, fetus-like cords drop from above onto the stage. Chion calls the intruders "organic cords"; others call them "sperm-like objects" or "spermy fetuses," while a Lacan enthusiast contends they are lamellae derived from "the sexed subject's initial loss of the life substance."[41] In a 1997 interview, assistant director Catherine Coulson admits to picking up fresh umbilical cords every night from a local hospital during that period of shooting, stating that she wore scrubs and stood outside the delivery room, "and they would come out with a jar of fresh bili cords," no questions asked.[42] Whatever the modified umbilical cord fetus invaders are, the show must go on for the Lady in the Radiator. Once the things impede her path, the performer stomps on their white goo-filled bodies with an impish grin. Olson's interpretation of her action is compelling: "In Lynch's cosmology, the chastely asexual, fetus-stomping Radiator Lady is like an anti-Christ to the Planet Man's Universal Procreational Lever-Puller in the sky."[43]

Looking beyond the gross-out factor and the evident wish-fulfillment fantasy that the fetus-stomping must represent for Henry as he copes poorly with his sick, unwanted offspring, the stomping sequence further advances the pipe-dominant narrative of the film by showing that plumbing grows in bodies as well as in homes. The Fats Waller "Stompin' the Bug" tune to which the squashing occurs was recorded in Camden, New Jersey, in 1927 on the Estey pipe organ of an old Baptist church that had been converted into a recording studio.[44] "Lenox Avenue Blues," another Fats Waller tune used in the film, was also recorded on the same pipe organ. The originator of the Estey company, Jacob Estey, has a rags-to-riches story with serendipitous relevance to *Eraserhead*. Orphaned at age four, then adopted and abused until he ran away at age thirteen, Estey began an apprenticeship to a manufacturer of lead pipes and pumps. At age twenty-one, he took all of his savings and went into the plumbing business.[45] Estey had no musical background, but he successfully transitioned from one pipe business to another. What better instrument to accompany the Lady in the Radiator than a pipe organ fathered by a plumber? Moreover, the music of Fats Waller embodies the coexistence of sacred and profane so natural to the Lynchian universe. Waller's first paid musical job was playing organ for the silent movies at the Lincoln Theatre, or as his father called it, "the house of Satan."[46] In Lynch's world, Fats Waller and Jacob Estey's pipe organ herald the angel of a hellhole's heaven.

The separation of interior and exterior that Lynch perpetually erases through sonic bridges becomes so tenuous by this point in the film that the same umbilical fetuses from the stage now invade Henry's bed. The next time the Lady in the Radiator appears, no establishing shot or zoom to the radiator is necessary. The boundaries between the outside and inside of the radiator are as fluid as the boundaries between dream and reality. An interviewer once asked Lynch, "Is Henry dreaming the film up? Or is he being dreamt?" In his typical fashion, the director replied, "See, that's something I can't say."[47] And little does it matter. The permeability of space makes the entire film appear to reside inside a radiator or inside the fever dream that comes from living in an environment as pressurized, industrial, and steam-filled as a radiator. When the Lady in the Radiator makes this latest appearance, she now sings about heaven, the promise of escape to a place where "everything is fine." When she finishes her song, Henry joins her on stage and takes her hand. What follows is the sequence that inspired the film and its title, the meaning of which I will not attempt to unravel or to explain in detail. Suffice it to say, Henry's head, which is pushed out of place by a growing phallic baby head, falls to the stage, sinks through a puddle, and then plummets from the sky and splats onto the pavement. A young boy picks the head up and takes it to a factory, where it is made into pencil erasers and tested by a factory employee. This sequence of Henry as a literal eraserhead might be described as the mutant filmic offspring of Italian neorealism coupled with Fernand Léger's *Ballet mécanique* (1924). For some, the sequence signals a gnostic drive to erase matter, self-effacement as rebirth.[48] Eraser dust, brushed into the air after testing, hovers against a black background like stars in the heavens. All sense of scale is lost, as is all sense of interiority and exteriority. The eraser cosmos image fades to Henry in bed, hands over ears and elbows pointing up at the ceiling. Slowly, he parts his elbows in a manner that gives the impression of a head emerging from between spread legs—an image that supports the theory of Henry's radiator sequence as rebirth. But there's still that fussy baby to contend with before Henry will ever be free.

The final minutes of *Eraserhead* are what, for many, push the film into the horror genre.[49] Whether out of curiosity or malice, Henry takes scissors to the baby's gauze only to find no skin underneath to keep the organs in place. From the center, the body opens like two stage doors, offering a close-up view of abject body horror, or if you're Lynch, a view of beautiful textures. Something of an ejaculatory castration ensues, followed by bizarre and gruesome transformations of the baby. The convulsing, metamorphosing baby is intercut with shots of a flickering lamp and sparking electrical sockets as if to suggest an affinity between the electrical field and the creature. The Man in the Planet, the ally of baby production, works his levers in vain as sparks fly from the base. Then a shift in sound and image introduces Henry to the white-hot steam of radiator heaven. The Lady in the Radiator warmly greets Henry with a loving embrace. Eyes closed, his expression at last peaceful, Henry lingers with his head resting on her shoulder. Everything is fine. Only the steady roar of steam occupies this island of space, and for Henry, the white noise is probably as blissful as the sound-vibration-thought that Lynch has been accessing for twenty minutes twice a day since 1973.

Postscript: Painting Out the Radiator

In the early (and only) script of *Eraserhead*, Henry was to meet his demise inside the gaping mouth of the giant mutant baby.[50] Instead, Lynch began to see the radiator from Henry's point of view, and everything changed. Lynch explains, "And then I saw the radiator in my head. And it was the instrument for producing warmth in a room; it made me sort of happy—like me as Henry, say. I saw this opening to another place."[51] Lynch ran into the room with the radiator and studied it more closely, noticing for the first time "a little kind of chamber, like a stage in it." He continues, "I'm not kidding you. It was right there, and it just changed everything."[52] Thanks to radiator restoration specialist Pierre Lemieux at Ecorad, I can offer a solution to the mystery of the unexpected chamber: Henry's radiator is a gas-fired steam radiator, and the stagelike space is for the combustion.[53] The fortuitous chamber allowed Lynch to build small doors and a stage into the structure, thereby granting the radiator the status of a magical theater—an important trope in Lynchian cosmology. The post-script change saves Henry from victimization in an Oedipal narrative and instead offers radiator heaven's version of a ride off into the sunset. According to Lim, the conclusion is classic Lynch: "A happy ending that may not be one."[54]

In place of consumption (the baby that devours the father), *Eraserhead* ends in a planetary explosion and the triumph of a white-hot radiator-steam atmosphere. As the last in a series of radiator-related scenes, the steamy ending with the sweetly chaste hug envelops the cinema screen in white. The stage either has overtaken the screen or has dissolved into pure screen. To decide which is as futile and unnecessary as separating dream from reality in the film. Nevertheless, a look back at the radiator scenes discussed above reveals a clear visual logic that moves progressively from exteriority to interiority and finally to a dissolution of boundaries. First, when Henry drapes his wet sock on the radiator, the camera and Henry contemplate its external structure. The slow pan along the moss and dirt at the iron base helps "plant" the radiator in the space. Second, the radiator is seen from the ground up, and for the first time, light shines from inside the coils. Third, a more active zigzagging camera movement into the coils initiates the "Stompin' the Bug" scene. Fourth, the radiator stage no longer requires an establishing shot. The lengthy "eraserhead" sequence cuts straight to the stage, which becomes permeable when Henry's head falls through a puddle, into the sky, and onto the pavement. Finally, the white steam of the ending melts into pure atmosphere. Those in favor of gnostic readings of the film will find validation in what appears to be a move toward immateriality. Another way to read the ending is as a move toward the ground zero of decor, the baseline of *Eraserhead*'s room tone: industrial steam and a unified sonic hum.

Nothing could be more Lynchian than the American Radiator Company's "Colonial Model House" exhibit at the 1904 St. Louis World's Fair. With the open facade of a doll's house, the two-story walk-in set displayed "the simplicity of the modern warming outfit" and the ways in which radiators can harmonize with draperies and other furnishings.[55] A view of the house published in the company's 1905 booklet *Radiation and Decoration* shows the colonial home surrounded by a white picket fence (a favorite Lynchian trope) made entirely of radiators, and an arched gateway made of two boilers and overhead connecting pipes. Inside the fence grow hedges of radiators and round radiator bases topped with ferns. Throughout the house, ornate painted radiators demonstrate their compatibility with floral wallpaper and tasteful furnishings—a happy confluence of organic and industrial growth. Michel Foucault calls sites such as these (fairs, the cinema, and the theater) "heterotopias"—sites that contain contradictory impulses. The oldest heterotopias, Foucault recalls, are ancient Persian gardens that represent the world in microcosmic space and place a fountain at the center "like an umbilicus."[56] The heart of the world converges with plumbing. Foucault also notes that the patterns of Persian rugs were meant to evoke those heterotopian gardens. In other words, we may not know it, but heterotopias exist in our home decor. For Lynch, this is certainly the case. Lynch's heterotopian radiator is a convergence of piping of all kinds—organic, industrial, and musical.

I cannot help but wonder how, exactly, Lynch painted the Keelers' radiator in 1965. Did he use more than one color? Did he paint it the same color as the bathroom walls? Common decorating practice took two approaches to overcoming the unwelcome view of bare iron: camouflage and ornamentation. To overcome the industrial look, radiator companies offered embellished patterns with floral and Italianate motifs. As a *Good Housekeeping* article from 1918 explains, "manufacturers have striven to make the radiator more ornamental by wreathing its brazen coils with blobby cast-iron roses or petrified Roman garlands painted in brilliant colors," but the results have been "highly unfortunate."[57] The American Radiator Company's lavish *Radiation and Decoration* suggests that a tasteful paint job "subdues" or "paints the radiator out."[58] In other cases, bold color and pattern create a theatrical effect that embraces the radiator as a sculptural object. Did Lynch "paint out" the Keelers' radiator? Did he add a contrasting color to make it a focal point? Did the Keelers' radiator have a floral pattern to mask its industrial nature? In all likelihood, the Keelers wanted their radiator to

Fig. 12.2. The American Radiator Company's exhibit at the 1904 St. Louis World's Fair (American Radiator Company, 27).

disappear, to be painted out. But maybe, while staring into every nook and cranny of that radiator for a solid day, nineteen-year-old David Lynch, the art school dropout, saw something worth looking at.

Notes

1. Rodley, 31.
2. See Chion, *David Lynch*, 37.
3. Lynch, 31.
4. See Olson, 87.
5. Rodley, 42–43.
6. Saban and Longacre, 5.
7. Rodley, 56.
8. Olson, 62–63.
9. Dufour, 8 (translation mine).
10. See Rodley, xi. As Rodley observes, we should not confuse Lynch's "frequent use of the absurd or the incongruous" with surrealism.
11. Lynch, 121.
12. Lim, 13.
13. Rodley, 27.
14. Ibid., 64.
15. Ibid., 32.

16. Olson, 88.
17. Chion, *David Lynch*, 44.
18. Indiana, 11.
19. "2014," Criterion DVD bonus feature, *Eraserhead*.
20. Chion, *David Lynch*, 38. Chion is incorrect about the "electronic" organ, however, as I later explain.
21. Rodley, 72–73.
22. Lim, 32.
23. Lynch, 4.
24. Ibid.
25. Chion, *David Lynch*, 44.
26. Ibid., 45.
27. R. Martin, 70.
28. See R. Martin, 76; Nieland, 13.
29. Veronica Gangem, cited in a footnote in Hoberman and Rosenbaum, 236.
30. Nieland, 14.
31. Ibid., 18.
32. Ibid., 12.
33. Lynch, 119.
34. Ibid., 15.
35. See Fales and Northend.
36. Aldis, 79.
37. Bates, 158–59.
38. Ibid., 161.
39. Olson, 72.
40. Indiana, 14.
41. Chion, *David Lynch*, 32; R. Martin, 145; Hoberman and Rosenbaum, 214; McGowan, 32.
42. "1997," Criterion DVD bonus feature, *Eraserhead*.
43. Olson, 78.
44. Kirkeby, 218.
45. Nadworny, 50.
46. Kirkeby, 25.
47. Rodley, 72.
48. For gnostic readings on Lynch, see Olson, 80; Wilson, 43.
49. See Schneider for an example of someone arguing for the film's adherence to genre conventions.
50. Olson, 88.
51. Rodley, 65.
52. Rodley, 65–66.
53. Thanks also to Patricia Cloutier for facilitating the hunt for the *Eraserhead* radiator. For a manual on this type of radiator, see Clow.
54. Lim, 47.
55. American Radiator Company, 27.
56. Foucault, 25.
57. Fales and Northend, 56.
58. American Radiator Company, 10.

13

PILLS

AN OBVIOUS BUT CRUCIAL DESIGN FEATURE THAT SETS pills apart from the other household objects in this book is the fact that pills are meant to be ingested. The same might also be true of certain houseplants, such as potted herbs, but most would agree that a living plant differs significantly from a pill. In fact, in one of the films discussed in this chapter, fresh herbs stand in violent opposition to vitamin pills. Even though vitamins have a metonymic link to nature, as do capsules of herbal supplements, the pill as a delivery system guarantees a connection to science and medicine, to institutions and forces culturally encoded as entities distinct from the natural world. Many theorists, however, have discarded dichotomous thinking about nature and culture in favor of integrated and continuous concepts such as Donna Haraway's "naturecultures"—a term that fuses the biological and social binary into a connected whole.[1] Pharmaceuticals exemplify the complexity of naturecultures because they act in ways that define what is natural and what requires medical intervention. Furthermore, their reach extends from the macro level of political institutions to the microsphere of molecular being. As sociologist Johanne Collin remarks, scholarship is beginning to take "a biographical approach to the study of pharmaceutical drugs" by including the full life cycle of the objects from design to distribution and consumption.[2] In short, pills have lives. As the coauthors of "Living Drugs" argue, "as much as we live through drugs, they live through us."[3]

Pills inhabit broad social structures, human bodies, and posthuman molecular environments. Pills are actors, a fact that explains why their presence on screen is rarely that of mere set decor. Pills engage characters. Pills drive narrative, as Morpheus makes clear in *The Matrix* (1999): "You take the blue pill, the story ends.... You take the red pill, you stay in Wonderland, and I show how deep the rabbit hole goes." The science fiction pill is always mind-bending. In horror, a pill is always suspect, always ready to act on the human body in ways that force the viewer to reconsider motives, actions, and interpretative frameworks. A pill is fast-acting unreliable narration. In horror, pills are weapons or, conversely, talismanic objects that enhance or protect the body. Pills mutate their host for better or worse. The pills in the films covered in this chapter have life-and-death consequences for the characters. The pill-actors include vitamins to fortify a psychopathic child, sleeping pills that beg to be weaponized, prenatal supplements that compete with herbal drinks to control the fetal development of Satan's spawn, and anticonvulsants that take on Christianity in court. In each case presented here, pills act on gendered (female) racially encoded (white) bodies, which is not surprising, given the pervasive presence of white women's bodies as fetishized objects in both the horror genre and advertising media for pharmaceuticals.[4] The three films—*The Bad Seed* (1956), *Rosemary's Baby* (1968), and *The Exorcism of Emily Rose* (2005)—encompass pregnancy, childhood, and adulthood. Each media text also portrays distinct ways in which pills script the human body—for example, through vitamins, which posit and then supplement an inherent lack; through sleeping pills, which assert temporal normativity and also hold great potential for abuse; and through medications that influence neurotransmission to suppress conditions that would have been grounds for exorcism or sterilization in times past.

Medicated Motherhood and Vitamin-Enriched Childhood

The Bad Seed, the 1954 William March novel adapted for stage that same year and then for screen two years later, presents a debate on the problem of evil that argues for genetic determinism but clings to moralistic environmental factors. No one and everyone is to blame for the crimes of an unlikely villain. Rhoda Penmark (Patty McCormack) is a prim and proper eight-year-old who knows what she wants and will get it by any means necessary. With her vaguely menacing Aryan features and platinum-blonde Brynhildr braids to match, Rhoda is tailor-made for model citizenship and murderous hidden agendas. Her family is a picture of 1950s American values. Her doting (although frequently absent) father is a military colonel, and her mother, Christine (Nancy Kelly), is an elegant if somewhat anxious exemplar of upscale midcentury housewifery. Rhoda's predilection for shiny treasures such as the best penmanship medal won by her lower-class

Fig. 13.1. Christine gives new "vitamins" to Rhoda in *The Bad Seed* (1956).

schoolmate Claude Daigle triggers the murderous instincts of the dainty runner-up. Like a homicidal version of Shirley Temple, Rhoda taps her troubles away by striking Claude with the metal heel taps of her shoes until he drowns in a bay during a school picnic. When resident handyman and fellow takes-one-to-know-one sociopath Leroy Jessup (Henry Jones) claims to have retrieved evidence of the crime, she sets him on fire. As Christine's suspicions mount and her countenance worsens, urbane landlady and indulgent gift giver Monica Breedlove (Evelyn Varden) offers haggard Christine a bottle of adult vitamins and a bottle of sleeping pills. Once Christine learns that her daughter is indeed a killer—a bad seed from a criminal bloodline kept hidden from her by her adoptive father—she blames herself for having passed on the gene and concludes that murder-suicide is the only reasonable solution. She will give Rhoda a handful of "new vitamins" and then shoot herself. What could possibly go wrong?

The Bad Seed is rife with paradox, but the logical inconsistencies make perverse sense when viewed in the context of the changing 1950s relationship between medicine, psychiatry, and morality. Christine's infanticidal logic is baffling but passes for the best course of action in the film. Horror springs less from the attempted murder-suicide than from the hospital waiting-room revelation that Christine has failed on both counts. Her self-inflicted gunshot wound to the head did not kill her, and worse, the sound of the gunshot drew help to Rhoda before the overdose of sleeping pills had taken full effect. To satisfy requirements of the Hays Code, which stipulated a crime-never-pays moral stance, the film adaptation tacks on a deus ex machina lightning strike to finish off the little devil. The supposed morality of the revised ending, however, essentially puts a divine stamp of approval on Christine's choice to kill her daughter. Heaven's own electric chair metes out justice and corrects maternal failure. After all, what else could have been done? Medication? Incarceration? Therapy? No, Rhoda's precocious psychopathy and criminal genes fate the girl to follow in the footsteps of her absent grandmother, Bessie Denker, a beautiful for-profit serial killer who poisoned her own children except for the hiding toddler Christine. Richard Bravo (Paul Fix)—a proponent of nurture over nature—chose to conceal his adopted daughter's sordid heritage and fails to see anything but perfection in granddaughter Rhoda.

Clearly, Mr. Bravo is wrong. Rhoda is a born monster despite her privilege—or perhaps because of her privilege. In spite of the titular "bad seed" philosophy, the environment gets its share of the blame. Like Patrick Bateman (Christine Bale) in *American Psycho* (2000), Rhoda is the embodiment of the values of her time: ambition, materialism, good looks, dissimulation—in short, everything a capitalist society could want in a productive citizen. "Rhoda darkly embodies the American family dream," writes Tony Williams in his study of the family in American horror.[5] Williams argues that social causes are behind Rhoda's problems, not genes: "Rhoda merely enacts on a local scale the logical consequences of her father's Cold War—Pentagon activities."[6] Monica Breedlove incessantly enables Rhoda's greed and sense of superiority with gifts. She gives the girl rhinestone-framed glasses to look like a "Hollywood actress," a necklace and two different birthstones for being "such a natural little girl" who is not afraid to ask for what she wants, and a second popsicle since she's not one of those "fat, self-indulgent little blobs." Appearance is everything. Tellingly, each of Monica's gifts signals duplicity: the glasses reference star-quality acting, while the two different birthstones and the second popsicle give a sense of Rhoda as two children in one. Christine, meanwhile, reinforces Rhoda's two-faced tendencies through discipline rather than gifts. When Rhoda lies, Christine critiques her acting skills: "It is not a very good act. Now, you may perfect it enough to convince someone who doesn't know you, but right at present, it is quite easy to see through." However bad Christine may feel, her reaction on hearing her daughter's confession to two murders is to engage in a cover-up. Only after Leroy burns alive in front of Christine does the mother abandon hope of saving Rhoda. After witnessing firsthand what her daughter is capable of, Christine accepts that Rhoda is a born criminal—a conclusion that nevertheless does not stop her from believing that she alone bears the responsibility for what her daughter has done.

The relative ease with which Christine accepts infanticide as her best option reflects a pervasive cultural bias against "defects" that was only beginning to fall out of favor in the aftermath of the Second World War. Had Christine known about her genetic heritage, she would never have had children. Her culpability stems from passing on the gene, which skips a generation according to every summary, analysis, or review of *The Bad Seed*. And although by all accounts, that is how March intended the criminal gene to manifest itself, the fact remains that Christine performs the same infanticidal act as her mother, even to the point of adopting the same methods. Given her childhood trauma with poison, Christine has good reason to tell Monica, "I really don't like sleeping pills. I'm afraid of them." Christine's attempted murder stems not from greed but from the logic that those "poor deformed children born without pity" are monsters who never should have been born. The problem with Rhoda is the same one that led three juries to acquit Bessie Denker: a deformity that evades the social and medical gaze. Again, both society and genetics are to blame. When Christine asks if Bessie was ever found out, criminologist Reggie Tasker (Gage Clarke) replies, "Not in this country. Three juries looked at that lovely dewy face and heard that melting cultured voice and said she couldn't have done it." Reggie's preface, "not in this country," indicts Americans for being blinded by beauty and social standing. Bad seeds like Bessie "present a more convincing picture of virtue than normal folk."

A virtually forgotten film that might be read as a companion piece to *The Bad Seed* is *The Black Stork* (1917), the "eugenic love story" based on the real-life case of Dr. Harry J. Haiselden in which the doctor refuses to save the life of a deformed newborn and advises the young parents that the baby is better off dead.[7] After a vision from God of the child's painful and criminal future, the mother agrees to let the baby die, and Jesus receives its soul. *The Black Stork* enjoyed a long commercial run in American theaters throughout the 1920s after being retitled *Are You Fit to Marry?* in 1918. A revised rerelease came out in 1927 and continued to play in traveling shows and in small theaters as late as 1942.[8] It is not difficult to imagine that the character Christine in *The Bad Seed*, or any audience member in 1956, might have been influenced by the ideas behind *The Black Stork*. When Dr. Haiselden admitted to routinely letting deformed infants die, he did so not as a confession but as part of a public advocacy agenda for the elimination of lives not worth living. The list of well-known backers of Haiselden's viewpoint is disturbingly long and includes celebrated doctors, nurses, judges, historians, the founder of the Food and Drug Administration, the National Medico-Legal Society, and shockingly, Hellen Keller.[9] By the time *The Black Stork* hit theaters, sixteen states had already passed laws to legalize the sterilization of criminals, the mentally handicapped, the insane, and epileptics.[10] In 1927, the year of *The Black Stork*'s rerelease, the Supreme Court infamously ruled 8–1 in *Buck v. Bell* that an eighteen-year-old girl in the Virginia State Colony for Epileptics and Feeble Minded could be forcibly sterilized after she had given birth to a "mentally defective" child. Justice Oliver Wendell Holmes argued that "three generations of imbeciles was enough."[11] The list of "degenerate protoplasm" created by the Eugenics Record Office included people with physical or mental disabilities, certain diseases, addictions, and weak constitutions, as well as the poor.[12] When Hitler began mass sterilizations, the superintendent of Virginia's Western State Hospital complained, "Hitler is beating us at our own game!"[13]

Although it would be nice to believe that eugenics ended with the war, Dorothy Porter's statement in her study of public health is probably more accurate: "The revelations of mass murder under the Third Reich temporarily undermined the authority of eugenics."[14] Ideas taught at high schools and colleges across the nation do not die overnight. Instead, questions of heredity and environment surfaced elsewhere, including in pills, which straddle the nature/nurture conundrum by promising to supplement deficiencies and to intervene biologically where individuals fall short of standards deemed "normal." One of the most pervasive pill interventions is vitamins. Casimir Funk coined the word *vitamine* in 1912 in a seminal paper about the relationship between diet and health. He identified four "vitamines" (from "vital anime") according to the diseases they fought: antiberiberi, antirickets, antiscurvy, and antipellagra.[15] Although vitamin pills came later, as scientists learned to isolate and synthesize more vitamins, Funk laid the conceptual groundwork for the widespread belief that supplements could fight disease and hence optimize bodies. Little did it matter that most children were not at risk for diseases such as scurvy and rickets; the allure of a vital force hidden in foods developed a market for supplements, whether they were needed or not.

A consequence of vitamin advertising beginning as early as the 1930s is the fear of subclinical deficiencies. The Food and Drug Administration attempted to control spurious claims by vitamin manufacturers, but their efforts and governmental authority were undermined by the U.S. military's use of vitamin tablets. Regulations were consequently postponed until the 1960s, leaving companies ample time to promote vitamin supplements as essential remedies for ostensibly widespread and yet undetectable deficiencies.[16] "Vitamania" seized the country, and belief in the power of vitamins far exceeded scientific evidence.[17] Thanks to the synthesis of vitamins, widespread vitamin enrichment became possible. In the 1940s, companies began to enrich processed flour with thiamine, niacin, and riboflavin, and milk with vitamin D.[18] Vitamin fortification and vitamin supplements resulted in an abstraction of food that Gyorgy Scrinis has called "nutritionism." The problem, says Scrinis, is that "taking vitamin supplements is nevertheless a reductive, one-dimensional, and fragmented approach to food and the body."[19] Swallowing a vitamin pill does not equate to eating vitamins as they naturally occur in foods. From a broader standpoint more relevant to *The Bad Seed*, nutritionism medicalizes motherhood. Belief in subclinical threats to children makes mothers into extensions of medical authority while advertisers sell products by generating fear of maternal incompetency. "Are you bringing up your children properly?" asks an ad for vitamin-rich Grape-Nuts cereal. "It is possible to give children all the food they can possibly eat—and still their little bodies can be under-nourished."[20] Due to nutritionism, even food not artificially enriched with vitamins becomes first and foremost a vitamin delivery system. In the 1950s, the "golden decade" for vitamin sales, often every member of the household, pets included, took at least one vitamin pill a day.[21] By the 1950s, nutritionists genuinely believed they had solved all of the big questions and had discovered all of the vitamins.[22] It is against that optimism that the horror of *The Bad Seed* emerges.

The missing actors in discussions of whether Rhoda is spoiled rotten or just born rotten are the pills that participate so heavily in the plot. Pills occupy a moral space and a medical space in the story and are a source of horror because they fail at every turn. Monica, a self-proclaimed expert in psychoanalysis and the film's strongest advocate of pills, is also the most blind to Rhoda's psychopathy. From Monica's point of view, Christine is the one in need of bionormative intervention, not Rhoda. "Do you take vitamins regularly?" asks Monica, noticing how distraught Christine has become. "No . . . no, I don't," replies Christine, in what sounds like the lead-in to a vitamin commercial. "Well, you should, darling. That's one of the things we do know." By "we," Monica means herself and the broader modern scientific and medical community—what might be called a "medical we" or the majestic plural of the medicalized consumer. Monica has internalized the advertising of her day to become an enthusiast of pill-based interventions. She has "an awfully good combination" that she promises to bring down to Christine. Not yet finished with her prescriptions, Monica then asks, "Do you sleep enough?" When Christine responds, "No, not always," Monica again uses "we" in a manner that aligns her with modern research: "You must have some sleeping pills; that much we can do." Monica presents the "things we do know" and the thing "we can do," but Rhoda is evidence that we do not know much and can do very little.

Women are pill dispensaries in *The Bad Seed*, not unlike the middle-class mothers of the 1940s and 1950s who were expected to serve emergent nutritionist and bionormative regimes with the help of the local drugstore. Christine supplements her child while Monica supplements Christine. The brand of sleeping pills given to Christine and then deployed by her against Rhoda is not mentioned, but in all likelihood, the pills were barbiturates. At least a dozen brands of barbiturates were in common use by 1950, and more than two thousand different kinds had been synthesized.[23] Efforts to combat the "lullaby pill peril" (as *Newsweek* labeled the problem in 1939) only became more difficult after the Second World War, with returning soldiers already primed for barbiturate and amphetamine consumption by their service.[24] The overproduction (enough for twenty-four pills for every American in 1948) and extramedical use of barbiturates rivaled the opiate problems of the nineteenth century.[25] Had *The Bad Seed* been written a little later, Monica might have offered Christine some Miltown (meprobamate), the "miracle cure for anxiety" first released in 1955 and taken by one in twenty Americans by 1956.[26] Instead, Christine receives an unnamed brand of sleeping pill, which she repurposes for euthanasia, just as the Nazis had done with the previously fashionable sleeping drugs Luminal and Veronal.[27]

The Bad Seed sits uneasily at the cusp of far-reaching medical shifts whose theoretical frameworks had yet to be articulated. The rumblings of phenomena such as Foucault's notion of biopower and related theories of biopolitics, biomedicalization, pharmaceuticalization, and molecularization were present in the 1950s at most in "larvated" form (to use one of Monica Breedlove's psychoanalytic terms).[28] That is, companies marketing vitamin supplements, barbiturates, and other pill-based solutions to problems, including those anxiety-producing deficiencies labeled "subclinical," trained women as the maternal arm of medicine in the home to identify, shop for, and distribute supplements and drugs as risk-prevention against unseen abnormalities. This is not to say that ideological forces conspired to wrest maternal authority from the home or to reconstruct the subject of medicine to the point of treating molecules instead of patients; rather, the point is to acknowledge those transformations as a complex network of actors, including pills, which, as Collin argues, participate as more than "material avatars of larger social forces."[29] Today, the notion that "cultures are literally folded into the materiality of certain drugs" (arguably, *all* drugs) is increasingly evident.[30] It is impossible to unpack all of those cultures and forces here, but a key idea (and a Cold War obsession) that has insinuated itself into everyday objects such as vitamin supplements is risk prevention.

The Bad Seed is horror about risk, and pills are the (failed) solution to eliminating that risk. Christine's justification for giving her daughter an overdose of sleeping pills is that Rhoda will kill again and again if not stopped. Death is more humane than institutionalization in her mind, and so it was in the thinking of the general public given the state of institutions at the time.[31] Moreover, the criminal justice system failed to convict Bessie Denker, so the odds of institutional justice are slim. The psychoanalysis with which Monica is so infatuated was better at naming mental illnesses than treating them. As sociologist Nikolas Rose explains, "Many of the troubles of psychiatry in the 1950s and 1960s flowed from its inability to demonstrate organic correlates of its diagnoses," which left the field impotent in the assessment of criminal responsibility.[32] The rise of psychopharmacological drugs and the coincident surge in the mind's perceived malleability had not quite arrived when Marsh published *The Bad Seed*. Neurochemical selfhood can be constructed only as psychiatric drugs move from the general (sedatives and stimulants) to the specific—"chlorpromazine for psychosis, reserpine for hypertension, the benzodiazepines for anxiety, imipramine for depression," all beginning from the 1950s onward.[33] Monica's "awfully good combination" of vitamins and her sharing of sleeping pills demonstrate a readiness for the designer drugs of the future but a reality of blunt instruments. According to Collin and numerous other scholars of medicine, "the mid-20th century marked the beginning of a major reconfiguration of the relationship between signs, symptoms and pathologies."[34] A growing pharmaceuticals industry, increased medical specialization, and data analysis led to "normal curves" or "statistical benchmarks for identifying at-risk groups."[35] An ounce of prevention was just a pill away.

Pills as risk prevention promise to optimize bodies and eliminate disease before it happens. Pills offer to fulfill some of the goals of eugenics but without the ideological toxicity. Nutritional consciousness made vitamins a quick fix for poor populations or those judged to have weak constitutions. Where sterilization is no longer a socially acceptable form of biopower, supplementation and medication step in. At-risk populations might be brought to standards of normalcy through pills rather than procedures. Among the negative risks associated with pills—side effects excluded—is abuse or neglect by women (mothers in particular) who are simultaneously the target demographic pill consumers and pill distributors as surrogate nurses in the home. Not coincidentally, the two women serial killers mentioned in *The Bad Seed* are both poisoners. When Reggie discusses his criminological reporting at a lunch party hosted by Christine, he mentions Mrs. Allison, a nurse who killed nine patients for their life insurance with "almost as many different poisons." And then there's Bessie Denker, a homicidal and infanticidal mother who "never used the same poison twice." Instead of the risk of the incompetent mother, the frequent subtext of drug and vitamin advertising, the two women serial killers are the embodiment of medicalized motherhood at its most toxic.

In the age of modern psychopharmacology, Christine's logic no longer works. The killing of "bad seeds" now requires an immediate threat. In *The Good Son* (1993), a weakening grip on two children hanging over the edge of a cliff forces a mother to choose which child to save. In *Orphan* (2009), the "child" turns out to be a thirty-three-year-old woman, but even then, her death is justified as self-defense. Alternatively, the child to be killed must have superhuman powers derived from satanic or alien forces, such as the towhead alien seed of *Village of the Damned* (1960) and *Children of the Damned* (1964) or the changeling Antichrist in *The Omen* (1976). Christine's bedtime poisoning scheme no longer registers as fair play, but the bridge between behavior and neurochemistry was still under construction as Christine was accepting her fate as a deadly nurse-mother figure. The pills at Christine's disposal hold no answer for Rhoda's condition other than as a tool for euthanasia. As Reggie tells Christine, the brains of bad seeds are irretrievably anachronistic; they are "born with the kind of brain that may have been normal in humans 50,000 years ago." The sleeping pills that Christine uses as "vitamins" to extinguish Rhoda nevertheless contain a germ of hope, not for reptilian-brained bad seeds like Rhoda but for milder deviations from the norm like Christine and her bad sleeping patterns. When a pill becomes a tool that can alter biology to accommodate the requirements of modern life, when nature is no longer seen through the lens of genetic determinism, and when pharmaceutical intervention can reshape the neurological self, the only thing left to fear is the bad pill.

Rosemary's Prenatal Vitamins

Rosemary's Baby is the story of a pregnant woman's fight to take prenatal vitamins rather than drink alternative herbal concoctions. Sure, that woman also happens to be carrying the spawn of Satan, but some might argue that the horrors of prenatal care are sufficiently chilling even if "little Andy or Jenny" (as she calls the fetus) turns out to be the progeny of a narcissistic actor and not the Antichrist. Never has a film made vitamin supplements as fraught as they are in *Rosemary's Baby*. No less than two doctors, a coven of witches, a husband, and a bevy of friends weigh in on Rosemary's (Mia Farrow) prenatal care and supplements. After decades of vitamania and its concomitant trust/blame game with regard to women as pill dispensaries, the mid-1960s mark the beginning of an exponential increase in fetal surveillance and maternal responsibility. The it-takes-a-coven-to-raise-a-fetus mind-set of Rosemary's neighbors is hardly hyperbolic given the unprecedented public attention at the time to women's reproductive rights (or lack thereof). More than ever, the maternal and fetal bodies were viewed as objects—often oppositional ones—open to collective scrutiny.[36] But Rosemary is not a reproductive rights activist, and hot-button issues like "the pill" and abortion are peripheral to the plot at best.[37]

In the final paragraph of a tepid review for the *New Yorker*, Penelope Gilliatt dismisses Polanski's venture as a waste of his talent and "an exercise in Gynecological Gothic"—an unfortunate critique but a perfect description of the film's architectural approach to the body.[38] When Rosemary and Guy (John Cassevetes) go apartment hunting on the Upper West Side of Manhattan and fall in love with the Bramford (the historic Dakota Apartments)—an eccentric old building with crumbling tiles in the hallway, gloomy decor, and a violent past that includes cannibalism, witchcraft, abandoned babies, and suicides—they may as well be relocating to Dracula's castle. The previous tenant, Mrs. Gardenia, has passed away, leaving behind her furnishings and dozens of sickly, wilting plants. "Did a little gardening on the side," says Rosemary, running her hand along a shelf of one of the gardening benches in the study. Naturally, Rosemary knows her herbs. She begins to list them for Guy—"Mint, basil." Meanwhile, the realtor suggests, "This room would make a lovely nursery." That bit of salesmanship and remodeling advice just four minutes into the film establishes a relation between plants, babies, and nurses. Etymologically, nursery derives from the French word for wet nurse (*nourrice*). By definition, nurseries for plants and nurseries for babies and young children attend to the growth, feeding, and cultivation of the young apart from the care of the mother (human or mother earth). For a plant, that means, for example, starting life in a constructed environment like a greenhouse or a container on Mrs. Gardenia's potting bench as opposed to the life of a seedling in the wild. For a baby, the nursery signals a form of foster care, a stand-in for an absent mother. A supplement to ensure proper growth is therefore embedded in the name of the designated modern domestic space associated with infancy. Architecturally and etymologically, a nursery guarantees maternal separation as much as it implies child care. Through the nursery reference, the Bram Stoker–esque Bramford takes a decisive shift to the Gynecological Gothic before Rosemary is even pregnant. Herbal supplements, medical intervention, and extramaternal influences thus figure into the tour of Guy and Rosemary Woodhouse's future home.

Once moved in, Rosemary essentially paints out the visible Gothic by redecorating with bright white paint, subtle floral wallpaper, and contemporary furniture. Nevertheless, one important Gothic architectural trope remains: a secret passage in the linen closet that communicates with the apartment of the satanist couple next door. In a compelling analysis of the Ira Levin source novel, Sharon Marcus connects the linen closet passage to the urbanization of the Gothic and to the disproportionate concern in society about domestic electronic surveillance (i.e., "bugs") compared to fetology's invasion of a pregnant woman's privacy in changing approaches to obstetrics. According to Marcus, both Rosemary and her apartment are "split by a faulty partition that can neither divide external from internal nor prevent incursion on one side by the other."[39] The bodily equivalent to the faulty linen closet partition is the placental barrier. Until the mid-1960s, the placenta was seen as a shield, or, in the words of a 1958 public affairs pamphlet, "a silent nurse, constantly on duty, protecting him from almost every kind of poison."⁴⁰ The wall-nurse-organ separates the fetus from the mother and serves as a living fortress discarded as afterbirth once its job is complete. The maternal body is therefore part of a ruins narrative, with the placenta as a fortress that crumbles with parturition. In the early 1960s, pills forced a revision of that narrative when thalidomide, a tranquilizer often used by pregnant women to fight nausea, was revealed to have caused widespread birth defects.⁴¹ The placental barrier had been a hidden passageway all along. Marcus argues that just as the false partition in Rosemary's closet facilitates surveillance and intrusion by the neighbors, the reassessment and sudden permeability of the placenta became a justification for increased surveillance of pregnancy, including the expectant's "paranoid self-surveillance" to "protect the fetus from her own dangerousness."⁴²

In addition to the thalidomide horror, rubella epidemics between 1962 and 1964 further amplified fears of birth abnormalities. As a consequence, prenatal diagnosis became more common, epidemiology took new interest in reproductive surveillance, and birth defects registries were established regionally, nationally, and internationally.⁴³ On the surface, the specter of eugenics drifts uncomfortably through the climate of renewed political and medical interest in the unborn subject, but the concern with fetal anomalies after thalidomide was not restricted to the groups targeted by eugenicists, nor was it a top-down act of institutional control over reproductive rights. Bourgeois households were now heavily invested in the conversation. After a fight to terminate a pregnancy complicated by pills containing thalidomide, picture-perfect all-American mother and children's television show star Sherri Finkbine helped shift the discourse from bad seeds to bad medicine and strengthened arguments in favor of abortion rights.⁴⁴ Trust in medicine and science plummeted in the wake of the pharmacological betrayal.⁴⁵

Paradoxically, fear and skepticism surrounding medicine only spurred on technological monitoring. Imaging technologies and other interventions for scanning and screening fetal bodies enabled medicine to claim care over the fetus as opposed to the maternal body. In a study of fetal citizenship, Deborah Lupton observes, "Through these technologies, the foetus is constructed as 'the patient', seen to have its own rights, which may differ from or conflict with those of its mother. Mothers as individual subjects, indeed, may 'disappear' from the view of health care providers when all the focus is on the foetal patient."⁴⁶ A consequence of "direct contact with the fetus," according to sociologist Ann Oakley, is that obstetricians are able to "dispense with mothers as informants on fetal status."⁴⁷ But this was not yet the case in *Rosemary's Baby*. Just as *The Bad Seed* barely precedes the rise of psychopharmacological drugs, *Rosemary's Baby* predates the general availability and routine use of ultrasound and other screening mechanisms.⁴⁸ While it is true, as Marcus asserts, that Levin "mapped the invasion of women's privacy in pregnancy onto the invasion of privacy effected by home surveillance," technological womb surveillance was minimal for all but high-risk women in the 1960s. There is no ultrasound in *Rosemary's Baby*. Significantly, the Gynecological Gothic relies on fetal invisibility to generate dread. The notion of a placental barrier was indeed crumbling in the 1960s, but the newly permeable womb was not yet visually available.⁴⁹ Rosemary cannot view the tiny cloven hooves and budding horns of her unborn child. Hers is a haunted womb because "little Andy or Jenny" eludes visual capture—the success of the conspiracy to gestate the Antichrist depends on it. Influence over the baby comes down to vitamins or herbal drinks. Even Satan's baby needs supplements.

Before Roman (Sidney Blackmer) and Minnie Castevet (Ruth Gordon) and their geriatric coven strike a secret Faustian bargain with Guy Woodhouse—his wife's womb in exchange for a successful acting career—Minnie vets Rosemary's fertility by asking about her siblings and their children. The conversation occurs in Minnie's kitchen near an impressive array of potted herbs. "I'd like to have a spice garden someday," says Rosemary. And this is not mere polite conversation. Rosemary's interest in herb gardening is such that near the end of the film, after Rosemary has been told that the baby died, Guy believes he can cheer her up with the promise of relocating to "the beautiful hills of Beverly with a pool and a spice garden." Despite Rosemary's love of plants, her first instinct when it comes to prenatal care is not to explore alternative medicine and herbal supplements but rather to find a conventional doctor and to take a daily vitamin pill. Dr. Hill (Charles Grodin) draws her blood (the extent of the medical procedures) and reminds her, "Don't forget the pills"—conventional care. Rosemary does not venture into herbal drinks until after Minnie insinuates herself (like "an ersatz modern midwife," according to some) into Rosemary's care by setting up an appointment with eminent obstetrician and secret coven member Dr. Sapirstein (Ralph Bellamy).⁵⁰

Long before the myth of the placental barrier gave way, vitamin supplements were marketed as indispensable tools for a healthy pregnancy.⁵¹ In the 1930s, experiments measuring the intelligence of B1-deficient rats led to the recommendation that "human mothers take an extra supply of vitamins before and after childbirth."[52] Numerous animal experiments in the 1940s posited maternal dietary deficiencies as a cause of fetal malformation.[53] A study from 1945 to 1952 involving 2,400 women and 800,000 vitamin pills concluded that the children of women given vitamins during pregnancy and lactation scored higher on intelligence tests. The beneficial results were identified only in women "under certain circumstances" (by which they meant poor and black), but in practice, the promotion of vitamins was more likely to reach white middle-class women with easy access to a rich and varied diet—in other words, those least in need of supplements.[54] In the mid-1960s, the same fear of subclinical risk that had helped fuel vitamin sales in previous decades brought folate deficiency into the public eye and set up the fetus as an at-risk potential consumer. As historian Al-Gailani observes in his study of vitamins and risk reduction, the megaloblastic anemias and neural tube defects associated with folate deficiencies most often afflicted peoples in poor living conditions in tropical and subtropical areas, and yet healthy pregnant women became, "in haematological terms, akin to the poorly nourished populations in the 'underdeveloped' world most vulnerable to this condition."[55] Folic acid follows the same risk-driven path to mass adoption as other vitamin supplements and anticipates the pattern followed by ultrasound in the decade to come. What begins as an intervention reserved for high-risk cases is soon adopted as a routine part of prenatal care for every pregnancy. Subclinical risk therefore introduces a new degree of fear into pregnancy.

In order to get Rosemary to switch from vitamin pills to herbal shakes, Dr. Sapirstein appeals to public skepticism about pills and safety. "No pills," he says. "Minnie Castevet has an herbarium. I'm going to have her make a daily drink for you that will be fresher, safer, and more vitamin-rich than any pills of the market." In contrast to the young Dr. Hill, who represents the norm of modern medicine, Dr. Sapirstein combines the reassuring authority of a respectable, older doctor with the post-thalidomide mistrust of the system. Sapirstein delivers all of the "society babies," which makes him both venerable and "in." His preference for fresh herbs over "the market" is an appealing countercultural alternative to the ills of modernity. Outside the context of a horror film, even coven membership might be a selling point rather than a deterrent in the minds of late-1960s hipsters. A priest's 1968 review of *Rosemary's Baby* remarks, "Today the preternatural has become an 'in' thing."[56] The reviewer quotes the October 1968 issue

Fig. 13.2. Rosemary drinks an herbal shake supplement in *Rosemary's Baby* (1968).

of the fashionable magazine *Eye*, which claims, "You can't go to a party anymore in the village without meeting at least seven girls who claim to be witches."[57] Rosemary is more interested in trends (like her Vidal Sassoon haircut) than in hippie counterculture, but Sapirstein allows her to access a hippie-chic nostalgia for unadulterated nature packaged in a reassuringly high-society context.

Sapirstein's acceptance as an eminent doctor within the system shuts down any objections to his practice. Rosemary's friend Hutch dismisses the visible signs of Rosemary's declining health when he learns that Sapirstein is her doctor. When Roman Castevet stops by, the shot frames Rosemary between the two older men as they discuss her care. "Mrs. Castevet makes a vitamin drink for me every day from fresh herbs she grows," says Rosemary, whereupon Roman interjects, "Yes, all according to Dr. Sapirstein's directions, of course. He's inclined to be suspicious of commercially prepared vitamin pills." Roman thus appeals to (male) medical authority and to mistrust of commercial manufacture. Hutch counters, "Indeed? But surely they're manufactured under every imaginable safeguard." Roman replies by shifting the blame to distribution and sales: "That's quite true, but commercial pills can sit for months on a druggist's shelf and lose a great deal of their original potency." Hutch admits, "I hadn't thought of that." For her part, Rosemary now embraces primitivism in opposition to pills: "I like the idea of having everything fresh and natural. I'll bet expectant mothers chewed bits of tannis root when nobody'd even heard of vitamin pills." Even though Rosemary's dietary intake has been determined for her by Sapirstein, she has come to view her diet as primitive, natural, instinctive, and matriarchal.

Pills align their users with social values and communities. From an anthropological perspective, Mark Nichter and Nancy Vuckovic suggest that commercial drugs associate their users with modernity, whereas "a return to herbal medicines may constitute a 'line of flight' to 'traditional' or 'alternative' values."[58] Rosemary's shift in allegiance, however, occurs within the medical system. Her herbal drinks do not grant her a place in the maternal order of romanticized tannis-chewing primitives any more than Minnie's participation as a pseudomidwife with a blender wrests prenatal care from the patriarchy. When Rosemary escapes from the Bramford to seek refuge with Dr. Hill, she fails to realize that, coven or no coven, doctors Hill and Sapirstein are part of the same fraternity of medicine, and within that community, Dr. Hill defers to the eminent Dr. Sapirstein, to whom Rosemary belongs as a patient. Doctors and the fetus trump the expectant woman. Sapirstein's threat to institutionalize Rosemary if she does not behave demonstrates her utter helplessness in the face of biopower.

During the conversation with Hutch and Roman, Rosemary realizes for the first time that she has no idea what tannis root is: "It's one of the herbs she puts in the drink. Or is it an herb? Can a root be an herb?" So much for Rosemary's botanical knowledge. Hutch peeks through Rosemary's silver filigree tannis-root charm and remarks that the foul-smelling stuff looks more like a mold or a fungus. Rosemary's trust in the substance quickly erodes once she sees it as something other than an herb. She blames the drinks for her pain and begins to pour them secretly down the drain. Rosemary argues with Guy: "I want vitamins and pills like everyone else!" On the advice of friends, Rosemary informs Guy that she has decided to return to Dr. Hill. At the height of the argument, the pain suddenly stops, and the baby moves. "It's alive!" cries Rosemary with an unintentional irony not lost on those familiar with the same declaration in *Frankenstein* (1931). "Guy, it's moving! It's alive! It's all right." Here again, the Gynecological Gothic relies on an occulted womb rather than on technological fetal surveillance. Instead, the surveillance emanates from the fetus, whose awareness of its mother's intention to change doctors prompts it to thump like a ghost making its presence known. Marcus compares the fetus to a "miniaturized and invisible transmitter" or a "bug transplanted in her internal corporeal space," and indeed, the well-timed sign of life does indicate eavesdropping followed by a telegraphed message clearly intended to placate Rosemary.[59] Thus appeased, Rosemary jumps back on board with her drink regimen without further question.

Three weeks shy of her due date, Rosemary finally learns that tannis is not an herb after all but a fungus called devil's pepper. Tannis, she reads, is used in rituals that predate Christianity. The "spongy matter derived from swampy regions" is "considered to have special powers."[60] Further reading and some Scrabble-tile anagram sleuthing help Rosemary identify Roman Castevet as the son of a satanist. Despite the connection between the Castevets and Sapirstein, Rosemary's faith in medicine and in her doctor never falters. For the final few weeks of her pregnancy, Sapirstein reassures Rosemary by prescribing pills instead of Minnie's drinks. Relieved to finally have "pills like everyone else," Rosemary never bothers to question what the capsules contain. The form alone is reassuring. Guy now manages the pregnancy at home just as he managed the conception right down to the charting of her cycle on the kitchen calendar. Guy pops pills in Rosemary's mouth and hands her a glass of water. Although Rosemary comes to suspect a broader conspiracy, she is slow to implicate Sapirstein. Finally seeking refuge at the office of Dr. Hill, Rosemary stares at the bottle of pills and repeats, "Monsters . . . monsters"—a repudiation of pharmaceuticals with real-world analogs.[61]

Of the many inversions of Christian iconography in the film (Guy as Joseph, Rosemary as Mary, etc.), the one most pertinent to the pharmaceutical self may pass unnoticed. The moment occurs postpartum, as Guy hands Rosemary a pill to keep her bedbound and docile. A close-up shows Guy stretching forth his hand, a pill artfully posed on it. Rosemary reaches for the pill like a mirror image of Adam receiving the breath of life from God in the Michelangelo fresco. Guy's gesture is literally underhanded, the opposite of God's overhanded gift of life, but like an inverted cross, the form is unmistakable. The scene recalls Rosemary's drug-induced vision of the Sistine Chapel as the coven carries her semiconscious body horizontally through the linen closet to be impregnated by Satan. Now stretched out on her bed, Rosemary receives pharmaceutical communion for the last time. In the novel, Rosemary thinks, "The pills, of course, were the answer."[62] She pretends to take them, stores them up, and uses them to drug her caretaker before crossing through the linen closet to find her baby. In Polanski's adaptation, Rosemary pretends to take the pills and stashes them like

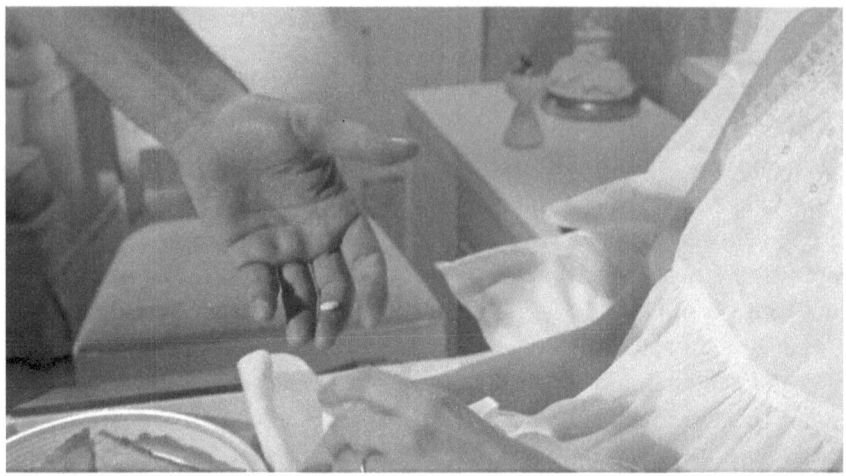

Fig. 13.3. Guy hands Rosemary a pill in *Rosemary's Baby* (1968).

mortar between the bricks by her bed, but she does not use them against the coven. Rosemary's rejection of pills is the only reason for their presence in the final act. This is her one victory. Shockingly, Rosemary's renunciation of pills leads to an acceptance of monstrosity that would have been unimaginable to Christine in *The Bad Seed*. Rosemary will love her tannis-baby no matter what. Unconditional love, in the end, is more frightening than abortion or infanticide.

A magazine shown briefly in the film offers a piece of relevant cultural insight into postpartum care, and the magazine is not the controversial April 6, 1966, *Time* cover "Is God Dead?" that Rosemary sees on a side table in Sapirstein's waiting room. Rather, as a postscript commentary, I propose a look inside the June 1966 issue of *Reader's Digest* that Laura-Louise (Patsy Kelly) reads at Rosemary's bedside in the final act. Beginning on page 66 of the 6/66 issue, an alarmist article, "Pills, Glue, and Kids: An American Tragedy," stokes fears of domestic pill horror beyond prenatal care. The first sentence begins, "Crime is mushrooming at such a shocking rate in our nation that decent citizens must wonder in alarm what is causing this moral decay."[63] The verb *mushrooming* conveniently conflates drug use with nuclear annihilation. The authors describe an "explosion of senseless crime" by children from good homes and the real-life horror of an honor student-turned-killer.[64] The head of the San Francisco narcotics squad blames parents for not caring about this "pill and glue stuff."[65]

The article ends with a disturbing fatalism and a call for increased surveillance by parents: "For the segment of the younger generation already on drugs, it is too late. But for the rest of the kids, let their parents keep track of what they are doing and help prevent them from getting into big trouble."[66] In a nation inundated with drugs, fetal surveillance is only the beginning of a lifelong surveillance process. Pills do more than create monsters; they create surveillance states.

Demonizing a Pill, or Satan's Little Helper

Christianity is predicated on turning losses into wins, so it should come as no surprise that the loss of life after an exorcism and the subsequent conviction of a priest on charges of negligent homicide end up a win-win in *The Exorcism of Emily Rose* (2005). Emily Rose (Jennifer Carpenter), through self-sacrifice, becomes an all-but-canonized modern saint, while Father Moore (Tom Wilkonson), who is convicted but sentenced to time served, gets to tell Emily's faith-promoting story in court despite the reluctance of the archdiocese to put religion on trial. The losers in this courtroom procedural–horror hybrid are pills, which enter the court as evidence for the prosecution but wind up as scapegoats for the defense. In the possession of Emily Rose, prescription pills become Satan's little helpers, spirit-numbing facilitators of demonic possession. Like horror's answer to Morpheus, bright-red capsules take Emily down the rabbit hole and into hell. The pills create in Emily a receptive state for possession and then lock her into that state, according to the defense. What A. O. Scott called "propaganda disguised as entertainment" is therefore not merely a pro-Christian exercise but also an antipharmaceutical diatribe, or at minimum an argument that the fight for Emily's body and soul is not limited to Satan and God but also includes a pharmaceuticals industry every bit as concerned with worldwide evangelization as Christianity.[67]

The Exorcism of Emily Rose is loosely based on the story of Anneliese Michel, a student in a small Bavarian town who died of starvation and battery in 1976 after months of exorcisms by two priests who were subsequently charged with negligent homicide for their failure to seek appropriate medical help.[68] Scott Derrickson and cowriter Paul Harris Boardman (the voice of religious skepticism in the team) transplant the story to a nonspecified city in the United States with drab costuming meant to look timeless. Timeless style or not, the reception of the film is very much tied to a specific post-9/11 come-to-Jesus moment for Hollywood. The success of Mel Gibson's blockbuster *The Passion of the Christ* (2004) made even the most cynical studio executives fight for some "Passion dollars" by catering to the Christian masses.[69] In July 2005, *March of the Penguins* (or "The Passion of the Penguins" to conservative radio host and critic Michael Medved) attracted some of those dollars as the religious right co-opted the nature documentary in support of intelligent design and heterosexual monogamy.[70] In September, Derrickson's film brought in more than $30 million its opening weekend ($10 million higher than its budget), proving that horror was, as the young director had said, "the genre where a Christian could connect with mainstream culture."[71] The marketer for the Sony Screen Gems film "tried to make exorcisms newsworthy" with online polls, newsletters, and special screenings and interviews touting Derrickson's Bible school background—an approach that won positive coverage by the conservative group Focus on the Family and the Catholic News Service.[72] After the DVD release of Derrickson's film, the Christianity Today publication *Ignite Your Faith* gave a list of scriptures and discussion ideas to enhance home viewing beginning with questions such as "Was Emily possessed or were her symptoms strictly psychological? Why?" and ending with the prompt "Write your own script of the Legion story or turn it into a homemade horror movie with friends."[73]

Not all Christian critics recommended belief in demons as a surefire stepping-stone to faith in God.[74] Derrickson's professed agenda was, in any case, less ambitious; he aimed instead to "persuade people to consider the plausibility or non-plausibility of belief."[75] But belief in what, exactly? Here is what attorney for the defense, Erin Bruner (Laura Linney), asks the jury to believe in her closing argument: "I'm not asking that you believe everything that Father Moore believes. I'm simply asking that you believe in Father Moore." This is what A. O. Scott finds so disturbing, the notion that the sincerity of the believer should be "conflated with the plausibility of his beliefs." *The Exorcism of Emily Rose*, for Scott, "suggests an improbable alliance of postmodern relativism and absolute religious faith against the supposed tyranny of scientific empiricism."[76] That improbable alliance received a name three years later with the publication of "Notes on Post-secular Society" by sociologist Jürgen Habermas. Postsecularism, which soon became an academic buzzword, indicates for Habermas "a change in consciousness" toward the continued importance of religion in the public arena.[77] Postsecularism signals the academic secularist's acknowledgment that rumors of religion's death have been greatly exaggerated. *The Exorcism of Emily Rose* placed the problematic hybrid of secularism and religious belief in a generically hybrid courtroom horror drama, and it did so, coincidentally, at the same time that a federal case (*Kitzmiller v. Dover Area School District*) about teaching intelligent design in public schools was playing out on the nightly news. Little did it matter that in both cases religion lost. The story was getting out there, not in a church but in a secular arena.

The Exorcism of Emily Rose is without a doubt a postsecular film, one that asks viewers to engage in the new acrobatics of tolerance: to believe in the believer regardless of one's belief. Postsecularism's pluralistic inclusivity mirrors the jury's recommendation and judge's decision to sentence Father Moore to time served, to reintegrate the religious figure into society rather than continue his sequestration. The most antagonistic part of Father Moore's trial is the fight between medicine and religion as competing communities of interpretation. The dogmatism revealed on both sides of the debate surrounding Emily's pills suggests anything but the peaceful coexistence of faith in God and in medicine, not because there is no common ground but rather because there is a turf war over the same ground. The idea of a demonized pill points to a deeply embedded religious discourse within a supposedly secular field. Richard DeGrandpre, a scholar of drugs with a doctorate in psychopharmacology, uses the term *pharmacologicalism* to describe the ideology that portrays drugs as either angels or demons, as sacred others to be praised or feared. Ritalin, for example, is an angel, whereas cocaine is a demon, even though their pharmacological actions are virtually identical.[78] According to DeGrandpre, the social construction of psychoactive drugs endows "certain molecules with potency and meaning" in the same way that ancient magic accorded special powers to certain substances.[79] Pharmacologicalism posits potentialities within the chemical structure of the drug to "take hold of and transform both brain and behavior."[80] The words *take hold of* are particularly relevant to *The Exorcism of Emily Rose* because the heart of the case is about seizing control of Emily. The prosecution speaks of "seizures" while the defense speaks of "possession," but to seize is by definition to possess or take hold of something. Emily is seized either by demons or by spontaneous electrical discharges in the brain. Religious ritual and pharmaceutical ritual present ongoing therapeutic interventions into Emily's body and soul (or her molecular being), regimens that constitute rites/rights of possession in their own manner.

"Demons exist, whether you believe in them or not," says Father Moore to his agnostic attorney. The same unwavering dogmatism is evident in the testimonies of the prosecution's medical experts. Dr. Mueller (Kenneth Welsh) testifies that he first suspected illegal drugs (pharmacologicalism's demons) as the cause of Emily's problems. After drug tests came back negative, Mueller diagnosed Emily with epilepsy and prescribed Gambutrol (most likely a fictionalized stand-in for the anticonvulsant Gabatril, or Tiagabine). Emily's problem, says Mueller, is that, on Father Moore's advice, she stopped filling her prescriptions. Dr. Briggs (Henry Czerny) argues that the lack of proper medical treatment allowed Emily's epilepsy to evolve "into a condition known as psychotic epileptic disorder." According to Briggs, Emily's experiences—auditory and visual hallucinations, extreme paranoia, locked joints, bodily contortions, and dilated pupils—are evidence of a violent psychosis induced by epilepsy. The drug Gambutrol would have controlled that condition, and Emily would still be alive had she continued to take it. Briggs says he would have force-fed Emily and treated her with electroconvulsive therapy against her will to save her life. Father Moore killed Emily by telling her to stop treatment.

Gambutrol appears visually three times in *Emily Rose*. First, the word *Gambutrol* is seen in all caps on a Post-it on Bruner's legal pad shown in an extreme close-up. Bruner has drawn a box around the word and written beneath it, "Side Effects?" About fifteen minutes later, while Father Moore tells Bruner about Emily's first hospital visit, we see a close-up of the bottle large enough to easily read the drug's name and dosage. The third appearance of Gambutrol is a cutaway during Bruner's remarks in court about Father Moore's sincerity contrasted with the failure of medicine. An extreme close-up shows the printed text "Gambutrol 25 mg" on a white label. The shot is followed by an extreme close-up of two bright-red Gambutrol capsules, then Emily's hand picking them up and putting them into her mouth. A series of close-ups and slow-motion shots with amplified eating sounds suggests that Emily is experiencing one of the unbearable side effects of the drug. The three appearances of the word *Gambutrol*, always in close-up or extreme close-up, serve as ominous intertitles, clinical and yet incantatory, familiar as pharmacological speech but not decipherable by those unversed in the lexicon of drugs. Gambutrol may just as well be the name of a demon summoned by three intertitle-like repetitions of its name.

Gambutrol, according to the Yale- and Cambridge-educated anthropologist and witness for the defense, Dr. Adani (Shohreh Aghdashloo), has "an

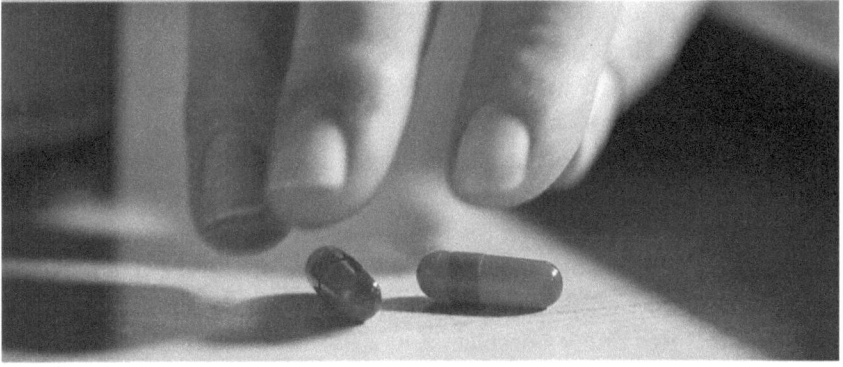

Fig. 13.4. Two sequential extreme close-ups of Gambutrol in *The Exorcism of Emily Rose* (2005).

intoxicating effect on the brain" that interferes with the "psycho-spiritual shock that exorcism is intended to provide." Adani represents a scientific perspective that Bruner needs for the defense—a voice from the scholarly community willing to assert that exorcism is a "scientifically verified and culturally universal phenomenon." The prosecution wants to dismiss Adani's testimony on grounds of "silliness," to which Scott's review responds, "Sustained," but in fact, Adani represents the broadening of interpretive frameworks in postsecularist society. As prosecutor Ethan Thomas (Campbell Scott) well knows, silliness is not legitimate grounds for objection in a court of law. The only thing preventing a silly defense is a lawyer who is afraid of looking silly. And to the dismay of her firm and the skittish archbishop, Erin Bruner has become fearless in her defense of possibilities. "This trial isn't about facts," says Bruner in her closing arguments with no hint of irony. "This trial is about possibilities. . . . Facts leave no room for possibilities."

Dr. Adani has her real-world counterparts—academics open to vast realms of possibilities. Consider, for example, Professor Stafford Betty's article "The Growing Evidence for 'Demonic Possession': What Should Psychiatry's Response Be?" published in the *Journal of Religion and Public Health* just five months before the release of *The Exorcism of Emily Rose*. Betty claims that there is "mounting evidence today that evil spirits do oppress and even occasionally possess the unwary, the weak, the unprepared, the unlucky, or the targeted."[81] Betty wonders, should psychiatry embrace alternative spiritual therapies and "place them alongside the brain-altering drugs and electroconvulsive therapies (ECT) presently used" just as "science learned a generation ago to accept chiropractic?"[82] He believes so. "No one can say why ECT works, but there is no question that it does," says Betty, who clearly would have made an ideal witness for the defense of Father Moore.[83] Bruner argues that Father Moore helped "in a different way" than conventional doctors. Bruner learns late in the game that Moore invited a trusted psychiatrist, Dr. Cartwright (Duncan Fraser), to the exorcism in order to get the opinion of a medical professional. Cartwright meets with Bruner and assures her that Emily was neither epileptic nor schizophrenic nor psychotic. Cartwright recognizes the impotence of medicine to solve Emily's problem and speaks to Bruner of his renewed faith since his frightening encounter with evil. But Cartwright as a figure of religion and science walking hand in hand is too good to be true, or at least too good to survive the freak accident that befalls him on the eve of his day in court.

In the end, all possibilities are left intact. Emily refused continuing medical treatment, so she died. Who's to say if ECT might have saved her? Emily also refused (after a vision of the Virgin Mary) Father Moore's continuing regimen of exorcisms, which places exorcism in the discontinued treatment camp along with medicine rather than in the failed treatment category. Emily's martyrdom, if anything, qualifies her as a saint of possibilities. Bruner, despite a series of encounters with the supernatural, is not converted to any particular religion. Father Moore tells her at one point, "You sound more like a mystic than an agnostic." As a multivalent concept, mysticism is probably a good stance for Bruner if she believes her own closing arguments. Even the Virgin Mary keeps out of denominational concerns, promising Emily in a vision that through this story many would see "that the realm of the spirit is real." Moore offers, finally, a conciliatory approach to any antagonism between religion and medicine. He leaves room for separate spaces: "I never said she should quit seeing her doctors. That would be quite wrong. Medical care is not my field." But he did tell Emily to stop taking Gambutrol. Medicine is fine, Moore's testimony suggests, but drugs remain in a different category than medicine, one subject to spiritual judgment. Pills are angels or demons. They may have never been secular, let alone postsecular. On this, too, medicine and religion seem to agree—and that is what makes the possibility of a postsecular pill so hard to, well, you know . . . so let's proceed to sentencing:

"You are guilty, Father Moore. And you are free to go," says the judge.
You are guilty, Gambutrol. And you are free to go, says no one.

Notes

1. See Haraway, 8.
2. Collin, 73.
3. Fraser, Valentine, and Roberts, 124.
4. On whiteness and pharmaceuticals, see Wolf-Meyer.
5. T. Williams, 87.
6. Ibid., 88.
7. Pernick, 41.
8. Ibid., 6.
9. Ibid.
10. Porter, 170.
11. Ibid., 172.
12. Offit, 102.
13. Ibid., 122.
14. Porter, 194.
15. See Combs, 15.
16. See Apple, 127–29.
17. See Scrinis, 67.
18. Ibid., 65.
19. Ibid.
20. Levenstein, 153.
21. Apple, 73.
22. Scrinis, 71.
23. Pieters and Snelders, 99.
24. Ibid.
25. Ibid., 100.
26. Metzl, 241.
27. Pieters and Snelders, 100.
28. A recent book on biomedicalization contains as many thirty-five related "-ization" categories. See Bell and Figert, 13. See Paltrinieri for a review of the theoretical permutations of biopower. See Nichter and Vuckovic for an examination of ten micro- and macrolevel

interconnected themes of an "anthropology of pharmaceutical practice." Although his main focus is the twenty-first century, Nikolas Rose's *The Politics of Life Itself* puts some of the most important ideas about medicine in a clear, historical context.

29. Collin, 74.
30. Fraser, Valentine, and Roberts, 125.
31. See Pernick, 10.
32. Rose, 199.
33. Ibid., 203.
34. Collin, 77. Among other scholars mentioned by Collin, see especially Conrad; Clarke et al.; Armstrong; Greene.
35. Collin, 77.
36. See Lupton, 331.
37. For the ways in which abortion does appear, see Valerius.
38. Gilliatt, 89.
39. Marcus, 136.
40. Quoted in Marcus, 135.
41. See A. Martin and Holloway, 301.
42. Marcus, 138.
43. Löwy, 292.
44. See Valerius, 117.
45. Harris polls saw public trust in medicine decline from 73 to 42 percent. See Quinlan, 316–17.
46. Lupton, 335.
47. Oakley, 155.
48. Although research in ultrasound began in the mid-1950s, the technology was not commonly used in prenatal surveillance until the late 1970s. See Oakley, 166.
49. The April 30, 1965, *Life* magazine photo essay on the fetus is sometimes cited as an example of the newly visible fetus, but the photographs have nothing to do with current imaging technology available to pregnant women. In fact, what viewers were seeing in many of the photos were surgically removed fetuses, often on the brink of death.
50. On Minnie as midwife, see L. Fischer, 446; Valerius, 127.
51. Al-Gailani, 279.
52. Harrell, Woodyard, and Gates, 3.
53. Ibid., 6.
54. On the study, see Harrell, Woodyard, and Gates, 59–62. On advertising of prenatal vitamins, see Molyneaux.
55. Al-Gailani, 280.
56. Hughes, 488.
57. Ibid.
58. Nichter and Vuckovic, 1510.
59. Marcus, 145.
60. Tannis or devil's pepper as described in *Rosemary's Baby* does not exist. Devil's pepper is a real (and poisonous) plant, not a fungus. The name *tannis* feels vaguely herbal as it evokes tannins and is also evocative of pre-Christian cultures because of the Egyptian city of Tanis and its ties to ancient artifacts.
61. See Valerius, 125.

62. Levin, 229.
63. Earl Selby and Anne Selby, "Pills, Glue and Kids: An American Tragedy," *Reader's Digest*, June 1966, 66.
64. Ibid., 69–70.
65. Ibid., 70.
66. Ibid.
67. A. O. Scott, "Dancing with the Devil, Then with a Prosecutor," *New York Times*, September 9, 2005.
68. For the story of Anneliese Michel, see Goodman.
69. Hanna Rosin, "Can Jesus Save Hollywood?" *Atlantic*, December, 2005, 161.
70. Jonathan Miller, "March of the Conservatives: Penguin Film as Political Fodder," *New York Times*, September 13, 2005, http://www.nytimes.com/2005/09/13/science/march-of-the-conservatives-penguin-film-as-political-fodder.html.
71. Chattaway, 102.
72. Kate Kelly, "How Sony Courted Christian Audiences for 'Emily Rose,'" *Wall Street Journal*, September 16, 2005.
73. Todd Hertz, "Entertaining Faith," *Ignite Your Faith*, January/February 2006, 29.
74. For representative examples see Jason Byassee, "Devil in the Details: When Faith Is Ruled by Fear," *Christian Century*, November 1, 2005; and Peter T. Chattaway, "Devil in the Details?" *Christianity Today* 49, no. 12 (2005): 102.
75. Quoted in Chattaway.
76. Scott.
77. Habermas, 20.
78. That is, their actions are identical "when taken in comparable doses and circumstances." DeGrandpre, 28.
79. Ibid., 242.
80. Ibid., 209.
81. Betty, 14.
82. Ibid., 19.
83. Ibid., 21.

14

SHOWER CURTAIN

Prologue: Reddit and YouTube Users React to *Psycho* (1960)

I never knew that that horror-tune came from this . . . (TheUnfriendlyGhost1)

Am I the only one that thinks this lady looks way too happy to be taking a shower? (scs1156320)

The scariest thing in this scene is how she didn't wait for the shower to heat up. (hitmandude360)

Nooooo, he got her right in the chocolate syrup! (Emmanuel Gapud)

Who's the director? (Marta Alegret)

Roommate just bought a clear shower curtain for his bathroom. When I asked why he'd want a clear shower curtain, he looked at me and said "No mildew and no murderers." (smithson23)

I know a lot of women, myself included, who lock the bathroom door when taking a shower because of having watched that film. (corcyra)

> I know a lot of people, myself included, who lock the bathroom door whenever they enter the bathroom at all because that's just a basic human thing to do in a room where most of the activities involve your genitals. (deleted)

My dad told me when he saw this movie as a kid (he was born in 1955, so not when it premiered in theaters) that he was terrified to take a shower with the curtain drawn for years afterward. Even when I was a kid all the bathrooms in our house had clear liners and curtain hooks so you could always see out while in the shower. Now that I'm grown with a house of my own, I can't bring myself to have anything but clear liners and curtain hooks in the bathroom. The thought of someone attacking you while in the shower has haunted me since I was a child, long before I ever saw the film because of how it impacted my father. (sunshine_rex)

Why not just shower with a gun? (zeCrazyEye)

Shower Scene Overkill

It is customary when writing about *Psycho* and its celebrated shower murder scene to begin with superlatives such as "It's no exaggeration to say that the scene is *the* most analyzed, discussed, and alluded to scene in film history."[1] Condolences, Odessa Steps sequence from *Battleship Potemkin* (1925). It should go without saying that no book, much less a short book chapter, can represent more than a small fraction of *Psycho* scholarship. To echo Raymond Durgnat's *A Long Hard Look at "Psycho,"* it is "impossible here to review the many interpretations of *Psycho*, which must by now be well into three figures."[2] Among the scores of books and articles I have read about the film, bonus points for hubris go to William Rothman's contextualization of his own contribution to *Psycho* shower scene interpretations: "Although the shower murder is perhaps the most celebrated sequence in all of Hitchcock's work, it has never, to my knowledge, been subjected to more than rudimentary analysis."[3] This claim is hard to believe, but what Rothman may be referring to is the disproportionate amount of writing devoted to an activity best described as "geeking out" over the shots, setup, montage, and the like. Favorite points of contention include what constitutes the beginning and end of the shower scene, how to count the shots, how to subdivide the sequence (three parts? five acts?), how to speak of the POV, and how well Hitchcock's montage fits Eisenstein's techniques. Those discussions have trickled down into the consciousness of film buffs to such a degree that when Alexandre O. Philippe's *78/52: Hitchcock's Shower Scene* (2017) debuted at the Sundance Film Festival, the documentary neither had nor needed an explanatory postcolon title. A still of a blurred figure behind a shower curtain and the numbers alone sufficed to indicate the subject matter, even if the exact number of setups and cuts were not on the tip of the average festivalgoer's tongue.

Equally customary in any discussion of *Psycho* is the perpetuation of certain narratives about audience response—the terror and the titillation, the screams and the scandals, not to mention how shocking it must have been back in 1960 to see for the first time a toilet flushing on-screen—the horror! Film critic David Thomson writes, "It really is quite exhilarating to see what tender creatures we were in 1960."[4] Were we, though? And are we the creatures that scholars tell us we are? Durgnat notes with skepticism how quickly theorists attribute "extreme moral debility to moviegoers," often equating viewers with a "libidinal Unconscious and infantile response."[5] According to Rothman, when Marion (Janet Leigh) starts to shower, "We can all but feel the water coursing over our bodies, awakening and arousing us, all but feel Marion's own pleasure, all but become Marion."[6] François Truffaut, in contrast, says, "In that whole picture there isn't a single character with whom a viewer might identify."[7] Hitchcock disagrees and feeds Truffaut a line about the audience that many critics have since cited and adopted as uncontested truth: "You might say I was playing them, like an organ."[8] The reality—that some audience members (both then and now) find humorous what others find terrifying—makes the myth of the normative viewer difficult to uphold.

Marion's enthusiastic self-cleansing and jarring demise simply cannot mean the same thing to all people. Kaja Silverman's influential work on suture theory, for example, provides a fascinating schematization of POV and montage, but as Linda Williams notes, "Silverman's psychoanalytic characterization of the viewer as 'castrated' comes close to presenting the experience of viewing the film as a form of punishment."[9] For some, it is. My own view is that psychoanalytic approaches become more interesting when reread structurally as models that include nonhumans as beings in their own right. In the "Refrigerator" chapter, for example, I argue that Julia Kristeva's formulation of the abject can explain the identity of a kitchen appliance from a material standpoint regardless of how the refrigerator feels about its mother. Similarly, as I note in the "Sewing Machine" chapter (chap. 7), Silverman's suture theory approach to *Psycho* need not exclude objects as participants in shot/reverse shot sequences. When Marion gazes at her showerhead, the showerhead gazes back. What Silverman sees as "obtrusive and disorienting," I argue, is nothing more than object POV. And the concept of being stitched into the discursive position of a thing need not imply psychological depth on the part of the object.[10] Material presence alone can implicate objects in meaningful structures, including those theories normally consumed by anthropocentrism. This is where Rothman's analysis is a welcome addition to the literature of the shower sequence. Rothman takes the showerhead POV seriously not as a disruption of the gaze but rather as a "source of the intimate views that follow."[11] My addition to the commentary on *Psycho*'s shower scene, if nothing else, contributes a sustained consideration of an object that tends to get pushed aside to make room for the violent cutting. My reading of the shower curtain in *Psycho* includes not only the filmmaker's authorial intent but also human-object interaction and the figural and literal plasticity of the curtain.

Hitchcock was delighted to have fooled audiences into thinking they were seeing gore and nudity in the shower murder that simply were not there. Sure, if you squint at a frame or two in some copies you might see the tip of the knife apparently breaking skin, or if you have an eagle eye for nipples, you might spot a hint of one, but nothing on-screen is as salacious or as gruesome as what some critics were convinced they had seen. As Robert Kolker remarks, the shower scene "alludes to a stabbing, without showing one."[12] The same phenomenon adds violence to Bill Krohn's mention of "the shredded curtain" and Rothman's proclamation that the "curtain has really been torn."[13] No direct curtain slashing or shredding occurs in the sequence other than the curtain popping out of its hooks as Marion grasps it for support while dying. The curtain's wounds—torn or empty spaces for metal grommets—are felt more than seen until Norman spreads the curtain on the floor during the murder clean-up. During the attack, the shower curtain, too, suffers death by allusion. Moreover, the death of the shower curtain is arguably more complicated and fraught with meaning than the death of Marion Crane. One might even say that Marion Crane's death is merely a vehicle for Hitchcock to murder a shower curtain. Absurd as it sounds, my assertion is wholly consistent with Hitchcock's approach to objects and coheres with the notion of "pure cinema" that so excited the director in his discussions with Truffaut.

There are at least two Alfred Hitchcocks behind every one of his films, and Joseph Stefano understood both of them perfectly when adapting Robert Bloch's novel for the screen. The first is the Freudian Hitchcock, the one that likes to plumb the depths of the human psyche. Stefano knew that the Freudian Hitchcock would bulldoze the censors into getting that flushing toilet on-screen. Says Stefano, "I thought, 'This is where you're going to begin to know what the human race is all about. We're going to start by showing you the toilet and it's only going to get worse.' We were getting into Freudian stuff and Hitchcock dug that kind of thing, so I knew we would get to see that toilet on-screen."[14] The second Hitchcock is the object-oriented Hitchcock, although he would never have put it in those terms. This is the Hitchcock for whom the hinged chest in *Rope* (1948) is as important as the dead body it houses. As Steven Jacobs writes in his study of Hitchcock's architecture, "Hitchcock's cinema is permeated by fetish objects, many of which have highly architectural or domestic connotations such as a bunch of keys, a doorknob, a closed door, a darkened window, or the top of a staircase."[15] Obviously, object-oriented

Hitchcock not only is compatible with but also serves Freudian Hitchcock, the toilet being an excellent example of "what the human race is all about." But Hitchcock's objects speak for the nonhuman as well. In the vertiginous echo of swirls from the toilet to the drain to Marion's dead eye and a rotating camera movement, Hitchcock arrives at something that object-oriented ontologists call a flat ontology. There, the camera eye and household plumbing are on equal footing with the human. To bring things back to humans as quickly as possible in such cases, psychoanalytic theorists upgrade from Freud to Lacan, which leads to utterances such as "She is the material residue of the negation of the Real by the Symbolic order. In this sense, she resists being completely absorbed by the system of the Other."[16] Okay, maybe that's true, but then again, perhaps she is just not that important anymore. Maybe the material we should be looking at is the polyvinyl chloride shower curtain that Norman (Anthony Perkins) wraps around her lifeless body.

Hitchcock famously told Truffaut, "I don't care about the subject matter; I don't care about the acting; but I do care about the pieces of film and the photography and the sound track and all the technical ingredients that made the audience scream. . . . It wasn't a message that stirred audiences, nor was it a great performance or their enjoyments of the novel. They were aroused by pure film."[17] The context of that statement is usually ignored. Truffaut was baiting Hitchcock by asking if *Psycho* was an experimental film. In other words, this was an invitation to geek out over the art of cinema, not to talk about John Gavin's stiff acting or the decision to cast a heartthrob in the role of Norman. "*Psycho*, more than any of my other pictures, is a film that belongs to film-makers, to you and me," says Hitchcock to Truffaut.[18] Of course, Hitchcock did care about the subject matter and the acting, but sitting there with Truffaut, director to director, cinephile to cinephile, was an occasion to talk about the essence of cinema. As George Toles explains, "I am sure that Hitchcock was not trying to deceive us when he said that the shower sequence had no meaning, as far as he was concerned. He placed it in that strangely aseptic realm of 'pure cinema,' where images, like poems, should not mean but be. For an image simply 'to be,' in Hitchcock's terms, it must be acknowledged as something with no depth—the screened image is both literally and ontologically flat."[19] Pure cinema recognizes the primacy of the image on-screen as the key form of the medium. In that flat ontology of the screened image, shower curtains are no different from movie stars.

Fig. 14.1. The shower curtain as cinematic screen in *Psycho* (1960).

When scholars talk about torn and shredded shower curtains in the shower murder scene, they are conflating the shower curtain with the movie screen—and for good reason. The shower curtain introduces, participates in, and literally wraps up the scene most associated with pure cinema. A curtain presupposes an audience, and the opening and closing of the shower curtain clearly alludes to theatricality. Marion's interaction with the curtain starts and finishes the spectacle of her murder. As Durgnat notes, "An actual moment of death is suggested—although uncertain—when Marion's fall brings down the curtain (a Hitchcock pun perhaps). Or, indeed *rings* down the curtain, for in low-angle close-up the curtain hooks jangle and dance in mid-air like crazy bells."[20] But this is cinema, not theater, and in its filmic context, the shower curtain serves not only as a sign of theatricality but also as a stand-in for the cinematic screen. David Sterritt sees Marion's entry into the shower uniquely as a theatrical gesture "that closes off two 'performances': the crime, of which she has now repented, and the 'act' she has unwittingly put on for her voyeuristic observer."[21] I propose instead that the theatrical closure be read as an overture to pure cinema. Marion sets the screen/scene as she steps into the shower and draws the semitranslucent curtain closed. The closing of the curtain becomes the opening of the screen.

At first, Marion establishes the screen by closing the curtain. Her nude body performs a primitive shadow play for our eyes (and those of the censors), a vague form of a woman as a screened image. Next, the shot cuts to place us inside the shower with her. We experience the shot/reverse shot exchange with the showerhead as well as a potentially disorienting series of shots that demonstrate the camera's ability to adjust our vantage point on a dime. Durgnat calls these sudden spatial disruptions a "collision of spatial orientation" in reference to Eisenstein's concept of montage collision.[22] The camera settles for a moment on an "Antonioni shot," defined by Durgnat as "a woman's face in a cold, blank space."[23] The Antonioni reference is apt here not only in the shot construction but also because Antonioni, perhaps even more than Hitchcock, famously viewed his actors as props. Here, as Marion's face occupies the lower right corner of the frame, the blank space of the curtain-as-screen regains prominence. Like an echo of the shadow play where we viewed Marion's figure from the opposite side of the curtain moments earlier, a new shadowy form appears on the curtain-screen. A pan-tilt drops Marion completely out of the picture for a moment, giving us a screened picture show that is not about Marion. On one level, our privileged (pre)view of the killer is a tool of suspense. As Philip Skerry explains in his book on the shower scene, "Hitchcock is using his 'tried and true' suspense technique of crossing the diegetic barrier by providing the audience knowledge that the character does not have."[24] On another level, Marion's momentary disappearance from the frame is as much about shifting our attention to the curtain-screen as it is about offering us information that Marion does not have.

According to Stefano's script, now in object-oriented mode, what we are about to experience is the slashing of the movie screen: "An impression of a knife slashing, as if tearing at the very screen, ripping the film."[25] Just as Marion closed the curtain-screen and initiated an erotic spectacle, the knife-wielding figure now thrusts the membranous plastic aside for a spectacle of violence that scholars have called "an act of visual frenzy" and an "unrelenting collision of images," a "vortex of violence," and an "attack on the spectator's vision, on the screen."[26] From a "pure cinema" perspective, the frenzy of montage fights to overcome the static boundaries of the screen. Hitchcock wages war on the screen itself, not only on Marion, not only on the audience. Here is montage in a death match with mise-en-scène, death by a thousand cuts ending in Hitchcock's downed shower curtain as a directorial mic drop. In his "shredded curtain" assessment, Krohn writes, "Hitchcock's most inspired visual metaphor was to make the shadow's stabbing thrusts, as the screenplay had said, an attack on the movie screen, represented by the shredded curtain and then by the expanse of Marion's unmarked belly, with the knife poised to strike at her navel."[27] The white expanse of Marion's belly in extreme close-up becomes, for Krohn, another screen under attack—Marion as a shower curtain.

Plasticity and the Horrors of Polyvinyl Chloride

Sometimes a shower curtain is just a shower curtain. Or rather, a shower curtain is *also* a shower curtain. Objects in films do more than prop up action, and they are more than symbols or metaphors. Objects, like actors, bring a surplus of presence and meaning that exist independently from directorial intent, qualities that in the best cases serendipitously harmonize with and add depth to the work. The shower curtains at the Bates Motel add plasticity and toxic modernity. They are relatable, ubiquitous, but not beloved companions to American rituals of hygiene. They are evidence of a takeover by plastics as disposable, homogeneous, synthetic, and as amorphous as the all-consuming ooze of *The Blob* (1958). According to the trade journal *Modern Plastics*, shower curtains, place mats, and decorative shelf papers alone could account for twenty-five million pounds of vinyl in American homes in 1959.[28] Sales of plastics steadily rose during the fifties and sixties, with annual production at more than six billion pounds by 1960.[29] Counter to the apocryphal tale of a "decline in sales of opaque shower curtains" mentioned in passing by Stephen Rebello and subsequently parroted as fact in nearly every work on *Psycho* ever since, I have found no evidence to support anything but steady growth in shower curtains, opaque or otherwise (not that curtain opacity was to blame for Marion's death).[30] As satisfying as it would be to substantiate the legend, *Psycho* had no discernable impact on shower curtain sales in the 1960s and, sadly, never gets mentioned in the plastics trade journals that would have so benefitted from a Bates Motel remodel spread or a column on curtain rod self-defense moves. Today, however, one can easily lose a few hours browsing and reading Amazon reviews for *Psycho*/slasher-inspired shower curtains with blood or shadowy figures. "I considered some of the other bloody curtains," notes one discerning customer, "but I decided on the subtlety of the bloody hand smears. It's just the right amount of blood. In a small bathroom it actually looks like a decent amount of blood."[31] Maybe things have changed just a little since 1960.

Shower curtains represent plastic at its worst. Consider that new shower curtain smell, which the *Washington Post* describes as "a sweet, sharp, dead

Fig. 14.2. The shower curtain participates in the clean-up in *Psycho* (1960).

smell, a smell like a blend of sun-heated tarpaulin, bus exhaust, the banality of evil and a day at the beach in East Germany." Many people love the smell of a new car, the article notes, but with a shower curtain, "it's a bad chemical smell that makes you think of words like 'mutation' and 'derailed tank car.'"[32] Search the internet for "PVC shower curtain," and the results turn up a mixture of articles about toxic chemicals and advertisements for PVC-free shower curtains. Volatile organic compounds, phthalates (plasticizers phonetically too Lovecraftian to be safe), lead, and other toxic emissions infuse shower curtains with a dread unknown to the 1960s spectator. Even during the heyday of proplastics propaganda after the Second World War, shower curtains were a sticking point. Design historian Jeffrey Miekle explains that many postwar plastics were poorly processed from rejected military scrap: "Consumers expressed disdain for tacky raincoats and shower curtains made from improperly plasticized vinyl sheeting. 'They smell, they sweat, the print comes off and they get brittle,' an editorial in *Modern Plastics* reported; enough rejected sheeting existed in storage to 'curtain the whole world.'"[33] Americans were thus purchasing the detritus of the military production in the form of raincoats, shower curtains, place mats, and other subpar housewares marketed as the very substance of modernity. Of the many polyvinyl chloride products in the home in 1960, a shower curtain is the most nakedly plastic, especially in the plain, semitranslucent blankness of *Psycho*, where there is no mistaking the sheet for natural fabric. Purely utilitarian and yet not particularly durable, the material has as more in common with plastic packaging than with fabric. The white PVC shower curtain appears hygienic but in an industrial, clinical manner. To shower behind a plasticized PVC curtain in a shower-bath is to turn a space for bathing into a decontamination chamber.

"Arggh, Why Does the Shower Curtain Attack Me?" asks a science feature on NPR. The answer, as far as we know, is a vortex of violence curiously in keeping with Hitchcock's swirling imagery. The rush of water from the shower, according to computer models by David Schmidt, turns the air inside the shower into a sort of spinning vortex like a hurricane. The low pressure at the eye of the hurricane sucks the shower curtain in (or at least does so with cheaper lightweight curtains within the right distance of the shower), giving the showering person an unwelcome but thankfully psycho-free attack of clinging plastic.[34] The attacking shower curtain grabs the skin like shrink-wrap on a cut of beef. When Marion, in her final moments of life, reaches for the wet shower curtain for support, the tactile experience of plastic against skin registers with anyone who has ever touched or been attacked by a wet shower curtain. Plasticized polyvinyl chloride offers tenuous support for Marion, as do we, when her outstretched hand reveals the limits of the slashed screen. Marion's gaze is not directed at the viewer, and her hand reaches not beyond the screen but instead at the curtain-screen that she grasped at the beginning of the screen-scene. The curtain yields, falls, and drapes itself alongside Marion over the tub, ready in its polyvalent plasticity to serve as a shroud, a body bag, packaging material ready for transport.

The shower curtain participates in the clean-up and the ignominious burial as both accomplice and victim. Norman turns off the shower, grabs the curtain, and spreads it—grommet wounds momentarily visible—on the hotel room floor. The vinyl's impermeability to liquids enables a tidy disposal process, while its visual permeability keeps the object of disposal dimly within the eye's grasp. According to Stefano, Hitchcock "acted out every move, every gesture, every nuance of wrapping the corpse in the curtain."[35] The shower scene, as some imagine it, has already ended with the swirling drain and Marion's sightless eye, but the shower curtain scene continues. Norman positions the curtain to protect the carpeting, drags Marion's body onto the plastic, and then washes his bloody hands and the bathroom surfaces. With a meticulous grace that might be mistaken for

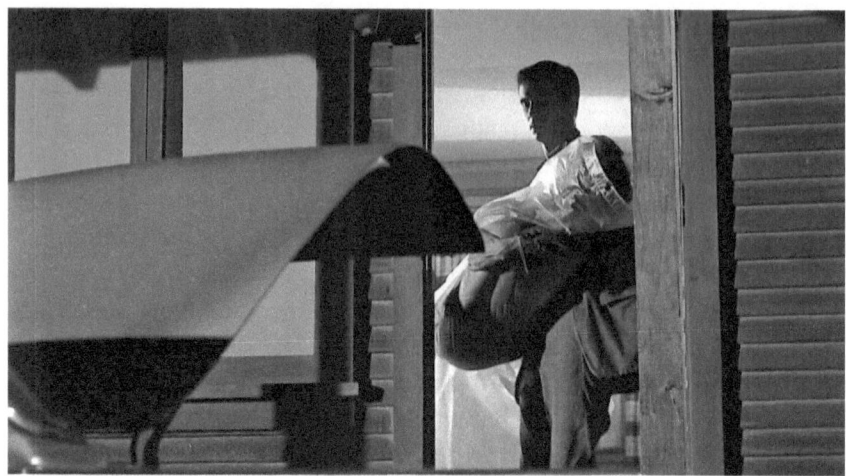

Fig. 14.3. Norman puts Marion's shower-curtain-wrapped body in the trunk in *Psycho* (1960).

reverence under different circumstances, Norman folds the shower curtain over the body from each side, ensuring that no blood will spill as he transfers the enshrouded figure to the trunk of Marion's used car. Durgnat compares the curtain scooped up in Norman's arms to a wedding dress "carried over the threshold—the wrong way."[36] Whether Hitchcock imagined the exit as a perverse counterpoint to a wedding tradition is anyone's guess, but the twisted humor certainly fits Hitchcock's style. In addition, Marion's used 1957 Ford Custom 300 Sedan—the same make and model (possibly the same exact prop) used by the quintessential all-American TV family, the Cleavers, in *Leave It to Beaver*—adds another Hitchcockian critique of American traditional values.[37] Satirically speaking, Hitchcock kills three birds with one stone: a naked blonde inside a plastic curtain inside a family sedan—a veritable turducken (an irresistibly tacky but appropriately avian metaphor) of midcentury America. Into the muck sinks Marion, the all-American girl Friday, but also Janet Leigh, the movie star wrapped in a plastic shower curtain, metonymically attached to the booming modern plastics industry and all of its accompanying falsity (to use a term Norman likes), and the curtain as a movie screen metaphor, a sign of theatricality, and perhaps as film itself (as cellulose triacetate film stock belongs under the broad umbrella of plastics), all wrapped inside a Ford sedan, a part of the car culture that built and then destroyed the Bates Motel. Add Marion's luggage and her stolen cash wrapped in newspaper, and you've got materialism and media going down for the ride as well. As they say in Hollywood, it's a wrap.

Epilogue: Amazon Customers React to "LiBa Mildew Resistant Anti-Bacterial PEVA 8G Shower Curtain Liner, 72x72 Clear-Non Toxic, Eco-Friendly, No Chemical Odor, Rust Proof Grommets"—Annotated

> No scent! And I like that, so far as plastic goes, it's kind-of-sort-of not-so-bad for the earth. Or, that's my understanding. (Riles)

The North Pacific Subtropical Gyre is roughly seven to nine million square miles of circulating ocean currents that spiral inward like a vortex. Within that gyre is nested another gyre known as the Pacific Garbage Patch or the Eastern Garbage Patch.[38] This vortex within a vortex is often characterized in the media as an island of plastic, as in the article "There's a Trash Pile in the Ocean Bigger Than Texas."[39] But the island eludes visual capture despite its enormity. Most of the circulating debris is composed of tiny particles—a microplastic soup whose plasticization of the ocean has yet to be fully understood. Bans on microbeads—plastic particles used in products such as exfoliating face and body wash, toothpaste, and cosmetics—demonstrate the emergence of the plastic leviathan in the public consciousness, though by no means are microbeads the sole offenders. As environmental scholar Jennifer Gabrys observes, "The packaging, films, fragments and assorted objects that cycle around gyres may remain there for many decades to come, eventually forming new oceanic environments and influencing organisms and food webs."[40] To Hitchcock's beloved vortices of the flushing toilet, the shower drain, and Marion Crane's lifeless eye, we can now add a garbage patch vortex swimming with particles of the material that envelops Marion's body as it sinks into the swamp.

> Excellent, doesn't make your bathroom smell like a plastic factory like other vinyl liners. (Ben Dubin)

> This item attracted me because of all the hype going around about toxic shower curtains, chemicals, and PVC found in other products. (Rollingdice)

PVC is a hard, brittle substance, but thanks to chemical additives called plasticizers, a shower curtain can take on qualities such as flexibility, mold resistance, and fire resistance. Because plasticizers do not bind chemically to polymer chains, they tend to leach from plastic products and enter other bodies, including human bodies, where they act as endocrine disruptors. Environmental scientist Max Liboiron explains, "This may result in nothing notable—a gene that expresses itself out of turn may just create extra or malformed, harmless proteins. On the other hand, various plasticizers have been correlated with infertility, recurrent miscarriages, feminization of male foetuses, early-onset puberty, obesity, diabetes, reduced brain development, cancer and neurological disorders such as early onset senility in adults and reduced brain development in children."[41] Causation is difficult to prove, however, given the number of variables and the complex "cocktail" of plasticizers in the body.[42] The CDC has found that every person in the United States and Canada has plastic chemicals in their body. Persistent organic pollutants (POP) such as the plasticizers in the PVC shower curtain at the Bates Motel are classified "by their lack of a discernable half-life, their ability to bioaccumulate, high levels of toxicity and the tendency to travel long distances."[43]

> Need to wrap a dead body before dumping in the river? Haven't tried it, but I think it would work well for that too. (Brandon N. Wirtz)

Norman would probably agree.

> Best shower curtain I've ever bought. It truly is mildew-resistant. And the clear design means I'm not having mental images of Psycho while I'm showering. (David W. Hensley)

> Love my new clear shower curtain liner! Ever since the movie Psycho, I have had this "thing" about taking a shower and not being able to see outside the curtain. (WizGeek; ArtulCutie)

No one knows how many clear shower curtains have been purchased as a direct result of *Psycho*, but those who have opted for a clear curtain have in fact made their bathrooms a little more like the Bates Motel, given the relative transparency of the curtain in the film. Moreover, those customers have extended the viewing experience of Hitchcock's curtain-screen to the home. Showering behind a translucent curtain, the *Psycho*-traumatized person looks at and through the plastic just as the audience does when placed in the shower with Marion. Hitchcock has made the solitary routine shower its own form of cinematic spectacle.

> Purchased for my Grandmother. If she didn't complain it must be alright. (Avon)

Notes

1. Skerry, 285.
2. Durgnat, 3.
3. Rothman, 299.
4. Thomson, 56.
5. Durgnat, 111.
6. Rothman, 303.
7. Truffaut, 206.
8. Ibid., 207.
9. L. Williams, 168.
10. Silverman, 211.
11. Rothman, 301.
12. Kolker, "The Form, Structure, and Influence of *Psycho*," 242.
13. Krohn, 230; Rothman, 309.
14. Rebello, 46.
15. Jacobs, 26.
16. Samuels, 144.
17. Truffaut, 211.
18. Ibid.
19. Toles, 129.
20. Durgnat, 117.
21. Sterritt, 107.
22. Durgnat, 115.
23. Ibid.
24. Skerry, 315.
25. The December 1, 1959, version of Stefano's script can be found online at http://www.imsdb.com/scripts/Psycho.html.
26. Kolker, "The Form, Structure, and Influence of *Psycho*," 247; Skerry, 321; Krohn, 225.
27. Krohn, 230.
28. R. L. Van Boskirk, "The Plastiscope," *Modern Plastics*, September, 1959, 212.
29. Meikle, 2.
30. Rebello, 172. Rebello gives no source, and everyone else cites Rebello. Annual retail sales reports do not itemize housewares down to the level of shower curtains. Trade journals such as *Modern Plastics* report steady growth in shower curtain sales during the period after *Psycho*'s release.
31. James, May 22, 2016, https://www.amazon.com/Spinning-Hat-Blood-Shower-Curtain/dp/B00ABH1SR6/ref=sr_1_1?ie=UTF8&qid=1514016544&sr=8-1&keywords=psycho+shower+curtain#customerReviews.
32. Henry Allen, "Plastics. And That's Vinyl. From Celluloid to Lucite to Mel Mac to Tupperware, It's a Synthetic with Real Staying Power," *Washington Post*, October 31, 1993, https://www.washingtonpost.com/archive/lifestyle/1993/10/31/plastics-and-thats-vinyl-from-celluloid-to-lucite-to-mel-mac-to-tupperware-its-a-synthetic-with-real-staying-power/60213def-6d67-4b76-ae9b-722858e485d3/?utm_term=.c851e0b1719e.
33. Miekle, 166.
34. See Joe Palca, "Arggh, Why Does the Shower Curtain Attack Me?," *NPR*, November 4, 2006, https://www.npr.org/templates/story/story.php?storyId=6430581.

35. Kolker, 47.
36. Durgnat, 134.
37. Legend has it on the Internet Movie Cars Database (IMCDB) that after the Cleavers switched from the Ford Custom 300 (the first two seasons) to a Plymouth, Hitchcock used the same car in *Psycho*. If so, it was without the wheel covers and trailer hitch and with a different license plate. See http://www.imcdb.org/vehicle_373429-Ford-Custom-300-1957.html.
38. See Gabrys, 203–4.
39. Sophie Kleeman, "There's a Trash Pile in the Ocean Bigger Than Texas—Here's What You Need to Know," *Mic*, October 27, 2015, https://mic.com/articles/127391/theres-a-trash-pile-in-the-ocean-bigger-than-texas-heres-what-you-need-to-know#.jH9cqtX6j.
40. Gabrys, 208.
41. See Liboiron, 294–97.
42. Ibid., 299.
43. Ibid., 284, 303.

CONCLUSION...

In the introduction, I call this book the insomniac's answer to *Goodnight Moon* because like the classic children's book, *Household Horror* treats domestic objects as coequals to be reckoned with. Unlike *Goodnight Moon*, this book aims to keep the reader up at night—at least long enough to suspect, as one does in the dark, that objects contain more than meets the eye, long enough "to reveal the hidden density of a unit," to explode "the innards of things."[1] Ian Bogost refers to the practice as the "realism of multitude"—a turn of phrase not unlike Charles Baudelaire's description of walking among crowds as a "bath of multitude," a "debauch of vitality at the expense of the human species."[2] Bogost and Baudelaire are essentially playing the same game. The nineteenth-century flaneur wanders the city as a solitary figure bathed in multitude, attentive to fleeting connections and enjoying the "feverish delights" that come from imagining the inner being of strangers.[3] The twenty-first-century object-oriented philosopher engages the alien nature of objects poetically through metaphor and allusion, and warily through the hubris of anthropomorphism. At best, as Graham Harman suggests, poetic speculation multiplies signs that point toward an object's depth: "This indirect access is achieved by allowing the hidden object to deform the sensual world, just as the existence of a black hole might be inferred from the swirl of light and gases orbiting its core."[4] To engage objects is thus to witness terrifying density through monstrous deformations. Object-oriented ontology (with its ghostly wail of an acronym: OOO) is a horror story.

This book has used the half light of horror to allude to the unfathomable being of objects as seemingly benign as refrigerators, microwave ovens, sheets, and shower curtains. Rich interpretive possibilities emerge from the mundane once we see things no longer "hazily as bland instruments of our will" but rather as beings "marked by sincerity"—that is, as things that exhibit their own inner life.[5] We can never really know what it's like to be a houseplant or a remote control or a sleeper sofa, but we can, like *Goodnight Moon*, salute our fellow objects. We can walk through a house of objects bathed in multitude and see a vitality that questions human exceptionalism. This book is a record of paths taken to allude to objects. Some of those paths are playful, others rigorously methodic, but none prescriptive. A map is anathema to the flaneur. The object-oriented "bath of multitude" is at once solitary and crowded. "Multitude, solitude: identical terms, and interchangeable by the active and fertile poet," writes Baudelaire.[6] The object-oriented wanderer celebrates the multitude by adding to it. "Deprived of access to the real objects that lurk beneath perception and all other contexts, we produce our own real objects in the midst of them," writes Harman.[7] Or to quote Bogost, "Instead of understanding [an object], the best we can do is trace the edges of its dark noise."[8] Interchangeable with appreciating objects through multitude is recognizing their solitude—hence the object-oriented philosopher's love of Lovecraftian excess (multitude) on one hand and bare-bones lists on the other (solitude). The two work in tandem to argue for inner richness amid detachment. In that spirit, *Household Horror* takes a simple inventory of household objects, explores the deformations caused by their presence in cinematic horror, and produces new objects as readings. The book begins as a list, defined by Bogost as "a group of items loosely joined not by logic or power or use but by the gentle not of the comma."[9] And now it must end, not with one point but with the gentle void of an ellipsis . . .

Notes

1. Bogost, *Alien Phenomenology*, 58.
2. Ibid., 58; Baudelaire, 20.
3. Baudelaire, 20.
4. Harman, *Weird Realism*, 238.
5. Ibid., 44.
6. Baudelaire, 20.
7. Harman, *Weird Realism*, 260.
8. Bogost, *Alien Phenomenology*, 107.
9. Ibid., 38.

FILMOGRAPHY

Alien (1979, UK/USA, Ridley Scott)
American Psycho (2000, USA, Mary Harron)
The Amityville Horror (1979, USA, Stuart Rosenberg)
Annabelle (2014, USA, John R. Leonetti)
The Bad Seed (1956, USA, Mervyn LeRoy)
Ballet mécanique (1924, France, Fernand Léger)
Battleship Potemkin (*Bronenosets Potemkin*, 1925, Russia, Sergei M. Eisenstein)
Black Christmas (1974, Canada/USA, Bob Clark)
Black Sabbath (*I tre volti della paura*, 1963, Italy/France, Mario Bava)
The Black Stork (1917, USA, Leopold Wharton and Theopold Wharton)
The Blob (1958, USA, Irvin S. Yeaworth Jr. and Russell S. Doughten Jr.)
Blow Out (1981, USA, Brian De Palma)
Body Snatchers (1993, USA, Abel Ferrara)
Brick (2005, USA, Rian Johnson)
Carrie (1976, USA, Brian De Palma)
Children of the Damned (1964, UK, Anton Leader)
A Clockwork Orange (1971, UK/USA, Stanley Kubrick)
The Conjuring (2013, USA, James Wan)
Death Bed: The Bed That Eats (1977, USA, George Barry)
Detour (1945, USA, Edgar G. Ulmer)
Dial M for Murder (1954, USA, Alfred Hitchcock)
Dressed to Kill (1980, USA, Brian De Palma)
Dr. Strangelove, or How I Learned to Stop Worrying and Love the Bomb (1964, UK, Stanley Kubrick)
Eraserhead (1977, USA, David Lynch)
E.T. the Extra-Terrestrial (1982, USA, Steven Spielberg)
Evil Laugh (1986, USA, Dominick Brascia)
The Exorcism of Emily Rose (2005, USA, Scott Derrickson)
The Exorcist (1973, USA, William Friedkin)
Eyes without a Face (*Les yeux sans visage*, 1960, France/Italy, Georges Franju)
Final Destination (2000, USA, James Wong)
Final Destination 2 (2003, USA, David R. Ellis)
The Fly (1986, Canada, UK/USA, David Cronenberg)
Frankenstein (1931, USA, James Whale)
The Freakmaker (a.k.a. *The Mutations*, 1974, UK/USA, Jack Cardiff)
Full Metal Jacket (1987, UK/USA, Stanley Kubrick)
Garden of Death (a.k.a. *The Gardener*, 1974, USA, James H. Kay)
Ghost in the Machine (1993, USA, Rachel Talalay)
A Ghost Story (2017, USA, David Lowery)
The Good Son (1993, USA, Joseph Ruben)

Gremlins (1984, USA, Joe Dante)
Halloween (1978, USA, John Carpenter)
The Hills Have Eyes (1977, USA, Wes Craven)
The Hills Have Eyes (2006, USA, Alexandre Aja)
The House on Sorority Row (1983, USA, Mark Rosman)
Indiana Jones and the Temple of Doom (1984, USA, Steven Spielberg)
Inglourious Basterds (2009, USA/Germany, Quentin Tarantino and Eli Roth)
The Innocents (1961, UK, Jack Clayton)
The Invasion (2007, USA/Australia, Oliver Hirschbiegel and James McTeigue)
Invasion of the Body Snatchers (1956, USA, Don Siegel)
Invasion of the Body Snatchers (1978, USA, Philip Kaufman)
I Saw What You Did (1965, USA, William Castle)
It (TV miniseries, 1990, USA/Canada, Tommy Lee Wallace)
It (2017, USA/Canada, Andy Muschietti)
It Chapter Two (2019, USA, Andy Muschietti)
It Follows (2014, USA, David Robert Mitchell)
Ju-on: The Grudge (*Ju-on*, 2002, Japan, Shimizu Takashi)
The Last House on the Left (1972, USA, Wes Craven)
The Last House on the Left (2009, USA, Dennis Iliadis)
The Little Shop of Horrors (1960, USA, Roger Corman and Charles B. Griffith)
Long Distance (1941, USA Bell System Film)
Looper (USA/China, 2012, Rian Johnson)
M (1931, Germany, Fritz Lang)
March of the Penguins (2005, France, Luc Jacquet)
The Matrix (1999, USA, Lana Wachowski and Lilly Wachowski)
May (2002, USA, Lucky McKee)
Memories of Murder (*Salinui chueok*, 2003, South Korea, Bong Joon-ho)
Microwave Massacre (1983, USA, Wayne Berwick)
Misery (1990, USA, Rob Reiner)
The Nation at Your Fingertips (1951, USA, Bell System Film)
A Nightmare on Elm Street (1984, USA, Wes Craven)
The Night Walker (1964, USA, William Castle)
Noriko's Dinner Table (*Noriko no shokutaku*, 2006, Japan, Sono Shion)
Oldboy (*Oldeuboi*, 2003, South Korea, Park Chan-wook)
The Omen (1976, UK/USA, Richard Donner)
Orphan (2009, USA/Canada/Germany, Jaume Collet-Serra)
The Others (2001, USA/Spain, Alejandro Amenábar)
Our Shrinking World (1946, USA, Young America Films, Inc.)
The Passion of the Christ (2004, USA, Mel Gibson)
Peeping Tom (1960, UK, Michael Powell)
Phone (*Pon*, 2002, South Korea, Ahn Byeong-ki)
Pieces (1982, Spain/Italy/Puerto Rico/USA, Juan Piquer Simón)
Poltergeist (1982, USA, Tobe Hooper)
Poltergeist II: The Other Side (1986, USA, Brian Gibson)
Possession (1981, France/West Germany, Andrzej Zulawski)
Powers of Ten (1977, USA, Charles Eames and Ray Eames)

Psycho (1960, USA, Alfred Hitchcock)
Pulse (*Kairo*, 2001, Japan, Kiyoshi Kurosawa)
Pulse (2006, USA, Jim Sonzero)
Rear Window (1954, USA, Alfred Hitchcock)
Rent a Family, Inc. (2012, Denmark, Kaspar Astrup Schröder)
Repulsion (1965, UK, Roman Polanski)
Ringu (1998, Japan, Nakata Hideo)
The Ring Virus (*Hangul*, 1999, South Korea, Kim Dong-bin)
Room 237 (2012, USA, Rodney Ascher)
Rope (1948, USA, Alfred Hitchcock)
Rosemary's Baby (1968, USA, Roman Polanski)
Scream (1996, USA, Wes Craven)
The Secret Life of Plants (1978, USA, Walon Green)
Se7en (1995, USA, David Fincher)
78/52: Hitchcock's Shower Scene (2017, USA, Alexandre O. Philippe)
The Shining (1980, UK/USA, Stanley Kubrick)
The Silence of the Lambs (1991, USA, Jonathan Demme)
Sisters (1973, USA, Brian De Palma)
The Sixth Sense (1999, USA, M. Night Shyamalan)
Sorry, Wrong Number (1948, USA, Anatole Litvak)
Strait-Jacket (1964, USA, William Castle)
Suicide Club/Suicide Circle (*Jisatsu Sākuru*, 2001, Japan, Sono Shion)
Superstition (1982, USA, James W. Roberson)
A Tale of Two Sisters (*Janghwa, Hongryeon*, 2003, Korea, Kim Jee-woon)
Tetsuo: The Iron Man (*Tetsuo*, 1989, Japan, Tsukamoto Shin'ya)
The Texas Chainsaw Massacre (1974, USA, Tobe Hooper)
2001: A Space Odyssey (1968, UK/USA, Stanley Kubrick)
Txt (2006, Philippines, Michael Tuviera)
Un chien andalou (1929, France, Luis Buñuel)
Untold Scandal (*Seukaendeul—Joseon namnyeo sangyeoljisa*, 2003, South Korea, Lee Je-yong)
Urban Legend (1998, USA, Jamie Blanks)
Village of the Damned (1960, UK, Wolf Rilla)
When a Stranger Calls (1979, USA, Fred Walton)
Whispering Corridors (*Yeogo goedam*, 1998, South Korea, Park Ki-hyeong)
Whispering Wires (1926, USA, Albert Ray)
The Willies (1990, USA, Brian Peck)
Wolfen (1981, USA, Michael Wadleigh)
The World at Your Call (1950, USA, Jam Handy Organization)

BIBLIOGRAPHY

Aldis, Dorothy. *Everything and Anything*. New York: Minton, Balch, 1927.
Al-Gailani, Salim. "Making Birth Defects 'Preventable': Pre-conceptional Vitamin Supplements and the Politics of Risk Reduction." *Studies in History and Philosophy of Biological and Biomedical Sciences* 47 (2014): 278–89.
Allen, Thomas B. *Possessed: The True Story of an Exorcism*. New York: Doubleday, 1993.
Althusser, Louis. *Lenin and Philosophy and Other Essays*. Translated by Ben Brewster. New York: Monthly Review, 1971.
American Radiator Company. *Radiation and Decoration*. Chicago: American Radiator Company, 1905.
American Telephone and Telegraph Company. *The Telephone in America*. New York: Information Department, AT&T, 1942.
Amis, Kingsley. *The King's English: A Guide to Modern Usage*. New York: St. Martin's, 1998.
Apple, Rima D. *Vitamania: Vitamins in American Culture*. New Brunswick, NJ: Rutgers University Press, 1996.
Armstrong, David. "The Rise of Surveillance Medicine." *Sociology of Health and Illness* 17, no. 3 (1995): 393–404.
Arnold, Keith. "The Subject of Radical Change." *Philosophical Studies: An International Journal for Philosophy in the Analytic Tradition* 33, no. 4 (1978): 395–401.
Ashkenazi, Michael, and Jeanne Jacob. *The Essence of Japanese Cuisine: An Essay on Food and Culture*. Philadelphia: University of Pennsylvania Press, 2000.
Asimov, Isaac. "Forward: The Role of the Heretic." In *Scientists Confront Velikovsky*, edited by Donald Goldsmith, 7–15. Ithaca, NY: Cornell University Press, 1977.
Aumont, Jacques. "Lumière Revisited." *Film History* 8, no. 4 (1996): 416–30.
Bachelard, Gaston. *La poétique de l'espace*. Paris: Presses universitaires de France, 1974.
———. *The Poetics of Space*. Translated by Maria Jolas. Boston: Beacon, 1994.
Backster, Cleve. *Primary Perception: Biocommunication with Plants, Living Foods, and Human Cells*. Anza, CA: White Rose Millennium, 2003.
Ballantyne, Jeanette. "Women as Law Stenographers." In *Proceedings of the New York State Stenographers Association*, 72–76. Troy, NY: Daily Press Book Publishing House, 1881.
Barthes, Roland. *The Rustle of Language*. Translated by Richard Howard. Berkeley: University of California Press, 1989.
Bates, Arlo. *A Book O' Nine Tales*. Boston: Roberts Bros., 1891.
Baudelaire, Charles. *Paris Spleen: 1869*. Translated by Louise Varèse. New York: New Directions, 1947.
Baudrillard, Jean. *Le système des objets*. Paris: Gallimard, 1968.
Bauer, Henry H. *Beyond Velikowsky: The History of a Public Controversy*. Chicago: University of Illinois Press, 1984.
Baxter, John. "Kubrick in Hell." In *Stanley Kubrick's "The Shining": Studies in the Horror Film*, edited by Danel Olson, 15–54. Lakewood, CO: Centipede, 2015.

Bell, Susan E., and Anne E. Figert, eds. *Reimagining (Bio)Medicalization, Pharmaceuticals, and Genetics: Old Critiques and New Engagements*. New York: Routledge, 2015.

Bellamy, Robert V. Jr., and James R. Walker. *Television and the Remote Control: Grazing on a Vast Wasteland*. New York: Guilford, 1996.

Benson-Allott, Caetlin. *Remote Control*. New York: Bloomsbury Academic, 2015.

Betty, Stafford. "The Growing Evidence for 'Demonic Possession': What Should Psychiatry's Response Be?" *Journal of Religion and Health* 44, no. 1 (2005): 13–30.

Biskind, Peter. *Seeing Is Believing: How Hollywood Taught Us to Stop Worrying and Love the Fifties*. New York: Pantheon Books, 1983.

Bogost, Ian. "The Aesthetics of Philosophical Carpentry." In *The Nonhuman Turn*, edited by Richard Grusin, 81–100. Minneapolis: University of Minnesota Press, 2015.

———. *Alien Phenomenology, or What It's Like to Be a Thing*. Minneapolis: University of Minnesota Press, 2012.

Borgé, Guy, and Marie Borgé. *Les Lumière: Antoine, Auguste, Louis et les autres . . .* Lyon: Éditions lyonnaises d'art et d'histoire, 2004.

Bozung, Justin. "Interview with Brian Cook (Assistant Director)." In *Stanley Kubrick's "The Shining": Studies in the Horror Film*, edited by Danel Olson, 697–705. Lakewood, CO: Centipede, 2015.

———. "Interview with Gordon Stainforth." In *Stanley Kubrick's "The Shining": Studies in the Horror Film*, edited by Danel Olson, 637–58. Lakewood, CO: Centipede, 2015.

———. "Interview with Greg MacGillivray." In *Stanley Kubrick's "The Shining": Studies in the Horror Film*, edited by Danel Olson, 601–22. Lakewood, CO: Centipede, 2015.

———. "Interview with Shelley Duvall." In *Stanley Kubrick's "The Shining": Studies in the Horror Film*, edited by Danel Olson, 367–76. Lakewood, CO: Centipede, 2015.

Brenner, Eric D., Rainer Stahlberg, Stefano Mancuso, Jorge Vivanco, Frantisek Baluska, and Elizabeth Van Volkenburgh. "Plant Neurobiology: An Integrated View of Plant Signaling." *Trends in Plant Science* 11, no. 8 (2006): 413–19.

Brodeur, Paul. *The Zapping of America: Microwaves, Their Deadly Risk, and the Cover-Up*. New York: W. W. Norton, 1977.

Brown, Margaret Wise. *Goodnight Moon*. Pictures by Clement Hurd. New York: Harper and Row, 1947.

Brunner, Bernd. *The Art of Lying Down: A Guide to Horizontal Living*. Translated by Lori Lantz. Brooklyn: Melville House, 2012.

Brunvand, Jan Harold. *Encyclopedia of Urban Legends, Updated and Expanded Edition*. Santa Barbara, CA: ABC-CLIO, 2012. Accessed February 24, 2017. Via ProQuest ebrary.

Bryson, Bill. *A Short History of Nearly Everything*. Toronto: Anchor Canada, 2004.

Buffler, Charles R. *Microwave Cooking and Processing: Engineering Fundamentals for the Food Scientist*. New York: Van Nostrand Reinhold, 1993.

Bulkeley, Kelly. *Visions of the Night: Dreams, Religion, and Psychology*. Albany: State University of New York Press, 1999.

Burgess, Anthony. *On Going to Bed*. New York: Abbeville, 1982.

Burke, Michael B. "Cohabitation, Stuff and Intermittent Existence." *Mind* 89, no. 355 (1980): 391–405.

Cagle, Robert L. "Diary of a Lost Girl: Victoriana, Intertextuality, and *A Tale of Two Sisters*." In *Korean Horror Cinema*, edited by Alison Peirse and Daniel Martin, 158–72. Edinburgh: Edinburgh University Press, 2013.

Cameron, Allan. "Colour, Embodiment and Dread in *High Tension* and *A Tale of Two Sisters*." *Horror Studies* 3, no. 1 (2012): 87–103.
Cameron, Allan, and Richard Misek. "Time-Lapse and the Projected Body." *Moving Image Review and Art Journal* 3, no. 1 (2014): 38–51.
Campbell, Gavin James. "Mortification, Mockery and Dissembling: Western Adventures in Japanese Etiquette." In *Manners and Mischief: Gender, Power, and Etiquette in Japan*, edited by Jan Bardsley and Laura Miller, 86–99. Berkeley: University of California Press, 2011.
Castle, William. *Step Right Up! . . . I'm Gonna Scare the Pants off America*. New York: Putnam, 1976.
Chamovitz, Daniel. *What a Plant Knows: A Field Guide to the Senses*. New York: Scientific American/Farrar, Straus and Giroux, 2012.
Chapuis, Robert J. *100 Years of Telephone Switching (1878–1978) Part 1: Manual and Electromechanical Switching*. New York: North-Holland, 1982.
Chion, Michel. *David Lynch*. Translated by Robert Julian. London: British Film Institute, 1995.
———. *Le cinéma et ses métiers*. Paris: Bordas, 1990.
Choi, Jinhee. *The South Korean Film Renaissance: Local Hitmakers, Global Provocateurs*. Middletown, CT: Wesleyan University Press, 2010.
Ciesielski, Andrew. *Introduction to Rubber Technology*. Shrewsbury, UK: Smithers Rapra, 2001.
Ciment, Michel. *Kubrick: The Definitive Edition*. Translated by Gilbert Adair and Robert Bonnono. New York: Faber and Faber, 2001.
Cinotto, Simone. "'Everyone Would Be around the Table': American Family Mealtimes in Historical Perspective, 1850–1960." *New Directions for Child and Adolescent Development*, no. 111 (2006): 17–34.
Clarke, Adele E., Laura Mamo, Jennifer Ruth Fosket, Jennifer R. Fishman, and Janet K. Shim, eds. *Biomedicalization: Technoscience, Health, and Illness in the US*. Durham, NC: Duke University Press, 2010.
Clow, James B. *Clow Gasteam Heating Systems*. Chicago: James B. Clow, 1929.
Cocks, Geoffrey. *The Wolf at the Door: Stanley Kubrick, History, and the Holocaust*. New York: Peter Lang, 2004.
Coffin, Judith. "Credit, Consumption, and Images of Women's Desires: Selling the Sewing Machine in Late Nineteenth-Century France." *French Historical Studies* 18, no. 3 (1994): 749–83.
———. *The Politics of Women's Work: The Paris Garment Trades, 1750–1915*. Princeton: Princeton University Press, 1996.
Colin, Armand. "La querelle du sofa: Étude sur le rapport entre gloire et diplomatie." *Histoire, économie, et société* 20, no. 2 (2001): 185–97.
Collin, Johanne. "On Social Plasticity: The Transformative Power of Pharmaceuticals on Health, Nature and Identity." *Sociology of Health and Illness* 38, no. 1 (2016): 73–89.
Combs, Gerald F. Jr. *The Vitamins: Fundamental Aspects in Nutrition and Health*. Burlington, VT: Elsevier Science, 2007.
Conrad, Peter. *The Medicalization of Society: On the Transformation of Human Conditions into Treatable Disorders*. Baltimore: Johns Hopkins University Press, 2007.
Copeland, Gary A., and Karla Schweitzer. "Domination of the Remote Control during Family Viewing." In *The Remote Control in the New Age of Television*, edited by James R. Walker and Robert V. Bellamy Jr., 155–68. Westport, CT: Praeger, 1993.

Cowan, Ruth Schwartz. *More Work for Mother: The Ironies of Household Technology from the Open Hearth to the Microwave.* New York: Basic Books, 1983.
Crébillon, Claude-Prosper Jolyot de. *Le sopha, conte moral.* 2 vols. Paris: Prault, 1742.
Creed, Barbara. *The Monstrous-Feminine: Film, Feminism, Psychoanalysis.* London: Routledge, 1993.
Cropper, Corry. "*Réintroduction à la littérature fantastique*: Enlightenment Philosophy, Object-Oriented Ontology, and the French Fantastic." *Nineteenth-Century French Studies* 44, nos. 1–2 (2015–2016): 25–45.
Curtiss, Ursula Reilly. *Out of the Dark.* New York: Dodd, Mead, 1963.
Cwiertka, Katarzyna. *Modern Japanese Cuisine: Food, Power and National Identity.* London: Reaktion Books, 2006.
Dahl, Roald. *The Gremlins: The Lost Walt Disney Production, a Royal Air Force Story by Roald Dahl.* Introduction by Leonard Maltin. Milwaukie, OR: Dark Horse Books, 2006.
Darwin, Charles. *The Power of Movement in Plants.* London: John Murray, 1880.
Davies, Eric. "New Functions for Electrical Signals in Plants." *New Phytologist* 161 (2004): 607–10.
Davies, Margery W. *Woman's Place Is at the Typewriter: Office Work and Office Workers, 1870–1930.* Philadelphia: Temple University Press, 1982.
DeGrandpre, Richard. *The Cult of Pharmacology: How America Became the World's Most Troubled Drug Culture.* Durham, NC: Duke University Press, 2006.
DeJean, Joan. *The Age of Comfort: When Paris Discovered Casual—and the Modern Home Began.* New York: Bloomsbury, 2009.
Deleuze, Gilles. *The Fold: Leibniz and the Baroque.* Translated by Tom Conley. London: Continuum, 2006.
Derry, Charles. *Dark Dreams 2.0: A Psychological History of the Modern Horror Film from the 1950s to the 21st Century.* Jefferson, NC: McFarland, 2009.
Domosh, Mona. "Selling Civilization: Toward a Cultural Analysis of America's Economic Empire in the Late Nineteenth and Early Twentieth Centuries." *Transactions of the Institute of British Geographers*, n.s., 1, no. 4 (2004): 453–67.
Donaldson, Barry, and Bernard Nagengast, with an introductory essay by Gershon Meckler. *Heat and Cold: Mastering the Great Indoors.* Atlanta: American Society of Heating, Refrigerating and Air-Conditioning Engineers, 1994.
Dostoyevsky, Fyodor. *The Idiot.* Translated by Henry and Olga Carlisle. New York: Signet Classics, 2010.
Douglas, Mary, and Jonathan Gross. "Food and Culture: Measuring the Intricacy of Rule Systems." *Social Science Information* 20, no. 1 (1981): 1–35.
Dufour, Éric. *Le cinéma d'horreur et ses figures.* Paris: Presses universitaires de France, 2006.
Dumas, Chris. *Un-American Psycho: Brian De Palma and the Political Invisible.* Bristol, UK: Intellect, 2012.
Dupuy, Coraline. "'Why Don't You Remember? Are You Crazy': Korean Gothic and Psychosis in *Tale of Two Sisters*." *Irish Journal of Gothic and Horror Studies* 3 (2007): 64–77.
Durgnat, Raymond. *A Long Hard Look at "Psycho."* London: British Film Institute, 2002.
Earls, Alan R., and Robert E. Edwards. *Raytheon Company: The First Sixty Years.* Charleston, SC: Arcadia, 2005.
Eco, Umberto. *Travels in Hyperreality.* Translated by William Weaver. San Diego: Harcourt, 1986.

Elias, Norbert. *The Civilizing Process: Sociogenetic and Psychogenetic Investigations.* Edited by Eric Dunning, Johan Goudsblom, and Stephen Mennell. Translated by Edmund Jephcott. Malden: Blackwell, 2000.
Epstein, Jean, and Stuart Liebman. "Magnification and Other Writings." *October* 3 (1977): 9–25.
E. Remington and Sons. *The Type-Writer! A Machine to Supersede the Pen.* Ilion, NY: E. Remington and Sons, 1875.
Fales, Winnifred, and Mary Northend. "Camouflaging the Radiator." *Good Housekeeping*, July 1918, 56–57.
Fernandez, Nancy Page. "Creating Consumers: Gender, Class, and the Sewing Machine." In *The Culture of Sewing: Gender, Consumption and Home Dressmaking*, edited by Barbara Burman, 157–68. Oxford: Berg, 1999.
Fischer, Claude S. "Gender and the Residential Telephone, 1890–1940: Technologies of Sociability." *Sociological Forum* 2, no. 4 (1988): 11–33.
Fischer, Lucy. "Birth Traumas: Parturition and Horror in *Rosemary's Baby*." In *Dread of Difference*, edited by Barry Keith Grant, 439–58. Austin: University of Texas Press, 2015.
Flusser, Vilém. *Gestures.* Translated by Nancy Anne Roth. Minneapolis: University of Minnesota Press, 2014.
Forman-Brunell, Miriam. *Babysitter: An American History.* New York: New York University Press, 2009.
Foucault, Michel. "Of Other Spaces." Translated by Jay Miskowiec. *Diacritics* 16, no. 1 (1986): 22–27.
Fraser, Suzanne, Kylie Valentine, and Celia Roberts. "Living Drugs." *Science and Culture* 18, no. 2 (2009): 123–31.
Freud, Sigmund. "The Uncanny." Translated by Alix Strachey. In *Creativity and the Unconscious*, 122–61. New York: Harper and Row, 1958. First published 1919.
Gabrys, Jennifer. "Monitoring and Remediating a Garbage Patch." In *Research Objects in Their Technological Setting*, edited by Bernadette Bensaude Vincent, Sacha Loeve, Alfred Nordmann, and Astrid Schwarz, 201–14. London: Taylor and Francis, 2017.
Galston, Arthur W., and Clifford L. Slayman. "The Not-So-Secret Life of Plants: In Which the Historical and Experimental Myths about Emotional Communication between Animal and Vegetable Are Put to Rest." *American Scientist*, May–June 1979, 337–44.
Gateward, Frances. "Waiting to Exhale: The Colonial Experience and the Trouble with *My Own Breathing*." In *Seoul Searching: Culture and Identity in Contemporary Korean Cinema*, edited by Frances Gateward, 191–218. Ithaca, NY: State University of New York Press, 2007.
Gaycken, Oliver. *Devices of Curiosity: Early Cinema and Popular Science.* Oxford: Oxford University Press, 2015.
———. "The Secret Life of Plants: Visualizing Vegetative Movement, 1880–1903." *Early Popular Visual Culture* 10, no. 1 (2012): 51–69.
Gentilcore, David. *Pomodoro! The History of the Tomato in Italy.* New York: Columbia University Press, 2010.
Gilliatt, Penelope. "Anguish under the Skin." *New Yorker*, July 15, 1968.
Goldgar, Anne. *Tulipmania: Money, Honor, and Knowledge in the Dutch Golden Age.* Chicago: University of Chicago Press, 2008.
Goodman, Felicitas D. *The Exorcism of Anneliese Michel.* Garden City, NY: Doubleday, 1981.

Gordin, Michael D. *The Pseudo-science Wars: Immanuel Velikovsky and the Birth of the Modern Fringe.* Chicago: University of Chicago Press, 2012.
Grant, Barry Keith. *Invasion of the Body Snatchers.* BFI Film Classics. New York: Palgrave Macmillan in association with the British Film Institute, 2010.
Greenberg, Lewis M., ed. *Velikovsky and Establishment Science.* Glassboro, NJ: Krono, 1977.
Greene, Jeremy A. *Prescribing by Numbers: Drugs and the Definition of Disease.* Baltimore: Johns Hopkins University Press, 2007.
Grover and Baker Sewing Machine Company. *A Home Scene, or Mr. Aston's First Evening with Grover and Baker's Celebrated Family Sewing Machine.* New York: Grover and Baker Sewing Machine Company, 1860.
Habermas, Jürgen. "Notes on Post-secular Society." *New Perspectives Quarterly* 25, no. 4 (2008): 17–29.
Halberstam, Judith. "Skinflick: Posthuman Gender in Jonathan Demme's *The Silence of the Lambs*." *Camera Obscura* 27 (1991): 37–52.
Halligan, Peter W., Christopher Bass, and John C. Marshall, eds. *Contemporary Approaches to the Study of Hysteria.* Oxford: Oxford University Press, 2001.
Haraway, Donna. *The Companion Species Manifesto: Dogs, People, and Significant Otherness.* Chicago: Prickly Paradigm, 2003.
Harman, Graham. "Time, Space, Essence, and Eidos: A New Theory of Causation." *Cosmos and History: The Journal of Natural and Social Philosophy* 6, no. 1 (2010): 1–17.
———. *Weird Realism: Lovecraft and Philosophy.* Winchester, MA: Zero Books, 2012.
Harrell, Ruth F., Ella Woodyard, and Arthur L. Gates. *The Effect of Mothers' Diets on the Intelligence of Offspring: A Study of the Influence of Vitamin Supplementation of the Diets of Pregnant and Lactating Women on the Intelligence of Their Children.* New York: Teachers College, Columbia University, 1955.
Hastings, Sally A. "A Dinner Party Is Not a Revolution." In *Manners and Mischief: Gender, Power, and Etiquette in Japan,* edited by Jan Bardsley and Laura Miller, 100–117. Berkeley: University of California Press, 2011.
Heidegger, Martin. "Being Dwelling Thinking." In *Basic Writings from "Being and Time" (1927) to "The Task of Thinking" (1964),* edited by David Farrell Krell, 347–63. San Francisco: HarperSanFrancisco, 1993.
Hemingway, Ernest. *The Collected Poems of Ernest Hemingway.* New York: Haskell House, 1970.
Herkimer County Historical Society. *The Story of the Typewriter, 1873–1923.* New York: Andrew H. Kellogg Company, 1923.
Hoberman, J., and Jonathan Rosenbaum. *Midnight Movies.* New York: Harper and Row, 1983.
Horwood, Catherine. *Potted History: The Story of Plants in the Home.* London: France Lincoln, 2007.
Huffington, Arianna. *The Sleep Revolution.* New York: Harmony Books, 2016.
Hughes, Herman S. "All of Them Witches." *America* 119, no. 16 (1968): 488–89.
Indiana, Gary. "Good Eraserhead: Indiana." In *David Lynch: Interviews,* edited by Richard A. Barney, 9–18. Jackson: University Press of Mississippi, 2009.
Ireland, Jeannie. *History of Interior Design.* New York: Fairchild Books, 2009.
Isoda, Kōichi. "The Dilemma of Domestic Sensibilities." Translated by Alan Tansman. *Journal of Japanese Studies* 21, no. 1 (1995): 49–63.
Jackson, Tom. *Chilled: How Refrigeration Changed the World, and Might Do So Again.* London: Bloomsbury Sigma, 2015.

Jacobs, Steven. *The Wrong House: The Architecture of Alfred Hitchcock*. Rotterdam, Netherlands: 010, 2013.
Jameson, Fredric. *Signatures of the Visible*. New York: Routledge, 1990.
Joel, A. E. Jr., and Bell Telephone Laboratories staff. *A History of Engineering and Science in the Bell System: Switching Technology (1925–1975)*. United States: Bell Telephone Laboratories, 1982.
Johnson, Catherine. "Tele-branding in TVIII: The Network as Brand and the Programme as Brand." *New Review of Film and Television Studies* 5, no. 1 (2007): 5–24.
Katayama Jun'nosuke (attributed to Fukuzawa Yukichi). *Seiyō ishokujū*. Edo, Japan: Katayama-shi Zōhan, 1867.
Kearney, Mary Celeste. "Birds on the Wire: Troping Teenage Girlhood through Telephony in Mid-Twentieth-Century US Media Culture." *Cultural Studies* 19, no. 5 (2005): 568–601.
Keesey, Douglas. *Brian De Palma's Split-Screen: A Life in Film*. Jackson: University Press of Mississippi, 2015.
Keister, W. "The Evolution of Telephone Switching." *Bell Laboratories Record*, June 1965, 197–203.
Kermode, Mark. *The Exorcist*. 2nd ed. London: BFI, 1998.
Kidwell, Claudia Brush. "Gender Symbols or Fashionable Details?" In *Men and Women: Dressing the Part*, edited by Claudia Brush Kidwell and Valerie Steele, 125–43. Washington, DC: Smithsonian Institution Press, 1989.
King, Stephen. *Carrie*. New York: Doubleday, 1974.
———. *Misery*. New York: Viking, 1987.
———. *The Shining*. New York: Pocket Books, 1977.
Kirkeby, Ed. *Ain't Misbehavin': The Story of Fats Waller*. New York: Da Capo, 1975.
Kittler, Friedrich A. *Gramophone, Film, Typewriter*. Translated and with an introduction by Geoffrey Winthrope-Young and Michael Wutz. Stanford: Stanford University Press, 1999.
Kiver, Milton S., and Milton Kaufman. *Television Electronics: Theory and Servicing, Eighth Edition*. New York: Van Nostrand Reinhold Company, 1983.
Kolker, Robert. *A Cinema of Loneliness: Penn, Stone, Kubrick, Scorsese, Spielberg, Altman*. Oxford: Oxford University Press, 2011.
———. "The Form, Structure, and Influence of *Psycho*." In *Alfred Hitchcock's "Psycho": A Casebook*, edited by Robert Kolker, 206–255. Oxford: Oxford University Press, 2004.
Kriel, Johanet. "A (Tall) Tale of Two Sisters: Integrating Rhetorical and Cognitive-Pragmatic Approaches to Explore Unreliable Narration in Film." *Acta Academica* 47, no. 2 (2015): 34–53.
Kristeva, Julia. *Powers of Horror: An Essay on Abjection*. Translated by Leon S. Roudiez. New York: Columbia University Press, 1982.
Krogness, Karl Jakob, and David Chapman, eds. *Japan's Household Registration System and Citizenship: Koseki, Identification and Documentation*. London: Routledge, 2014.
Krohn, Bill. *Hitchcock at Work*. London: Phaidon, 2000.
Kubrick Archive. University of the Arts, London.
Kwapisz, Jan. *The Greek Figure Poems*. Leuven, Belgium: Peeters, 2013.
Lafond, Frank. *Joe Dante: L'art du je(u)*. Pertuis, France: Rouge Profond, 2011.
Larson, Reed W., Angela R. Wiley, and Kathryn R. Branscomb, eds. *Family Mealtime as a Context of Development and Socialization*. No. 111 of *New Directions for Child and Adolescent Development*. San Francisco: Wiley Periodicals, 2006.

Lastra, James. "Buñuel, Bataille, and Buster, or, the Surrealist Life of Things." *Critical Quarterly* 51, no. 2 (2009): 16–38.
Lavery, David. "'No More Unexplored Countries': The Early Promise and Disappointing Career of Time-Lapse Photography." *Film Studies* 9 (2006): 1–8.
Lee, Hunju. "The New Asian Female Ghost Films: Modernity, Gender Politics, and Transnational Transformation." PhD diss., University of Massachusetts Amherst, 2011.
Leeder, Murray. *Devil's Advocates: Halloween*. New York: Auteur, 2014.
Leung, Wing-Fai. "From *A Tale of Two Sisters* to *The Uninvited*: A Tale of Two Texts." In *Korean Horror Cinema*, edited by Alison Peirse and Daniel Martin, 173–86. Edinburgh: Edinburgh University Press, 2013.
Levenstein, Harvey A. *Revolution at the Table: The Transformation of the American Diet*. Oxford: Oxford University Press, 1988.
Levin, Ira. *Rosemary's Baby*. New York: Random House, 1967.
Liboiron, Max. "Plasticizers: A Twenty-First-Century Miasma." In *Accumulation: The Material Politics of Plastic*, edited by Jennifer Gabrys, Gay Hawkins, and Mike Michael, 283–314. London: Taylor and Francis, 2013.
Lieberman, Daniel E. *The Story of the Human Body: Evolution, Health, and Disease*. New York: Pantheon Books, 2013.
Liegey, Paul R. "Microwave Oven Regression Model." Bureau of Labor Statistics. Accessed April 7, 2017. https://www.bls.gov/cpi/quality-adjustment/microwave-ovens.htm.
Lim, Dennis. *David Lynch: The Man from another Place*. Boston: New Harvest, 2015.
Loadman, John. *Tears of the Tree: The Story of Rubber—a Modern Marvel*. Oxford: Oxford University Press, 2005.
Löwy, Ilana. "Prenatal Diagnosis: The Irresistible Rise of the 'Visible Fetus.'" *Studies in History of Philosophy of Biological and Biomedical Sciences* 47 (2014): 290–99.
Lubar, Steven. "Men/Women/Production/Consumption." In *His and Hers: Gender, Consumption, and Technology*, edited by Roger Horowitz and Arwen Mohen, 7–38. Charlottesville: University Press of Virginia, 1998.
Lumière, Louis. "The Lumière Cinématograph." In *A Technological History of Motion Pictures and Television: An Anthology from the Pages of the* Journal of the Society of Motion Picture and Television Engineers, edited by Raymond Fielding, 49–51. Berkeley: University of California Press, 1967.
Lupton, Deborah. "'Precious Cargo': Foetal Subjects, Risk and Reproductive Citizenship." *Critical Public Health* 22, no. 3 (2012): 329–40.
Lynch, David. *Catching the Big Fish: Meditation, Consciousness, and Creativity*. New York: Jeremy P. Tarcher, 2006.
Mage, Shane. *Velikovsky and His Critics*. Grand Haven, MI: Cornelius, 1978.
Maier, Thomas. *Dr. Spock: An American Life*. New York: Harcourt Brace, 1998.
Marc, Olivier. *Psychology of the House*. Translated by Jessie Wood. London: Thames and Hudson, 1977.
Marcus, Sharon. "Placing *Rosemary's Baby*." *differences: A Journal of Feminist Cultural Studies* 5, no. 3 (1993): 121–53.
Marinelli, Lydia. *Die Couch: Von Denken im Liegen*. Munich: Prestel, 2006.
Martin, Aryn, and Kelly Holloway. "'Something There Is That Doesn't Love a Wall': Histories of the Placental Barrier." *Studies in History and Philosophy of Biological and Biomedical Sciences* 47 (2014): 300–310.
Martin, Richard. *The Architecture of David Lynch*. New York: Bloomsbury, 2014.

Martin, Tovah. *Once upon a Windowsill: A History of Indoor Plants.* Portland, OR: Timber, 1988.
Martineau, Harriet. Letter to Helen Bourn Martineau Tagart. May 12, 1825. In *Harriet Martineau: Selected Letters*, edited by Valerie Sanders, 287. Oxford: Clarendon, 1990.
Mather, John C., and John Boslough. *The Very First Light: The True Inside Story of the Scientific Journey Back to the Dawn of the Universe.* New York: Basic Books, 2008.
Mayer, Andreas. *Sites of the Unconscious: Hypnosis and the Emergence of the Psychoanalytic Setting.* Chicago: University of Chicago Press, 2013.
McAvoy, Catriona. "Creating *The Shining*: Looking beyond the Myths." In *Stanley Kubrick: New Perspectives*, edited by Tatjana Ljujić, Peter Krämer, and Richard Daniels, 280–307. London: Black Dog, 2015.
McDonald, J. C., J. M. Harris, and G. Berry. "Sixty Years On: The Price of Assembling Military Gas Masks in 1940." *Occupational and Environmental Medicine* 63, no. 12 (2006): 852–55.
McGowan, Todd. *The Impossible David Lynch.* New York: Columbia University Press, 2007.
McLuhan, Marshall. *Understanding Media: The Extensions of Man.* New York: McGraw-Hill, 1964.
McLuhan, Marshall, and Quentin Fiore. *The Medium Is the Message.* New York: Bantam, 1967.
Meeker, Natania, and Antónia Szabari. "From the Century of the Pods to the Century of the Plants: Plant Horror, Politics, and Vegetal Ontology." *Discourse* 34, no. 1 (2012): 32–58.
Meikle, Jeffrey L. *American Plastics: A Cultural History.* New Brunswick, NJ: Rutgers University Press, 1995.
Metzl, Jonathan. "'Mother's Little Helper': The Crisis of Psychoanalysis and the Miltown Resolution." *Gender and History* 15, no. 2 (2003): 240–67.
Molyneaux, Heather. *In Sickness and in Health: Representations of Women in Pharmaceutical Advertisements in the "Canadian Medical Association Journal," 1950–1970.* PhD diss., University of New Brunswick, 2009.
Montfort, Nick, and Ian Bogost. *Racing the Beam: The Atari Video Computer System.* Cambridge, MA: MIT Press, 2009.
Morton, Timothy. *Hyperobjects: Philosophy and Ecology after the End of the World.* Minneapolis: University of Minnesota Press, 2013.
———. *Realist Magic: Objects, Ontology, Causality.* Ann Arbor, MI: Open Humanities, 2013.
Muir, John Kenneth. *Wes Craven: The Art of Horror.* Jefferson, NC: McFarland, 1998.
Murphy, Sheila C. *How Television Invented New Media.* New Brunswick, NJ: Rutgers University Press, 2011.
Musser, George. *Spooky Action at a Distance.* New York: Scientific American, 2015.
Nadworny, Milton J. "The Perfect Melodeon: The Origins of the Estey Organ Company, 1846–1866." *Business History Review* 33, no. 1 (1959): 43–59.
Nichter, Mark, and Nancy Vuckovic. "Agenda for an Anthropology of Pharmaceutical Practice." *Social Science and Medicine* 39, no. 11 (1994): 1509–25.
Nieland, Justus. *David Lynch.* Urbana: University of Illinois Press, 2012.
Oakley, Ann. *The Captured Womb: A History of the Medical Care of Pregnant Women.* New York: Basil Blackwell, 1984.
Offit, Paul A. *Pandora's Lab: Seven Stories of Science Gone Wrong.* Washington, DC: National Geographic, 2017.
Oh, Eunha. "*Mother's Grudge* and *Woman's Wail*: The Monster-Mother and Korean Horror Film." In *Korean Horror Cinema*, edited by Alison Peirse and Daniel Martin, 60–72. Edinburgh: Edinburgh University Press, 2013

Olivier, Marc. "Gidget Goes Noir: William Castle and the Teenage Phone Fatale." *Journal of Popular Film and Television* 41, no. 1 (2013): 31–42.

———. "Glitch Gothic." In *Cinematic Ghosts: Haunting and Spectrality from Silent Cinema to the Digital Era*, edited by Murray Leeder, 253–70. New York: Bloomsbury Academic, 2015.

Olson, Greg. *David Lynch: Beautiful Dark*. Lanham, MD: Scarecrow, 2008.

Omote, Mami. "Transition of 'Home Circle with Having Family Meal Together' Described in the Home Economics Textbook at the Taisho Era and the Preceding Term of Showa Era." *Journal of Home Economics of Japan* 58, no. 1 (2007): 5–15.

Pally, Marcia. "*Double* Trouble." In *Brian De Palma Interviews*, edited by Laurence F. Knapp, 92–107. Jackson: University Press of Mississippi, 2003.

Paltrinieri, Luca. "Biopouvoir, les sources historiennes d'une fiction politique." *Revue d'histoire moderne et contemporaine* 60, no. 4 (2013): 49–75.

Paquet, Darcy. *New Korean Cinema: Breaking the Waves*. London: Wallflower, 2009.

Parissien, Steven. *Interiors: The Home since 1700*. London: Laurence King, 2009.

Park, Julie. *The Secret Life of Things: Animals, Objects, and It-Narratives in Eighteenth-Century England*. Stanford: Stanford University Press, 2010.

Parks, Lisa. "When Satellites Fall: On the Trails of Cosmos 954 and USA 193." In *Down to Earth: Satellite Technologies, Industries, and Cultures*, edited by Lisa Parks and James Schwoch, 221–37. Piscataway, NJ: Rutgers University Press, 2012.

Parks, Lisa, and James Schwoch. "Introduction." In *Down to Earth: Satellite Technologies, Industries, and Cultures*, edited by Lisa Parks and James Schwoch, 1–16. Piscataway, NJ: Rutgers University Press, 2012.

Pascal, Susan M. *Images of America: Agoura Hills*. Charleston, SC: Arcadia, 2013.

Peretz, Eyal. *Becoming Visionary: Brian De Palma's Cinematic Education of the Senses*. Stanford: Stanford University Press, 2008.

Pernick, Martin S. *The Black Stork: Eugenics and the Death of "Defective" Babies in American Medicine and Motion Pictures since 1915*. Oxford: Oxford University Press, 1996.

Phillips, Kendall R. "Unmasking Buffalo Bill: Interpretive Controversy and *The Silence of the Lambs*." *Rhetoric Society Quarterly* 28, no. 4 (1998): 33–47.

Pieters, Toine, and Stephen Snelders. "From King Kong Pills to Mother's Little Helpers—Career Cycles of Two Families of Psychotropic Drugs: The Barbiturates and Benzodiazepines." *Canadian Bulletin of Medical History* 24, no. 1 (2007): 93–112.

Polt, Richard. *The Typewriter Revolution: A Typist's Companion for the 21st Century*. New York: Countryman, 2015.

Porter, Dorothy. *Health, Civilization and the State: A History of Public Health from Ancient to Modern Times*. London: Routledge, 1999.

Powell, Anna. *Deleuze and Horror Film*. Edinburgh: Edinburgh University Press, 2005.

Quinlan, Sean M. "Demonizing the Sixties: Possession Stories and the Crisis of Religious and Medical Authority in Post-Sixties American Popular Culture." *Journal of American Culture* 37, no. 3 (2014): 314–30.

Randell, Alexander C., James A. Surrell, and Stephen D. Cohle. "Microwave Oven Burns to Children: An Unusual Manifestation of Child Abuse." *Pediatrics* 79, no. 2 (1987): 255–60.

Rebello, Stephen. *Alfred Hitchcock and the Making of "Psycho."* New York: Dembner Books, 1991.

Redfern, Mary. "Getting to Grips with Knives, Forks and Spoons: Guides to Western-Style Dining for Japanese Audiences, c. 1800–1875." *Food and Foodways* 22, no. 3 (2014): 143–75.
Reed, Christopher. "Off the Wall and onto the Couch! Sofa Art and the Avant-Garde Analyzed." *Smithsonian Studies in American Art* 2, no. 1 (1988): 32–43.
Rees, Jonathan. *Refrigerator*. New York: Bloomsbury, 2015.
———. *Refrigeration Nation: A History of Ice, Appliances, and Enterprise in America.* Baltimore: Johns Hopkins University Press, 2013.
Renard, Jean-Bruno. *Rumeurs et legends urbaines*. Paris: Presses universitaires de France, 1999.
Robinson-Morris, Matthew (2nd Baron Rokeby). Letter to Elizabeth Robinson. United Kingdom, 1740. Via Domestic Interiors Database (AJV1027). http://csdi.rca.ac.uk/didb/detail.php?ID=3731.
Rodley, Chris, ed. *Lynch on Lynch*. London: Faber and Faber, 1997.
Rose, Nikolas. *The Politics of Life Itself: Biomedicine, Power, and Subjectivity in the Twenty-First Century*. Princeton: Princeton University Press, 2007.
Rothman, William. *Hitchcock: The Murderous Gaze*. Ithaca: State University of New York Press, 2012.
Roubaux, Félix. *La France médicale et pharmaceutique*. Paris, 1859.
Rubinstein, Richard. "The Making of *Sisters*: An Interview with Director Brian De Palma." In *Brian De Palma Interviews*, edited by Laurence F. Knapp, 3–14. Jackson: University Press of Mississippi, 2003.
Russell, Cristine. "AAAS Takes on the World." *BioScience* 25, no. 3 (1975): 217–19.
Russell, Edmund. *War and Nature: Fighting Humans and Insects with Chemicals from World War I to Silent Spring*. Cambridge: Cambridge University Press, 2001.
Ryang, Sonia. *Japan and National Anthropology: A Critique*. New York: Routledge Curzon, 2004.
Saban, Stephan, and Sarah Longacre. "*Eraserhead*: Is There Life After Birth?" In *David Lynch: Interviews*, edited by Richard A. Barney, 3–8. Jackson: University Press of Mississippi, 2009.
Sadoul, Georges. *Louis Lumière*. Paris: Seghers, 1964.
Sagan, Carl. "An Analysis of *Worlds in Collision*." In *Scientists Confront Velikovsky*, edited by Donald Goldsmith, 41–104. Ithaca, NY: Cornell University Press, 1977.
———. "Life in the Universe." In *All about Venus*, edited by Brian Aldiss, 141–47. New York: Dell, 1969.
Sagan, Carl, and George Mullen. "Earth and Mars: Evolution of Atmospheres and Surface Temperatures." *Science*, n.s., 177, no. 4043 (1972): 52–56.
Samuels, Robert. *Hitchcock's Bi-textuality: Lacan, Feminisms, and Queer Theory*. Albany: State University of New York Press, 1998.
Sand, Jordan. *House and Home in Modern Japan: Architecture, Domestic Space and Bourgeois Culture, 1880–1930*. Cambridge, MA: Harvard University Asia Center, 2003.
Sanders, Steven M. "Picturing Paranoia: Interpreting *Invasion of the Body Snatchers*." In *The Philosophy of Science Fiction Film*, edited by Steven M. Sanders, 55–72. Lexington: University of Kentucky Press, 2008.
Schantz, Ned. *Gossip, Letters, Phones: The Scandal of Female Networks in Film and Literature*. Oxford: Oxford University Press, 2008.

Scheible, Jeff. *Digital Shift: The Cultural Logic of Punctuation*. Minneapolis: University of Minnesota Press, 2015.
Schneider, Steven Jay. "The Essential Evil in/of *Eraserhead* (or, Lynch to the Contrary)." In *The Cinema of David Lynch*, edited by Erica Sheen and Annette Davidson, 5–18. London: Wallflower, 2004.
Schroeder, Natalie. "Stephen King's *Misery*: Freudian Sexual Symbolism and the Battle of the Sexes." *Journal of Popular Culture* 30, no. 2 (1996): 137–48.
Sconce, Jeffrey. *Haunted Media: Electronic Presence from Telegraphy to Television*. Durham, NC: Duke University Press, 2000.
Scrinis, Gyorgy. *Nutritionism: The Science and Politics of Dietary Advice*. New York: Columbia University Press, 2013.
Seet, K. K. "Mothers and Daughters: Abjection and the Monstrous-Feminine in Japan's *Dark Water* and South Korea's *A Tale of Two Sisters*." *Camera Obscura* 71, no. 2 (2009): 138–59.
Seo, Hyun-suk. "That Unobscure Object of Desire and Horror: On Some Uncanny Things in Recent Korean Horror Films." In *Horror to the Extreme: Changing Boundaries in Asian Cinema*, edited by Mitsuyo Wada-Marciano and Jinhee Choi, 163–78. Hong Kong: Hong Kong University Press, 2009.
Shaviro, Steven. *The Universe of Things: On Speculative Realism*. Minneapolis: University of Minnesota Press, 2014.
Shin, Chi-Yun. "The Art of Branding: Tartan 'Asian Extreme' Films." In *Horror to the Extreme: Changing Boundaries in Asian Cinema*, edited by Mitsuyo Wada-Marciano and Jinhee Choi, 85–100. Hong Kong: Hong Kong University Press, 2009.
Shoemaker, Peter. "The Furniture of Narrative in Crébillon's *Le Sopha* and Laclos's *Les Liaisons Dangereuses*." *Romanic Review* 101, no. 4 (2010): 689–708.
Sholes and Glidden. *The Sholes and Glidden Type-Writer*. Boston: George and Martin, 1874.
Silverman, Kaja. *The Subject of Semiotics*. Oxford: Oxford University Press, 1983.
Singer Sewing Machine Company. *Genius Rewarded, or The Story of the Sewing Machine*. New York: Singer Sewing Machine Company, 1880.
Skerry, Philip J. *The Shower Scene in Hitchcock's "Psycho": Creating Cinematic Suspense and Terror*. Lewiston: Edwin Mellen, 2005.
Slocum, W. H. "Pen Paralysis." In *Proceedings of the New York State Stenographers Association*, 77–84. Troy: Daily Press Book Publishing House, 1881.
Sloterdijk, Peter. *Spheres Volume 3: Foams: Plural Spherology*. Translated by Wieland Hoban. South Pasadena, CA: Semiotext(e), 2016.
Soister, John T., Henry Nicolella, Steve Joyce, Harry H. Long, and Bill Chase. *American Silent Horror, Science Fiction and Fantasy Feature Films, 1913–1929*. Vol. 2. Jefferson, NC: McFarland, 2012.
Spock, Benjamin. *Baby and Child Care*. New York: Hawthorn Books, 1968.
Stapledon, Olaf. *Star Maker*. London: Methuen and Company, 1938.
Steele, Valerie. "Dressing for Work." In *Men and Women: Dressing the Part*, edited by Claudia Brush Kidwell and Valerie Steele, 64–91. Washington, DC: Smithsonian Institution Press, 1989.
Sterne, Jonathan. *MP3: The Meaning of a Format*. Durham, NC: Duke University Press, 2012.
Sterritt, David. *The Films of Alfred Hitchcock*. Cambridge: Cambridge University Press, 1993.
Strom, Sharon Hartman. *Beyond the Typewriter: Gender, Class, and the Origins of Modern American Office Work, 1900–1930*. Chicago: University of Chicago Press, 1992.

Sturrock, Donald. *Storyteller: The Authorized Biography of Roald Dahl*. New York: Simon and Schuster, 2011.
Telotte, J. P. "Tangled Networks and Wrong Numbers." *Film Criticism* 10, no. 3 (1986): 36–48.
Tharp, Julie. "The Transvestite as Monster: Gender Horror in *The Silence of the Lambs* and *Psycho*." *Journal of Popular Culture* 19, no. 3 (1991): 106–13.
Thévenot, Roger. *A History of Refrigeration throughout the World*. Translated by J. C. Fidler. Paris: International Institute of Refrigeration, 1979.
Thomas, Benjamin. *L'attrait du vent*. Liège, Belgium: Yellow Now, 2016.
Thomson, David. *The Moment of "Psycho": How Alfred Hitchcock Taught America to Love Murder*. New York: Basic Books, 2009.
Thornton, Peter. *Authentic Décor: The Domestic Interior, 1620–1920*. London: Weidenfeld and Nicolson, 1985.
Tobin, Joseph J. "Introduction: Domesticating the West." In *Re-made in Japan: Everyday Life and Consumer Taste in a Changing Society*, edited by Joseph J. Tobin, 1–41. New Haven, CT: Yale University Press, 1992.
Toles, George. "If Thine Eye Offend Thee . . . : *Psycho* and the Art of Infection." In *Alfred Hitchcock's "Psycho": A Casebook*, edited by Robert Kolker, 120–145. Oxford: Oxford University Press, 2004.
Tompkins, Peter, and Christopher Bird. *The Secret Life of Plants*. New York: Avon Books, 1973.
Tourn, Lya. "Des chambres de parents, des nuits d'enfants." In *Rêves d'alcôves: La chambre au cours des siècles*, 174–192. Paris: Réunion des musées nationaux, 1995.
Travers, Peter, and Stephanie Reiff. *The Story behind "The Exorcist."* New York: Crown, 1974.
Trigg, Dylan. "'The Horror of Darkness': Toward an Unhuman Phenomenology." *Speculations: A Journal of Speculative Realism* 4 (2013): 113–21.
———. *The Thing: A Phenomenology of Horror*. Winchester, MA: Zero Books, 2014.
Truffaut, François. *Hitchcock*. New York: Simon and Schuster, 1998.
Tullett, Barrie. *Typewriter Art: A Modern Anthology*. London: Laurence King, 2014.
Valerius, Karyn. "*Rosemary's Baby*, Gothic Pregnancy, and Fetal Subjects." *College Literature* 33, no. 2 (2005): 116–35.
Vaz da Silva, Francesco. "Red as Blood, White as Snow, Black as Crow: Chromatic Symbolism of Womanhood in Fairytales." *Marvels and Tales* 21, no. 2 (2007): 240–52.
Velikovsky, Immanuel. *Worlds in Collision*. New York: Macmillan, 1950.
Velikovsky Reconsidered. Editors of *Pensée*. Garden City, NY: Doubleday, 1976.
Vincent, Bev. "The Genius Fallacy: *The Shining*'s 'Hidden' Meanings." In *Stanley Kubrick's "The Shining": Studies in the Horror Film*, edited by Danel Olson, 293–310. Lakewood, CO: Centipede, 2015.
Wagner, Neal R. "The Sofa Problem." *American Mathematical Monthly* 83, no. 3 (1976): 188–89.
Walker, James R., and Robert V. Bellamy Jr. "The Remote Control Device." In *The Remote Control in the New Age of Television*, edited by James R. Walker and Robert V. Bellamy Jr., 3–14. Westport, CT: Praeger, 1993.
Warner, Maria. "Freud's Couch: A Case History." *Raritan* 31, no. 2 (2011): 146–63.
Westerbeck, Colin L., Jr. "The Banality of Good." *Commonweal*, March 1, 1974.
Western Electric Company. *The Step-by-Step Dial Telephone System, Telephone Systems Training, Course: Central Office Equipment, Lesson No. 3*. United States: Western Electric Company and Hawthorn Works, 1958.

Whippo, Craig C., and Roger P. Hangarter. "The 'Sensational' Power of Movement in Plants: A Darwinian System for Studying the Evolution of Behavior." *American Journal of Botany* 96, no. 12 (2009): 2115–27.

Willcox and Gibbs. *Willcox and Gibbs Noiseless Family Sewing Machine*. New York: Willcox and Gibbs Sewing Machine Co., 1864.

Willes, Margaret. *And So to Bed*. London: National Trust, 1998.

Williams, Linda. "Discipline and Fun: *Psycho* and Postmodern Cinema." In *Alfred Hitchcock's "Psycho": A Casebook*, edited by Robert Kolker, 164–204. Oxford: Oxford University Press, 2004.

Williams, Tony. *Hearths of Darkness: The Family in the American Horror Film, Updated Edition*. Jackson: University Press of Mississippi, 2014.

Wilson, Eric G. *The Strange World of David Lynch: Transcendental Irony from "Eraserhead" to "Mulholland Dr."* New York: Continuum, 2007.

Wilson Sewing Machine Company. *The Wilson Shuttle Sewing Machines*. Wilson Sewing Machine Company, 1871.

Wolf-Meyer, Matthew. "Biomedicine, the Whiteness of Sleep, and the Wages of Spatiotemporal Normativity in the United States." *American Ethnologist* 42, no. 4 (2015): 446–58.

Wyckoff, W. O. *The Type-Writer Magazine*. Ithaca, NY: W. O. Wyckoff, 1878.

Yoshida, Mitsukuni. *Naorai: Communion of the Table*. Edited by Mitsukuni Yoshida and Tsune Sesoko. Hiroshima: Mazda Motor Companion and Cosmo Public Relations Corporation, 1989.

Young, Elizabeth. "*The Silence of the Lambs* and the Flaying of Feminist Theory." *Camera Obscura* 27 (1991): 5–35.

Zielenziger, Michael. *Shutting Out the Sun: How Japan Created Its Own Lost Generation*. New York: Nan A. Talese, 2006.

Zipes, Jack. *The Enchanted Screen: The Unknown History of Fairy-Tale Films*. New York: Routledge, 2011.

———. *The Trials and Tribulations of Little Red Riding Hood: Versions of the Tale in Sociocultural Context*. South Hadley: Bergin and Garvey, 1983.

Zŏng, In-sŏb. *Folk Tales from Korea*. New York: Greenwood, 1969.

INDEX

Numbers in italics refer to illustrations.

abject, the, 12, 13, 19–20, *21*, 23, 25–26, 247–48, 263, 298
acid rain, 155, 169, 177
acoustic space, 50, 51, 52, 62, 70
actors as props, 302
Adler Universal 39 typewriter, 211, 216, *216*, 217, 218, 234n25
Alexa and humans, 121, 123
Alien, 29, 32, 246
Althusser, Louis, 121
Amenábar, Alejandro, 203
American Association for the Advancement of Science, 160, 162, 174–75
American Institute of Biological Sciences, 160
American Psycho, 23, 271
Amityville Horror, The, 95, 115
Annabelle, 6
anthropocentrism, 2, 6, 149, 158, 163, 173, 195, 208, 298
anthropomorphism: against anthropocentrism, 2, 311; and characters, 3; in *Goodnight Moon*, 4; and plants, 155, 163; of refrigerator, 13; and the sofa, 98, 100, 104; and telephones, 62
Are You Fit to Marry? See *Black Stork, The*
armoire, 118, 237–38, *239*, 241, 244, 248
asbestos scandal, 38
Atari 2600, 118; games, 120
atmoterror, 38–42
atomic bombing, 39

Baby and Child Care. See Spock, Benjamin
Bachelard, Gaston, 199, 238, 241, 245
Backster, Cleve, 160, 161–62
Bad Seed, The, 269–72, *270*, 274–75
bad seeds, killing of, 277
Ballet mécanique, 263

barbiturates, 275, 276
Baudelaire, Charles, 311, 312
Baudrillard, Jean, 191, 238, 241, 244
bed(s): as battlefield in *The Exorcist*, 191; body as an "it" in, 208; and childhood fear, 187; convergence of bed in *The Exorcist*, 191; eleven, in *The Exorcist*, 184–85; frame of, as altar, 190–91; as nocturnal comfort, 183; problems in *The Exorcist*, 185; sheet as layer of the, 202; and temptations, 187
bedtime stories as bedroom-centric horror, 192
Berlin Wall, 13, 14, 21
Bible, 127, 129, 131, 186, 209n4, 209n15
Big Bang, 119, 123
Bird, Christopher, 154, 161, 162
Birth of a Flower, The, 158
Black Christmas, 54–55, *55*, 56, 56–57
Black Sabbath, 73n52
Black Stork, The, 272–73
Blatty, William, 189
Blow Out, 96
Body Snatchers (1993), 172
Bogost, Ian, 1, 311–12
Bose, J. C., 161
Bray, Charles, 61
Brick, 144
Brodeur, Paul, 37–38
Brown, Margaret Wise. See *Goodnight Moon*
bubbles, immunity, 201
Buck v. Bell, 273
Burgess, Anthony, 187

caller ID, 56, 57
"call is coming from the house," 54–65, 72n25
Cameron, Allan, 157, 158
cannibalism, 134, 136, 137, 144, 145, 278

331

Carpenter, John, 203, 204
Carrie, 126, 128, 129–30, 131, 132
Castle, William. *See I Saw What You Did*
cell phone. *See* mobile phone
chabudai, 75, 78, 80, 81, *81*, 82, 83, 84, 87
Chamovitz, Daniel, 162, 163
channel hopping, 110, 123
chemical signals in animals, 160
chest, 103, 299
Children of the Damned, 277
Chion, Michel, 256–58, 260
chora, 21, 22
Christian propaganda, 287
Chumash people, 115, 116, 123
Ciment, Michel, 213, 214–15
Cinotto, Simone, 79
Clockwork Orange, A, 156, *156*, 214
coffin, refrigerator as, 23
cold chain, 17–18, 19, 25, 26
Cold War: anxiety and, 156, 164, 180n62; climate in *Possession*, 26; espionage, 37; obsession of as risk prevention, 276
Colonial Model House, 265, *266*
Conjuring, The, 247
containers nested, 242, 244, 245
controller, 118, 120, 121
conversion disorder, 189
cordless landline, 70
corpse cooler, 24, 25
couch POV, 147, 148, 149
Craven, Wes. *See Hills Have Eyes, The; Last House on the Left, The; Nightmare on Elm Street, A*
Crébillon, Claude, 100
Creed, Barbara, 246–47
Cronenberg, David, 2, 150
Cropper, Corry, 203

Dahl, Roald, 40–41
Dante, Joe, 40, 41
Darwin, Charles, 158
Davies, Eric, 159, 162
Death Bed: The Bed That Eats, 193
death by allusion, 299
"defects," cultural bias against, 272
denial strategy, 71

Demme, Jonathan, 137
DePalma, Brian, 95; and Hitchcock, 102–3, 109n27; inspiration of, for *Sisters*, 105; and split-focus diopters, 130–31
Detour, 47
Dial M for Murder, 47
dining room, 79–80, 88, 89
Disney, Walt, 40, 41
divine, the, 22
Dostoyevsky, 5, 8
Dressed to Kill, 96
Dr. Strangelove, 214
drugs, psychiatric, 276
Durgnat, Raymond, 297, 301, 302, 306

Ebert, Roger, 29, 30, 31
electroconvulsive therapies (ECT), 292
electronic switching systems (ESS), 57–58, *58*, 59, 69, 72n29
environmentalism, 176
enzyme detergents, 38
epilepsy, 290, *291*, 293
Epstein, Jean, 63
Eraserhead, 253–54, *254*, 258, 260–63
Estey, Jacob, 262
E.T. the Extra Terrestrial, 28, 42
eugenics, 272, 273, 277, 280
Evil Laugh, 31
exorcism: and excision, 189; as treatment, 292
Exorcism of Emily Rose, The, 269, 287–93
Exorcist, The, 183, 184–85, 188–92, *190*
expulsion, 19–20, 21, 22, 23, 25
Eyes without a Face, 73n38

family circle, 75, 76, 78, 82, 84, 86
Family Circle business, 75, 82, 84, 85–86, 87, 88
family mealtime, 79–80, 84
film noir, 44, 47, 48, 52
Final Destination, 6–7
Finkbine, Sherri, 280
flashbacks, 66, 81, 142, 242, 243, 249
flat ontology, 300
Flusser, Vilém, 57, 64
Fly, The, 150

food refusal, 81
Ford sedan, 306
forest primeval. *See* telephonic forest
Foucault, Michel, 265, 275
Frankenstein, 144, 284
Freakmaker, The, 3
Freud, Sigmund, 106, 107, 207, 300
Friends of the Earth, 166
Full Metal Jacket, 234n25
furniture monuments, 238, 244, 249n7

Galston, Arthur, 160, 162
Gambutrol, 290
Garden of Death, 3
gas masks, 38, 43n35
Gaycken, Oliver, 158
gender: assumptions about sewing, 139; identity, 137–38
genetic determinism, 269
genius fallacy, 216
Ghost in the Machine, 31
Ghost Story, A, 210n49
God, 12, 17, 22, 26, 129
Goldilocks, 192
Goldman, William, 224
golem, 12, 13, 16, 19, 26
gongan narrative tradition, 240
Goodnight Moon, 1, 4, 8, 311
Good Son, The, 277
Gospel of Thomas. *See* Bible
Gremlin mythology, 40–41
Gremlins, 29–30, *30*, 32, 39, 42
Gremlins effect, 35
grex, 173, 174, 175, 176, 180n62
guilt personified, 241

Haikyo.com, 85, 86, 89
Haiselden, Harry J., 272
Halberstam, Judith, 137–38
Halloween, 44, 63–64, *64*, 73n54, 203–5
Harman, Graham, 3, 204, 311, 312
haunting and repressed history, 115
heating and ventilation, 259
heat pumps, 17–18, 23
Helvetica font, 220–21, 235n42
herbal shakes, 279, 281, 283–85

heterotopias, 265
Hills Have Eyes, The, 71
Hitchcock, Alfred, 299–300, 302
Hitler, 39, 273
Holmes, Oliver Wendell, 273
Hooper, Tobe. *See Poltergeist*
House on Sorority Row, The, 193
Hunt, Walter, 127

ice, 6, 17–19, 25
ie, 79, 84, 85, 87
ie sei, 79, 84, 85
illusion of vision, 50
imaging technologies, 280, 294n49
Indiana Jones and the Temple of Doom, 29
Indian burial ground trope, 114–15, 123, 124n10
infanticide: as editing, 220; in *The Bad Seed*, 272, 276; in *Eraserhead*, 260–63; unconditional love and, 286
Inglourious Basterds, 40
Innocents, The, 203
intertextuality, 110
Invasion, The, 207
Invasion of the Body Snatchers (1956), 29, 164, 166, 169, 172
Invasion of the Body Snatchers (1978), 155, 163–67, 170, 172–78
I Saw What You Did, 44, 45, 47–49, *49*, 51–53
It adaptations, 4
It Follows, 5
it-function, 5

Jack and Jill, 144–45, 147, 148, 149
Jackson, Tom, 17, 18
Jacob's ladder, 13, 157
Jews, 39, 40
Johnson, Rian, 144
Ju-on: The Grudge, 249

Kant, Immanuel, 204
katei, 79
"keep him on the line" trope. *See* trace race
Keller, Helen, 273
King, Stephen, 130, 218, 220, 224

kitchen, as feminine space, 11
Kmetz, John M., 160
Kolker, Robert, 220, 299
Korean: feature films, 242; identity and Japanese rule, 248–49
Kristeva, Julia, 19–20, 21, 22, 23, 25, 298
Kubrick archive, 212, 218–19, 222, 223, 224, 234n29
Kubrick, Stanley: hidden messages from, 216; June Randall and, 216–17; secretary of, types pages, 222–23; treatment of Shelley Duvall, 215; typewriter of, 217
Kubrick, Vivian, 215, 217

Lady in the Radiator, 257, 260, 261, 262
Lang, Fritz, 60
Last House on the Left, The, 31, 32
Lemieux, Pierre, 264
Levinas, Emmanuel, 4, 150, 207, 208
Lewis, C. S., 247
Liberace, 230, 231
Lieberman, Daniel, 187
Little Red Riding Hood, 44, 52, 192
locality, 111
Lumière, Auguste, 146
Lumière, Louis, 146, 153n51
Lynch, David, 253, 255, 256, 265–66
Lynch, Peggy, 256

M, 60
Ma Bell, 44, 54, 61, 69
Mannheim, Robbie, 188–89, 190
March of the Penguins, 288
mass murder, 273
Matrix, The, 268
mattress: Beautyrest, 192; foam, 193, 198; as permeable membrane, 196; in *Psycho*, 193; raw egg test on, 192; sink and bounce of, 193, 202
May, 142–45, *143*, 150–51
McLuhan, Marshall: on acts of typewriter, 231; Gutenberg man of, 70; pretypographic man of, 62; and medium as message, 110; on ourselves as media, 111; on sight and sound, 50; on television as mosaic, 119; on Westerns, 116

medicalized motherhood, 274, 277
Meiji period, 77, 78, 80, 84–85
menstruation, 129, 130, 132, 248
Michel, Anneliese, 287
microwave: appeal of, 32, 33; damage from exposure, 36; embassy scandal, 37; sickness, 36, 37; and temporality, 33; as torture device, 31; urban legends of, 30, 35, 42n16
Microwave Massacre, 31
miscarriage, 12, 16, *16*, 19
Misek, Richard, 157, 158
Misery, 224–33
Mister Rogers' Neighborhood, 112, 116, 124
mobile phone, 70, 71, 73n54
mono no aware, 89
Morton, Timothy, 3, 4, 123

naturecultures, 268
nesting box of containers. *See* containers nested
Nieland, Justus, 258
Nightmare on Elm Street, A, 193–97, *196*, 200–201
911 (emergency number), 68, 69, 70
Nonhuman Turn, The, 1
nonlocality, 111, 123
Noriko's Dinner Table, 75, 80–89, *81*, 89
North Pacific Subtropical Gyre, 307
nutritionism, 274

object-centric, 6
object-oriented ontology (OOO), 1, 2, 3, 4, 100, 123, 204, 238, 300, 311
object POV, 298
objects, 203–4, 209n15, 238, 255, 299, 311–12
obscene phone call, 63–65
oil spill, 166, 179n32
Oldboy, 237
Omen, The, 277
Orphan, 277
Others, The, 203, 205–7, *206*, 237, 243
Oudart, Jean-Pierre, 147, 213–14

Passion of the Christ, The, 288
patchwork, filmmaking as, 144, 147

patriarchal: authority, 84; figure, 192, 247; order, 240; system, 78, 241
Peeping Tom, 108n4
pen as phallic potency, 227
penmanship compared to type, 229
pen paralysis, 226–27
Pfeffer, Wilhelm, 158
pharmacologicalism, 289
Phone, 71
phone company films, 45
phone fatale, 44, 47, 70, 71n3
piano compared to harpsichord, 218
pickpockets, sofas as, 95
Pieces, 193
pills: as actors, 268; as euthanasia, 277; human body, 269; interventions, 273; life of, 268; moral and medical space of, 274; and narrative, 269–70; as risk prevention, 277; in *Rosemary's Baby*, 285, 286; women as dispensaries, 275, 278
placental barrier, 279–80, 281
plants: anthropomorphize, intelligence, 163; fear felt by, 162; graceful vitality of, 157; humans coexist with, 155; humans depend on, 157; invite sex, 157; neuroscience, 163; reaction to violence, 155; telepathic reaction to man, 156; and time-lapse, 157
plasticizers, 308
Plastic Man, 194–95
plumbing and reproduction, 258
pod invasion, 164, 167, 170, *170*
Poltergeist, 110, 111–12, 118–19, 122–24, 246
Poltergeist II: The Other Side, 115
poltergeist, etymology of, 117
polyvinyl chloride, 303–5
Possession, 11–16, 19, 20–23
postsecularism, 288–89
Powers of Ten, 163
prenatal vitamins, 278, 282
"Princess and the Pea, The," 192
Psycho, 29, 101–2, 105, 108, 132, 149, 193, 296–300
Psychology of the House, 245
psychopharmacological drugs, 281
Pulse, 71
pure cinema, 300, 301, 302

radiation: microwave, 30, 36; nuclear, 33, 36; thermal, 34
radiator: bathroom, 253; as eyesore, 259; heterotopian, 265; picket fence made of, 265; as sculptural object, 265; sequences in *Eraserhead*, 260–61, 263; sounds of, 256; as spiritual center of *Eraserhead*, 256; stage in, 264; white-hot steam of heaven, 263
"Radiator Lions," 260
Raytheon "Radarange," 34
Rear Window, 51, 101
recuperation of memory, 107
refrigerator: as active prop, 13; as cadaver, 23; as coffin, 26; cold as raison d'être for, 23; post-Katrina graveyard of, 23; replaces icebox, 19; as woman's domain, 14; as womb, 26
Reiner, Rob, 224
Remington and Sons, 226
remote control: and advertising avoidance, 117; first use of term, 115; gratification from, 120; signaling, 112–13; showdown, 112, *112*, *113*, 113–14; space played by, 121; television played by, 121
Rent a Family, Inc., 76
Repulsion, 248
Ringu, 118
Roe v. Wade, 55
room tone, 256–57, 264
Room 237, 119, 211
Rope, 101, 103, 109n27
Rosemary's Baby, 67, 68, 269, 278–86, 283, 286
Rothman, William, 297, 298, 298
Ruin.com. *See* Haikyo.com

Sagan, Carl, 169, 175
Sand, Jordan, 76, 78, 79
Sanskrit text of Upanishads, 259
satellites, 119, 121–22
Scheherazade, 100, 226, 232
Schreber's bed harness, 187–88
Sconce, Jeffrey, 122
Scream, 70
Secret Life of Plants, The, 154, 155, 158, 160, 163, 177

seizure, 289
serial killer and publishing, 232
Se7en, 220
78/52: Hitchcock's Shower Scene, 297
sewing and filmmaking, 145–46
sewing machine: as burdened religiously, 126; as foe to tailor, 139; gender of the, 141; as iron sartor, 139, 141, 227, 235n63; Margaret White's, 126, *128*; used by Christian consumers, 127, 128; for women, 140–41
sheeted dead, 199, 201, 202, 203, 205, 207
Shining, The, 115, 211–24, *212*, *216*, 225, 232–33
shower curtain: as body bag, 305, *306*; as cinematic screen, *301*; and clean up, *304*, 305; Marion as, 303; murder of a, 299; as wrap, 300, 301
showerhead POV, 298, 302
shower scene, 296–97, 298
Silence of the Lambs, The, 132–37, *133*, 137–38, 141–42
Silverman, Kaja, 146–47, 149, 298
Singer Sewing Machine Company, 127
Sisters, 95–98, 100–102, *102*, 104–6, *107*, 107–8
Sixth Sense, The, 206, 237, 243
sleeping, 186–87
Sloterdijk, Peter, 38, 198–99
slow motion and human figure, 157, 158
snow. *See* television static
sofa: ability of, to conceal, 103; bed, invention of, 107; definition of, 99; as De Palma's favorite trope, 96; enables illicit behavior, 98; etymology of, 98; and the French, 99–100; and psychoanalysis, 106, 109n32
Sony products, 117
Sorry, Wrong Number, 47
sound atmosphere, 256
sound-vibration-thought mantra, 257, 263
Spencer, Percy, 34, 42n12
Spielberg, Steven, 29, 40, 110
split diopter, 130
Spock, Benjamin, 185–86, 209nn4–5
sterilization, 273
Sterne, Jonathan, 61
Stoicism, 135, 136

"Stompin' the Bug," 261, 262
Strait-Jacket, 71n1
Suicide Club/Suicide Circle, 75, 81, 86
Superstition, 31
surveillance, 280, 287
suture horror, 150
suture theory, 146–49, 151, 213, 298

table event, 75–76, 88–89
table: Japanese history of, 76–78; Western-style, 79, 80, 82, 84
Tale of Two Sisters, A, 237, 238–41, 242, 243–44, 248
Tappan "Time Machine," 33–34
teenage girls and telephones, 48, 54, 67
telephone: cord and umbilical cord, 67, 68; exchange (*see* electronic switching systems [ESS]); poles (*see* telephonic forest)
telephonic: film, 44, 67; forest, 44–45, *46*, 53, 55, 70; horror, 61, 62, 67, 70, 71
telephony, 45, 53, 54, 60, 61, 204
television static, 118–19
Tetsuo: The Iron Man, 150
thalidomide, 280
time-lapse and plants, 155–58, 164, 177
tin-can-and-string metaphor, 59, 60
there is (*il y a*), 4, 207, 208
Thimonnier, Barthélemy, 127
three drops of blood trope, 131–32
Todorov, Tzvetan, 203
tomato pincushion, 128
Tompkins, Peter, 154, 161, 162
trace race, 58–60
tray, 78, 80, 87
Trigg, Dylan, 207, 208
Truffaut, François, 298, 299, 300
trust in medicine, 280, 294n45
TV POV, 147, 148, 149
2001: A Space Odyssey, 220, 221
Txt, 71
typeface, 220–21
typewriter: and linguistic dismemberment, 214; as mechanical bride, 228; in *Misery*, 225, 26, 231, 233; as object of terror, 214; and pen paralysis, 226–27, 233; as piano,

230; and secretary gender, 229; in *The Shining*, 233; as Trojan horse, 228; as weapon, 213
typing and weaponry, 219
typographic dysfunction, 225

umbilical fetuses, 261, 262
Un chien analou, 151
unhumanity, 207
urban legend, 30, 35, 42n16, 65
Urban Legend, 31

Velikovsky, Immanuel, 174, 175, 180n64
vitamins, 273–74, 276, 278, 281–84
voyeurism, 50, 73n52, 96–97, 100, 107–8, 301

Waller, Fats, 262
wardrobe. *See* armoire
weaponize appliance, 30–38
westerns, movie compared to television, 116

Wever, Ernest, 61
When a Stranger Calls, 44, 65–67, 68, 69
Whispering Wires, 72n25
white noise. *See* womb: white noise simulates
White Sewing Machine Company, 127
Willies, The, 31, 42n6
wireless phone. *See* mobile phone
Wolfen, 115
womb: armoire as, 242, 245–46, 247; bubble bath like a, 200; oven as, 11; refrigerator as, 26, 248; white noise simulates, 118
Wonder, Stevie, 155, 178

zapping. *See* channel hopping
Zapping of America, The. See Brodeur, Paul
Zenith: Flash-Matic remote, 114; Space Command remote, 112, 113, 114, 116, 117, 123
Zipes, Jack, 52, 53
Zulawski, Andrzej. See *Possession*
Zyklon B, 38, 39

MARC OLIVIER is Professor of French Studies at Brigham Young University.